# Jewish Masculinities

# Jewish Masculinities

*German Jews,*
*Gender, and History*

Edited by
Benjamin Maria Baader, Sharon Gillerman,
and Paul Lerner

INDIANA UNIVERSITY PRESS

*Bloomington & Indianapolis*

This book is a publication of

Indiana University Press
601 North Morton Street
Bloomington, Indiana 47404-3797 USA

iupress.indiana.edu

| *Telephone orders* | 800-842-6796 |
| *Fax orders* | 812-855-7931 |

MANUFACTURED IN THE UNITED STATES OF AMERICA

**Library of Congress Cataloging-in-Publication Data**

Jewish masculinities : German Jews, gender, and history / edited by
Benjamin Maria Baader, Sharon Gillerman, and Paul Lerner.
   p. cm.
Includes bibliographical references and index.
ISBN 978-0-253-00213-6 (cloth : alk. paper) — ISBN 978-0-253-00206-8
(pbk. : alk. paper) — ISBN 978-0-253-00221-1 (e-book) 1. Jewish men—
Germany—History—Congresses. 2. Jews—Germany—History—Congresses.
3. Jews—Germany—Identity—Congresses. 4. Subculture—Germany—
Congresses. 5. Masculinity—Germany—Congresses. 6. Germany—Ethnic
relations. I. Baader, Benjamin Maria. II. Gillerman, Sharon, [date] III. Lerner,
Paul Frederick.
   DS134.23.J49 2012
   305.892'4043—dc23
                                                                    2011049672

1 2 3 4 5 17 16 15 14 13 12

*To our fathers:*

*Gerhard Baader, Joseph Gillerman, and Jack Lerner*

# CONTENTS

10. Family Matters
    German Jewish Masculinities among Nazi Era Refugees

# ACKNOWLEDGMENTS

Our shared interest in masculinity, difference, and German Jewry stretches back many years, and we began to engage intensely with the topic in the late 1990s when all three of us were in Los Angeles. Several years later, together with Stefanie Schüler-Springorum, Deborah Hertz, Steven Lowenstein, and Monika Richarz, we formed a working group on gender and German Jewish history, and starting in 2003, after a conference in Hamburg on gender and women, the group turned its attention to masculinity. Deborah Hertz generously agreed to host a conference on Jewish masculinities at the University of California, San Diego, which allowed us to bring our ideas and vision to fruition. In addition to the other members of the working group, we would also like to express our gratitude to Atina Grossmann, Paula Hyman, and Marion Kaplan for inspiring our work and for supporting this project from its early stages.

The San Diego conference in December 2005 was a great success, still memorable for its absorbing, thought-provoking, and often heady discussions and for the unique dialogue it created between scholars of rabbinic studies, modern German history, and gender studies. In addition to those already mentioned, we are deeply grateful to David Biale, Darcy Buerkle, Ute Frevert, Sander Gilman, David Myers, Ofer Nur, Todd Presner, Gideon Reuveni, Ishay Rosen-Zvi, and Miriam Rürup for their participation. We would also like to acknowledge the extremely helpful input we received from Till van Rahden, Stefanie Schüler-Springorum, and Daniel Wildmann as we set about conceptualizing this volume, and we thank the volume's contributors for their openness to critique and their patience throughout this process.

USC Dornsife College and Hebrew Union College–Jewish Institute of Religion provided important financial assistance. We are especially grateful to Stephan Haas, vice dean of USC Dornsife, and Michael Marmur, vice president for academic affairs at HUC-JIR. We also thank Shayna Kessel and Evan Bernier for their editorial assistance with the manuscript.

At Indiana University Press, Peter Froehlich has been extraordinarily helpful, responsive, and gracious, and we thank June Silay for skillfully shepherding the manuscript through the publication process. Warm thanks to our copyeditor, Merryl Sloane, for her infinite patience and keen judgment. The two anonymous referees gave us many useful comments and suggestions, and we are enormously grateful to our editor, Janet Rabinowitch, for taking this project on and guiding us with her incisive comments and thoughtful advice.

Benjamin Maria Baader, Winnipeg
Sharon Gillerman, Los Angeles
Paul Lerner, Los Angeles

September 2011

# Jewish Masculinities

# German Jews, Gender, and History

PAUL LERNER, BENJAMIN MARIA BAADER,
AND SHARON GILLERMAN

This volume, an exploration of maleness and manliness among German Jews, presents innovative historical investigations of the lives, experiences, and identities of Jewish men. Its chapters stretch from the early modern period through the late twentieth century and treat German Jews in Germany, as well as in exile and emigration in North America, Palestine, and Israel. Its contributors engage with traditional Jewish texts, Jewish and non-Jewish social and religious practices, and anti-Semitic discourses on Jews; at the same time, *Jewish Masculinities* focuses closely on German and German Jewish cultures and contexts. The book builds on a growing body of scholarship on gender and Jewish culture and uses the categories of gender, Jewishness, and Germanness to offer new perspectives on identity, community, and difference in German Jewish history and beyond.

The idea that Jewish men differ from non-Jewish men by being delicate, meek, or effeminate in body and character runs deep in European history. In the thirteenth century, for example, the French historian Jacques de Vitry reported that his contemporaries believed Jewish men suffered from a monthly flux of blood and had become "unwarlike and weak even as women."[1] It is not clear how widespread this notion was in the Middle Ages or how much of a role gender played in discourses on the Jews in that period, but by the sixteenth century, various images—such as the sinful Jew who bled annually during Easter, and the melancholic, passive Jew whom medical treatises described as suffering from hemorrhoids—had coalesced into a common belief that Jewish men were deficient as men and possessed some womanly characteristics.[2] Even Abbé Grégoire, a renowned defender of Jewish rights, noted that Jewish men "almost all have scanty beards, a common mark of effeminate temperaments."[3] Still, Grégoire, in his pro-emancipation treatise of 1789, *Essai sur la régéneration physique, morale et politique des Juifs* (Essay on the Physical, Moral and Political Regeneration of the Jews), forcefully denounced the notion of male Jews' menstruation as an unfounded prejudice.

The notion that Jewish men suffered from a distorted masculinity or carried certain female traits did not figure prominently in the intense debates about Jewish emancipation and Jewish civil rights of the late eighteenth century and early nineteenth. The issue of Jewish masculinity arose only occasionally, when contemporaries—generally opponents of Jewish emancipation—argued that Jewish men were unfit for military service. Likewise, German Jewish men were at times excluded from manly practices such as duels.[4] On the other hand, some non-Jews considered Jewish populations well prepared for civil society, and significant numbers of Germans and other Western Europeans came to believe that Jews possessed an exemplary family life, in which faithful spouses, devoted fathers and mothers, and obedient sons and daughters formed tightly knit units.[5]

The tone changed toward the end of the nineteenth century, when racialized anti-Semitism spread through Central and Western Europe. Soon, non-Jewish commentators began to express serious concern about inappropriate gender expressions among Jewish men and women, and the trope of the effeminate Jewish man became the target of pervasive and vicious anti-Semitic critique. Two decades after the founding of the German empire, many Germans turned to an increasingly aggressive and exclusivist nationalism, which together with the enhanced status of militarism, Germany's emergence as an imperial power, and the spread of reactionary forms of military masculinity shaped the peculiar gender and cultural order of the Wilhelmine period.

At least since Carl Schorske's pathbreaking essays of the 1970s, historians have been fascinated by the many contradictions of this era in Germany and Austria-Hungary: the breathless experimentation and cultural innovation that occurred alongside growing demagoguery, colonial brutality, and xenophobia.[6] More recently, scholars, most notably Sander Gilman, have been exploring the impact of these developments on Jewish men's self-identity, and studies of figures like Otto Weininger have called attention to the self-hatred with which some highly acculturated Jewish men in Germany and Austria reacted to the pressures of exclusive nationalism and anti-Semitism, a self-hatred often expressed within a framework of gender and sexual difference.[7]

An alternative response to both Jewish and non-Jewish defamations of Jews' virility occurred among Zionists and other proponents of a new, "muscular Judaism" in the early twentieth century. Zionist activists like Max Nordau sought to reverse the alleged degeneration of diaspora Jewry by leading Jews out of the unhealthy conditions of European cities and towns to the salutary fields and farms of the Yishuv (the Jewish settlement in Palestine). Simultaneously, new Jewish heroes, such as the strongman Siegmund Breitbart, and increasingly popular movements, like gymnastics and physical culture, spread images of healthy, strapping Jewish men and a regenerated, muscular Jewry.[8]

Discourses concerning the distorted gender of Jewish men were not unique to the German and Austrian cultural milieu, and beginning in the late eighteenth century they also entered the repertoire of Jewish and non-Jewish modernizers in Eastern Europe, where they were often voiced by male *maskilim* (supporters of the Jewish Enlightenment). Some *maskilim,* and at times also non-Jews, averred that Jews married off their children too early and that these unhealthy early marriages robbed young Jewish men of their adolescence and led to precocious sexual involvement and, ultimately, masculine frailty. The unproductive, bookish Jewish men who devoted their lives to religious learning accordingly became dependent on dominant wives, who took over male roles and earned the family income, rather than restricting themselves to the private sphere.[9] Colored of course by the gender assumptions of their authors, these descriptions reflect a normative thinking that was typical in Enlightenment discourse; in their condemnations of traditional ways of life as immoral, unhealthy, and unnatural, they promoted a middle-class gender order and subscribed to bourgeois ideas of male authority and privilege. Nevertheless, such negative depictions of Jewish family life in the shtetl by modernizing Jews remained influential throughout the twentieth century and continue to shape ideas and stereotypes of the Eastern European past today. Only recently have historians begun to conduct systematic research on the social reality of family patterns and gender organization among Jewish populations in the Pale of Settlement, and a more nuanced picture has begun to emerge.[10]

Significantly, scholars are transcending the framework of anti-Semitic representations and internal Jewish self-critiques, and are now seeking alternative perspectives for the study of Jewish masculinities and Jewish male identities. The Talmudist Daniel Boyarin helped open up such new interpretive possibilities with his provocative and controversial claim that Jewish culture has fostered a distinct Jewish gender order and a unique Jewish mode of masculinity that resonated from ancient times into the twentieth century.[11] In his 1997 book, *Unheroic Conduct,* Boyarin argued that the rabbis of the Talmudic era 2,000 years ago propagated a nonphallic, gentle patriarchy as a strategy of cultural resistance in opposition to prevailing gentile ideals of manliness. According to Boyarin, this particular Jewish gender order, with its ideal of a sensitive and emotionally accessible masculinity, still reverberated in the modern period, so much so that major figures of German-speaking Jewry such as Sigmund Freud and Theodor Herzl wrestled with and sought to overcome its influence and legacy.

*Unheroic Conduct* has provoked a great deal of debate among scholars of Jewish cultural studies and rabbinics, and has certainly increased the visibility and enhanced the profile of gender as a category of analysis. However, Boyarin's work has been slower to make its impact felt among historians, who have only recently begun to engage with its arguments and implications.[12] Several of the contributors to *Jewish Masculinities* evaluate the significance of Boyarin's work for historical scholarship and subject some of its claims to the scrutiny of empirical historical research into Jewish religious, cultural, and intellectual traditions in a variety of settings.

The chapters in this volume explore the problem of Jewish masculinity from a Judaic studies perspective, to be sure, but they are simultaneously rooted in the concerns of German history and historiography. After all, the Jewish men whose lives and experiences are the subject of this book were Germans too, and thus the history of German Jewish masculinities also needs to be seen as part of the history of German masculinities. The latter field was largely founded by a scholar who, not coincidentally, also published pathbreaking works on German Jewish history, George L. Mosse. Mosse and subsequent historians of Germany, such as Ute Frevert and Karen Hagemann, have used the prism of gender history to examine evolving cultures of maleness as part of the process of German nation building and the rise of nationalism and militarism.[13]

The history of masculinities began—in the words of historian Deborah Hertz—as a "child of gender history and a grandchild of women's history."[14] Several historians of Germany who did early research on women's history turned to men as historical subjects in the late 1980s and early 1990s. This move, the attempt to regard men too as gendered beings, was intended to open up new horizons for the history of women and to provoke a reenvisioning of German history along feminist lines.[15] Thus in 1992, Hanna Schissler expressed the hope that the historical study of men would complement what women's studies had accomplished in the preceding two decades. "If the goal of the feminist project is to disrupt the excessive emphasis on and the normative aggrandizement of the male [*Überhöhung des Männlichen*]," she declared, "it is important to study men *as men* in order to gain insight into how the life worlds are constructed that constantly reproduce the inequality between the sexes."[16]

*Jewish Masculinities* thus draws on the rich body of scholarship on Jewish women and the Jewish family that has emerged over the last several decades. It foregrounds the changing character of German Jewish masculinities and explores constructions and deconstructions of the gender of German Jewish men. It builds on the works by the founding mothers of German Jewish women's and gender studies, above all Marion Kaplan's groundbreaking investigations of the Jewish middle class in the nineteenth century, Jewish families under the Nazis, and the Jüdischer Frauenbund (Jewish Women's League); and Monika Richarz's foundational research on Jewish experience and daily life.[17] We have conceived of this volume as a kind of feminist "grandchild of women's history"—to use Hertz's term—and hope that it will contribute to the understanding and even challenging of existing gender regimes.

Critics of masculinity studies have charged that writing the history of masculinity can efface women and thus risks subverting feminist goals, constituting an "atavistic return to research on men."[18] The authors in this volume are sensitive to such concerns; even as they focus their attention on men and masculinity, they are careful not to elide women nor reproduce "atavistic" historical narratives. Their chapters are situated within the framework of feminist analyses which see gender as relational and which therefore dictate the historical study of women *and* men, femininity *and* masculinity. In this way, the volume interrogates hierarchies and regimes of power between men and women as well as between men and men, and its chapters proceed from the assumption that masculinity as a historical category includes both men and women. The contributions thus seek to discover whether particular modes of masculinity were accessible to women and to inquire into the relationships between (what contemporaries positioned as) the two sexes.

By exploring masculinities and the gender constructions of men without losing sight of women and femininity, this volume resists an erasure that appears to be intrinsic to the operation of difference. Inquiries into women as historical agents and into women's positions in historical processes necessarily involve some degree of engagement with the men in relation to whom women as a category are defined. This is not the case for accounts of men. The ontological status of "man" is by definition absolute, self-reflexive, and self-contained. Rather than requiring the naming of the Other in relation to which the subject position "man" acquires standing, manhood silences and obfuscates its relational Other, "woman."

The categories "German" and "Jew" operate in a similar manner in the discursive field of German and German Jewish history. Thus, when we write the history of German Jews, we cannot avoid doing so in relation to a German historical narrative which has a similarly absolute ontological status. Within this historiographic terrain, Jewish Germans remain unmentioned unless scholars make an effort to render them visible. This is not simply a reflection of the fact that Jews have always been a numerically small group within the German population; it is also a consequence of a regime of power in which "Germans" constitute the norm and "Jews" mark sites of difference, and it is part of a process by which structuring, master narratives obscure and obliterate difference.[19] The study of German Jewish masculinities, then, forces a consideration of the operation of difference on several levels, as it interrogates the workings of regimes of both gender difference and Jewish difference in German history and historiography.[20]

Thus, the chapters in *Jewish Masculinities* take up some of the key concerns that continue to preoccupy historians of Germany and German Jewry: the tensions between Jewish integration and the maintenance of a separate identity, the texture of Jewishness, the notion of Jewish distinctiveness, and the boundaries of the Jewish community. These investigations into the history of Jewish masculinities offer insights into the complex dynamics by which German Jews lived sameness as Germans and difference as Jews. The volume questions the conception of the modernization of Jewish society and culture in Germany as a monolithic and linear process and argues for the existence of multiple modernities, which are defined as much by gender, class, and culture as by the more traditional categories of religious affiliation and observance. Along similar lines, *Jewish Masculinities* builds on feminist reevaluations of German Jewish modernity but takes them in new directions, influenced above all by discourse analysis, social theory, and the toolkit of the new cultural history.[21] Several of the chapters combine current gender studies approaches with insights about culture and difference from cultural studies and postcolonial theory, and thereby extend and broaden feminist analyses to reexamine the foundations of Jewish self-perception and Jewish life worlds.[22]

Because the figure of the unmanly Jew was an extraordinarily powerful image in Germany and Austria at the turn of the twentieth century, German-speaking Europe provides an ideal terrain for this first systematic, historical exploration of Jewish masculinity. Indeed, much of the scholarship on anti-Semitic notions of Jewish masculinity and Jewish sexuality pertains to the German cultural setting.[23] Germany also constitutes a particularly compelling context for exploring the meanings of Jewish masculinities because of its long-standing status as the paradigm of modernity in Jewish studies scholarship. As nineteenth-century German Jews fought for emancipation and embraced the norms and values of the German middle classes, they adapted Jewish culture and religion to modern needs and bourgeois sensibilities. In the process they helped create some of the key intellectual and religious movements that shaped modern Judaism, including the tradition of modern Jewish historiography, Jewish scholarship in the form of *Wissenschaft des Judentums* (the science, or scholarly study, of Judaism), Reform Judaism, modern Orthodoxy, and the intellectual foundations of American Conservative Judaism. Of course, similar developments occurred elsewhere, notably in Italy, France, the Netherlands, Britain, Hungary, the Levant, and the Americas. However, due to the specific pressures of the German situation, German Jews seem to have been particularly prolific and self-conscious producers of modern Jewish cultural forms and of innovative religious movements. Within Jewish history and historiography, German Jews have also profited from the prestige of German culture from Beethoven and Mozart to Kant, Hegel, Marx, and Nietzsche. And perhaps most important, German cultural influence over Eastern Europe made the world's largest Jewish populations look to the German case as a model for modern, middle-class, cultivated Jewish life. Thus, from the mid-nineteenth century to the 1990s, the German Jewish path to modernity was widely accepted as representing the normative, if not the universal, Jewish experience; it served as a standard against which the histories of Jewish communities in other countries were measured and assessed.[24]

Among the shortcomings of this German-centric approach to Jewish history is its failure to do justice to the experience of most world Jewries; at the same time, it also obliterates the German dimension of German Jewish history and culture. As David Biale has argued in *Cultures of the Jews: A New History,* what figures as "Jewish culture" in a particular historical and geographic setting is always a reworking of aspects of local cultures in the course of which Jews create what is then Jewish.[25] From this perspective, German history not only has formed the background for German Jewish history and provided the ingredients for the German elements in the compound concept of "German Jewish," but the "Jewish" in "German Jewish" can be seen as partly German, too. Yet, German Jewish history is not fully contained within German history, but rather forms part of the history of Jewish particularities, communities, and cultural identities that together constitute a Jewish history perspective to which *Jewish Masculinities* is committed. Thus, most of the chapters in this volume frame their analyses in terms of German history *and* Jewish history, and by operating on both levels at once, they reveal the rich and complex interrelationships between Jewish and non-Jewish worlds.

Until recently, Jewish studies and Jewish historical scholarship have been dominated by the tendency to see the history of Jewish civilization as self-contained. Some scholars have studied the Jewish people as an ethnic group that has succeeded in surviving adversity and maintaining its cohesiveness and traditions, while others have traced the intellectual and religious lineages of Judaism from the world of the Talmudic rabbis to towering figures like Rashi, Maimonides, the Baal Shem Tov, Moses Mendelssohn, and Franz Rosenzweig, and then to the origins and development of modern Jewish movements, such as Reform or modern Orthodoxy.[26] With all its erudition and richness, this body of scholarship has for the most part been a fairly insular enterprise. Although a multitude of individual studies on Jewish religious and intellectual movements, Jewish personalities, and Jewish communities through the centuries and across the continents have explored the lines of continuity of Jewish life, they have too often treated Jewish cultures in isolation, inquiring infrequently into their interactions with the social and cultural fabrics of their host societies.[27]

At the same time, since World War II and the Holocaust, scholars of German history and of German Jewish history have often de-emphasized the Jewishness of German Jews and instead stressed their Germanness. This tendency, we believe, represented an attempt to overcome the legacies of National Socialism and a desire to reassert German Jews' membership in and identification with German society and culture, but it may have gone too far in its downplaying of Jewish distinctiveness. Indeed, Nazi ideology shattered the once-nuanced matrix of "German," "German Jewish," and "Jewish" identities. The Nazi worldview imagined Germans and Jews as two distinct and mutually exclusive racial groups which were locked in an existential struggle, and the National Socialist state implemented a murderous policy of purging Jews from the German *Volkskörper* (national body). Against this background, historians came to conceive of the process of German Jews' integration and acculturation into German society as a development whose limits were set solely by anti-Semitism, ignoring the appeal that Jewish identity and Jewish communal life continued to have. Postwar scholars of both German and German Jewish history tended to shy away from treating Jewish Germans as a collective that, as a part of world Jewry, was engaged in a process of maintaining difference and reworking age-old modes of particularity in a modern framework. A significant number of historians examined the Jewish population in Germany as a segment of German society that stood out by its unique social profile, cultural preferences, and religious practices—or, at least, religiously defined family background—but they often overlooked the historical agency of their subjects, that is the ways some German Jews negotiated the challenge of trying to remain at once fully German and distinctly, even deeply Jewish.[28]

We believe that new methods of cultural history and theory, perhaps most of all postcolonial studies, offer extremely useful insights into the minority experience of Jews in German culture and society. Postcolonial studies provide fresh perspectives that allow us to transcend the sometimes artificial and awkward divisions between Germanness and Jewishness that persistently vex historians of the German Jewish past. As scholars of empire have investigated the consequences of the encounter between colonizer and colonized in African, Asian, and Latin American settings, they have created a vocabulary that can be applied to the experience of Jews, who for centuries figured as Europe's quintessential Other. In colonial settings, the imposition of the economic and cultural hegemony of Europeans has rarely led to the seamless erasure of the ethnic, cultural, and religious particularities of indigenous populations. Rather, colonization entailed processes of co-optation, transformation, and mutual interpenetration in the course of which multiple new forms of identity and cultural practice emerged, and neither the colonizer nor the colonized remained unchanged. Resistance then materialized not as a frontal assault on the cultural regime of the European invader, but from within new hybrid cultural configurations, shaped and informed by indigenous traditions, European cultural patterns, and distinctly colonial modes of thought and conduct.[29] Along similar lines, scholars have explored the mechanisms of the social and cultural subjugation of people of color in the First World itself, and in Jewish studies, researchers have begun to examine how German Jews of the nineteenth century asserted Jewish distinctiveness and dignity as Jews from within the German culture they had come to embrace.[30]

Applying this methodology to the study of German Jewry constitutes a breakthrough not only for Jewish history, but also for the study of German and European society and history as a whole. The scholars who have created a voluminous body of literature on the processes of Jewish emancipation, integration, and acculturation into—and exclusion from—German society have until recently treated German Jews as a minority population that faced a well-defined, even monolithic German society. Today the very conception of a

German mainstream society in relation to which Jews have figured as the Other is in question. Rather, historians are beginning to understand nineteenth- and twentieth-century Germany as consisting of culturally diverse and distinct individuals and groups with multiple, constantly evolving identities that together shaped "a public space of common culture."[31] Thus, conceiving of German Jews as Germans while employing a culturally sensitive and specific conception of this population's (varied expressions of) Jewishness means redefining the terms of both Jewish history and German history.[32]

This volume's chapters evoke a new, decentered, multivalent German and German Jewish history specifically through the lens of gender. Gender analyses in postcolonial studies have provided windows into the makeup of and the relationships between different social, cultural, ethnic, and religious groups. Scholars have also focused on gender expressions, gender relations, and norms of gendered behavior, treating them as sites where regimes and elites try to impose boundaries and hierarchies, where individuals probe and contest community and belonging, and where men and women enact religious and ethnic identities. The study of masculinities in this context has proven particularly fruitful, as maleness has typically been predicated on domination, superiority (over women), and privileged access to material goods and other resources.[33]

As a whole, *Jewish Masculinities* applies these kinds of insights to the field of German Jewish gender history. Its contributors ask how the concept of masculinity played out in the German Jewish social, political, and cultural matrix. They explore how German Jewish men and women responded to, resisted, adopted, and adapted gender ideals and gendered social and cultural practices from the cultures in which they lived; how they reinvented their Jewishness; and how Jewish men made sense of themselves as men, as Germans, and as Jews.

This volume assumes that the content of German culture and the boundaries of German society were never natural and self-evident, but emerged through the participation and involvement of Jews, Catholics, feminists, Afro-Germans, various groups of immigrants, and other "outsiders" and "foreigners." Similarly, the boundaries of German culture have exceeded the often shifting and unstable territorial bases of German polities and regimes. Thus, these chapters not only explore Jewish masculinities and the lived experiences of men and women in Germany proper, but also extend beyond Germany's borders to Austria and even Eastern Europe. Likewise, several chapters in *Jewish Masculinities* follow German-speaking Jews in emigration and exile, to Palestine (later, Israel) and to the United States.

We begin with a chapter by Andreas Gotzmann, who challenges and updates common assumptions about premodern Jewish masculinity and male behavior. Gotzmann explores the case of Veith Kahn, a philandering and deceitful Jewish businessman who lived in Frankfurt in the late seventeenth century and early eighteenth. He uses the lurid details of Kahn's personal life and business ventures to shed light on Jewish life and gender relations in the period. He shows, for example, that the ideal of the pious, gentle-mannered, and peace-loving family father existed side by side with Jewish men actually comporting themselves as truly virile "real men," who were fully capable of sexual harassment and other improper and aggressive behaviors. This distinction between cultural ideals and norms, on the one hand, and social practices, on the other, Gotzmann argues, was not a sign of the decay of Jewish society but indeed was integral to Jewish culture. Furthermore, using the records of Kahn's criminal proceedings, Gotzmann documents that even a Jewish man who failed to live up to contemporary ethical and social standards stood above women in the social hierarchy and was perceived as powerful and masculine by Jews and Christians alike.

Gotzmann's research gives us insights into the gender order of early modern Ashkenazi Jewry and into concepts of Jewish manliness at that time which go significantly beyond what we knew from the memoirs of Glikl of Hameln, our most important and most heavily relied upon source up to now.[34] Gotzmann, furthermore, shows the inadequacy of stereotypes which depict Jewish men as weak, modest, defenseless, and most of all dedicated Talmud scholars. His chapter suggests that neither the tension between (Jewish) norms and the actual behavior of Jews nor the distinction between religious and profane life worlds are functions of the modern Jewish condition.

Central to the next several chapters, which focus on the nineteenth century, is the program and culture of *Bildung,* the uniquely German ideal of the harmonious formation of the heart and the intellect. These authors ask, in different ways and from different perspectives, how the ideal of *Bildung* and the practices by which German Jews pursued it—in conjunction with a variety of forms of Jewishness and varying degrees of engagement with Jewish cultural and religious traditions—informed the masculinities and identities of German Jewish men. Benjamin Baader focuses on the writings of three Jewish leaders from different religious movements: the Reform preachers Gotthold Salomon of Hamburg and Adolf Jellinek of Vienna, and the Frankfurt founder of modern Orthodoxy, Samson Raphael Hirsch. Baader shows that these rabbis and preachers not only developed and promoted an emotionalized culture of bourgeois religiosity in which they assigned a central place to women, but Hirsch and Jellinek also believed in and advocated a gentle and affectionate form of Jewish masculinity and declared femininity to constitute the principle of the Jewish religion. Even though the tender manliness they celebrated was clearly an expression of the contemporary culture of bourgeois sensitivity, these Jewish leaders contended that it was a distinctively Jewish character trait, and they might have contributed to the rise of twentieth-century ideas of the effeminate Jewish male.

In a similar vein, Robin Judd's discussion of two types of Jewish ritual practitioners in the nineteenth century, *shochetim* (kosher slaughterers) and *mohelim* (performers of circumcision), shows that Jewish men adopted the contemporary ideals of an educated and balanced manhood. They not only expressed German cultural sensibilities and demonstrated their affiliation with the German middle class, but the poise, orderliness, and self-control they sought to exhibit were also intended to embody a dignified Jewishness. Such attributes of a refined manliness may have been especially important given the ongoing German debates about kosher slaughtering and the controversies around circumcision, in which anti-Semites described Jewish rites and practices as archaic, disorderly, and uncivilized.

In the volume's next chapter on nineteenth-century German Jewish masculinities and bourgeois culture, Stefanie Schüler-Springorum presents the case of Aron Liebeck, a Jewish businessman born in 1856, who left an extremely detailed and rich memoir. Schüler-Springorum analyzes the text closely and pays attention to Liebeck's language and narrative choices. She shows that Liebeck portrayed himself as a man who adhered steadfastly to rigorous standards of honor, and who engineered his and his family's social and economic advancement with great determination and integrity. Yet Liebeck characterized himself as a "soft hero." He was a fighter and an achiever, but he was also a family man who, like Baader's protagonists, rejected military standards of manhood and celebrated male beauty and gentleness in his friends and associates.

Lisa Fetheringill Zwicker, in her chapter on Jewish and Catholic student fraternities and male honor in Wilhelmine Germany, takes a comparative perspective, which places middle-class German Jewish masculinities in broader contexts and therefore helps us assess their uniqueness. Zwicker offers a detailed analysis of two incidents in which male students perceived an affront to their honor and sought satisfaction. Due to the papal prohibition on dueling, the devout Catholic student eschewed the duel and appealed to university authorities to restore his honor. The Jewish student, on the other hand, belonged to a Jewish dueling fraternity, which gave him the ability to defend his name and reputation with force. Significantly, as Zwicker argues, the renewed popularity and visibility of dueling in this period (among non-Jews and Jews) can be seen, at least in part, as a backlash against the entrance of women into German universities.

While Zwicker's contribution is largely based on university records, the next chapter, by Sander Gilman, draws on scientific and medical literature from the late nineteenth and early twentieth centuries. Specifically, Gilman looks at material on hermaphroditism and sex and gender identity, and also at a number of autobiographical accounts in which, from the late nineteenth century on, authors explored issues of sexual difference. One of the most interesting of these published memoirs is the story of "N. O. Body," which appeared in 1907 with an epilogue by the prominent German Jewish sexologist Magnus Hirschfeld. Under the pseudonym of N. O. Body, Karl M. Baer, born into a Jewish family in

1885, related how he had been taken for and raised as a girl (Martha), but as an adult decided to live as a man, after a medical examination determined his sex to be male. Gilman uses Baer's testimony to reflect on the meanings of Jewish and gender identities in Imperial Germany. In the terms of nineteenth-century science, Gilman argues, Jewish identity, like other ethnic and national identities, was racialized, meaning it was understood as having an underlying and immutable biological basis. The same applied to sexual identity, around which no ambiguity could be tolerated. Gilman thus interrogates a process in which both masculinity and Jewishness were turned into essentialized categories and were mapped and inscribed onto bodies.

Gilman's contribution is followed by Etan Bloom's chapter, which moves the discussion from Germany to Palestine/Israel and focuses on Zionism, Israeli culture, and the body. Bloom uses the modern Hebrew handshake to get at a series of larger issues, including the rise of a hegemonic masculinist Israeli body language. According to Bloom, the decidedly firm handshake, together with a forceful slap on the back, neck, or shoulder, which gained currency among Jewish men in pre-state Palestine, exemplifies a particular type of masculinist physicality that the German Jewish Zionist and scientist Arthur Ruppin and the Palestine Office (which promoted and monitored Jewish immigration to Palestine) succeeded in popularizing. In a highly original fashion, Bloom uses Pierre Bourdieu's concept of the habitus and a set of related ethnographic and semiotic categories to examine the inscription of social practices and ideologies on the bodies and movements of Israeli men. Bloom argues that the ultimately influential group of Zionists around Ruppin had internalized European notions of the degenerate character of diaspora Jewry and consciously engaged in the project of creating a physically fit, phallic Hebrew man.

The next two chapters are case studies exploring the array of choices available to individuals who lived masculinity and Jewishness in interwar Germany and Austria, and the dilemmas these Jewish men faced. First, Ann Goldberg presents an in-depth, psychoanalytically informed reading of the voluminous correspondence between Friedrich Gundolf, a reactionary literature scholar from Heidelberg, and Elisabeth Salomon, his (Jewish) "new woman" lover and, later, wife. On the one hand, Gundolf was a Jewish Wagnerian. He rejected his Jewishness and belonged to a group of male intellectuals around the homosexual poet Stefan George, who espoused an anti-modernist, anti-feminist, and philosophically anti-Semitic worldview. On the other hand, Gundolf bonded with Salomon as a Jew and adored and encouraged her free-spirited and independent femininity. Yet he also feared the power of Salomon's womanhood and cast himself as the feminized, racialized Other who submitted to his "black mistress." At his best, Gundolf advocated the "doubleness of the German Jew" and envisioned an intellectual realm where Jewish men and women could recreate themselves while remaining Jews.

Siegmund Breitbart, the Jewish strongman whom Sharon Gillerman discusses, likewise navigated complex sets of gendered, racial, and ethnic identities that contemporaries and scholars often think of as mutually exclusive. Yet Breitbart did so with significantly greater success and ease than did Gundolf, as he shifted his repertoire according to the tastes and preferences of his multiple audiences. Gillerman finds that Breitbart simultaneously personified Jewish working-class images of physical prowess *and* ideals of soft-heartedness, Jewish learnedness, and German *Bildung,* while he could also embody the strong Zionist protector and even the Imperial German military hero. Breitbart operated and performed within a field of overlapping and shifting discourses and identities, and in his performances and in his offstage persona he borrowed from and transformed both the Jewish and the German cultural contexts. Drawing on postcolonial theory, Gillerman proposes an understanding of Breitbart that undercuts simplified oppositions between the rabbinic culture of learnedness and Zionist "muscle Jews" as well as between German and Jewish, Western and Eastern, modern and traditional modes of masculinities, which gives us insight into the complexity and fluidity of both East European Jewish and German norms and practices of masculinity.

From the discussions of these two exceptional individuals, who pushed the boundaries of public and private Jewishness in the Weimar period, we return in the volume's final chapter to the lives of more common Jewish men. Simultaneously we shift from historical and cultural studies analyses to the methods of historical sociology, as Judith Gerson inquires into the gender identities and gendered practices of Jewish men under National Socialism and its aftermath. Through her analysis of a body of memoirs by German Jewish refugees who settled in New York, Gerson is able to rework our understanding of Jewish families' responses to life under Nazi rule and after emigration. Gerson's work builds on previous scholarship as she shows that male refugees typically dwelled on their military service in World War I and their families' long loyalty to the German nation, thus expressing particular male concerns and sensibilities. Yet her findings also challenge earlier research on the gendered behavior of Nazi era refugees, as Gerson shows how these men wrote for the benefit of family members and consistently emphasized family matters and domestic affairs. In contrast to Aron Liebeck, whose memoir revolved around his personal feats and accomplishments, these men emplotted their lives within broader narratives that stressed family continuities and German Jewish historical trajectories.

One significant topic not covered in this volume is Jewish masculinities under National Socialism. The impact of the Nazi dictatorship on Jewish masculine identity, on the representations and constructions of Jewish masculinity, and indeed on the ways that Jewish men performed their gender roles is an area of study with enormous potential that still awaits systematic research and analysis. Nazi propaganda about Jews was certainly gendered, and the Nazis drew on a whole range of age-old stereotypes about Jewish men, including depicting them as flaccid and unmanly and constantly warning about their deceitful, corrupt, and sexually rapacious ways. While some representations recycled notions of the alleged weakness and physical deficiencies of male Jews, others attributed enormous powers to Jewish men, claiming that they controlled high finance and capitalism and commanded Soviet Russia, the United States, and international networks of spies. Furthermore, Nazi propaganda contrasted the Jew's alleged mobility, cleverness, and amorality with the Aryan's deliberateness, steadiness, and rootedness, and claimed to be protecting the latter from the devious machinations of the former.

Nazi racialism left no room for nuanced distinctions or subtle notions of identity. Jews—whether from Germany or Eastern Europe, from big cities or small towns, devout or indifferent—constituted a racial category to be defined (by the hastily written and maladroit Nuremberg Laws of 1935), marked, and weeded out of the *Volksgemeinschaft* (national community). The Nazis thus negated the complexities and subtleties of German Jewish subjectivity. They rendered moot the ongoing challenge of balancing German citizenship and cultural affiliation with Jewish communal solidarity and religious practice—the defining drama of some two centuries of German Jewish history and an issue of existential import to so many of the individuals who are featured in this volume's chapters, from Aron Liebeck through Karl M. Baer, from the religious leaders of Baader's chapter and the *mohelim* and *shochetim* of Judd's chapter through the Jewish Wagnerian, Friedrich Gundolf, discussed by Goldberg, and Gerson's German Jewish refugees, who clung to their World War I medals and reclaimed their families' deep German lineages.

Nazi policy toward Jews can also be viewed as a systematic emasculation of Jewish men. Starting soon after the Nazi assumption of power in 1933, increasing numbers of Jewish men were barred from carrying out their occupations, thus preventing them from being breadwinners and the protectors of their families. Nazi propaganda often became self-fulfilling prophecy, as Michael Berkowitz points out in his superb study of the myth of Jewish criminality.[35] Depriving Jews of legitimate means of earning a living and herding them into overcrowded, disease-ridden ghettos turned some Jews (by necessity) to crime and infected them with disease, giving a patina of truth to spurious stereotypes and vilifications. Similarly, rhetoric about the failure of Jewish men to carry out their masculine roles was reinforced by the effects of Nazi policies, which pushed them out of the public sphere, barred them from the military, and stripped them of their positions and livelihoods.

Thanks to the work of several historians, above all Marion Kaplan, we now know a great deal about Jewish families in Nazi Germany and the ways women struggled to hold families together, to sustain beleaguered communities, and to organize emigration.[36] Kaplan's work focuses largely on women's experiences.

Scholars have yet to provide a detailed analysis of what Nazi persecution meant for Jewish men as men, or to thematize the masculinity of Jewish men in National Socialist Germany in a systematic and sustained manner. Thus at this point we have far too little insight into the psychological impact of Nazi propaganda and policy, or of the experience of street violence, physical intimidation and humiliation, deportation, and life in the concentration camps on masculine self-identity in those years.[37]

Of course National Socialism ultimately failed in its attempts to cleanly separate Jews from non-Jews and to excise Jews from German and European life. And while the Nazi period obviously marked the absolute nadir of Jewish life in Germany, it did not put an end to the complex interconnectedness of German and Jewish histories and identities. In fact, relations between German and European Jews and what the Nazis considered Aryan Germans continued throughout the darkest years of Nazi persecution and genocide and began to assume their post-Holocaust configurations immediately after the war, when more than 180,000 Jewish survivors from Eastern Europe found temporary homes in the displaced-person camps of occupied Germany.[38] While it was common in the second half of the twentieth century to refer to "Jews" and "Germans" as if the two terms designated mutually exclusive groups, scholars have argued that the Nazi genocide of European Jewry by no means disentangled the German-Jewish cultural matrix. On the contrary, as soon as the killings ended and the events began to enter historical consciousness, the reality of (non-Jewish) German guilt and Jewish victimhood created new webs of German-Jewish interrelatedness and reinscribed the "Jewish question" into the fabric of (West) German national identity. As Auschwitz developed into a fixture in the symbolic landscape of postwar Europe, the German extermination project that is known today as "the Holocaust" became a pillar of Jewish identity worldwide; at the same time, a "negative symbiosis" emerged which ties together Jews who live in Germany and other Germans.[39]

And once again, even as we write these lines, Jewish life in Germany is undergoing a dramatic transformation. Immigrants from the former Soviet Union have revitalized Jewish communities and doubled, tripled, and even quadrupled their numbers in some cases. Berlin, above all, has reemerged as a dynamic, cosmopolitan metropolis and is now home to large and conspicuous populations of Russian, Israeli, and North American Jews, who are updating and reimagining their identities and, hand in hand with the more established segment of contemporary German Jewry, actively creating their own twenty-first-century German-Jewish symbioses. These populations, together with the far greater numbers of Turkish, Arabic, and Southern and Eastern European residents, present a serious challenge to German ethno-nationalism and are at last helping to decouple German ethnicity from national belonging.[40] At the same time, Berlin appears to have regained its position at the forefront of avant-garde artistic movements and cultural experimentation and, fittingly, as a space for new articulations of Jewish gender identity.[41] Amid the current resurgence of Jewish life in Germany, our three organizing categories—Jewishness, gender, and Germanness—thus once again interact and intersect in challenging and provocative ways.

These observations are not meant to suggest that discrimination, anti-Semitism, and racism have disappeared, nor that Jews in Germany today live with complete ease in the shadows of the Third Reich. Indeed, the burdens of history remain palpable; they are etched into the landscape, and everyday interactions are still encumbered by their often suffocating weight. Nevertheless, despite these tangible obstacles, the stories told in this volume are open-ended and the themes are ongoing. Jews—both living and dead, in Germany and beyond—remain inextricably bound up with German narratives and German national identity, and Jewish history and German history will continue to be intertwined indefinitely.

The academic world is changing too. As Jews in North America and Europe are more solidly and centrally established in the political and cultural matrices of their societies and are more self-confident than ever before, Jewish studies has reached the mainstream of the academic enterprise, and the walls are breaking down. Our generation of scholars and those who follow us are increasingly literate and fully at home in multiple fields, such as Judaic studies, German studies, and gender studies. While Jewish studies and Jewish history scholars labored largely in vain for more than a century to engage the luminaries of German studies and German history in dialogue, today's German studies scholars in North America turn to "Jewish topics" in order to give their field new impulses.[42] Moreover, as we discussed above, postcolonial and other decentering readings of German history challenge the time-honored master narratives in the field. Likewise, women's studies and gender studies have been revolutionizing all disciplines, as they open new vistas in well-explored areas of investigation and provide key insights into the operation of difference. In this significantly altered scholarly, intellectual, and cultural landscape, Jewish studies researchers have started to go beyond seeking dialogue with representatives of mainstream (German) history schools and rather choose to practice Jewish history and gender studies from within German history and other traditionally hegemonic scholarly fields. We hope that the chapters in this volume offer a glimpse of the potential for this new generation of scholarship. We also hope that future scholars will pick up where this book leaves off and continue to explore and investigate German Jewish masculinities along the intertwined axes of German history, Jewish history, and gender history.

NOTES

1. Quoted in David Biale, *Blood and Belief: The Circulation of a Symbol between Jews and Christians* (Berkeley: University of California Press, 2007), 105; Sander Gilman, *Jewish Self-Hatred: Anti-Semitism and the Hidden Language of the Jews* (Baltimore, MD: Johns Hopkins University Press, 1986), 74–75; Irven M. Resnick, "Medieval Roots of the Myth of Male Jewish Menses," *Harvard Theological Review* 93, no. 3 (2000): 258–260.

2. Willis Johnson, "The Myth of Jewish Male Menstruation," *Journal of Medieval History* 24 (1998): 273–295; David S. Katz, "Shylock's Gender: Jewish Male Menstruation in Early Modern England," *Review of English Studies* 50 (1999): 440–462. See also Biberman, who claims that the hypermasculine "Jew-Devil" was the anti-Jewish stereotype of medieval Europe that only in the early modern era was replaced by the notion of the "Sissy-Jew." Michael Biberman, *Masculinity, Anti-Semitism and Early Modern English Literature* (Burlington, VT: Ashgate, 2004).

3. Quoted in Ritchie Robertson, "Historicizing Weininger: The Nineteenth-Century German Image of the Feminized Jew," in Bryan Cheyette and Laura Marcus, eds., *Modernity, Culture and "the Jew"* (Stanford, CA: Stanford University Press, 1998), 25.

4. Baader, this volume; Baader, "Jews, Women, and Germans: Jewish and German Historiographies in a Transatlantic Perspective," in Karen Hagemann and Jean Quartaert, eds., *Gendering Modern German History: Rewriting Historiography* (Oxford: Berghahn, 2007), 182; Ute Frevert, *A Nation in Barracks: Modern Germany, Military Conscription and Civil Society* (Oxford: Berg, 2004), 65–69; Robertson, "Historicizing Weininger," 25–27; Kevin McAleer, *Dueling: The Cult of Honor in Fin-de-Siècle Germany* (Princeton, NJ: Princeton University Press, 1994), esp. 155.

5. Paula E. Hyman, *The Emancipation of the Jews of Alsace: Acculturation and Tradition in the Nineteenth Century* (New Haven, CT: Yale University Press, 1991), ch. 4; Hyman, "Introduction," in Steven M. Cohen and Paula E. Hyman, eds., *The Jewish Family: Myth and Reality* (London: Holmes & Meier, 1986), 3–4; Hyman, "The Modern Jewish Family: Image and Reality," in David Kraemer, ed., *The Jewish Family: Metaphor and Memory* (New York: Oxford University Press, 1989), 179–193.

6. Carl E. Schorske, *Fin-de-Siècle Vienna: Politics and Culture* (New York: Vintage, 1981). See also, among others, Steven Beller, ed., *Rethinking Vienna 1900* (New York: Berghahn, 1991); Suzanne Marchand and David Lindenfeld, eds., *Germany at the Fin de Siècle: Culture, Politics and Ideas* (Baton Rouge: Louisiana State University Press, 2004); Kevin Repp, *Reformers, Critics and the Paths of German Modernity* (Cambridge, MA: Harvard University Press, 2000).

7. John Efron, *Medicine and the German Jews: A History* (New Haven, CT: Yale University Press, 2001), 142–150, esp. 145; Frevert, *Nation in Barracks;* Sander Gilman, *Franz Kafka, the Jewish Patient* (New York: Routledge, 1995); Gilman, *Freud, Race, and Gender* (Princeton, NJ: Princeton University Press, 1993); Gilman, *The Jew's Body* (New York: Routledge, 1991); Gilman, *Jewish Self-Hatred: Anti-Semitism and the Hidden Language of the Jews* (Baltimore, MD: Johns Hopkins University Press, 1986), esp. 243–246; Klaus Hödl, *Die Pathologisierung des jüdischen Körpers: Antisemitismus, Geschlecht und Medizin im Fin de Siècle* (Vienna: Picus, 1997), 164–232; Nancy A. Harrowitz and Barbara Hyams, eds., *Jews and Gender: Responses to Otto Weininger* (Philadelphia: Temple University Press, 1995); David Luft, *Eros and Inwardness in Vienna: Weininger, Musil, Doderer* (Chicago: University of Chicago Press, 1989); Paul Reitter, *The Anti-Journalist: Karl Kraus and Jewish Self-Fashioning in Fin-de-Siècle Europe* (Chicago: University of Chicago Press, 2008); Paula E. Hyman, *Gender and Assimilation in Modern Jewish History: The Roles and Representation of Women* (Seattle: University of Washington Press, 1995), 134–160; Céline Kaiser and Marie-Luise Wünsche, eds., *"Die Nervosität der Juden" und andere Leiden an der Zivilisation:*

*Konstruktionen des Kollektiven und Konzepte individueller Krankheit im psychiatrischen Diskurs um 1900* (Paderborn: Ferdinand Schöningh, 2003); George Mosse, *The Image of Man: The Creation of Modern Masculinity* (New York: Oxford University Press, 1996); Mosse, *Nationalism and Sexuality: Respectability and Abnormal Sexuality in Modern Europe* (New York: Howard Fertig, 1985), 36–37, 133–152; Chandak Sengoopta, *Otto Weininger: Sex, Science and Self in Imperial Vienna* (Chicago: University of Chicago Press, 2000).

8. Michael Berkowitz, *Zionist Culture and West European Jewry before the First World War* (Chapel Hill: University of North Carolina Press, 1993), esp. 99–118; Sharon Gillerman, "Samson in Vienna: The Politics of Jewish Masculinity," *Jewish Social Studies* 9 (2003): 65–98; Gillerman, "More than Skin Deep: Histories of the Modern Jewish Body," *Jewish Quarterly Review* 95 (2005): 470–478; Todd Presner, "'Clear Heads, Solid Stomachs, and Hard Muscles': Max Nordau and the Aesthetics of Regeneration," *Modernism/Modernity* 10, no. 2 (2003): 269–296; Presner, *Muscular Judaism: The Jewish Body and the Politics of Regeneration* (London: Routledge, 2007); Michael Stanislawski, *Zionism and the Fin de Siècle: Cosmopolitanism and Nationalism from Nordau to Jabotinsky* (Berkeley: University of California Press, 2001); Daniel Wildmann, *Der veränderbare Körper: Jüdische Turner, Männlichkeit und das Wiedergewinnen von Geschichte in Deutschland um 1900* (Tübingen: Mohr Siebeck, 2009); Wildmann, "Jewish Gymnasts and Their Corporeal Utopias in Imperial Germany," in Michael Brenner and Gideon Reuveni, eds., *Emancipation through Muscles: Jews and Sports in Europe* (Lincoln: University of Nebraska Press, 2006), 27–43.

9. David Biale, "Childhood, Marriage and the Jewish Family in the Eastern European Jewish Enlightenment," in Cohen and Hyman, eds., *The Jewish Family*, 45–61; Biale, *Eros and the Jews: From Biblical Israel to Contemporary America* (New York: Basic, 1992), 149–175; Shulamit S. Magnus, "Sins of Youth, Guilt of a Grandmother: M. L. Lilienblum, Pauline Wengeroff, and the Telling of Jewish Modernity in Eastern Europe," in ChaeRan Y. Freeze, Paula E. Hyman, and Antony Polonsky, eds., *Jewish Women in Eastern Europe* (Oxford: Littman Library of Jewish Civilization, 2005), 87–120.

10. ChaeRan Y. Freeze, *Jewish Marriage and Divorce in Imperial Russia* (Hanover, NH: Brandeis University Press, 2002); Freeze, Hyman, and Polonsky, eds., *Jewish Women in Eastern Europe*; Immanuel Etkes, "Marriage and Torah Study among the *Lomdim* in Lithuania in the Nineteenth Century," in David Kraemer, ed., *The Jewish Family: Metaphor and Memory* (New York: Oxford University Press, 1989), 153–178; Gershon Hundert, "Approaches to the History of the Jewish Family in Early Modern Poland-Lithuania," in Cohen and Hyman, eds., *The Jewish Family*, 17–28; Hyman, *Gender and Assimilation*, 50–92; Shaul Stampfer, *Families, Rabbis, and Education* (Oxford: Littman Library of Jewish Civilization, 2010).

11. Daniel Boyarin, *Unheroic Conduct: The Rise of Heterosexuality and the Invention of the Jewish Man* (Berkeley: University of California Press, 1997).

12. Some historical studies of Jewish masculinity are Gregory A. Caplan, "Germanising the Jewish Male: Military Masculinity as the Last Stage of Acculturation," in Rainer Liedtke and David Rechter, eds., *Towards Normality? Acculturation and Modern German Jewry* (Tübingen: Mohr Siebeck, 2003), 159–184; Caplan, "Militärische Männlichkeit in der deutsch-jüdischen Geschichte," *Die Philosophin* 22 (2000): 85–100; Caplan, "Wicked Sons, German Heroes: Jewish Soldiers, Veterans, and Memories of World War I in Germany," Ph.D. diss, Georgetown University, 2001; Till van Rahden, "Jews and the Ambivalences of Civil Society in Germany, 1800 to 1933—Assessment and Reassessment," *Journal of Modern History* 77, no. 4 (2005): 1045; Stefanie Schüler-Springorum, "'Denken, Wirken, Schaffen': Das erfolgreiche Leben des Aron Liebeck," in Andreas Gotzmann, Rainer Liedtke, and Till van Rahden, eds., *Juden, Bürger, Deutsche: Zur Geschichte von Vielfalt und Differenz, 1800–1933* (Tübingen: Mohr, 2001), 369–393.

13. George L. Mosse, *German Jews beyond Judaism* (Bloomington: Indiana University Press, 1983); Mosse, *Image of Man;* Mosse, *Nationalism and Sexuality.* See also Stanley G. Payne, David J. Sorkin, and John S. Tortorice, eds., *What History Tells: George L. Mosse and the Culture of Modern Europe* (Madison: University of Wisconsin Press, 2004); Ute Frevert, *Men of Honor: A Social and Cultural History of the Duel* (Cambridge: Polity, 1995); Frevert, *Nation in Barracks;* Karen Hagemann, "*Männlicher Muth und Teutsche Ehre*": *Nation, Militär und Geschlecht in Preußen zur Zeit der Antinapoleonischen Kriege* (Paderborn: Ferdinand Schöningh, 2002); McAleer, *Dueling;* and Paul Lerner, *Hysterical Men: War, Psychiatry and the Politics of Trauma in Germany, 1890–1930* (Ithaca, NY: Cornell University Press, 2003).

14. Deborah Hertz, "Männlichkeit und Melancholie im Berlin der Biedermeierzeit," in Kirsten Heinsohn and Stefanie Schüler-Springorum, eds., *Jüdische Geschichte als Geschlechtergeschichte: Studien zum 19. und 20. Jahrhundert* (Göttingen: Wallstein, 2006), 291.

15. For the crucial contributions of Ute Frevert and Karen Hagemann to women's history, see Frevert, *Women in German History: From Bourgeois Emancipation to Sexual Liberation* (Oxford: Berg, 1989); Hagemann, *Frauenalltag und Männerpolitik: Alltagsleben und gesellschaftliches Handeln von Arbeiterfrauen in der Weimarer Republik* (Bonn: Dietz, 1990).

16. Hanna Schissler, "Männerstudien in den USA," *Geschichte und Gesellschaft* 18 (1992): 220.

17. Marion Kaplan, *The Jewish Feminist Movement in Germany: The Campaigns of the Jüdischer Frauenbund, 1904–1938* (Westport, CT: Greenwood, 1979); Kaplan, *Between Dignity and Despair: Jewish Life in Nazi Germany* (New York: Oxford University Press, 1998); Kaplan, *The Making of the Jewish Middle Class: Women, Family, and Identity in Imperial Germany* (New York: Oxford University Press, 1991); Monika Richarz, ed., *Jewish Life in Germany: Memoirs from Three Centuries,* trans. Stella P. Rosenfeld and Sidney Rosenfeld (Bloomington: Indiana University Press, 1991); Richarz, ed., *Die Hamburger Kauffrau Glikl: Jüdische Existenz in der Frühen Neuzeit* (Hamburg: Christians, 1991). Other feminist-inspired works related to women and the family include Harriet Freidenreich, *Female, Jewish, and Educated: The Lives of Central European University Women* (Bloomington: Indiana University Press, 2002); Deborah Hertz, *Jewish High Society in Old Regime Berlin* (New Haven, CT: Yale University Press, 1988); Gudrun Maierhof, *Selbstbehauptung im Chaos: Frauen in der jüdischen Selbsthilfe 1933–1943* (Frankfurt: Campus, 2002); Elisabeth Malleier, *Jüdische Frauen in Wien, 1816–1938: Wohlfahrt—Mädchenbildung—Frauenarbeit* (Vienna: Mandelbaum, 2003); Sibylle Quack, *Zuflucht Amerika: Zur Sozialgeschichte der Emigration deutsch-jüdischer Frauen in die USA, 1933–1945* (Bonn: Dietz, 1995). The eminent volume on Jewish gender history, Paula Hyman's *Gender and Assimilation,* touches on Germany only in passing. On this body of literature, see also Baader, "Jews, Women, and Germans," 175–178.

18. Hertz, "Männlichkeit und Melancholie," 291. This issue was the subject of lively and at times heated debate at the Jewish Masculinities Conference, where the contributions to this volume were originally presented.

19. For a thought-provoking discussion of master narratives and difference, see Prasenjit Duara, *Rescuing History from the Nation State: Questioning Narratives of Modern China* (Chicago: University of Chicago Press, 1995), esp. introduction and ch. 1.

20. For a literary and cultural-historical approach to this problematic, see Mark H. Gelber, ed., *Confrontations/Accommodations: German-Jewish Literary and Cultural Relations from Heine to Wassermann* (Tübingen: Niemeyer), 2004.

21. For examples of this scholarship, see Benjamin Maria Baader, *Gender, Judaism, and Bourgeois Culture in Germany, 1800–1870* (Bloomington: Indiana University Press, 2006); Sharon Gillerman, *Germans into Jews: Remaking the Jewish Social Body in the*

*Weimar Republic* (Stanford, CA: Stanford University Press, 2009); and Alison Rose, *Jewish Women in Fin de Siècle Vienna* (Austin: University of Texas Press, 2008).

22. For the new Jewish cultural studies and examples of postcolonial readings of German Jewish modernity, see Jonathan Boyarin and Daniel Boyarin, eds., *Jews and Other Differences: The New Jewish Cultural Studies* (Minneapolis: University of Minnesota Press, 1997); Daniel Boyarin, Daniel Itzkovitz, and Ann Pellegrini, eds., *Queer Theory and the Jewish Question* (New York: Columbia University Press, 2003); Matti Bunzl, "Jews, Queers, and Other Symptoms: Recent Work in Jewish Cultural Studies," *GLQ: A Journal of Lesbian and Gay Studies* 6, no. 2 (2000): 321–341; Bunzl, *Symptoms of Modernity: Jews and Queers in Late-Twentieth-Century Vienna* (Berkeley: University of California Press, 2004); Susannah Heschel, *Abraham Geiger and the Jewish Jesus* (Chicago: University of Chicago Press, 1998); Jonathan Hess, *Germans, Jews and the Claims of Modernity* (New Haven, CT: Yale University Press, 2002); Christian Wiese, *Challenging Colonial Discourse: Jewish Studies and Protestant Theology in Wilhelminian Germany* (Leiden: Brill, 2005); and Derek J. Penslar and Ivan Davidson Kalmar, eds., *Orientalism and the Jews* (Waltham, MA: University Press of New England, 2004).

23. See, for example, Dagmar Herzog, "How 'Jewish' Is German Sexuality? Sex and Antisemitism in the Third Reich," in Neil Gregor, Mark Roseman, and Nils Roemer, eds., *German History from the Margins, 1800 to the Present* (Bloomington: Indiana University Press, 2006), 185–203.

24. For a challenge to this German-centered perspective, see Todd M. Endelman, "The Englishness of Jewish Modernity in England," in Jacob Katz, ed., *Toward Modernity: The European Jewish Model* (New Brunswick, NJ: Transaction, 1987), 225–246; Pierre Birnbaum and Ira Katznelson, eds., *Paths of Emancipation: Jews, States and Citizenship* (Princeton, NJ: Princeton University Press, 1995); David B. Ruderman, *Jewish Enlightenment in an English Key: Anglo-Jewry's Construction of Modern Jewish Thought* (Princeton, NJ: Princeton University Press, 2000).

25. David Biale, ed., *Cultures of the Jews: A New History* (New York: Schocken, 2002).

26. For some classic, large-scale Jewish history accounts with an ethnic approach, see H. H. Ben-Sasson, ed., *A History of the Jewish People* (Cambridge, MA: Harvard University Press, 1976); Simon Dubnow, *Weltgeschichte des jüdischen Volkes,* 10 vols. (Berlin: Jüdischer Verlag, 1925–1930); Heinrich Graetz, *Geschichte der Juden von den ältesten Zeiten bis auf die Gegenwart,* 11 vols. in 12 (Leipzig: Oskar Leiner, 1866–1877). For a textbook that exemplifies the intellectual history approach and that can serve as a guide through the main trends of the traditional Jewish studies themes and literature, see Robert Seltzer, *Jewish People, Jewish Thought: The Jewish Experience in History* (Upper Saddle River, NJ: Prentice Hall, 1980).

27. An early exception is the work of Salo Wittmayer Baron, who took great interest in the ways in which Jewish populations formed part of the non-Jewish societies in which they lived. Baron, *A Social and Religious History of the Jews,* 2nd ed., 18 vols. (New York: Columbia University Press, 1952–1983).

28. On this problem, see Baader, "Jews, Women, and Germans"; Gillerman, *Germans into Jews,* 8–9. More or less explicitly, this approach characterizes almost all scholarship on the social, cultural, and political history of German Jewry in the nineteenth and twentieth centuries. Exceptions are studies on Jewish religious culture, modern Jewish thought, and Jewish movements such as Zionism, as well as works that have pioneered in reevaluating the German Jewish condition, such as David Sorkin's study of the German Jewish subculture in the late eighteenth and early nineteenth century. Sorkin, *The Transformation of German Jewry, 1780–1840* (New York: Oxford University Press, 1987).

29. Homi Bhabha, *The Location of Culture* (London: Routledge, 1994); Paul Gilroy, *The Black Atlantic: Modernity and Double Consciousness* (Cambridge, MA: Harvard University Press, 1993); Ranajit Guha, "On Some Aspects of the Historiography of Colonial India," in Ranajit Guha and Gayatri Chakravorty Spivak, eds., *Selected Subaltern Studies* (Oxford: Oxford University Press, 1988), 37–45; Ania Loomba, *Colonialism/Postcolonialism* (New York: Routledge, 1998); and Catherine Hall, "Histories, Empires and the Post-Colonial Moment," in Iain Chambers and Lidia Curti, eds., *The Post-Colonial Question: Common Skies, Divided Horizons* (New York: Routledge, 1996), 65–76.

30. Heschel, *Abraham Geiger;* Hess, *Germans, Jews and the Claims of Modernity;* Wiese, *Challenging Colonial Discourse.*

31. Till van Rahden, "Jews and the Ambivalences of Civil Society in Germany, 1800 to 1933—Assessment and Reassessment," *Journal of Modern History* 77 (2005): 1043. See also Robert Gellately and Nathan Stolzfus, eds., *Social Outsiders in Nazi Germany* (Princeton, NJ: Princeton University Press, 2001); Gregor, Roseman, and Roemer, eds., *German History from the Margins;* Till van Rahden, *Juden und andere Breslauer: Die Beziehungen zwischen Juden, Protestanten und Katholiken in einer deutschen Großstadt von 1860 bis 1925* (Göttingen: Vandenhoeck & Ruprecht, 2000); and Joyce Marie Mushaben, *The Changing Faces of Citizenship: Social Integration and Political Mobilization among Ethnic Minorities in Germany* (New York: Berghahn, 2008).

32. For some other works that challenge established frameworks and go beyond inserting Jews into the familiar master narrative of German history, see Peter Eli Gordon, *Rosenzweig and Heidegger: Between Judaism and German Philosophy* (Berkeley: University of California Press, 2003); Robin Judd, *Contested Rituals: Circumcision, Kosher Butchering, and Jewish Political Life in Germany, 1843–1933* (Ithaca, NY: Cornell University Press, 2007); Todd Presner, *Mobile Modernity: Germans, Jews, Trains* (New York: Columbia University Press, 2007). And for cultural studies and visual studies perspectives on these issues, see the essays by Paul Lerner, Leora Auslander, Na'ama Rokem, Darcy Buerkle, and Lisa Silverman in "Round Table: Jewish Studies Meets Cultural Studies: New Approaches to the German-Jewish Past," *Journal of Modern Jewish Studies* 8 (March 2009): 41–120.

33. See, for instance, Sikata Banerjee, *Make Me a Man! Masculinity, Hinduism, and Nationalism in India* (Albany: State University of New York Press), 2005; David Eng, *Racial Castration: Managing Masculinity in Asian America* (Durham, NC: Duke University Press, 2001); Philippa Levine, *Prostitution, Race and Politics: Policing Venereal Disease in the British Empire* (New York: Routledge, 2003); Anne McClintock, *Imperial Leather: Race, Gender and Sexuality in the Colonial Context* (New York: Routledge, 1995); Mrinalini Sinha, *Colonial Masculinity: The "Manly Englishman" and the "Effeminate Bengali" in the Late Nineteenth Century* (Manchester, England: Manchester University Press, 1995); Gayatri Chakravorty Spivak, "Can the Subaltern Speak?," in Cary Nelson and Lawrence Grossberg, eds., *Marxism and the Interpretation of Culture* (Urbana: University of Illinois Press, 1988), 271–313; Ann L. Stoler, "Making Empire Respectable: The Politics of Race and Sexual Morality in 20th Century Colonial Cultures," *American Ethnologist* 16, no. 4 (1989): 634–660; John Tosh, *Manliness and Masculinities in Nineteenth-Century Britain: Essays on Gender, Family, and Empire* (New York: Pearson, Longman, 2005), ch. 10.

34. Glückel of Hameln, *The Memoirs of Glückel of Hameln,* trans. Marvin Lowenthal (New York: Schocken, 1977).

35. Michael Berkowitz, *The Crime of My Very Existence: Nazism and the Myth of Jewish Criminality* (Berkeley: University of California Press, 2007).

36. Kaplan, *Between Dignity and Despair;* Maierhof, *Selbstbehauptung im Chaos.*

37. See Victor Klemperer's diaries for an extremely valuable primary source: Klemperer, *I Will Bear Witness: A Diary of the Nazi Years*, trans. Martin Chalmers (New York: Random House, 1998).

38. See Atina Grossmann's important book *Jews, Germans and Allies: Close Encounters in Occupied Germany* (Princeton, NJ: Princeton University Press, 2007) for a treatment of the "entangled histories" of Germans and Jews (and Americans) in the immediate postwar period and for a gender-historical analysis which stresses reproduction, sexuality, and the history of the body among Jewish survivors.

39. The term "negative symbiosis" was originally used by Hannah Arendt in a 1946 letter to Karl Jaspers. See Dan Diner, "Negative Symbiose: Deutsche und Juden nach Auschwitz," in Diner, ed., *Ist der Nationalsozialismus Geschichte? Zu Historisierung und Historikerstreit* (Frankfurt: Fischer, 1988), 185–197, reprinted in translation as "Negative Symbiosis: Germans and Jews after Auschwitz," in Peter Baldwin, ed., *Reworking the Past: Hitler, the Holocaust and the Historians' Debate* (Boston: Beacon, 1990), 251–261. See also Sander Gilman, "Negative Symbiosis: The Reemergence of Jewish Culture in Germany after the Fall of the Wall," in Klaus Berghahn, ed., *The German-Jewish Dialogue Reconsidered: A Symposium in Honor of George L. Mosse* (New York: Lang, 1996), 207–232; Anson Rabinbach, "The Jewish Question in the German Question," *New German Critique* 44 (1988): 159–192; Jack Zipes, "The Negative German-Jewish Symbiosis," in Dagmar C. G. Lorenz and Gabriele Weinberger, eds., *Insiders and Outsiders: Jewish and Gentile Culture in Germany and Austria* (Detroit, MI: Wayne State University Press, 1994), 144–154.

40. See Y. Michal Bodemann, ed., *New German Jewry and the European Context: The Return of the European Jewish Diaspora* (London: Palgrave, 2008); Jeffrey Peck, *Being Jewish in the New Germany* (New Brunswick, NJ: Rutgers University Press, 2007).

41. See Bunzl, *Symptoms of Modernity*; and Peck, *Being Jewish*. Beyond Berlin, see Caryn Aviv and David Shneer, eds., *New Jews: The End of the Jewish Diaspora* (New York: New York University Press, 2005), for studies of dynamic sites of Jewish life and new possibilities for nontraditional modes of Jewish life and Jewish gender identity.

42. David Brenner and Michael Berkowitz, "German History, Jewish History and German Jewish Studies: Old Wine in New Bottles?," in David P. Benseler, Craig W. Nickisch, and Cora Lee Nollendorffs, eds., *Teaching German in Twentieth-Century America* (Madison: University of Wisconsin Press, 2001), 79–88; Noah Isenberg, "Recent Developments in German-Jewish Studies (1980–Present)," *AJS Perspectives* (Spring–Summer 2004): 6–7.

# 1

## Respectability Tested

### *Male Ideals, Sexuality, and Honor in Early Modern Ashkenazi Jewry*

ANDREAS GOTZMANN

Veith Kahn was everything a seventeenth-century Jewish man was not supposed to be. In business, he was no more than an agent for other members of the Frankfurt Jewish community. He sporadically dealt in the linen trade, and his attempts to mix with the merchant elite proved disastrous. In fact, Kahn seemed cursed with bad fortune. He declared bankruptcy at least twice in his lifetime, when he lost his businesses in Hamburg and in Amsterdam. According to his own account, Kahn was so aggressively hounded by creditors that he was forced to leave Frankfurt. Kahn was captured after an attempt to flee the city and incarcerated in Frankfurt's asylum, possibly the worst jail in the city. Eventually, the city council banned Kahn from Frankfurt, after which he wandered through towns and villages.

Veith Kahn's marriage, which was designed to secure his social standing, ironically seems to have been the source of his terrible fortune. Veith came neither from the best nor the worst class of Frankfurt's Jewish community, while his wife, Blümle, came from a very upstanding family; Veith's match appeared to be enviously good. As she emphatically told the Frankfurt city council in 1672, Blümle was the daughter of people who were among the most respectable in the Jewish community. Members of her grandfather's and her mother's families had served on the community board, and both families were well known for their integrity, their *Redlichkeit*.[1]

The couple was anything but harmonious. After twenty years of marriage to Blümle, Veith and several other members of the community accused Blümle of cooperating with her family in an attempt to end the marriage because she allegedly despised Kahn.[2] They called Blümle wicked, an evil wife, a *bös Frau*, and years later she admitted that her brothers had tried to force Veith to divorce her in order to save what remained of her social status and her properties, most of which Veith was said to have spoiled and plundered. Faced with debts and creditors, Veith sued his mother-in-law in the local rabbinical court for money that had been designated as his wife's dowry in their *ketubah* (marriage contract), and he won the suit. Although quarreling with family was not looked on favorably, some members of the community might have approved of the suit, as Veith was within his rights to claim the money. On the other hand, the community did *not* condone Kahn's behavior when he slapped Blümle's face and gave her a good *Maulschelle* (box on the ears) for bringing him in front of the community board.[3]

Within the Jewish community, it was not unusual or too shameful for men and women to strike servants of either gender, or for men to trade blows. It was, however, considered appalling if a "proper" Jewish man beat his own or another man's wife. Thus, when in 1744, members of the Jewish community of Karlsruhe, the new capital of the margrave of Baden, wanted to rid themselves of their supposedly insufficiently trained and incompetent chief rabbi, Nathan Uri Kahn of Metz, they accused him of having maltreated women. They claimed that Kahn had "run into other people's houses and treated their wives with blows." Rabbi Kahn's conduct was considered particularly unacceptable because his position as a religious functionary obliged him to serve as an example to others.[4]

Clearly, in striking Blümle, Veith Kahn had violated the Jewish community's standards of acceptable behavior. To add insult to injury, Blümle, her brothers, and others depicted Veith as a professional failure and a drunkard. Financially desperate and unable to support Blümle and their four children, Kahn pawned tin dishes and pots from his wife's kitchen. Faced with the reality that her marriage was in trouble and her husband wholly unable to support their family, Blümle, like any proper Jewish housewife and mother, decided to leave Kahn. Blümle complained to her family that all her money had been squandered on her husband's fruitless transactions or, even worse, on drinking. But despite Kahn's offensive behavior and failure to support his family—both of which fell short of a Jewish man's ideal comportment—his legal and social position as a man helped him force Blümle and the children to return to the family home.

After Blümle's return, life in the Kahn home did not change for the better, and Veith tried to use his wife's silverware as currency to pay his debts. Blümle could not tolerate more of her husband's unseemly behavior so, fed up, she packed all the silver cutlery and candlesticks into a chest which she then deposited with her father. When Kahn approached his father-in-law and dared to ask him to pawn these valuables, Blümle's father and brothers assaulted Veith so severely that it took him seventeen weeks in bed to recover. Years later, Veith tried to convince the authorities that he had needed to pawn the valuables to get money to buy food; according to Veith's logic, he had not failed his family but instead behaved exactly as a proper husband and father should. Unfortunately for Veith, his long history of behavior unbecoming to a Jewish man left a trail of evidence to the contrary.

Although the law remained on Veith's side, Blümle and her family soon found a flaw that could not be so easily dismissed. The unhappy marriage seemed to be at an end when Veith, a veritable *shmendrik* (weak, stupid, unsuccessful person), became a *schmuck* (contemptible person): accused of impregnating Ritzge, the unmarried daughter of a poor member of the community, Veith was arrested and brought before the court. In this case, the arbiters of propriety were Ritzge's parents, Joseph zum Tannenbaum and his wife. As there was no way to force an already married man into marrying a pregnant girl, Ritzge's parents pressed Veith for damages and financial support for their daughter and grandchild. Ritzge's father explained that they expected Veith to procure the money from his well-to-do relatives.

Throughout the legal proceedings in this case, Veith swore that Ritzge's child was not his and that he had never had relations with her. He implied that she was nothing but a lying whore. Yet evidence introduced in court showed that Veith had previously yielded to zum Tannenbaum's demands and had signed a promissory note to Ritzge's underage brother.[5] Even during Veith's incarceration, Frau zum Tannenbaum continued to demand money from him and told him through the bars of the jail window that her family would produce another father as soon as Veith had paid them. Veith only laughed at this proposal.

These details suggest that the entire case might have been—as Veith claimed all along—nothing but an attempt to blackmail him, and Veith had been sober enough not to admit in the note to Ritzge's brother why he owed the boy 200 *Reichstaler*. According to his own testimony and that of other witnesses, Veith had signed the promissory note in order to prevent zum Tannenbaum's accusations from spreading, and he feared most that his relatives or, worse, Blümle would hear about them. For this reason, he had agreed to the strange promissory note. After all, Veith depended on Blümle's family for help, despite the vicious assault.

Veith's fears were soon proved justified, and the family jumped at the opportunity of charging him with the additional *Schimpf* (dishonor) of adultery. Blümle's brothers reported Veith's allegedly adulterous behavior to the authorities as soon as they learned of it, for they knew the crime of adultery would further weaken Veith's already tenuous position, especially in light of the fact that he was now destitute. Veith later complained that he could not afford a lawyer and that his family had not even sent him food into the jail, as was the custom. As Veith had feared, the moment Blümle heard that her husband had been accused of adultery, she exploded. A witness told the city council that "she immediately got busy, pulled the bed from under him and did not tolerate him in the house any longer." Blümle and her brothers now attempted to rid themselves permanently of Veith, and tried to gain a rabbinical court order that would force him to grant Blümle a divorce. It appears that Veith thereupon sought (unsuccessfully) to file a countersuit at the rabbinical court, claiming that his in-laws' case against him was based on rumor alone.

We will never know whether Veith really committed adultery and fathered Ritzge's child, but three years after his conviction, Blümle, seemingly out of nowhere, pleaded on behalf of her husband and produced letters and witnesses to prove that he had been wronged in the zum Tannenbaums' blackmail attempt. In Blümle's words, the "pregnant whore" and her parents had invented the case in order to extort money from her family. War had broken out during Veith's incarceration, and as Blümle remained married to him and responsible for their children, she may have decided that, under the circumstances, having a husband at home was better than not having one. Whatever her reasons, she pleaded for her husband's return to her and the children so that he might "take care of them," thereby saving him from jail and securing the poor family's survival in the process.

Veith, then, was all that a proper Jewish man was not supposed to be: he had no respectability or prestige, and he was a poor husband and father, a failure in business who stayed out all night drinking with friends, and possibly an adulterer as well. But despite Veith's abundant shortcomings, the fact that he was married and had a family made him a "real man" and perhaps even protected him, although documents from this period do not explicitly state that marriage and procreation were crucial factors to establish a man's masculinity. However, evidently bachelors were not considered proper men, since they were excluded from influential roles in community affairs and from many religious rituals. Although Veith's alleged sexual escapades did not make him an ideal husband, they were signs of his virility. Veith's behavior is a prime example of the dissonance between the *ideal* of what male behavior ought to be and the *realities* of male conduct. Veith behaved in ways that fell far short of what was expected of a proper "house father," a *baal habayit*. His behavior violated the norms outlined by religious teachings, which conformed to the outlook of merchants. Nevertheless, Veith endured, albeit precariously, as a "real man." A "real man" did his best to make ends meet, he actively sought and took advantage of every opportunity to better his lot, yet he also pursued his pleasure.

Along similar lines, notes in the court's interrogation of Veith indicate that he took a distinctly male approach to matters that concerned both men and women. When asked about his family, Veith named four children and added that "about two or three have died." While the death of children after birth or at a very young age was common at the time, Veith's nonchalance provides evidence for the distance men could keep from such female spheres as the household and children, and gives insight into Veith's self-perception. Of course, Blümle would have been able to supply precise information about the children's deaths, but as a merchant, Veith was frequently away from home for long periods of time; exact knowledge about his children may have been beyond the realm of his concern. Contemporaries considered such diverging male and female perspectives normal and took it for granted that men and women related to the exigencies of life in different ways.

In early modern society, much of the actual behavior of Jews and Christians alike did not conform to the standards that communities and religious leaders tried to enforce. The bans on card games and gambling that the Frankfurt community board and the local rabbinical court repeatedly issued are a good example of this state of affairs. Except under very particular circumstances, both Christian and Jewish authorities considered card games and gambling immoral behavior,[6] and we know of several cases in the Frankfurt Jewish community in which men who engaged in such activities were punished. Punishment included losing the right to wear signs of an honorable reputation, such as the Shabbat cloak, hat, or collar, or losing the right to be called for the public reading of the Torah during synagogue services, sometimes for a period of years.[7] In ongoing quarrels within the community, transgressions such as gambling made for sensational news and appear to have permanently blemished the reputations of neighbors and community members.

In one of these cases, Moses Feist Hirschhorn, a man from a well-established family in the Frankfurt Jewish quarter, was convicted of playing cards and drinking with friends. Later, Hirschhorn, along with his three sons, was also accused of having committed acts of public slander on several occasions and of having physically attacked other men in the synagogue. This occurred during the Kann-Kulp conflict, a decade-long series of disputes within the Jewish community in the mid-eighteenth century, in which the powerful brothers Bär Löw and the rabbi Mosche Löw Isaac zur Kann, on the one hand, and David Meyer Juda, on the other hand, played the leading roles. Thus, Hirschhorn did not hesitate to identify David Meyer Juda, who was called zum Kulp after his family's house sign, as another gambler. Zum Kulp was said to have frequently played cards with other Jews in the nearby town of Offenbach, but he succeeded in avoiding punishment thanks to his family connections and social standing as a younger leader of the community.[8] Accordingly, while illegal behavior and deviation from the ideal could do damage to one's reputation, they were quite normal for men of various social ranks and therefore acceptable.

In contrast to Veith Kahn and the gamblers, the proper Jewish man of the house was supposed to be honorable, faultless in his dealings, and religious in his behavior, which included attending communal services, observing the ritual commandments of *kashrut* (dietary laws), and giving charity in accordance with his financial status. All of these virtues were to be reflected in a man's manners and clothing, which had to display and express his wealth and trustworthiness without being ostentatious. Men who obeyed the rules of good taste wore dark colors, good but not luxurious fabrics, and only a few items indicating prosperity, such as jewelry, silver buttons, or richly embroidered vests under their somber black cloaks.[9]

A man could express his status as a proper *baal habayit*, and his female counterpart that of a proper housewife, by wearing specific synagogue garb, which resembled the costumes worn at the Spanish court. The public outfit of Christian officials in Frankfurt differed from this Jewish garb only in the higher quality of its fabric and in intricate details on the pants, sleeves, and hat. Like the Jewish costume, the official attire of the city's mayors and patricians featured a beret—or sometimes a top hat—a round cloak, and a white collar. Therefore, at communal meetings and religious rituals as well as public appearances on holidays when such synagogue garb was mandatory, the low and bad ones were easily visible, as they were either forbidden to wear any of these special pieces of clothing or permitted to wear only individual components of them.

Restrictions on the clothing they could wear and exclusion from public activities were imposed on those who failed to pay taxes or who had committed a crime. A man whose wife had behaved badly—and who thus apparently had lost control over his household—could be punished in the same way. Men and women alike risked losing their seat in the synagogue or being completely banned from services. The loss of one's seat was particularly painful, as one was subsequently forced to stand during services, likely in a not very respectable place such as the students' section or the area reserved for strangers. Punishment could also include being banned from the great synagogue or its women's galleries, which would force someone to attend services in less-worthy houses of prayer, such as the least desirable place in Frankfurt am Main, the shul of the yeshiva. Only in very severe cases of moral or social transgression, such as those involving adultery or fraud, was partial exclusion from community rituals turned into a total ban from the public sphere. In those cases, offenders were forbidden from dining outside their own homes and attending any festivities, including religious celebrations; such restrictions often drove the offender from the community. This detailed system of penalties and fines, connected to concepts of honor and dishonor, acted as a powerful mechanism of social control by which most internal conflicts could be managed.[10] Within this system, the behavior of both men *and* women depended on and determined an individual's and a family's respectability.

Attacking any of the signs of a man's prestige and honor thus meant challenging his status as a man in the community. Ripping off a man's or a woman's hat or wig in public, tearing another person's clothing, or attacking a person's hair or beard were specific insults that constituted direct acts of aggression against the status and position of the other. For instance, in 1749, Rabbi Joel Engers insulted the chief judge of the Frankfurt rabbinical court by screaming at him, "You old rambling thief [*Gaudieb*], let me pull out your grey beard!" Engers's offense was twofold. First, he accused the judge of being dishonest and criminal, a common but serious charge among Jews whose profession as merchants depended on honesty and reliability. Second, in threatening to rip out the judge's beard, he attacked the judge's masculinity, his age, and the religious standing that the beard signified.[11]

In the hierarchy of offenses, physically assaulting another person—particularly with a walking stick or a real weapon—was considered worse than hurling insults, spitting, or making threatening gestures, such as shaking fists. But even worse than physical attacks were acts of aggression against the markers of male status that symbolized a man's place among honorable men, his embodiment of an ideal Jewish masculinity, and his status as a respectable house father. Threatening to rip out another man's beard, such as Engers did, was thus an extremely serious transgression that cost the offender his personal honor and bore immediate consequences for his business.

The matter of one's *shem tov*, one's good name or reputation, had different implications for men than it had for women. Within the discourse of honor, every man, Christian and Jew alike—although the discourses in Christian and Jewish settings do deviate from each other in certain respects—had not simply the right but the *obligation* to publicly secure and reinstate his honor. A man might begin working toward the restoration of his damaged honor by formally and publicly acknowledging his misdeeds in the synagogue as an act of atonement, begging for pardon, or asking for an appropriate penance.

The victim of public slander, on the other hand, ideally took immediate revenge or redirected the insult onto the attacker. For instance, when Bär Löw Isaac called Calme Bauer a "thief for whom the gallows were waiting" and expressed his desire "to get [Bauer] there as soon as possible," Bauer appropriately answered that the real culprit—meaning Isaac—would certainly meet the gallows as his fate.[12] Here, the victim responded to a verbal assault by turning the offensive remark against the aggressor. Such a retaliation on the same level was acceptable to both the Christian authorities and the Jewish community board and rabbis, because it did not aggravate the situation and left room for the religiously prescribed manner of dealing with this type of incident, such as conciliatory proceedings or lawsuits.

However, the offended often tried immediately to exceed the damage done.[13] In fact, one reason for the rise in dangerous conflicts in early modern societies was the heat and destructiveness of the victims' reactions, as tempers and sensitivities tended to flare easily. The honor of men (and women) defined their social status and thus had to be protected carefully. Moreover, concepts of honor and respectability not only had gendered dimensions, but being an honorable and reliable person had direct impact on the material welfare of individuals and families. This was particularly relevant for Jews, who tended to make their livings in commercial occupations.[14]

Yet again, there was a tension between the ideal behavior of a man and the ways in which contemporaries comported themselves in everyday life. At least in regard to the elite or the core of the Jewish community (people of wealth and high social standing from leading families), we have some information on how this discrepancy played out. Thus, early modern sources portray Jewish men at times, in conformity with the ideal, as peace-loving patriarchs who ruled over their families, maids, and servants in a strict yet benevolent manner. During the Kann-Kulp conflict, for example, one of the male servants in Bär Löw Isaac's house described the Isaacs' home along these lines. In court, he portrayed the household's family life in the same idealized manner in which Moritz Daniel Oppenheim envisioned it a century later in his romanticized paintings of Jewish family life: Isaac presided over the dinner table on Shabbat, and even though there were riots in the street in front of his house, no one rose from the table without his permission. On Isaac's orders, the servants closed the doors to the turmoil in the ghetto and thus kept out the strife and aggression of the street and safeguarded the peace and privacy of the household.[15]

As attractive as this idyllic scene may be, additional information reveals that the servant's description was not an entirely accurate report of matters at the Isaac family's home. It became evident that the servant's untypically expensive clothing was ruined after he left the supposedly peaceful home to join the riot. Further investigations brought to light that both Isaac's and his servants' behavior greatly differed from what had been testified at the courthouse earlier. It turned out that during the riots, it had not been unusual for some of Isaac's servants to be found on the house's doorstep or leaning out of windows, while others—together with various community members of low social standing—acted as foot soldiers on the street and insulted and even attacked adversaries according to Isaac's orders.[16]

Although court documents cannot give us direct insight into "normal" behavior, the principles that guided Jewish men's actions are quite evident in this investigation. Ideally, a man was to remain stoically calm whenever a conflict arose. However, the actions he took—or failed to take—defined his status as a man. In contrast to the ideal of sober calmness, the Jewish male who was a man knew which strings to pull, and rather than wait, he would for instance empty a chamber pot from his window over someone's head. He did not hesitate to let his opinion be known, to the point of being insulting and thereby potentially aggravating the situation. Jewish men acted in ways that contradicted the negative (albeit often subtle or indirect) Christian stereotype of male Jews as weak yet cunning, who dealt behind the backs of others rather than directly defending themselves in the face of male aggression. In fact, with certain specific exceptions, Jewish men behaved exactly as Christian men did.

Abraham zum Drachen, for instance, one of the leading figures of the Frankfurt Jewish community in the late seventeenth century, was accused of having served as an intermediary in a case of rape. As Abraham tried to extricate himself from the case, which was finally dealt with by the city's magistrate, he asserted to the mayors and judges that he had never been involved in the affair. The alleged offender was Meyer zum Trichter, the deaf son of a prominent member of the community, who was accused of having forced Bälle, a Jewish maid, to have sexual intercourse with him several times in plain view in the backyard and in the *Stube*, the central public room of the family's house. Bälle's uncle, who was called "lame Aron," from the nearby village of Niederhofheim tried several times to secure money from the man he believed to have fathered Bälle's child—which was more or less the standard procedure where the sexual exploitation of maids was concerned. In the case of daughters from respectable families, on the other hand, a man would have first attempted to force the alleged father to marry the girl in order to save her and her family's honor. But Aron knew that Meyer could not be forced to marry Bälle, as Meyer's social position forbade marriage to a poor country girl, so he sought the help of community leaders. Yet while we know that community leaders, or *parnasim*, sometimes resolved similar incidents by levying fines, "whoring" was a criminal act that fell under the jurisdiction of secular Christian courts, and in Bälle's case, the elders refused to get involved in the sordid business. Thus, Bälle's family asked Abraham to act as an intermediary. When, after Bälle had given birth, Aron learned that she would receive no compensation, he finally initiated a criminal suit at the city council, in the course of which Abraham zum Drachen was asked to clarify his role in the case.[17]

To avert any suspicion and prove his impeccable conduct in this distasteful affair, Abraham was forced to take an oath of cleansing in the presence of the plaintiff. Standing in the synagogue in front of the Torah scrolls, he and Aron had to swear that they had not lied. Aron categorically avowed his honesty without hesitation, but Abraham was quite cautious in his wording, since taking the oath already had damaged his social status. Aron mocked Abraham for his reluctance and repeatedly screamed into the other's face, accusing him of being a dirty liar and a man without integrity who could not be trusted. Abraham turned to neither the Christian court clerk nor the Jewish judge, or *dayan,* for aid, nor was he concerned about damaging the judge's honor, and he cared even less about the dignity of the synagogue: after screaming at Aron that he would rather pay a fine than be insulted any longer, he struck Aron so hard in the face that the other man's blood splattered everywhere.

Abraham was severely fined for this behavior, but he turned to the Christian judges and insisted that he had only defended his honor against an unworthy man. Abraham asked for a reduction of his fine and in the same breath proclaimed that he would rather give all the money to the poor than let his honor and his status as a man be subject to doubt. The Christian judges understood quite well that both a man's honor and his standing as a man were defined by how eagerly he defended himself, and they thus convicted Abraham merely of having violated the dignity of the synagogue and the ritual of oath taking. The judges did not fine him for having assaulted Aron.[18]

The stereotype of the cowardly and submissive Jew was widespread among Christians and particularly prevalent among guild members and the lower strata of society, such as the peasantry. In defiance of this perception, Jews were eager to defend themselves both verbally and physically. For instance, Jewish travelers frequently bore arms, a practice that was tolerated by the authorities, even though by law Jews were not permitted to carry weapons. Because of that restriction, Jews were often granted special safeguards by the authorities, and we know of many cases in which Jews waved such writs and letters of protection in the faces of their aggressors when they felt threatened, hoping to avert a physical attack. Jews were often victimized on their long travels through the countryside or even when they did business in the city, and they thus learned to take precautions. For instance, they avoided traveling alone.

Accordingly, a respectable Jewish woman, unlike Christian women, did not walk on her own through the streets of Frankfurt, and she certainly refrained from being on the roads outside the city without a companion. Also, after several dangerous incidents in the city, Jewish merchants and moneylenders no longer entered Christian houses without a business partner or a servant waiting for them on the street. Those who traded in coins or pawned goods usually made sure to do so only within the Jewish quarter, and they avoided carrying large sums of money through the city or even in the countryside. Everyday life was hazardous for Jews, and even a rumor that authorities might not be willing to fully protect a local community raised the specter of an anti-Jewish riot and endangered the Jewish population.[19] Yet whatever the threat, if forced, Jewish men did not hesitate to defend themselves and employed weapons that ranged from walking sticks to knives.

The following examples in particular belie the stereotype of the unmanly and powerless Jewish man. Several peasants, likely joined by mercenaries, attacked and injured a rabbi from Friedberg in Hesse while he was traveling in the year 1579. The act was clearly inspired by an anti-Jewish animus, as the men tortured the rabbi for sport. A few weeks later, the attackers made another attempt on the same elderly rabbi, as he was on his way to Frankfurt.[20] This time, however, a group of Jewish merchants was traveling nearby and hurried to save the old man. While the peasants humiliated the rabbi by pulling his hat down, exposing the barely healed wound on his head and telling him they would "crack it open once again," the Jewish rescuers stormed onto the scene. They not only assaulted the peasants, but also seized the swords and guns that the rabbi's tormentors carried and turned them against the attackers. Later, the rescuers delivered the weapons to the guards at the gates of nearby Frankfurt and reported the peasants. When the attackers foolishly tried to claim their property later, they were arrested and subsequently convicted.

We can observe a similar willingness to act aggressively in two incidents during the Kann-Kulp conflict in Frankfurt. Bär Löw Isaac, one of the protagonists in the dispute, was a *gabbai,* or treasurer of the community, and by blackmailing and handing out favors, he held a tight grip on a large segment of the population. At some point in the course of events, Isaac asked the mayors of Frankfurt to send guards into the Jewish quarter in order to prevent further rioting. Isaac's request was granted, but instead of posting the guards throughout the Jewish quarter, Isaac used them to further his own agenda. One night, he sent the guardsmen into his adversaries' homes. When the guards entered Löw Michel Goldschmidt's house, they found about eleven men, who were talking, smoking, and drinking together in defiance of the curfew that had been issued by the city council. The guards concluded that the men must be plotting against Isaac. Yet instead of yielding to the guards and submitting to the power of Christian authority, the men interrogated the soldiers about who had given them the right to break into a house late at night. The soldiers defended their actions as authorized by an official decree, issued in the interest of security and peace, and they advised the Jewish men to go home. But the men rightly understood these house searches to be another of Isaac's schemes to consolidate his position within the community and refused to leave. In the turmoil that followed, the guardsmen had no choice but to fight their way out of the house and into the street, as their commander later reported to the city's mayor.[21]

On the same night, soldiers in other parts of the Jewish quarter endangered the lives of the entire ghetto population by entering the wooden houses with burning torches, searching rooms and tossing beds. Typical of how Christian officers tended to treat Jews, some soldiers also harassed and injured an elderly couple. The guardsmen later reported that about a thousand Jewish men and some women had crowded into the narrow street in front of Isaac's house, all of them screaming and in no way afraid of the guards. The soldiers had to attach bayonets to their guns in order to hold the masses at bay, as they forced their way out of the ghetto. Similarly, when city guards tried some days later to break up the performance of the traditional *purim-shpil,* which had been forbidden for fear of more unrest, the students who acted in the play resisted. Again, these Jewish men behaved by no means like the helpless victims that Christian contemporaries expected Jews to be, or that historians have sometimes portrayed them as.[22]

No scholarly research has been conducted specifically on Jewish masculinity, male role models, or male sexuality in the early modern period, and studies on the so-called classical rabbinic period of late antiquity or on medieval Judaism are only of limited help for understanding early modern developments.[23] In fact, early modern texts themselves need to be read very critically when it comes to representations of masculinity, and publications about early modern history have so far heavily relied on highly ideological sources. Often, scholars have not done much more than unsystematically cite from a variety of rabbinic responsa, or *Mussar,* literature. Yet as we have seen, norms and social practices typically stood in a rather precarious relationship to each other.[24] Theological literature and legal prescriptions thus only provide us with a small part of the overall picture. Moreover, in early modern Jewish society, contemporaries understood laws not as actual realities, but rather as abstract ideals to which one might have recourse in situations where everyday practice fell short of resolving a conflict.

The most striking evidence for this distance that Jewish society kept from norms—including the strong legal tradition that has been perceived as the core of Jewish life—can be found in the organization of Jewish communities itself. In the seventeenth century and early eighteenth, western Ashkenazi communities introduced, in a rapid process, a new and more uniform system of electing their leadership. These new norms, regulating how and when elections were to take place, were designed to preserve the oligarchic structure of the community, while also allowing less wealthy and less influential groups to participate in governing the community. However, recent findings suggest that many, if not most, communities did not hold the periodic elections prescribed by these new regulations; on the contrary, most communities preferred to rely on the established practices that favored lifelong leadership by a small group of men. This older model of governance resembled the strictly hierarchical organization of Christian society and eighteenth-century political absolutism rather than reflecting the halakhic ideal of mutual cooperation and participation of all members of the community. Some communities, such as the Jewry of Karlsruhe in Baden, held elections only at extended intervals, although its Takkanot, or community bylaws, called for regular elections of the board every three years. Eventually, however, the government at least partially enforced the regulations of the Jewish community.[25] The same pattern is apparent in the much larger community of Frankfurt am Main, which certainly had older and more, and thus more highly organized, communal institutions. Only at times of conflict, when individuals or groups tried to compete with the established leadership in the ghetto, did newcomers to power cite existing laws and renegotiate norms. Later, however, the regulations fell back into oblivion.

Certain structural needs, especially in large communities like the one in Frankfurt, paved the way for the modern application of and relationship to law in early modern society. However, contemporaries were usually content with the abstract concept that their culture was law-based. Thus, the idea of Jewish society being regulated by law was tremendously vibrant for large parts of the Jewish population, but legal norms did not in fact govern social practices in everyday life.[26] Guided by essentialist and religious approaches, scholarly literature so far has interpreted the gap between religiously prescribed norms and actual practices as a rupture and a sign of the decay of Jewish culture at a time when Jewish society in Western Europe supposedly was undergoing a decline in the pre-emancipatory era. Yet the divide between legal norms and social practices played a constructive role in Jewish society. It was what positively defined

Judaism and enabled Jewish culture to survive under difficult social and economic circumstances.

Texts of rabbinic teachings, community bylaws, legal records, and other sources that have survived from the early modern period give us insight into the link between honor and manhood in Jewish culture in this era, and this literature shows the strong disjunction between the ideal comportment of the *baal habayit* and actual male behavior. Interestingly, Christian society developed a vast literature of so-called *Hausväter-Bücher* (books for the father of the house), which educated the male audience and informed readers how to conduct themselves in a variety of situations. Jewish moral literature of the time, however, had relatively little to say about these issues, which were instead largely addressed in legal texts.[27] Still, as we have seen in the criminal cases discussed above, Jewish men and women had a clear sense of proper male behavior, even though their actions only rarely conformed to the ideal. And this is not only a function of these sources being court records, which necessarily document overwhelmingly negative behavior. According to the entire range of available documents, the married Jewish man of early modern Germany was most of all expected to rule over his family and its servants; he was to conduct himself and to make decisions according to the values of rabbinic Judaism as well as economic considerations; and he was to act as the mediator between the family and the outside world.[28]

In contrast to the current and often-discussed ideas of a Jewish "soft masculinity," which is rooted in the anti-Semitic stereotype of the Jewish man as not truly male and even effeminate, the Jewish man of the pre-emancipatory period was far from passive or soft. Evidence from a variety of sources suggests that Jewish men acted "manly" and vigorously and at times displayed openly aggressive conduct, even when they found themselves in dangerous situations with few means of self-defense. They even tended to eschew shy or cautious behavior that might have been safer for them. Certainly, Jewish men of some standing did not engage in the coarse, belligerent male behavior that was characteristic of peasants and men from the lower classes of the urban population, whom Jews regarded as dangerous, rude, and uncultivated. Rather, Jewish ideals and social practices resembled those of Christian merchants and patricians.

Likewise, we find differences between the Jewish urban and the much larger Jewish rural population, but they were less pronounced than the comparable differences in the non-Jewish world. In Jewish society, the rural and urban spheres were closely interconnected and Jews highly valued the concept of a unified Jewish culture.[29] Although Jewish values and patterns of behavior undoubtedly differed in certain respects from those that were characteristic of Christian society, Judaism cannot be defined in relation and contradistinction to the standard—Christian—culture. As any other social and cultural formation, Jewish society must be seen as possessing a cultural reference system of its own.

Let us examine the case of a Jewish man whose manliness at first sight appears to exemplify the common idea of the weak Jewish male. In his autobiography, a famous rabbi and fierce critic of his time, Jacob Emden of Hamburg-Altona, tells us that he became depressed after he experienced himself as sexually inept and impotent on his wedding night.[30] His tale reads like a caricature of Jewish male sexuality and could be cited as a fair example of Jewish unmanliness. Yet Emden most probably included the comments on the fiasco of his wedding night quite purposefully. Like other rabbis did in their autobiographical accounts, Emden depicted himself as an *illui,* a young genius, whose constant reading and studying of religious literature created a holy life separated from the banal, everyday world. His elevation above mere physical matters thus had an impact even on the functions of his body, including his sexuality.

Emden certainly did not want to suggest that he was not a real man by informing his readers that he had not been able to hold an erection that night. Rather, by reporting on his impotence, Emden intended to convey that he was a scholar involved in work of the highest importance. The intense involvement in intellectual and spiritual pursuits had estranged him from the more worldly concerns of ordinary people, pure thoughts elevating even his body to a level of holiness. Emden's self-portrayal has little to do with later anti-Semitic stereotypes of Jewish men's sexual feebleness and impotence, though it does attest to a rabbinic ideal of male sexuality, according to which a man could be so entirely absorbed in spiritual matters that he became ignorant, and even forgetful, of his own body.

Emden's story seems to imply that religious life and sexuality were thought to be in conflict with each other. However, Emden's concern about his sexual failure may also have stemmed from the fact that in the Jewish theological tradition, the rabbinic concept of the "evil drive," or *yetzer ha'ra,* also stands for the zest for life and for life truly lived. Thus, rabbinic discussions on the sexual drive focused on the character of sexual passion and on how to control and direct it, since the unruly dimension of erotic desire was certainly seen as negative and dangerous.[31] But sex was also recognized as necessary for procreation, and so the rabbis did not perceive it as inherently negative, even though it could lead to evil. Perhaps Emden only intended to stress that he was *completely* absorbed in his studies and thus lacked sexual experience; after all, he also often presented himself as an ascetic.[32] Emden's otherworldliness supposedly made him somewhat akin to an innocent child or an angel who, unlike adult humans, did not need to negotiate those aspects of life which involved the potentially dangerous or even evil parts of creation and reproduction.[33]

Emden's anecdote, then, strikes a fine balance: while it points to and promotes a distinction between an idealized religious life and the worldly experience of average men, it does not negate Jewish male sexuality altogether. It rather endorses a worldview according to which all men's lived sexuality and scholars' preoccupation with matters of other than carnal or physical nature coexisted in a well-defined equilibrium. An examination of the vast theological and moral rabbinic literature of the time shows that the Jewish religious leaders of the early modern period were much concerned with human sexuality, which they sought to control and the expressions of which they tried to direct into appropriate modes of sexual conduct. According to these authorities, the precarious balance between the dangerous and destructive forces of nature and the positive aspects of the sexual instinct could only be achieved when sexual desire was contained within certain permissible channels and sexuality thus regulated and civilized.[34]

Beyond the realm of such philosophical and theological considerations, however, reports on incidents of sexual harassment suggest that sexuality was an important part of Jewish men's male identities. It was sexual virility, not childlike innocence, which shaped their masculinities. Virility was at the core of the entire range of expression of Jewish male behavior and sexuality; it characterized the sexual conduct of ideal husbands and fathers as much as that of rapists and adulterers. This is well illustrated by another case from the Frankfurt ghetto. In 1630, Samuel zum Elefanten, a lower-class Jew, was charged with having sexually harassed and having had intercourse with Bärbel Schantz, a Christian woman. Yet the matter was more complicated than it seems at first glance. Although Samuel appears to have committed these misdeeds, Bärbel and her husband had also deliberately staged one of Samuel's sexual infractions. After Samuel zum Elefanten had allegedly molested Bärbel more than once when he visited her for the purpose of some small business transaction, Bärbel and her husband devised a scheme for Samuel's next visit that would provide evidence of his transgressions and allow them to blackmail him. Thus, Samuel was again provided access to Bärbel, while her husband and another witness, the owner of the house, hid behind a curtain in an adjacent room. When Samuel tried to force himself on Bärbel, she not only accepted his improper advances, but tried to lure him into even more incriminating actions. She thus allowed Samuel to follow her upstairs to her bedroom, as the two other men watched from their hiding place.[35]

Later, at the trial, Samuel confessed to having committed immoral acts with Bärbel, but he also accused her of purposefully seducing him. In fact, if Bärbel had been a prostitute, it would not have been particularly scandalous for him as a Jewish man to have frequented her, and the judges would likely have understood it that way too.[36] Although, in theory, sexual intercourse between Jewish men and Christian women was punishable by death, actual sentences were rarely so extreme. The typical punishment Jewish men received for adultery— even when it was committed with Christian women—was merely a fine, albeit a harsh one. As far as we know, corporal punishment was imposed only in very serious cases and only occasionally did a Jewish perpetrator lose his privileges of protection, which usually forced him to leave the city.

According to the testimonies that both Samuel and Bärbel gave in court, Samuel was a sexually potent male. Bärbel and her husband portrayed Samuel in such a manner, since they accused him of having violated the prohibition of sexual contact between Jews and Christians. Sexual prowess only became problematic when it transgressed the boundaries of what contemporaries considered to be normal sexual behavior. Bärbel therefore attempted to portray Samuel as overly sexualized and testified that Samuel had boasted openly about his sexual prowess. According to her, he had claimed that he could help the "poor woman get pregnant." Bärbel's crippled husband, a former soldier, was allegedly unable to impregnate her, whereas Samuel could "do his own wife Sprenzle ten times a night."[37] Yet Bärbel understood that being sexually intimate with a Jew—not once, but several times—also undermined her own already questionable status as a respectable Christian wife. Thus, in order to make the court believe her assertion that she was the victim of sexual assault, she characterized Samuel as a sexual deviant. But although the details Bärbel provided successfully portrayed Samuel as a sex maniac, she could not make a good case as to why he would have chosen to have illegal sex with a Christian woman, enticing her with dried meat or money to consent, when he had a wife of his own. According to Bärbel, Samuel was attracted to her light skin because it differed from his wife's "uglier," darker complexion. The fact that Bärbel resorted to this anti-Jewish stereotype of Jewish women being dark and therefore unattractive shows that she found herself on the defensive in this trial against the man she accused of indecent behavior.

Notably, Samuel never refuted the central accusation of sexual assault, despite the seriousness of the charge. He knew that male virility was not considered a virtue in connection with the severe transgressions he was accused of, but he was also aware that these were not the charges that could put his life in danger. What threatened him more was that his behavior risked being seen as an expression of the unruly dimension of the sexual drive. Due to this supposedly dangerous aspect of human sexuality, the rabbis called sexual desire the "evil drive." While adultery and sexual intercourse between Jews and Christians certainly were perceived as criminal behavior, for Samuel the real danger at the trial lay in being characterized as oversexed and abnormal. Indeed, this aspect became the central issue in court: Samuel was accused of having exhibited his penis and having masturbated while touching Bärbel's breasts, which was considered highly improper. Moreover, he was said to have "whirled his member around like a windmill," ejaculated on the floor and on a bench, and even defiled the Schantz couple's bed with dirt- and manure-clogged shoes. References at the trial to his "enormous cut staff" further served to depict him as sexually abnormal, and systematically linked his being Jewish with his allegedly monstrous penis.

Supposedly, Samuel had also attempted sex with Bärbel while standing. She had rejected this position, which was considered an abomination at the time and seen as characteristic for sexual intercourse with prostitutes, whereupon Samuel had allegedly bragged that he and his wife were doing it frequently that way.[38] According to these accusations, Samuel had behaved in a way that was also "un-Jewish," counter, that is, to the Jewish ideal of a tame, restrained, and regulated male sexuality. This might have been another reason that Samuel denied having engaged in the type of unruly conduct that the Schantz couple and their witness described in graphic detail during the trial. Yet, seemingly against his best interests, Samuel allowed the general charge of sexual harassment to stand, even though this behavior was certainly immoral in the eyes of both Christians and Jews.

As a consequence, Samuel's credibility in court suffered. However, Samuel knew that the court had secured a witness who would testify to some of the charges made against him, and he must have recognized that he could not possibly disprove them. Perhaps he had resigned himself to paying a heavy fine for sexual harassment, knowing that only clear evidence of sexual intercourse would have endangered his life. Fortunately for Samuel, there was no proof that he did indeed have sex with Bärbel. The Schantzes' witness had left his hideout behind the curtains too soon, disgusted by what he had already seen. Moreover, as the witnessing landlord pointed out and the judges certainly noticed themselves, Bärbel Schantz's husband had devised the plot, in the course of which his wife was harassed and her honor endangered. This certainly threw a most unfavorable light on the couple themselves. Likewise, the Schantzes' subsequent attempt to blackmail Samuel had backfired. It severely discredited their cause when the court learned that Bärbel's husband had gathered a small gang and assaulted Samuel, grabbing his genitals and threatening to castrate him with a knife unless he signed a financial agreement. Samuel, on the other hand, raised his credibility by consistently denying ever having sexual intercourse with Bärbel. He did so even under threat of torture.[39]

Both Christians and Jews obviously distinguished between two different kinds of unacceptable behavior: one merely improper and the other veritably unruly and out of control. During the trial against him, Samuel conceded improper behavior. The Christian couple, on the other hand, whose scheme to blackmail Samuel evaporated as the legal proceedings progressed, found themselves on the defensive and therefore tried to mark what had been discussed earlier in the trial as improper behavior, as odd and unnatural. From a religious and moral perspective, the difference between unacceptable and truly unspeakable behavior was nothing more than a matter of gradation. But in practice, virility and vigor were considered normal characteristics of male sexual conduct (not so for female sexuality); only when sexual acts were deemed unnatural and filthy did male sexuality enter the realm of the abnormal. Christians and Jews would have agreed on this distinction between normal, albeit improper, behavior, on the one hand, and deviant or perverted sexual conduct, on the other hand. Yet there was a key difference in the way the two religious traditions approached sexuality. According to the Jewish view, the sexual drive should ideally be tamed; however, in all of its aspects—including those deemed uncultured or dangerous—the human drive for sexuality not only had the potential to harm gender relations but also stimulated and energized them. The potentially evil sex drive thus guaranteed procreation and the existence of the world. In the eyes of Christian contemporaries, though, this ambivalent conception of the nature of sexuality was highly inappropriate.

The boundaries of what Jewish society considered appropriate forms of masculinity were also defined in relation to standards of acceptable femininity, although the distinction between improper and utterly unacceptable behavior was different for women and men. In the case of adultery or other kinds of extramarital sexual activity, the truly unacceptable was clearly reached when an umarried woman became pregnant and gave birth to a child. Once a woman had crossed this line, she faced enormous difficulties when she tried to obtain financial support for herself or at least the child, and finding a man willing to marry her became almost impossible. Thus, she often did everything in her power to convince the father to wed her, or at least to admit his paternity. His doing so could restore some of the woman's devastated social position, while he only suffered a comparatively slight loss of respectability.

Women of high rank tended to be much more successful in these attempts, because they were able to avail themselves of powerful family connections to coerce the child's father. Maidservants and poor girls had virtually no chance of securing such concessions; these women could expect, at most, a payment for leaving quietly and not denouncing the father or, sometimes, even for falsely naming another man as the father. Such payments to unwed mothers were quite common, though they were strictly prohibited under the law, and both Jewish and Christian authorities certainly frowned upon them. Jewish leaders knew that such matters should be taken to the Christian courts, but still preferred to deal with them within the community. This practice is partly accounted for by a difference in emphasis: whereas the Jewish community tried most of all to secure at least some financial support for the child and to prevent the complete annihilation of the woman's honor, the Christian authorities focused primarily on punishing the adult transgressors.[40]

These payments were also intended to prevent or limit the spread of rumors about the sexual misconduct, but if matters had become public or could not be hidden, it was impossible to settle them in this way. Such was the case for Gutle Reis, the widow of a prominent Frankfurt Jew, who in 1663 gave birth to a child fathered by her servant, Menahem.[41] An entry in the Pinkas, or protocols, of the Frankfurt community board shows that Menahem subsequently lost his rights as a member of the Jewish community because of the shame that he and Gutle had brought on it. Moreover, he was banned from the community for three years—a harsh sentence which owed something to his low status as a servant. Gutle lost her seat in the women's section of the synagogue but, unlike Menahem, she was not totally excluded from all religious services. Public prayer was not a religious obligation for women as it was for men, and thus the proscriptions placed upon Gutle served mainly to stigmatize her within the community. She was forbidden to wear the customary synagogue garb, to have any private contacts, or to attend—or, even more so, to host—any festive gatherings. If she entered another person's home, no one was permitted to sit with her. Gutle owed it to her high social rank that she was not banned from the community like her lover was. Others of lower status who engaged in similar behavior were usually forced to leave the Jewish quarter, whereas Gutle was allowed to remain a marginal member of the community. Yet, on the whole, women had by far the less advantageous position.

Christians often considered Jewish men to be, first of all, men and only then Jews, while Jewish women were "nothing but women" in both cultures. Adulterous men commonly suffered fines, imprisonment, or banishment from the community, but women usually lost much more than this, and certainly more than the relatively privileged Gutle Reis. Even women who claimed to have been raped were usually regarded as common whores and were likely to face punishment. Christian authorities tended to sentence adulterous women to corporal punishment or even long-term slave labor; the Jewish community banned them; and often these unfortunate women were unable to ever return to normal life.[42]

These differences in the treatment of men and women attest to a transcultural imbalance of power between the sexes. The gender organization within Christian and Jewish social realms and the ideals of what constituted appropriate forms of masculinity and femininity in both societies were quite similar. Only at times did the different religious contexts lead to particular cultural differences and thereby to diverging values and practices in Christian and Jewish settings. Yet in both cultures, masculinity was conceived of as the natural counterpart to femininity, and vice versa. Thus, we must regard the different standards governing male and female sexual behavior as defining each other, and we must evaluate the expressions and norms of manhood and womanhood as mutually contingent. Any evaluation of male gender roles must take the corresponding female roles into consideration. Likewise, it is not enough to simply point out that a Jewish man was not considered a full man without a wife and children; *who* his wife was and *how* she behaved were also seen as reflections of the merit of the husband and therefore contributed to defining his social status. A wife who, for instance, gave charity to the poor and properly tended the home was regarded as an extension of her husband's virtue; it was usually he, after all, who provided her with the financial means necessary to lead such an exemplary life. Inscriptions on the tombstones of men and women speak to these stark gender differences and interrelations: whereas a man's distinction was a function of his social standing and his religious devotion, even the most virtuous woman was treated as nothing more than an *ateret baala*, a crown upon the head of her husband.[43]

We find the same pattern of men's central position and women's auxiliary though indispensable function in the sphere of public religious ritual, a predominantly male domain that was organized hierarchically. It mattered to contemporaries who among the men was first to be honored during the synagogue service, who was seated nearest to the eastern wall, who was entitled to express his concerns and his opinions, and most of all, who provided the ritual objects that embellished and symbolically elevated the sanctuary.[44] The embroidered fabrics for the curtain of the ark, the lecterns, the Torah mantles, and the ritual silverware of the period all served to honor and to glorify the "crown of the Torah." Yet at the same time, the large and in general centrally placed inscriptions on many of these objects showcased the names of their donors. Thus perhaps, in accordance with the Talmudic saying, it was the "crown of the good name"—or wealth and power—that tended to triumph in early modern synagogues.[45]

All of this took place almost entirely among men. Women, however, attended synagogue services more often than the rabbinic legal system demanded of them, and they formed the audience in front of which the spectacle of the men's worship unfolded.[46] As the women watched closely, the social order within the community played out in the main section of the sanctuary, and the men's wealth and status were projected onto the women's galleries. Yet the women were not merely passive receptacles. Not only did the location of their seats reflect the status of their husbands and families, but the female worshipers also participated in establishing the social ranking of the men by discussing and gossiping about them. They paid attention to the rituals by which the men achieved and expressed power, and they noted, for instance, who among the male worshipers had come first or who had received a jab in the ribs for moving his seat too close to his neighbor's. The women's acts of observing and retelling what took place in the men's section formed a necessary part of the process in which Jewish men's and Jewish families' social standing within the community took shape.

Although a woman was seen as an extension of her husband and as providing evidence for his virtue more than for her own, her husband needed her to bolster his respectability and offer support in periods of crisis. During the Kann-Kulp conflict in the mid-eighteenth century, when the Frankfurt Jewish community was divided into two rival factions, contenders used to publicly humiliate each other on their way to the synagogue or even during services. Members of one faction even threatened members of the other in attempts to discourage them from attending public worship. Yet neither side was willing to surrender this public arena to the adversary. The community elder Ruben Benedict Beyfuss was among those who had been threatened, but he defied the intimidation and made his way to the synagogue—only to find himself impeded, insulted, and spat upon by his adversaries. As they all left the synagogue, Beyfuss's opponents even confronted him with a puppet they had made to symbolize the allegedly illegitimate grandchild of David Meyer Juda, one of the chief participants in the conflict. Juda himself observed these events from his window, not daring to leave his house.[47]

Subsequently, Juda decided to organize a counterattack. He sent his wife to the synagogue to symbolically reclaim the public space from which he had been barred. As was the custom of wealthy and respected families, she went in her best apparel and accompanied by servants; Juda appears to have assumed that a woman of his wife's status would not be assaulted. Nonetheless, as she moved through a large crowd down the narrow streets of the ghetto, she too was confronted with the same paper doll, insulted, and screamed at by members of the opposing faction—humiliations her husband had been unwilling to experience. Finally, she successfully reached the synagogue and fought her way in.[48]

This is one of the many instances in which the close connection between the social status of men and that of women becomes evident. One certainly cannot conceive of the position of one without considering that of the other. Thus, we need to understand the matrix of gender relationships not only as a system of hierarchically organized, binary opposites of social ranking, but we should also take note of the processual interrelatedness of the ways in which both "male" and "female" were being staged in specific contexts. While less-dynamic models of gender relations tend to stress the differences between men and women and the gradings of the hierarchies between them, conceiving of gender as embedded in social acting is heavily relational and shows that neither men nor women can be understood without taking the other category into account.

Concluding these discussions about Jewish masculinity; appropriate, inappropriate, and unruly male sexuality; the alleged weakness and vigor of Jewish men; the discrepancies between religious prescriptions and social practices; and the interrelatedness of male and female social and cultural positions, I will return to the case of the hapless *shmendrik* Veith Kahn, with whose story we began. Kahn's image as a proper *baal habayit* was certainly damaged when his assertive wife gave him orders and forced him to leave the house, but had a woman been treated similarly, her fate would have been much worse. As a man, Kahn could wield power legitimately. His position was never in question. Even if he misused his power and transgressed moral norms, he was still perceived as powerful and masculine. A woman's transgressive behavior, on the other hand, inevitably called into question her status as a proper wife. Kahn may have been regarded as an inept weakling and a fraud, a laughingstock to other men, Christian and Jewish alike. Likewise, contemporaries, and Jews in particular, may have understood why Blümle Kahn acted the way she did. But it was ultimately her actions which were deemed unacceptable, because she challenged and usurped the male authority still embodied by her profligate husband. In other words, Blümle Kahn had threatened the structures that maintained and perpetuated the connection between masculinity and power and the principle of male superiority.

## Notes

1. Institut für Stadtgeschichte Frankfurt am Main (henceforth ISG Ffm), "Criminalia," fasc. XXX, 1388, Adulterim Veith Kahn, October 1672, esp. 29 October 1672 (oral examination of Veith Kahn according to the decree by the city council), 27 May 1675 (request of Blümle, wife of Veith Kahn, to readmit her husband: "Alle dieße Betrübnüßes tringen mit soviel schmertzlicher zu Hertzen, alß beydes ich und mein Ehe[mann] von dergleichen Eltern, welche unter der Judenschafft in großem Ansehn, und dero Vorsteher geweßen, entsprossen seynd; maßen mein Großvatter Moyßes zum [Weissen Kopf] allhier, und meine Mutter Meyer Caßel, wegen dero Redtlichkeyt annoch von iederman geprießen worden").

2. Ibid., 6 November 1672 (testimony by Veith Kahn, where he states that his "Schwäger, seien alle seine Tage seine grössten Feinde gewesen, wie noch jetzt und derglei-chen sei auch seine Frau; 2. es sei bekannt, dass solche [his brothers-in-law] mit der Hur [Blümle] ganz nah befreundet seien . . . , weil er Veith ein bös Frau habe, welche ihn alsbald würde hinweg gewiesen haben; auch weilen er, Gott erbarm es sein Stücklein Brod von seinen Freundten haben müsste").

3. Ibid. When asked during the examination of 29 October 1672 how he and his wife got along, Kahn answered: "Dieselbe seye ihm sein Lebtag nach Ehr und Glimpf gestanden, sampt ihren Freundten, wie auch dieselbe vor 17 Jahren mitt ihm zuzancken angefangen und zwar vor denen Baumeistern wegen geringer Ursach, als nemblich, daß er ihr sollte einen Mauschell gegeben haben; item daß er ir zuweilen mitt anderen habe einen Trunck gethan, und d.gleichen aber er habe recht behalten, und seine Frau habe wieder zu ihm kommen müßen."

4. Generallandesarchiv Baden (Karlsruhe), 74/3734, Löw Willstädter (deputy leader of the community of Karlsruhe) and David Bodenheimer (leader of the diet of the Jews living in the countryside of Baden-Durlach in Pforzheim) to the Margrave of Baden (31 October 1744). The community statutes of Hamburg put the responsibility for the moral conduct of servants on the man of the house. Thus, he was not allowed to hire someone of bad repute or a married woman. Likewise—similar to Christian mores, yet distinct—a husband was held responsible for the deeds of his wife and had to pay for the damages she caused or the fines levied against her. However, he could then reduce her *ketubah* accordingly. In this way, a married woman had to face the consequences of her actions, even though indirectly. In distinction to the general principle of Jewish law and to Christian practice, her husband mediated between her and the outside world, rather than acting as her master. Heinz Mosche Graupe, *Die Statuten der drei Gemeinden Altona, Hamburg und Wandsbek: Quellen zur jüdischen Gemeindeorganisation im 17. und 18. Jahrhundert* (Hamburg: Christians, 1973), 1:130, § 97 (MS AA).

5. ISG Ffm, "Criminalia," fasc. XXX, 1388, Adulterim Veith Kahn, 19 November 1672. In this document, Joseph zum Tannenbaum, the father of the pregnant girl, accuses Veith of being her violator. See also other testimonies and records of interrogations included in this file.

6. Leo Landman, "Jewish Attitudes toward Gambling," *Jewish Quarterly Review* 57, no. 4 (April 1967): 298–318, and *Jewish Quarterly Review* 58 (July 1967): 34–62.

7. Pinkas deKehila Keduscha deFrankfurt deMaina, University Library, Jerusalem, MS Hebr. 4, 622 (henceforth Pinkas Ffm), § 412, 176? (a general prohibition of such games); § 271, 1658 (Gabriel [Homburg] and his son Jakob were punished for playing cards on Shabbat); ISG Ffm, "Ugb," E 45 G, 1606 (Mosche zum Goldenen Apfel was punished by the community board for playing cards).

8. ISG Ffm, "Criminalia," 6546, 19 April 1751 (interrogation of the accused), 2 November 1751 (decision of the city's council), 4 May 1751 (Hirschhorn unsuccessfully asking for a reduction of his fine and interrogation of the witnesses), 21 December 1751 (review of the files by the city's lawyer Schudt); ISG Ffm, "Ugb," D 32, 65, Tom I, 59, 3 February 1750 (appeal of "peace-loving" Jews to the mayors and council of Frankfurt am Main that Juda frequently played "quite vigorously" with friends); Pinkas Ffm, § 412, 176? (prohibition of card playing), and § 271, 1658 (Gabriel [Homburg] and his son Jakob fined for gambling on Shabbat). We find similar prohibitions in other Jewish communities as well as in the Christian sphere. See, for instance, Graupe, *Die Statuten der drei Gemeinden*, 86, § 34 (MS AA); Stefan Litt, *Protokollbuch und Statuten der Jüdischen Gemeinde Friedberg (16.–18. Jahrhundert)*, in Andreas Gotzmann, ed., *Kehilat Friedberg* (Friedberg: Bindernagel, 2003), 2:441, § 222 (Takkanot).

9. In Hamburg, only married men and males after their bar mitzvah were allowed to wear a black hat on Shabbat and holidays. Bachelors were allowed to wear scarves as a sign of a low profession and street clothing at all times, but married men were allowed to wear such clothing just on holidays, while *parnassim* were never allowed to do so. Graupe, *Die Statuten der drei Gemeinden*, 86, § 33 (MS AA). Other customs surrounding clothing suggest that merchants by all means avoided flaunting their wealth in order not to stoke greed and resentment, which might pose a danger to themselves. Ibid., 160–162, §§ 176–181 (MS AA). Yet merchants still wanted to signal that they could afford expensive things, so they tended to wear black clothing with silver-thread buttons only on the sleeves, a small amount of jewelry, some embroidery, and no furs. Regulations for women's clothing were less strict, since women were perceived as vain. Martin Dinges, "Von der 'Lesbarkeit der Welt' zum universalisierten Wandel durch individuelle Strategien: Die soziale Funktion der Kleidung in der höfischen Gesellschaft," *Saeculum* 44 (1993): 90–112. Compare also Johann Jacob Schudt, *Jüdischer Merckwürdigkeiten* (1714), vol. 9. For regulations on which items of clothing were to be included in the mutual wedding gifts of a couple, see Litt, *Protokollbuch*, 395, § 10 (Pinkas); 441, § 221 (Takkanot).

10. Andreas Gotzmann, *Jüdische Autonomie in der Frühen Neuzeit: Recht und Gemeinschaft im deutschen Judentum* (Göttingen: Wallstein, 2008).

11. ISG Ffm, "Ugb," D32, no. 65, Tom I 71, B. L. Isaac and S. S. Stern (ca. 1749): "Du alter Gaudieb ich will dir deinen grauen Barth ausraufen"; Monika Preuß, *"Aber die Krone des guten Namens überragt sie": Jüdische Ehrvorstellungen im 18. Jahrhundert im Kraichgau* (Stuttgart: Kohlhammer, 2005), 80–102.

12. ISG Ffm, "Criminalia," 6532, B. L. Isaac, Benjamin Salomon, Abraham Stiefel, Calman Rothschild, and his son (complaint against real and verbal injuries), Actum Ffm, 29 May 1751.

13. For instance, the community regulations of Friedberg called on the *parnassim* (community leaders) to treat each other with honor, and stipulated that a *parnas* who

insulted a colleague had to pay a fine of one *kopfstück* (a small coin), while the offended colleague who answered with an insult paid only half a *kopfstück*. These regulations combined respect for the logic of the contemporary code of honor, according to which one had to defend one's honor, with legal thinking that preferred lawful actions, such as fines, to solve problems. Litt, *Protokollbuch*, 439, § 204 (Takkanot).

14. On the concept of honor among rural Jews, see Preuß, *"Aber die Krone des guten Namens."* On the situation in full-fledged Jewish communities, which differed from rural settings due to the more complex social structures, see Robert Jütte, "Ehre und Ehrverlust im spätmittelalterlichen und frühneuzeitlichen Judentum," in Klaus Schreiner and Gerd Schwerhoff, eds., *Verletzte Ehre: Ehrkonflikte in Gesellschaften des Mittelalters und der frühen Neuzeit* (Köln: Böhlau, 1995), 44–165.

15. Stadtarchiv Frankfurt am Main (henceforth StA Ffm), "Criminalia," 6534 (quarrels between Jews in the Jewish quarter), see, in particular, 8 March 1751 (the denunciation of the imperial court Jew David Meyer Juda to the judges of Frankfurt am Main), and 6 June 1751 (an interrogation in the same matter); ISG Ffm, "Criminalia," 6560, 1751 (on a fight in the Jewish quarter between Wolf Zunz and Löser [Rade?], in the course of which one of the men was cut in the face with a knife); ibid., 6534, 8 March 1751 (quarrels in the Jewish quarter, esp. letter by D. M. Juda, and compare the testimonies especially of Abraham Amschel Hahn and Löw Lazarus Oppenheimer in the same file).

16. See all of the sources cited in the previous note.

17. ISG Ffm, "Criminalia," fasc. XXIII, 1154, Adulterim Bälla von Niederhofheim/Meyer zum Dröchter, 14 June and 19 July 1655 (files include protocols of the examinations of Abraham zum Drachen and of Salomon zum Rothschild and Hirz zum Braiß, who were brought along as witnesses by Abraham).

18. Ibid., 17 July 1655 (Abraham zum Drachen said: "Du wer der . . . Schelm, was darfs tu mich schelten und schmähen, ich habe keinen Schaden bei dem Eid und ihm darauf hin eine Maulschellen gegeben in der Synagog, so dass ihm die Nase geschweizt und auf die Erde gefürkten, und als der Fleischschänzer zu Abraham gesaget, das sei nicht recht, du solltest nicht geschlagen haben, habe er nur gesagt, ich hoffe es vor Gott und der Welt wohl zu verantworten und will dies auch verantworten"); 24 July 1655 (request of Abraham zum Drachen: when he asked for a reduction of the fine, he explained that it was hurtful and unbearable to be called a villain who had committed perjury and, therefore, that he could not help but react violently).

19. Gotzmann, *Jüdische Autonomie*, 55, 749. This was the case in Frankfurt in 1609, before the Fettmilch riots. The Jewish communities in Germany were accused of treachery against the emperor and the reich, and the royal commission, in search of evidence against the community leaders and the rabbinate, intruded into the Frankfurt ghetto without the knowledge of the city council. The rumors that spread in this situation made guildsmen and the lower classes gather in front of the ghetto gates. In another setting, in the middle of the eighteenth century, the council ordered the city guards to patrol the Jewish quarter in order to prevent further unrest during the Kann-Kulp conflict. Jews, however, feared that the Christian population might understand the patrols as a sign of distrust or suspicion of the Jewish community by the authorities and might consequently attack or plunder the ghetto. ISG Ffm, "Ugb," D32, no. 65, Tom I, 48a, 5 January 1750 (Juda and Beyfuß reported to the mayor and the council of Frankfurt am Main that about a hundred non-Jewish people had gathered at the gates and had supposedly observed the entry of the commandos. Thus, there was fear that it could "gar leichtlich zu einer Plünderung kommen und die ganze Judengasse umgekehrt werden können").

20. Cilli Kasper-Holtkotte, "Jüdisches Leben in Friedberg (16.–18. Jahrhundert)," in Gotzmann, ed., *Kehilat Friedberg*, 1:228–234; Sabine Ullmann, *Nachbarschaft und*

*Konkurrenz: Juden und Christen in Dörfern der Markgrafschaft Burgau 1650–1750* (Göttingen: Vandenhoeck & Ruprecht, 1999); Maria R. Boes, "Jews in the Criminal-Justice System of Early Modern Germany," *Journal of Interdisciplinary History* 30, no. 3 (1999): 407–435.

21. ISG Ffm, "Ugb," D32, no. 65, Tom I, 10 (reports of the officer on duty of the *Hauptwache*, the guards' headquarters).

22. ISG Ffm, "Criminalia," 6534 (quarrels in the Jewish quarter, including a report from the city guards and protocols); see, for instance, 8 March 1751 (letter of D. M. Juda to the city's judges), 5 March 1751 (appeal of the students to the *Schultheissen* and *Schöffen* of the city of Frankfurt am Main).

23. Daniel Boyarin, *Carnal Israel: Reading Sex in Talmudic Culture* (Berkeley: University of California Press, 1993). On women's role in the early modern world, see Claudia Ulbrich, *Shulamit and Margarete: Power, Gender, and Religion in a Rural Society in Eighteenth-Century Europe* (Boston: Brill, 2004).

24. Andreas Gotzmann, Stefan Ehrenpreis, and Stephan Wendehorst, "Von den Rechtsnormen zur Rechtspraxis: Ein neuer Zugang zur Rechtsgeschichte der Juden im Heiligen Römischen Reich?," in Birgit Feldner et al., eds., *Ad Fontes: Europäisches rechtshistorisches Forum* (Frankfurt am Main: Lang, 2002), 97–119; Gotzmann, "At Home in Many Worlds? Thoughts about New Concepts in Jewish Legal History," *Jahrbuch des Simon-Dubnow-Instituts/Yearbook of the Simon Dubnow Institute* 2 (2003): 412–436. On the same phenomenon in Christian society, see Jürgen Schlumbohm, "Gesetze, die nicht durchgesetzt werden: Ein Strukturmerkmal des frühneuzeitlichen Staate?," *Geschichte und Gesellschaft* 23 (1997): 647–663.

25. Andreas Gotzmann, "Gemeinde als Gemeinschaft? Politische Konzepte der deutschen Juden im Absolutismus," *Jahrbuch des Simon-Dubnow-Instituts/Yearbook of the Simon Dubnow Institute* 1 (2002): 375–427.

26. At the same time, as far as we know, religious rituals (with a few exceptions of changing customs and local deviations) were closely tied to religious law.

27. Asriel Schochat, *Der Ursprung der jüdischen Aufklärung in Deutschland* (Frankfurt am Main: Campus, 2000), 287–308.

28. Helga Schnabel-Schüler, "Ego-Dokumente im frühneuzeitlichen Strafprozeß," in Winfried Schulze, ed., *Ego-Dokumente: Annäherung an den Menschen in der Geschichte* (Berlin: Akademie, 1996), 295–317.

29. Evidence for this includes, for instance, the forms of organization developed by rural Jewish populations, as they strove to realize what they considered the ideal setting for Jewish social life: the Jewish community. Although the structures that were typical for Jewish communities did not at all suit the needs of families who were scattered in rural areas, rural Jewries emulated community structures by creating the so-called *Landjudenschaften* (country Jewries). These *Landjudenschaften*—quite characteristic of such attempts to introduce communal forms of organization in the countryside—achieved a somewhat normative status, but consistently failed to meet the expectations of rural Jews. For regulations of rural communities, see Daniel Cohen, ed., *Die Landjudenschaften in Deutschland als Organe jüdischer Selbstverwaltung von der frühen Neuzeit bis ins neunzehnte Jahrhundert: Eine Quellensammlung*, 3 vols. (Jerusalem: Israelische Akademie der Wissenschaften, 1996–2001).

30. Jacob Joseph Schacter, "Rabbi Jacob Emden: Life and Major Works," Ph.D. diss., Harvard University, 1988, 37–40.

31. Boyarin, *Carnal Israel*, 62–75.

32. See, for instance, Jacob Emden, *Megilat Sefer*, ed. Abraham Beck (Jerusalem: Sifriyat Moreshet, 1979), 126–128, 275–277.

33. Boyarin, *Carnal Israel*, 62–75; Jonathan Wyn Schofer, "The Redaction of Desire: Structure and Editing of Rabbinic Teachings Concerning 'Yeser' ('Inclination')," *Journal of Jewish Thought and Philosophy* 12, no. 1 (2003): 19–53.

34. My book *Jüdische Autonomie* deals extensively with such aspects of communal control and the cultural autonomy of Jewish communities in the early modern period. See Gotzmann, *Jüdische Autonomie*: for rabbinic theology and the control of human nature and social behavior, see esp. ch. 3, "Ferne Ideale—Das rechte Leben im Recht," 191–196, and ch. 6, "Zügelungsversuche—Das Ideal des beherrschten Menschen," as well as "Beherrschung—Geregeltheit als Bollwerk gegen das Chaos," 713–745, 787–814.

35. ISG Ffm, "Criminalia," fasc. XIX, 950, 1630 (*unzüchtige Handlungen an einer Schuldnerin*); see, in particular, the testimonies from July 1630.

36. Ulinka Rublack, *Magd, Metz' oder Mörderin: Frauen vor frühneuzeitlichen Gerichten* (Frankfurt am Main: Fischer, 1998).

37. ISG Ffm, "Criminalia," fasc. XIX, 950, 1630 (*unzüchtige Handlungen an einer Schuldnerin*); see, in particular, the testimonies from July 1630.

38. Ibid.

39. Ibid., 17 July 1630 (interrogation of Johann Albrecht Hofmann, twenty-eight years old: "Er und Schanz sein daruf zugleich in Eifer hinein gestürm und Schanz ihn Juden sobald zu Boden geschlagen, und der Schantzen Mann zugleich die andere Tür hinein geloffen kommen, 33. Schnatz[!] hötte in dem mit Fluchen, und Schelten gesagt: Du Dieb und Schelm, weiter, auf diese Weis mich und meinen Frau zuschanden machen. 34. Sei auf der Erde gelegen und habe geschrieen, nein laßt mich doch gehen, 35. Schnatz habe dem Juden wie vorgemelt, und geschlagnen daß er [auf] dem der Erde ganz bloß gelegen, darum er Zeug ihm Juden bei seinem Glied erwischte und nach einem Messer zubringen geruffen, wollte ihn abschneiden, darauf Schanz in die Stuben ein Messer geholt und ihm Zeugen gegeben, hätte aber dem Juden damit nichts getan, dann derselbe ihm viel zugeben verheissen").

40. Gotzmann, *Jüdische Autonomie*, 633–642, 774–778.

41. Pinkas Ffm, § 292 (1663).

42. Ibid. On punishments in early modern Ashkenazi communities, see Gotzmann, *Jüdische Autonomie*, 259–291.

43. For a discussion of the concept of honor in rural Jewish communities in the early modern period, see Preuß, *Aber die Krone des guten Namens*, 60–71.

44. Graupe, *Die Statuten der drei Gemeinden*, 70, § 7; 75, § 11 (MS AA); 76, § 14 (MS AA; on bachelors being excluded from some of the Torah readings on certain holidays); 77, § 16 (MS AA; on the number of people for whom a *mi she'berakhs* could be said and for whom this was possible); 83, § 27 (MS AA; on the use of private Torah scrolls). For similar regulations in the Hessian town of Friedberg, see Litt, *Protokollbuch*, 396, § 11.

45. BT Avot 4, 17; Annette Weber, "Rekonstruktion von Synagogenausstattungen des 18. Jahrhunderts anhand der Photosammlung Harburger und die Rolle des Kultgerätes für die Tempelvorstellung," in Thomas W. Gaehtgens, ed., *Künstlerischer Austausch* (Berlin: Akademie, 1993), 3:455–465. For regulations of these practices in the Takkanot of the united communities of Hamburg-Altona-Wandsbek, see also Graupe, *Die Statuten der drei Gemeinden*, 67, §§ 1–4, 1685 (renewed 1726).

46. Thus, the alleged adulterer Samuel zum Elefanten remained at home on Shabbat and invited the Christian Bärbel Schantz to visit him, while his wife was in the synagogue; ISG Ffm, "Criminalia," fasc. XIX, 950, 1630 (*unzüchtige Handlungen an einer Schuldnerin*). See also David Kaufmann, ed., *Zikhronot marat Glikl Hamel mishnat tav-zaijn ad tav-ayin tet* (Frankfurt am Main: Kauffmann, 1896), 325–333.

47. ISG Ffm, "Criminalia," 6534, interrogations from March 1751: Moses Faist Hirschhorn, Hertz Abraham Geiger, Hayum Salomon Windmühl, Jacob Sal, Oppenheimer, etc.; and Joh, Eybinger, Joh. Georg Heinlein, and Joh. August Ziegler (Christian witnesses). See also Michaela Schmölz-Häberlein, "Ehrverletzung als Strategie: Zum sozialen Kontext von Injurien in der badischen Kleinstadt Emmendingen 1650–1800," in Mark Häberlein, ed., *Devianz, Widerstand und Herrschaftspraxis in der Vormoderne: Studien zu Konflikten im südwestdeutschen Raum (15.–18. Jahrhundert)* (Konstanz: Universitätsverlag, 1999), 137–163.

48. ISG Ffm, "Criminalia," 6534, interrogations from March 1751.

# 2

## Jewish Difference and the Feminine Spirit of Judaism in Mid-Nineteenth-Century Germany

BENJAMIN MARIA BAADER

In sermons, Bible commentaries, pedagogical literature, and a variety of other publications, nineteenth-century German Jewish preachers and rabbis lauded Jewish women. They praised the superior moral and religious temperament of the female sex, declared mothers and wives to be the pillars of modern Judaism, and developed a true cult of the Jewish mother and of feminine religiosity.[1] In this chapter, I will discuss how two Jewish leaders in this period, Samson Raphael Hirsch, who is often considered the founder of modern Orthodoxy in Germany, and the Reform rabbi Adolf Jellinek in Vienna took this exaltation of the female to another level by claiming that femininity constitutes the principle of the Jewish religion and that Jewish men stand out because of the character traits Hirsch and Jellinek called feminine.

In the middle of the nineteenth century, these Jewish leaders argued that Jewish culture and Jewish civilization rested on foundations that were domestic, spiritual, and feminine rather than political and manly, and according to Hirsch, Jewish manliness was not grounded in military and political power, but in domestic and feminine virtues. Jellinek postulated that Jewish women and Jewish men had a greater inclination toward gentleness, morality, and domesticity than other populations. He compared Jewish men favorably to non-Jews, praised their devotion to family life, and encouraged them to continue cultivating their tender and compassionate disposition.

With these ideas, Hirsch and Jellinek were operating within the parameters of nineteenth-century middle-class concepts of the manly and the feminine. By declaring that femininity represented the most beautiful, desirable, and religiously elevated qualities, the Jewish leaders expressed a view that was common within the framework of bourgeois culture at the time and that echoed the opinions of their Christian colleagues. Likewise, the ideal of the sensitive, emotionally expressive, and domestically inclined man fell within the realm of the well-balanced masculinity to which men aspired in the early and mid-nineteenth-century's German middle-class society. Thus, by lauding the gentle, moral, and domestic disposition of Jewish men, Hirsch and Jellinek expressed their acculturation and laid claim to Germanness.

However, Hirsch and Jellinek also affirmed Jewish distinctiveness when they contended that Jews differed from other people by having embraced and embodied feminine principles and character traits since antiquity. They advanced the notion that Jewish men possessed particular feminine character traits, an idea that became a hallmark of the anti-Semitic discourse on Jews at the turn of the twentieth century. Yet in the middle of the nineteenth century, the stereotype of the effeminate Jewish man appears not to have been common, and Hirsch and even more so Jellinek might have played a role in popularizing the concept that Jewish men were more soft-hearted and gentle-mannered than their non-Jewish contemporaries. However, further research is required into whether these Jewish leaders' sermons, religious texts, and various essays on the gender dimension of Jewish difference directly or indirectly inspired German and Austrian anti-Semites of the late nineteenth and early twentieth centuries. The material that I am presenting here should help us work toward a fuller understanding of how the concept of Jewish men's distinct gender traits developed in nineteenth-century Germany. But given the current state of the research, I will largely limit myself to shedding light on the nature of Hirsch's and Jellinek's notions of gender and Judaism, and I will explore the sources from which these Jewish clergymen drew the inspiration for their ideas.

## GOTTHOLD SALOMON AND A FEMINIZED BOURGEOIS RELIGIOSITY

One of the most influential promoters of the family- and woman-centered Judaism that became characteristic of the nineteenth-century German Jewish religious culture was Gotthold Salomon, who was born in 1784 in a village in Anhalt-Dessau. He attended a yeshiva in the town of Dessau, also pursued secular studies, and at the age of eighteen became a teacher at the Jewish Free School of Dessau, one of the leading institutions of the German Haskalah (Jewish Enlightenment) and home of the pathbreaking Jewish periodical *Sulamith*. Founded in 1806 by the director of the Dessau Free School, David Fränkel, and the *maskil* (promoter of the Jewish Enlightenment) Joseph Wolf, *Sulamith* pioneered in propagating the reform of Judaism and the embourgeoisement of Jewish culture and religion, trends that eventually became dominant among the German-speaking Jewries of Western and Central Europe.[2]

Salomon was a contributor to *Sulamith* from its inception, and he also played a leading role in introducing weekly edifying sermons in High German into German synagogues.[3] These novel sermons replaced the earlier, occasional, Yiddish-language *derashot* (hermeneutic explications of scripture), and their popularization constituted one of the most significant and universal aspects of the modernization of synagogue culture in nineteenth-century Germany. Since the later decades of the eighteenth century, Protestantism, under the influence of Pietism and Romanticism, had developed a homiletics that aimed at the heart of the worshiper. In a parallel development, German Jews cultivated a kind of sermon that expressed a new emotionalized religiosity and, by its high standards of rhetorical sophistication, was designed to testify to the German, middle-class status of the Jewish worshipers.[4]

In 1818, Gotthold Salomon became the second preacher of Germany's newly founded model Reform congregation, the Hamburg Temple, and together with his colleague Eduard Kley, he made Hamburg the capital of contemporary German Jewish homiletics.[5] As a preacher, Salomon served in a position that had previously not existed in Jewish communities but that, by the middle of the nineteenth century, German Jews had come to regard highly. Salomon gained significant fame for his talent as an orator and became known as the "father of modern Jewish homiletics" and as "the favorite preacher of the female sex."[6]

Salomon pioneered a style of preaching that dispensed entirely with transmitting concrete knowledge and rather focused fully on being "edifying, exciting, yes gripping [fortreißend]."[7] Contemporaries admired him as a preacher, because he "knew how to uplift the souls, to penetrate deep into the hearts, to illuminate and to embellish [verklären] the vibrations of the soul [Gemüthsstimmungen], to awaken thoughts in noble form . . . , and to shape warmly felt convictions."[8] His rousing delivery and the lively character of his sermons, distinguished by the frequent use of metaphors, parables, and rhetorical questions and interspersed with Bible verses and his own poetry, contributed to the success of the Hamburg Temple.[9]

As in German churches at the time, men and women sat in separate sections of the sanctuary, yet all worshipers at the Hamburg Temple appear to have relished Salomon's orations, and for some, the sermon became the main attraction of the synagogue service. The leading German Jewish newspaper, *Allgemeine Zeitung des Judenthums,* reported in 1838 that worshipers came to the Hamburg Temple merely to hear the sermon and left soon after the preacher had finished.[10] In a similar vein, the diary of Louis Lesser, a young man from a respectable though not wealthy Jewish family in Dresden, reveals that Lesser attended services primarily on high holidays and on other days on which the rabbi delivered a sermon.[11]

Yet women may have been particularly fond of Salomon and the modernized Jewish worship services. Eduard Kley described that during the winter of 1818–1819, "the oldest and the youngest ladies, not only from Hamburg but even from Altona streamed to the temple" in all kinds of weather.[12] Therese Gumpel, a worshiper in Brunswick, heard Salomon preach in the local synagogue on the occasion of the second rabbinical conference in June 1844, and lauded his beautiful and "moving words" in a letter to her fiancé.[13] In addition, the audience that Salomon reached with his sermons was far larger than those who came to hear him in person, as he—together with his colleague Eduard

Kley—published in the 1820s and 1830s no less than fifteen volumes of their sermons.[14]

In his devotional speeches, Salomon developed a theology that centered around women and the family. For example, in a collection of sermons entitled Das Familienleben (Family Life), published in 1821, he described the Jewish home as the house of God in which love inspires true religiosity: "parental love, the children's love, love between the spouses, Menschenliebe [love of humanity], [and] love of God."[15]

According to Salomon, women possessed the power to imbue the domestic sphere with love, piety, and faithfulness: "The home is your world, you women! You alone can and should give it the most pleasant form and transform it into a house of God."[16] Expounding on the verse from Proverbs which praises the woman of valor, eshet hayil, "Grace is deceptive, beauty is illusory; it is for her fear of the Lord that a woman is to be praised," Salomon then exalted the female virtues of piety, morality, and modesty that adorned a refined Jewish house.[17]

Salomon was propagating a set of ideas that had first been laid out in contributions to the journal Sulamith and that by the middle of the nineteenth century had become common in the culture of German Jewish bourgeois religiosity. In this era, Jewish men and women disengaged from ritual observances and from traditional forms of Jewish practice and sought in Judaism moral guidance within the parameters of German middle-class culture. Like their Christian contemporaries, German Jews wanted to be edified, morally uplifted, and emotionally engaged in beautifully orchestrated worship services. Christians and Jews both wished to find comfort in a domestic life that a spiritualized religiosity infused with warmth, dignity, and middle-class virtue. In this emotionalized culture of bourgeois religiosity that rabbis and preachers such as Salomon promoted in sermons, devotional literature, Jewish periodicals, and various other Jewish publications, women played a central role. According to nineteenth-century ideas of gender characteristics, the female sex was by nature endowed with a high propensity for morality and religious feeling, and women fulfilled indispensable functions as mistresses of the house, wives, and mothers.[18]

However, when a Jewish leader such as Gotthold Salomon sang the praises of the Jewish home, of a truly inspired Jewish religiosity, and of Jewish womanhood in his sermons, he was addressing Jewish men too. Salomon expected fathers along with mothers to raise their children with tenderness and devotion and to lead them toward love of God and piety. In a sermon for the Jewish New Year from the 1850s, Salomon lauded the biblical patriarch Jacob as a "deeply feeling, tenderly loving father," and he exhorted the men of his congregation to follow the example of Jacob and "to embed the principles of morality and religiosity in their [children's] spirit and soul [Gemüthe]."[19] In mid-nineteenth-century Jewish homiletics, gentle, tender, and caring fathers formed part of the ideal of a bourgeois Jewish family, and this was not confined to Reform circles.

## SAMSON RAPHAEL HIRSCH AND
## THE FEMININE SPIRIT OF JUDAISM

Like their counterparts in the Reform movement, modern Orthodox Jews adopted notions of a superior feminine religiosity, a home-based Judaism, and the paramount importance of the motherly influence in the religious realm. Samson Raphael Hirsch, who grew up in Hamburg in the era in which the founding of the Reform Temple deeply divided the Jewish community there and who became the leader and spokesperson of German Neo-Orthodoxy in the 1850s, indeed developed his own version of the nineteenth-century cult of the Jewish mother. In his education series in the modern Orthodox periodical *Jeschurun* from 1862, Hirsch turned with great urgency to the "women of the House of Jacob" and the "mothers of the Jewish people" and declared that it was they who had the power and the responsibility of ensuring the continuity of Judaism.[20] According to Hirsch, the future of Judaism depended on the commitment of future generations to Orthodox practice, Jewish children were in severe danger of being corrupted by modern ideas and mores, and mothers were destined to stem the tide. Hirsch exclaimed: "Take up the challenge, O Jewish mother, which the perversity of our era has thrown at the moral nobility of your children! Dedicate yourself to become a courageous fighter for the cause of God and to rescue your children! . . . Save your child for humanity and Judaism and raise him to be obedient to God!"[21]

As the leaders of the Reform movement did, Hirsch emphasized the crucial role that the home played in Jewish communal life, and he idealized the Jewish woman and the Jewish mother. Also in agreement with his Reform colleagues, Hirsch addressed men as well as women, since all Jewish clergymen thought of both sexes as the guardians of the Jewish religion and of religiosity within the family. Hirsch called upon both fathers and mothers to instill faithfulness toward the Jewish tradition in their children by fully observing the Sabbath in the home.[22] And at times, Hirsch turned specifically to men and urged them not to leave religious instruction entirely to the school. Fathers themselves needed to introduce their children to the biblical text, he claimed.[23] "The father's, and only the father's lips and face" can communicate to a child the full sanctity and seriousness of the holy text.[24] Thus, the formation of children's souls and hearts (*Geistes- und Herzensbildung*) required both parents' active involvement.[25] Nevertheless, Hirsch declared at the beginning of his series on pedagogy in *Jeschurun* that the influence of the mother and not that of the father was the decisive factor for the development of the intellectual capacities and religious sensitivities of a child.[26]

Every nineteenth-century educator is likely to have agreed with Hirsch in this matter. However, for the modern Orthodox leader more was at stake than pedagogical principles. He shared the high regard for the female sex with other rabbis, preachers, and pedagogues, but in his ideas on Judaism and femininity he went beyond what was common in the bourgeois religiosity that Gotthold Salomon had helped to popularize. Hirsch not only extolled and glorified the Jewish woman and the Jewish mother, but he regarded femininity as the highest form of Jewishness and as the essence of Judaism. Hirsch claimed that women lived on a morally and religiously higher plane than men: "The true woman is the noblest embodiment of man formed in the image of God."[27] As he explained in his much-noted Bible commentary, "the concept 'woman,' includes the notion of 'the good.'"[28] On these grounds Hirsch argued in his writings that women's more fully developed religious temperament resulted in their being exempt from active, time-bound *mitzvot* (religious commandments). According to Hirsch, the fact that Halakhah (Jewish ritual law) did not require women to perform these numerous ritual obligations neither expressed contempt for women nor marked an inferior status of the female sex. Rather, it was men who possessed the more fragile connection to God and who were exposed to various stimulations and temptations in their professional and public lives. Men required constant concrete reminders of their covenant with the Eternal, such as circumcision and regulated times and fixed formulas for prayers. Women, on the other hand, had a tendency to spontaneous fervor and faithfulness and were naturally drawn to God. Thus, due to women's strong innate spirituality, halakhic Judaism exempted them from the duty to perform the full array of religious commandments.[29]

This line of argument developed by Hirsch has become common in modern apologetics for women's inferior position in the religious economy of rabbinic Judaism and is still being promulgated by Orthodox leaders today. Through the second half of the twentieth century until today, it has served to defend women's exclusion—or, technically, exemption—from highly valued religious practices, such as the *mitzvot* of reciting Hebrew prayers at certain times of the day or of laying phylacteries, against the challenge of Jewish feminists.[30] In Hirsch's era, however, male Jewish leaders were not defending established customs against Jewish women who demanded equality and who criticized their marginal position in some of the most significant realms of Jewish religious practice. Rather, they were responding to Christian claims that the allegedly oriental, outdated, and archaic nature of Judaism resulted in the oppression of Jewish women.

Conversionists in Victorian England exploited this argument in their attempts to win Jewish women for Christianity, and publications by German Catholics in Germany, who as rationalist-pietist dissenters tended to support Jewish integration and emancipation, denounced Judaism and Jewish law as inherently misogynist.[31] Apparently, considerations of women's status in Judaism did not play a central role in the debates about Jewish emancipation in Germany, but Jewish leaders nevertheless were concerned about the charge that Judaism held women in disregard. Thus in 1806, David Fränkel sought to refute the

suggestion of women's inferior position in Judaism by claiming that the promi-
nence of women such as Deborah in the biblical text reflected the high regard
for women in Jewish society.[32] Perhaps the most distinguished Reform rabbi,
Abraham Geiger, on the other hand, acknowledged that Judaism treated wom-
en unfairly and needed to remedy its unfortunate subordination of the female
sex; and the participants in the rabbinical conferences of the 1840s attempted,
but failed, to emancipate Jewish women within the framework of Halakhah.
However, nineteenth-century rabbis, preachers, and educators integrated wom-
en and girls into programs of religious education and into synagogue services,
without making changes to the halakhic norms of rabbinic Judaism.[33] They
claimed that enlightened worship and instruction in the Jewish religion promoted the virtues, the morality, and the manners that qualified Jewish families
for citizenship while enabling mothers to imbue their children with religious
feeling and with loyalty to Judaism.

The modern Orthodox movement, led by Samson Raphael Hirsch, also put
great weight on a refashioned religious education for girls. In the school that
these deliberately modern yet observant Jews founded in Frankfurt in 1853,
girls received religious and secular instruction in the same classes as boys until
the community was able to establish a separate institution for the girls. In the
second half of the nineteenth century, the rabbi of Berlin's modern Orthodox
congregation, Esriel Hildesheimer, lectured to girls and women and advocated Talmudic learning for the female sex.[34] Thus, modern Orthodox Jews in
Germany adjusted their educational practices to modern sensibilities and even
moved toward giving women access to Talmud study. However, different from
all other German Jews, adherents of modern Orthodoxy remained committed to ritual observance and categorically rejected any changes to or reform of
Halakhah.

When Hirsch was pressed to reconcile the exclusion or exemption of
women from the highly valued, active, time-bound *mitzvot* with the great importance that he and his contemporaries ascribed to women's presence and
women's participation in the religious realm, he took recourse in a dualism inherent in rabbinic Judaism. Classical rabbinic literature distinguishes between
the prestige of rabbinic study, practiced most eminently by the educated male
elite, and the religious merit that the unlearned (almost all women and socially
disadvantaged men) could accumulate through acts of kindness, generosity, or
outstanding trust in God. Some texts indeed maintain that women possess a
particularly close, specifically feminine, not Halakhah-based relationship to
God, and at times they declare the meritorious deeds of women and others who
are weak and powerless to be superior in value to the religious merits of even
supremely dedicated and meticulously observant Talmud scholars.[35] By drawing on these precedents, Hirsch could praise female piety and exalt the role of
the Jewish mother, while at the same time confirming women's peculiar if not

inferior status in Halakhah. Yet when Hirsch lauded women's moral excellence, feminine religiosity, and the sublime nature of femininity, he was not merely concerned with women's place in Jewish practice, Jewish law, and the world of Jewish religiosity. Rather, his extolling of women and femininity formed part of a larger argument on the feminine spirit of Judaism.

Hirsch endorsed and defended the irrevocable validity and immutability of Halakhah and held Jews responsible for unremittingly observing the divinely revealed law. At the same time, Kantian and Hegelian ideas shaped his thinking, and he agreed with his more radically minded colleagues and many other educated Jews that a "spirit" or an "internal life principle," which was not contained in the performance of rituals, formed the core of Judaism.[36] This religious spirit of rabbinic Judaism Hirsch tended to gender feminine. The most true, pure, unspoiled essence of Judaism, according to Hirsch, was represented by the female principle of the Jewish religion and of Jewish history. In a sermon on fast days in the Jewish calendar, Hirsch stated: "The whole history of the Jews since the fall of Jerusalem is nothing but a triumph of the 'female' over the 'male.'"[37] According to Hirsch, this female principle embodied the "purely human," the spiritual, and the domestic realms of life, while maleness expressed itself in the civil realm, in political power, and in the state.[38] With the destruction of the Second Temple in 70 CE, however, Israel had lost all that is "merely power and sovereignty, stately splendor and civic honor," and had for centuries fully relied on values and principles that Hirsch considered to be feminine.[39] He claimed that what expressed itself in Jewish history was the ethical primacy of the human over the citizen and the house over the state. Since the Romans had overcome Israel in ancient times, Zion lacked the kind of manliness that associated male virtue with "sword and scepter," and instead Jewish society drew its strength from the spiritually more uplifted domestic sphere.[40]

Hirsch presented the Jews as having perfected the virtues of a diasporic people in 2,000 years of exile, and he linked their lack of power in the political and public realms with high standards of spiritual perfection, with moral superiority, and with femininity. Conceivably, Hirsch purposefully de-emphasized the national aspects of the Jewish collective existence at a time when German Jews were still struggling for full emancipation in the German states. However, if he intended to show that Jews were fit for citizenship, his suggestion that Jewish men had for centuries been estranged from a masculinity that expressed itself in the civic and political realms might seem surprising. In fact, Hirsch not only claimed that the "peculiarity [*Eigenthümlichkeit*]" of the Jewish nation consisted in its pursuit of "human perfection [*humaner Vollendung*]" rather than the quest for political power,[41] but he also encouraged men as well as women to practice renunciation and modesty, and even self-denial and submissiveness. Hirsch held that "the life of the woman contains even more renunciation," and indeed "her whole life is a self-denying devotion to the welfare of others, especially of her husband."[42] Yet rather than depicting the Jewish male as the independent, self-reliant, and assertive counterpart to the submissive female, Hirsch exhorted Jewish men to aspire to the same feminine ideals of renunciation and dutiful submission to the will of God.[43]

In his writings, Hirsch seems to have anticipated at least elements of Daniel Boyarin's claim that the rabbis of the Talmud and their descendants in the diaspora repudiated the imperial Roman culture of phallic manliness, embraced a feminized counter-masculinity, and cultivated male meekness. In regard to women's position in Jewish culture, Hirsch held that it was necessary to forcefully reject the idea that traditional Judaism was antiquated and out of step with the values of modern society in its supposedly oriental treatment and degradation of the female sex.[44] Apparently he was not concerned that Jewish men might be regarded as insufficiently masculine and unfit for emancipation due to their alleged lack of involvement in civic and political matters. On the contrary, Hirsch claimed that femininity and domesticity represented fundamental principles of Judaism, characterized Jewish culture, and should be the guiding values for Jewish men in the nineteenth century.

## ADOLF JELLINEK AND JEWISH MEN'S PARTICULAR GENTLENESS

The notion that a high regard for domesticity was a Jewish character trait appears to have been widely shared by Jews in mid-nineteenth-century Germany, and some contemporaries made explicit what Hirsch had only implied in his writings: the Jewish people had always been more family-oriented and more gentle-hearted than other nations. Abraham Geiger claimed in the essay "Nationality, Slavery, [and] Woman's Position" in a series on Judaism and Jewish history (originally published in 1863) that Israel had stood out through the ages for its high standards of family life and feminine virtue.[45] The Viennese preacher Adolf Jellinek expressed similar ideas in various sermons and publications, and like Hirsch he established a close connection between Judaism and femininity.

Born in Moravia in the early 1820s, Jellinek possessed a traditional Jewish education as well as university training and from 1854 on, served as preacher at the Vienna Reform synagogue. He believed in progress and was in favor of adapting Judaism to modernity, but he did not endorse radical and divisive reforms.[46] Like many of his contemporaries, Jellinek stressed the greater propensity of women for religion. He advocated religious instruction and confirmation ceremonies for girls and emphasized women's importance in modern Judaism as mothers and wives. For example, he devoted an entire sermon to praising the "motherly heart."[47] Yet Jellinek also asserted that the home and family life played a crucial role in the lives of Jewish men. In a sermon on the communal ordinances of the Israelites during their forty-year sojourn in the desert, Jellinek claimed that the ancestors of today's Jews had already possessed strong family ties in biblical times and had cared for family members with great devotion.[48]

In another sermon, Jellinek declared that Moses had erected Judaism and the social organization of the Jewish community on the principle of "family intimacy," which is an unusual term not only in English, but also in the original German (*Familieninnigkeit*).[49] In the same vein, Jellinek stated that "the most lively and most tender family spirit [*Familiensinn*] formed the deepest character trait of the Jewish people," and he asserted that Jews held their homes in higher esteem than they did synagogues, schools, and political institutions.[50] Jews stood out because of this innate family sense, which characterized Jewish culture and which inclined the hearts of the Jewish people toward mildness, compassion, and forgiveness. Biblical Israel, Jellinek declared, had distinguished itself from its neighbors by its loving and humane conduct. It had done justice to its own people as well as to foreigners and had possessed a great love of freedom. According to Jellinek, Jews had always been caring, gentle, and noble, and he called these qualities feminine and motherly. More than other people, the Israelites had cultivated "sweet [*traut*] domesticity" and "indulged in the soft, female emotions of mildness and kindness."[51]

Like Hirsch, Jellinek also argued that participation in the political and public realms did not lay the foundation for Jewish men's identities as Jews. Rather, feminine and motherly ideals informed Jewish religion and culture, since the values and sensibilities of family life had determined the national character and social institutions of the Jews since antiquity. Like their contemporaries, Hirsch and Jellinek held that women possessed a greater propensity for religion and bore special responsibilities in the domestic realm, and they also expressed a common view when they lauded the extraordinarily developed Jewish sense of domesticity. Yet Hirsch and Jellinek took these widely held notions a step further by claiming that Judaism was played out most importantly in the domestic realm and represented the feminine aspect of civilization. As unapologetic as Hirsch about the feminine values that supposedly shaped Jewish culture, Jellinek declared in 1866 that the Jewish religion "has room and sense enough for the most tender and soft . . . , the female aspects of humanity," even though "male sternness" characterized Judaism too, and manliness distinguished its *Weltanschauung*.[52] Jewish culture thought most highly of "noble femaleness," which according to Jellinek not only meant that women occupied a place of honor, but also that femininity was venerated as a principle.[53]

In an essay published in 1886, Jellinek made a similar argument and claimed that the feminine, tender, gentle, compassionate, humble, temperate, sober, and mild-hearted characteristics that distinguished Jews made the Jewish people operate on a morally higher plane than other nations. The text was indeed entitled "The Superiority of the Jewish Tribe in Respect of Ethics."[54] Unlike the Christians in "civilized Europe" who for centuries had taken pleasure in plundering and ravaging, in murder and destruction, Jellinek argued that history had proven that Jews had no tendency to commit brutal and violent acts. Endowed with soft hearts, even Jewish soldiers would never behave like their non-Jewish counterparts.[55] Because of their long history of suffering and due to the ethnic makeup and particularities of the Jewish tribe, Jews possessed a distinct Jewish spirit (*Geist*) and a "Jewish heart."[56] According to Jellinek, the Jewish spirit was practical, realistic, and goal-oriented, while the Jewish heart stood out because it had the noble characteristics of a woman's heart. However, the Jewish heart also had the defects of a female heart. At sad and at joyous occasions, men and women wept easily, Jellinek explained.[57] Here, the Viennese preacher hinted that it could not entirely be considered an advantage for a Jewish man to possess the emotional constitution of a woman. Yet overall Jellinek's message was unambiguous. Femininity is a most admirable and praiseworthy concept and principle, that is by definition linked to high standards of morality. What distinguishes the Jewish tribe from other nations and what makes Jews ethically superior is described by Jellinek as feminine. Thus, for Jewish men to be different from other men because of their feminine hearts and their feminine modes of conduct is something to be proud of and constitutes an integral part of Jewish men's Jewishness.

## CONCLUSION

In many respects, the fact that these nineteenth-century German Jewish religious leaders praised femininity and feminine virtues, and idealized what they understood as Jewish men's sensitive, tender, and feminine character traits is not surprising at all. Parallel to its masculinist and misogynist tendencies, the literature of rabbinic Judaism apparently also highly values female piety and feminine modes of behavior, and it lauds weakness, humility, and submissiveness for men and women.[58] Jewish men such as Salomon, Hirsch, Geiger, and Jellinek were certainly familiar with this textual tradition and its cultural implications. Daniel Boyarin has even argued that the weak, meek, submissive, sensitive, vulnerable, and penetrable man, who represented the ideal of Jewish masculinity in classical Jewish literature, was still culturally influential if not dominant in Jewish society in the nineteenth century. If one were to follow this interpretation, it would seem that when Samson Raphael Hirsch and Adolf Jellinek celebrated the gentleness and femininity of the Jewish male, they were propagating an updated version of ideas that were well established in Jewish culture. In a similar vein, Spinoza had claimed earlier that not only circumcision greatly contributed to maintaining Jewish distinctiveness, but that "the principles of their religion" more generally caused Jewish men's effeminacy.[59] In the same era, Glikl of Hameln in her much-noted autobiography had praised her husband as a devoted father and a model of pious meekness.[60] However, at the current stage of research we are far from having conclusive evidence that the concept of the sensitive, caring, and gentle-mannered Jewish man has indeed through the centuries been the guiding norm for male Jews' behavior, let alone the practice of most Jewish men.[61]

Moreover, whether Adolf Jellinek would agree or not, in the nineteenth century the exaltation of femininity was not an exclusively Jewish affair. The Jewish men under discussion here were all religious leaders, and the feminization of religion and of the clergy in nineteenth-century Western culture is a well-known phenomenon. Protestant and Catholic clergymen in Germany, in other European countries, and in North America lauded femininity and feminine religiosity and ascribed great importance to mothers in securing the religious faith of their children and their families. Christian ministers and priests preached to largely female audiences, and Christian functionaries shared interests and sensitivities with women. In a society in which politics, culture, and formal education were assuming an increasingly secular character, church leaders came to focus on the home as the location of Christian life and associated Christianity with domestic and feminine values.[62] Thus in nineteenth-century Germany, a whole range of factors helped turn religion into more of a female-oriented and feminine domain. Accordingly, when rabbis and Jewish preachers presented Judaism as a culture with a high regard for femininity and domesticity, and when they praised Jewish men and women for being exemplars of feminine virtue, they were endorsing a value system that they shared with Christian clergymen.

Likewise, male sensitivity and emotional expressiveness were integral to the culture of the emerging middle classes in the early and mid-nineteenth century. Since the late 1990s, scholars such as Rebekka Habermas and Anne-Charlott Trepp have qualified the results of earlier research on the polarization of sexual stereotypes and the gendered division of private and public realms in modern, civil, Western middle-class society.[63] The older scholarship had argued that modern society was shaped by a fundamentally dualistic sociocultural framework, in which prescriptions for the "disposition of the sexes" stood in a dialectic relationship to lived realities. In a world of binary gender conceptions, domesticity, passive qualities such as modesty, and the entire category of emotionality, including religious sensitivity, constituted female domains.[64]

This ideology of gender ascriptions and their practical applications had serious implications for men as well as for women. They formed the foundation of the nineteenth-century notion of parenting, according to which mothers played the key role in guaranteeing that a family's children grew into socially useful and morally competent adults. In contrast to this model, however, Habermas and Trepp found that in German middle-class families of the early part of the nineteenth century, educating children with love and tenderness was a responsibility that husband and wife shared.

Caring for the physical, emotional, moral, and religious well-being of children was of central importance in the relationships of couples who strove to lead a respectable and culturally refined lifestyle. Educators and ideologues advised fathers to be involved in the raising of children. In many families, fathers appear to have done so, and contemporaries experienced parental love and love between the spouses as closely connected. Spouses aspired to cultivate an intellectually stimulating and emotionally satisfying companionate relationship, and they aimed at being loving and thoughtful parents.

Already in the Enlightenment culture of the eighteenth century, men had cultivated close emotional bonds—preferably with other men—in a "cult of friendship"; they had engaged in practices of self-examination and introspection and exchanged letters and diaries with male and female friends. Thus, as family life gained a heightened intimate character in the nineteenth century, men were expected to become involved and emotionally vulnerable husbands and fathers in an emotionalized domestic culture. They came to highly value the domestic sphere as a space in which they would express and experience love and affection and in which their deepest personal needs would be fulfilled. Men were to embrace the values and embody the virtues in which contemporaries believed women to excel, such as tenderness, patience, sensitivity, and emotional expressiveness.[65] Accordingly, when Samson Raphael Hirsch and Adolf Jellinek sang the praises of a gentle masculinity, their explications were by no means unusual or remarkable. Indeed their ideas also fall within the parameters of what Karen Hagemann has defined as the model of masculinity that became hegemonic in German lands during the Napoleonic Wars from 1806 to 1815. This model of a patriotic and valorous (wehrhaft) masculinity "revolved around the notions of 'love of liberty,' 'honour' and 'fraternity,' 'piety' and the 'fear of God,' 'strength,' 'bravery' and loyalty,' but above all 'readiness to sacrifice,' 'patriotism,' and 'valour.'"[66] The concept of a nation that ought to be able to defend its honor and integrity by means of war clearly informs these attributes and virtues. Yet according to Hagemann, this valorous hegemonic masculinity is not to be understood as in conflict with contemporary ideals of male sensitivity:

> "Domesticity" and "sensibility" were regarded not merely as fundamental virtues of loving and caring fathers and husbands, but also as prerequisites for patriotism and valour. For only a man who loved his own family, home and fatherland from the bottom of his heart would be prepared to risk his life to protect and defend them.[67]

A militarization of German ideas of manliness occurred only later in the century, and at that time "men [had] ever fewer opportunities to cultivate these [domestic and feminine] virtues openly. They were no longer compatible with the military concept of 'soldierly combat readiness.'"[68]

Ute Frevert, in her study of the role of the military in German society, makes similar observations. According to her, the ideal man of the early nineteenth century was "typified by the ambition to get on with his career," while possessing "a sense of family and communal values."[69] Bourgeois notions of the harmonious male personality that combined physical fitness with the "intellectual culture of the sophisticated . . . mortal" had their roots in the Enlightenment. Yet equally old were concerns that Germany's "heroic sons" could degenerate into "dandified male puppets."[70] In the years of the Napoleonic Wars, demands of contemporaries such as the writer and ideologue Ernst Moritz Arndt in 1813 to educate citizens to be soldiers found increasing resonance, and Frevert traces the militarization of German society and of German ideas of masculinity in the nineteenth century.[71] However, she argues that the values of a militarized society came to dominate German concepts of masculinity only much later. Even in Imperial Germany, after 1871, when "the aura of this armed, soldierly masculinity" possessed significant influence in German society, martial notions of German manliness did not rule supreme.[72] While some scholars hold that by the turn of the twentieth century, an honor-driven, aristocratic, and conservative framework of masculinity formed part of an anti-democratic German *Sonderweg* (a special path leading to fascism), Frevert claims that at that time "the military triad comprising violence, discipline, and the readiness to sacrifice one's life" did not yet constitute a "hegemonic cultural model determining gender roles."[73] All scholars agree, however, that in Nazi Germany the language and the practice of a heroic, fully militarized, and deadly German manliness had become hegemonic.[74]

It appears that the domestic and sensitive masculinity which, according to Hirsch and Jellinek, characterized Jewish men and which these Jewish leaders lauded so highly did not, at least until sometime in the second half of the nineteenth century, fall outside of the realm of contemporary German conceptions of manliness. In fact, texts by these Jewish clergymen do not betray any indication that there was something problematic, inappropriate, or provocative about associating Judaism or Jewishness with femininity. Hirsch and Jellinek were not defensive and did not seem to have challenged existing norms when they discussed the feminine Jewish spirit and the feminine character of Jewish culture. While Boyarin suggests that the Talmudic rabbis purposefully "resisted the Roman imperial power structure through 'gender bending,'" and that Jews in early modern and modern times defied the European civilizing mission by maintaining a distinct and divergent gender order, the conception of Jewish masculinity that Hirsch and Jellinek advanced does not appear to have been counter-hegemonic or anti-colonial.[75]

The apparent fact that notions of a deviant Jewish masculinity played no significant role in the anti-Jewish or early anti-Semitic discourses of the first half of the nineteenth century further supports the conclusion that the gentle masculinity that the Jewish leaders advertised did not run counter to contemporary German standards of manliness. Christian Germans discussed at length whether Jews could or should be emancipated or whether their oriental origins and character rendered them unfit for German citizenship. Gentiles debated whether Jews were degenerate, corrupt, or otherwise morally and physically at odds with the norms of Western society. Yet contemporaries appear not to have been particularly concerned about whether Jewish men were sufficiently masculine. Even during the Napoleonic Wars, when German patriots accused the French adversary of being effeminate, Jewish men were not targeted in this manner. The critique of the feminine Jewish man that is so familiar to us from later decades appears not to have been current through the first half of the nineteenth century.[76]

In the early twentieth century, however, the figure of the effeminate Jewish man played a central role in a pervasive anti-Semitic critique, and at least some Jewish men came to feel deeply ambivalent about the ideas that Hirsch and Jellinek had expressed earlier. Best known for the phenomenon of Jewish self-hatred in this period is Otto Weininger, who committed suicide in 1903, just months after having completed his infamous and tremendously influential doctoral dissertation, *Geschlecht und Character* (Sex and Character). In this work, Weininger used a set of arguments that was similar to those advanced by the nineteenth-century Frankfurt rabbi Hirsch and Viennese preacher Jellinek, but Weininger radically reversed the valences. While nineteenth-century Jewish religious leaders had exalted the female sex and femininity and had equated both with morality, Weininger expressed boundless contempt for women and for all he considered feminine. He concurred with Hirsch and Jellinek that Jews stood out because of their feminine character traits, emotional expressiveness, and great attachment to domestic life and the family, but he thought of these Jewish particularities as deficiencies. According to Weininger, Jewish men were unable to form positive relationships to the state, since they lacked the rational and moral capacities of independent and self-reliant individuals. Weininger deployed the new racialized and medicalized discourse of the era, conceived of Jews and women as groups whose nature and character were biologically determined, and argued that both women and Jews—and most eminently Jewish women—were innately incapable of controlling their emotions and their sexual desires.[77]

Less than twenty years earlier, at a time when the anti-Semitic movement had already taken shape in imperial Germany and in Austria, Adolf Jellinek had still declared that femininity, *Familiensinn* (family spirit), and emotional accessibility constituted distinctive and positive character traits of Jewish men and Jewish women. However, the years around the turn of the twentieth century brought sweeping and dramatic changes. Martina Kessel asserts that at this time, the ideal of a well-balanced masculinity according to which a man was to cultivate emotional and social as well as intellectual and assertive capacities gave way to a body politics that associated femininity with hysteria and accentuated the differences between men's and women's gender identities. Upper middle-class men were pressured to focus their creative, sexual, and emotional energies on their careers and professional worlds, and if they failed, they ran the risk of being considered neurasthenic and insufficiently masculine.[78] In this context and in particular after the publication of Weininger's dissertation, the notion that Jewish men embodied femininity and displayed feminine character traits became problematic and fraught.

Accordingly, when in Weimar Germany the Jewish conservative intellectual Friedrich Gundolf exalted femininity and cast himself as feminine and even female in a dream, this was a more than ambivalent self-realization. In the cultural matrix of his time, Gundolf regarded the feminine within the male self as a source of creativity and transcendence. Yet his embracing femininity went hand in hand with what he experienced, with great pain, as his submitting to the domination of his too-powerful Jewish woman lover and partner.[79] Conversely, when nineteenth-century rabbis and preachers had lauded femininity and when Hirsch and Jellinek had held that Jewish men stood out because of their feminine character traits, their power and their social and intellectual superiority over women had not been in question.

To complicate things further, the memoir that the Jewish merchant Aron Liebeck composed in the 1920s shows no trace of the anguished self-feminization that characterizes Gundolf's and Weininger's texts. In line with nineteenth-century ideas of middle-class masculinity, Liebeck presented his manhood as striking a harmonious balance between the professional and the rational, on the one hand, and the domestic and emotional, on the other hand. Following a convention of the late nineteenth century, he portrayed himself as a "hero who succeed[ed] with honor in the momentous battle of commercial life."[80] Yet Liebeck described himself unabashedly as a family man, unambiguously rejected military values, and declared that male Jews possessed a specific kind of male Jewish beauty.[81]

Much more research is needed to put the experiences of and the programmatic statements by Hirsch, Jellinek, Weininger, Gundolf, and Liebeck into context and to establish the lines of continuity as well as the discontinuities in the self-representations of these men and in their conceptions of Jewish (and German) maleness. Perhaps a future study can determine if Adolf Jellinek played a role in shaping Otto Weininger's intellectual and emotional universe, as the more than sixty-year-old Jellinek published and preached in Vienna in the 1880s, when Weininger was a child.[82] Moreover, I suggest exploring the concepts of masculinity that Jewish clergy propagated in the interwar years and comparing their sermons and other writings to texts by Christian churchmen.

Much of the cult of femininity and of female spiritual and moral superiority that rabbis and Jewish preachers propagated in the middle of the

nineteenth century was not extraordinary or distinctly Jewish, but fell square-
ly within the parameters of the contemporary middle-class gender order. Yet
while sharing this gender order's value system with other Germans, Hirsch
and Jellinek postulated Jewish difference. They declared that Jewish culture
and religion represented the more noble, feminine aspect of civilization, and
thus claimed that Jews distinguished themselves from other people by possessing more of the elevated femininity that Jews as well as non-Jews cherished. Hirsch and Jellinek affirmed sameness and compatibility by saying "we
are like you; we share the same values," though at the same time, they asserted
distinctiveness by proclaiming "we are also different from you; we are better
at the values that we all share!" German Jews confirmed their cultural difference in the very process in which they integrated themselves into German
society. In the twentieth century, gender became an important site in the anti-
Semitic project of excluding Jews from the community of Germans. In the
nineteenth century, on the other hand, the Jewish romance with femininity
allowed German Jews to express Jewish distinctiveness as well as Germanness
in gendered terms.

However, in their remarks on the femininity of Jewish culture and on
Jewish manliness Hirsch and Jellinek also violated the conventions of the contemporary bourgeois gender order. Throughout nineteenth-century Europe and
North America, middle-class men cultivated modes of a sensitive masculinity,[83]
but as a rule, men did not consider their tender, loving, caring, and emotionally
expressive social and cultural practices and their attachment to the domestic
realm as feminine. They rather regarded their sensitive and emotional capacities
and skills to be expressions of their manliness. Conversely, Hirsch and Jellinek
called the Jewish tendency for compassion, morality, and gentle manners that
they postulated feminine. Hirsch not only held that Israel was deprived of manliness in the Roman sense, but he proudly characterized the virtues that distinguished Jewish men and women as feminine. Though he declared that Judaism
had masculine aspects too, Jellinek likewise described the noble and caring
conduct in which the Jewish tribe supposedly excelled as feminine rather than
manly. According to Jellinek, Jewish men did not possess a soft and compassionate manly heart, but what made Jewish men distinct and superior to non-
Jews is that they were endowed with a woman's heart.

The definition of femininity that Samson Raphael Hirsch and Adolf Jellinek
used was undoubtedly shaped by nineteenth-century bourgeois ideas of gender characteristics, and the qualities and the conduct that Hirsch and Jellinek
considered desirable in a man were those of middle-class culture. However, the
Jewish leaders conflated Jewishness and femininity in an extraordinary manner
and claimed that Jewish difference possessed a gendered dimension. In doing
so, they might have been drawing on currents in Jewish thought, yet only future research will show whether these inner Jewish impulses were decisive and

which role Hirsch and Jellinek may have played in laying the groundwork for the widespread anti-Semitic conception of the insufficiently masculine Jewish man of the twentieth century.

## NOTES

None of this work would have been possible without the friendship and support of a great many individuals. In particular, I am deeply grateful to Stefanie Schüler-Springorum and to my co-editors, Paul Lerner and Sharon Gillerman, for being, over many years, most precious companions in my intellectual and personal quests and adventures.

1. This chapter builds on my 2006 book but focuses on conceptions of Jewish masculinities rather than the position of women in nineteenth-century bourgeois Judaism; it takes the study of the gender order of nineteenth-century German Jewry in new directions by inquiring into the politics of Jewish distinctiveness. See Benjamin Maria Baader, *Gender, Judaism, and Bourgeois Culture in Germany, 1800–1870* (Bloomington: Indiana University Press, 2006), chs. 1–3.

2. Ibid., 19–41, 49.

3. Ibid., 49.

4. Alexander Altmann, "The New Style of Preaching in Nineteenth-Century Germany," in Altmann, ed., *Studies in Nineteenth-Century Jewish Intellectual History* (Cambridge, MA: Harvard University Press, 1964), 65–116; Baader, *Gender, Judaism, and Bourgeois Culture,* 140–143; Simone Lässig, *Jüdische Wege ins Bürgertum: Kulturelles Kapital und sozialer Aufstieg im 19. Jahrhundert* (Göttingen: Vandenhoeck & Ruprecht, 2004), 249–325; Michael A. Meyer, "Christian Influence on Early German Reform Judaism," in Charles Berlin, ed., *Studies in Jewish Bibliography, History and Literature in Honor of I. Edward Kiev* (New York: Ktav, 1971), 289–303.

5. Baader, *Gender, Judaism, and Bourgeois Culture,* 53–56.

6. Meyer Kayserling, *Bibliothek jüdischer Kanzelredner: Eine chronologische Sammlung der Predigten, Biographien und Charakteristiken der vorzüglichsten jüdischen Prediger: Für Rabbiner, Prediger und Lehrer und als Erbauungsbuch für die Familie* (Berlin: Springer, 1870–1872), 1:155; Kayserling, *Gedenkblätter: Hervorragende jüdische Persönlichkeiten des neunzehnten Jahrhunderts* (Leipzig: Th. Grieben, 1892), 72.

7. Kayserling, *Bibliothek jüdischer Kanzelredner,* 1:142.

8. Ibid., 1:154.

9. Ibid., 1:155.

10. *Allgemeine Zeitung des Judenthums* 2, no. 52 (1838): 210.

11. Christopher R. Friedrichs, *Jüdische Jugend im Biedermeier: Ein unbekanntes Tagebuch aus Dresden, 1833–1837* (Leipzig: Simon-Dubnow-Institut für jüdische Geschichte und Kultur, 1997), 12.

12. Leo Baeck Institute, Leopold Stein Collection, S 49/1. Altona, today a part of Hamburg, was at the time a separate city and belonged to Denmark.

13. Leo Baeck Institute, Max Markreich Collection, folder 6. See also Kayserling, *Bibliothek jüdischer Kanzelredner,* 1:555, and likewise note the album that a group of Jewish women prepared for Salomon on the occasion of his twenty-fifth anniversary as a preacher in Hamburg. Baader, *Gender, Judaism, and Bourgeois Culture,* 199–202.

14. Kayserling, *Bibliothek jüdischer Kanzelredner,* 1:54–56, 1:156–173; Phöbus Philippson, *Biographische Skizzen* (Leipzig: Leiner, 1864–1866), 2:254–257; David Sorkin,

*The Transformation of German Jewry, 1780–1840* (New York: Oxford University Press, 1987), 226–227.

15. Kayserling, *Bibliothek jüdischer Kanzelredner,* 1:179–209, quotation 180.

16. Ibid., 1:191.

17. Proverbs 31:30; Kayserling, *Bibliothek jüdischer Kanzelredner,* 1:191–199.

18. For a fuller elaboration of these ideas, see Baader, *Gender, Judaism, and Bourgeois Culture.*

19. Gotthold Salomon, *Festpredigten für alle Feiertage des Herrn, gehalten im neuen Israelitischen Tempel zu Hamburg* (Hamburg: Perthes-Besser & Mauke, 1855), 101, 113.

20. Samson Raphael Hirsch, "Woman's Role in Jewish Education," in *The Collected Writings: Samson Raphael Hirsch* (New York: Philipp Feldheim, 1992), 7:396.

21. Ibid., 7:398–399.

22. *Jeschurun* 2 (1855–1856): 264–270.

23. Ibid., 1 (1854–1855): 263–264.

24. Ibid., 8 (1861–1862): 317.

25. Ibid., 315.

26. Ibid., 58.

27. Samson Raphael Hirsch, "The Jewish Woman," in *Judaism Eternal: Selected Essays from the Writings of Rabbi Samson Raphael Hirsch,* trans. and ed. Isidor Grunfeld (London: Soncino, 1959), 2:57.

28. Mordechai Breuer, *Modernity within Tradition: The Social History of Orthodox Jewry in Imperial Germany* (New York: Columbia University Press, 1992), 122.

29. For instance, see Hirsch's commentary on Leviticus: Samson Raphael Hirsch, *Der Pentateuch: Übersetzt und erläutert von Samson Raphael Hirsch* (Frankfurt am Main: J. Kauffmann, 1873), 3:630–631. For additional references to texts in which Hirsch follows this line of argument, see Breuer, *Modernity within Tradition,* 428.

30. See, for instance, Chana Weisberg's blog from 1 June 2008, at www.chabad.org/blogs. Likewise, Moshe Meiselman quotes directly from Hirsch in Meiselman, *The Jewish Woman in Jewish Law* (New York: Ktav, 1978), 43–44. For the feminist challenge from within Orthodoxy, see Blu Greenberg, *On Women and Judaism: A View from Tradition* (Philadelphia: Jewish Publication Society of America, 1981); Tamar Ross, *Expanding the Palace of Torah: Orthodoxy and Feminism* (Waltham, MA: Brandeis University Press, 2004).

31. Baader, *Gender, Judaism, and Bourgeois Culture,* 203; Michael Galchinsky, *The Origin of the Modern Jewish Woman Writer: Romance and Reform in Victorian England* (Detroit, MI: Wayne State University Press, 1996), 35; Dagmar Herzog, *Intimacy and Exclusion: Religious Politics in Pre-Revolutionary Baden* (Princeton, NJ: Princeton University Press, 1996), 98–101.

32. Baader, *Gender, Judaism, and Bourgeois Culture,* 57–58.

33. Ibid., 58–73.

34. Daniel Boyarin, *Unheroic Conduct: The Rise of Heterosexuality and the Invention of the Jewish Man* (Berkeley: University of California Press, 1997), 320; Breuer, *Modernity within Tradition,* 123–125; Robert Liberles, *Religious Conflict in Social Context: The Resurgence of Orthodox Judaism in Frankfurt am Main, 1838–1877* (Westport, CT: Greenwood, 1985), 152–155.

35. Jacob Neusner, *Androgynous Judaism: Masculine and Feminine in the Dual Torah* (Macon, GA: Mercer University Press, 1993), 83–123.

36. Sorkin, *Transformation,* 166–171, quotation 166.

37. *Jeschurun* 4 (1857–1858): 182.

38. Ibid., 180.

39. Ibid., 181.

40. Ibid., 178, 182.

41. Ibid., 182–183.

42. Hirsch, "Jewish Woman," 57.

43. Ibid., 56–57.

44. See, for instance, ibid., 50.

45. *Jüdische Zeitschrift für Wissenschaft und Leben* 2 (1863): 194–204, esp. 200, 204. See also Abraham Geiger, *Judaism and Its History* (Lanham, MD: University Press of America, 1985), 1:49–60. On the limits of Geiger's appreciation of the feminine, see Ken Koltun-Fromm, *Abraham Geiger's Liberal Judaism: Personal Meaning and Religious Authority* (Bloomington: Indiana University Press, 2006), ch. 3; on Geiger as a reformer, see Michael Meyer, *Response to Modernity: A History of the Reform Movement in Judaism* (New York: Oxford University Press, 1988), 89–99.

46. Meyer, *Response to Modernity*, 192–193; Marsha Rozenblit, "Jewish Identity and the Modern Rabbi: The Cases of Isak Noa Mannheimer, Adolf Jellinek, and Moritz Guedemann in Nineteenth-Century Vienna," *Leo Baeck Institute Yearbook* 35 (1990): 110–111.

47. Adolf Jellinek, *Predigten* (Vienna: Herzfeld & Bauer, 1866), 3:69–89.

48. Adolf Jellinek, *Predigten* (Vienna: Carl Gerold's Sohn, 1863), 2:144–145.

49. Ibid., 2:236.

50. Ibid. (1866), 3:40–41, 213–228, quotation 218.

51. Ibid. (1863), 1:117. For the preceding sentences, see ibid., 2:172–178, and ibid. (1866), 3:217, 3:228.

52. Ibid. (1866), 3:94.

53. Ibid., 3:95.

54. Adolf Jellinek, "Die Superiorität des jüdischen Stammes in ethischer Beziehung," in Jellinek, ed., *Aus der Zeit: Tagesfragen und Tagesbegebenheiten* (Budapest: Sam. Markus, 1886), 3–19. I thank Till van Rahden for bringing this essay to my attention. See also Till van Rahden, "Jews and the Ambivalences of Civil Society in Germany, 1800 to 1933—Assessment and Reassessment," *Journal of Modern History* 77, no. 4 (2005): 1045.

55. Jellinek, "Superiorität," 4–5.

56. Ibid., 16.

57. Ibid., 16–17.

58. Neusner, *Androgynous Judaism*, 83–123.

59. Benedict de Spinoza, *The Political Works*, ed. and trans. A. G. Wernham (Oxford: Clarendon, 1965), 62–63.

60. Glückel of Hameln, *The Memoirs of Glückel of Hameln*, trans. Marvin Lowenthal (New York: Schocken, 1977), 34–35.

61. See Gotzmann, this volume.

62. Jens Blecher, "'Der Beruf der Frauen ist allein das Werk der Liebe': Weibliche Religiosität und Wohltätigkeit in Leipzig im 19. Jahrhunder," in Susanne Schoetz, ed., *Frauenalltag in Leipzig: Weibliche Lebenszusammenhänge im 19. und 20. Jahrhundert* (Weimar: Böhlau, 1997), 181–206; Norbert Busch, "Die Feminisierung der Frömmigkeit," in Irmtraud Goetz von Olenhusen, ed., *Wunderbare Erscheinungen: Frauen und katholische Frömmigkeit im 19. und 20. Jahrhundert* (Paderborn: Ferdinand Schöningh, 1995), 203–219; Ann Douglas, *The Feminization of American Culture* (New York: Knopf, 1978); Michael B. McDuffee, *Small-Town Protestantism in Nineteenth-Century Germany: Living Lost Faith* (New York: Peter Lang, 2003); Hugh McLeod, "Weibliche Frömmigkeit—männlicher Unglaube? Religion und Kirche im bürgerlichen 19. Jahrhundert," in Ute Frevert, ed., *Bürgerinnen und Bürger: Geschlechterverhältnisse im 19. Jahrhundert* (Göttingen: Vandenhoeck & Ruprecht, 1988), 134–156; Thomas Mergel, "Die subtile Macht der Liebe: Geschlecht, Erziehung und Frömmigkeit in katholischen Rheinischen Bürgerfamilien

1830–1910," in Irmtraud Goetz von Olenhusen et al., eds., *Frauen unter dem Patriarchat der Kirchen: Frauen und Religion vom Vormärz bis ins Dritte Reich* (Stuttgart: Kohlhammer, 1995), 22–47.

63. Rebekka Habermas, *Frauen und Männer des Bürgertums: Eine Familiengeschichte, 1750–1850* (Göttingen: Vandenhoeck & Ruprecht, 2000); Anne-Charlott Trepp, *Sanfte Männlichkeit und selbständige Weiblichkeit: Frauen und Männer im Hamburger Bürgertum 1770–1840* (Göttingen: Vandenhoeck & Ruprecht, 1996).

64. Karin Hausen, "Family and Role Division: The Polarization of Sexual Stereotypes in the Nineteenth Century: An Aspect of the Dissociation of Work and Family Life," in Richard Evans and W. R. Lee, eds., *The German Family: Essays on the Social History of the Family in Nineteenth- and Twentieth-Century Germany* (London: Croom Helm, 1981), 51–83, esp. 51, 55–56.

65. Habermas, *Frauen und Männer,* 365–394; George L. Mosse, "Friendship and Nationhood: About the Promise and Failure of German Nationalism," *Journal of Contemporary History* 17 (1982): 356–358; Anne-Charlott Trepp, "Anders als sein 'Geschlechtscharakter': Der bürgerliche Mann um 1800—Ferdinand Beneke (1774–1848)," *Historische Anthropologie* 4 (1996): 57–77, esp. 152; Trepp, *Sanfte Männlichkeit,* 221–222, 320–349, 397–398. See also Martina Kessel, "The 'Whole Man': The Longing for a Masculine World in Nineteenth-Century Germany," *Gender and History* 15, no. 1 (2003): 1–31.

66. Karen Hagemann, "German Heroes: The Cult of Death for the Fatherland in Nineteenth-Century Germany," in Stefan Dudink, Karen Hagemann, and John Tosh, eds., *Masculinity in Politics and War: Rewritings of Modern History* (Manchester, England: Manchester University Press, 2004), 124.

67. Ibid., 127–128.

68. Ibid. See also Karin Breuer, "Competing Masculinities: Fraternities, Gender and Nationality in the German Confederation," *Gender and History* 20, no. 2 (2008): 270–287.

69. Ute Frevert, *A Nation in Barracks: Modern Germany, Military Conscription and Civil Society* (Oxford: Berg, 2004), 27.

70. Ibid., 25.

71. Ibid., esp. 27.

72. Ibid., 221.

73. Ibid. For the *Sonderweg* argument, see Kevin McAleer, *Dueling: The Cult of Honor in Fin-de-Siècle Germany* (Princeton, NJ: Princeton University Press, 1994), esp. 208.

74. Frevert, *Nation in Barracks,* 247–259; McAleer, *Dueling,* 209–212.

75. Boyarin, *Unheroic Conduct,* xvii–xviii, quotation 6.

76. Hagemann, "German Heroes"; Karen Hagemann, *"Mannlicher Muth und Teutsche Ehre": Nation, Militär und Geschlecht in Preußen zur Zeit der Antinapoleonischen Kriege* (Paderborn: Ferdinand Schöningh, 2002).

77. Ritchie Robertson, "Historicizing Weininger: The Nineteenth-Century German Image of the Feminized Jew," in Bryan Cheyette and Laura Marcus, eds., *Modernity, Culture and "the Jew"* (Stanford, CA: Stanford University Press, 1998), 23–24. For the racialization of Jewishness and the medicalization of gender categories in this period, and in particular for the interconnectedness of both phenomena, see Gilman, this volume. On Weininger, see Nancy A. Harrowitz and Barbara Hyams, eds., *Jews and Gender: Responses to Otto Weininger* (Philadelphia: Temple University Press, 1995); and David Luft, *Eros and Inwardness in Vienna: Weininger, Musil, Doderer* (Chicago: University of Chicago Press, 1989). See also the introduction to this volume.

78. Kessel, "The 'Whole Man,'" 18–24. See also Sander Gilman, *Freud, Race, and Gender* (Princeton, NJ: Princeton University Press, 1993); Gilman, "The Jewish Psyche: Freud, Dora and the Idea of the Hysteric," in his *The Jew's Body* (New York: Routledge,

1991), 60–103; Paul Lerner, *Hysterical Men: War, Psychiatry, and the Politics of Trauma in Germany, 1890–1930* (Ithaca, NY: Cornell University Press, 2003), esp. ch. 1.

79. See Goldberg, this volume.

80. Kessel, "The 'Whole Man,'" 14. For Aron Liebeck, see Schüler-Springorum, this volume, 103.

81. Schüler-Springorum, this volume, esp. 102.

82. Alison Rose has laid some of the groundwork for such an exploration by discussing Jellinek's approach to women, femininity, and Jewish superiority in the context of her examination of the conflation of images of Jews and women in fin-de-siècle Viennese culture. Alison Rose, *Jewish Women in Fin de Siècle Vienna* (Austin: University of Texas Press, 2008), 57–67, 84–86, 221.

83. John Tosh, *A Man's Place: Masculinity and the Middle-Class Home in Victorian England* (New Haven, CT: Yale University Press, 1999); Donald Yacovone, "'Surpassing the Love of Women': Victorian Manhood and the Language of Fraternal Love," in Laura McCall and Donald Yacovone, eds., *A Shared Experience: Men, Women, and the History of Gender* (New York: New York University Press, 1998), 195–221.

# 3

## Moral, Clean Men of the Jewish Faith

### *Jewish Rituals and Their Male Practitioners, 1843–1914*

ROBIN JUDD

In September 1887, the leadership of the Frankfurt-based Free Association for the Interests of Orthodox Judaism contacted their member rabbis as part of a newly launched investigation into the character and training of local *mohelim* (ritual circumcisers). Earlier that summer, several of the organization's key leaders had publicly articulated concern over the reputation and integrity of ritual practitioners. At a moment when anti-Semites were increasingly identifying Jewish ritual practices as worrisome and when German-speaking Jews appeared to be relaxing certain standards of Jewish religious observance, the Free Association's leadership worried that some *mohelim* failed to exemplify a morally upstanding lifestyle. That autumn the Orthodox group commenced an investigation into the professional, cultural, and ethical standards of their circumcisers. As part of this inquiry, the leadership asked member rabbis: "Do your *mohelim* display good religious and moral character[?] . . . how do you envision training young men within this profession to attain the necessary moral fiber and knowledge . . . ?"[1] The Free Association was not alone. Over the course of the nineteenth and early twentieth centuries, many German Jewish writers and communal leaders similarly examined the ethical character of *shochetim* (kosher butchers). They offered analogous formulations of their idealized kosher butchers, seeking men who were "good, [and] reputable."[2]

Between 1843 and 1914, a group of German Jewish physicians, ritual practitioners, communal leaders, and rabbis participated in hundreds of published and spoken forums in which they interrogated the character of *shochetim* and *mohelim*.[3] In guidebooks for ritual practitioners, popular literature (such as joke books), and pamphlets, these leading figures in the Jewish community asked what it meant to be a "reputable" *shochet* and a "moral" *mohel*. Their calls offered varying—and sometimes competing—idealized images of the Jewish male communal servant. Even before the advent of a radicalizing anti-Semitism that envisioned ritual practitioners as bloodthirsty and supersexualized, the discussants of the ritual questions (*Ritualfragen*) touted a romanticized *mohel* or *shochet,* who embodied the ideals of a "reputable" manhood.

The contributors to the debates on *Ritualfragen* did not discuss the gender of *mohelim* or *shochetim* because they understood the rituals and their practitioners as fundamentally and unambiguously male. Historically, only men served as circumcisers or kosher butchers; women did not perform these tasks, and few if any of the discussants would have imagined it feasible for women to conduct circumcisions or kosher butchering.[4] The lack of explicit references to gender in their contributions, however, did not signify a disinterest in masculinity. To the contrary, just as masculinity was and is fundamentally involved in the creation and maintenance of hierarchies, meanings of gender difference also played an important role in how these diverse Jewish leaders and scholars envisioned the Jewish rites. Circumcision and kosher butchering establish and reinforce differences and hierarchies between men and women and between Jewish and non-Jewish men. Only boys born to Jewish parents are introduced into the covenant through *brit milah,* an issue that was contentious during the period under review here, and only men were envisioned as candidates for positions as ritual practitioners. When contributors to the *Ritualfragen* wrestled with the physicality and interiority of *mohelim* and *shochetim,* they were—in essence—discussing matters of masculinity.

Masculinity, writes the Russian historian Barbara Evans Clements, refers to "a set of normative assertions about the nature of the adult male and his conduct in society."[5] Between 1843 and 1914, discussants in the *Ritualfragen* articulated understandings of a Jewish masculinity that reflected the contemporary values and images of German bourgeois respectability. Their portraits moved away from images of Jewish manhood offered by anti-Semites and distanced themselves from notions of masculinity embraced by the culture of the abattoir and surgery.

## THE RITUAL QUESTIONS

The discussions concerning Jewish ritual practitioners were part of larger contemporary deliberations regarding the Jewish rites of kosher butchering and circumcision. During the nineteenth and twentieth centuries, four generations of Jews and non-Jews expressed interest in these Jewish rituals.[6] Such a wide range of participants paid attention to the rites in part because the *Ritualfragen* offered them ways to come to terms with their rapidly changing state and society. The period under review included German nation building, political revolutions, industrialization, accelerated economic growth, and downturns. Unification and emancipation in 1871 signaled additional political, economic, and social shifts within German Jewish and non-Jewish life. These shifts not only changed the political landscape in which Jews interacted with non-Jewish authorities and other minority and majority groups, they also encouraged dramatic changes within the German-speaking Jewish world. During this period, Jews acculturated, adopted the mores of the German middle class, and adapted their religious lives to accommodate the world around them. The debates on *Ritualfragen* thus offered an arena in which participants in the controversies could consider these dramatic transformations. These disputes encouraged participants to make sense of the complex reciprocal relationships between structures of power, authority, and dominance in a changing world.[7]

Discussions concerning circumcision preceded the "kosher butchering question [*die Schächtfrage*]," although the latter would soon outpace the former. The circumcision debates began in earnest in the early 1840s when a few German Jewish fathers refused to allow their sons' circumcisions and when a group of physicians, government officials, and academics simultaneously considered the medical benefits and dangers of the rite.[8] In the following decades, two interrelated questions formed the core of the circumcision debates. One set of discussions examined the relationship of the rite to standards of Jewish communal membership, if not Jewish identity more generally. The second set of deliberations concerned the safety issues surrounding the ritual and the possibility of governmental and medical intervention into the previously autonomous realm of ritual behavior. The debates about circumcision practices became increasingly radical in the 1890s, with some non-Jewish opponents linking the rite to charges of Jewish brutality, blood thirst, and economic greed.[9]

In almost all cases, the coterminous debates over kosher butchering began as part of larger animal protection campaigns. During the late nineteenth century and early twentieth, German animal protectionists, much like their European counterparts, lobbied for the licensing of slaughterers, the restriction of the abattoir to men only, and the implementation of stricter inspection procedures. Concerned that the slaughter of conscious animals allowed creatures to feel their own murder, animal advocates also called for changes to animal cruelty codes and for laws that would mandate the stunning of animals into a state of unconsciousness before slaughter. This latter reform had the potential of influencing Jewish life significantly and was the subject of the kosher butchering disputes. Jewish law dictates that an animal must be conscious when slaughtered. When local, regional, and state governments implemented laws that mandated the stunning of animals before slaughter, they potentially affected the practices of Jewish communities. Some authorities exempted their Jewish communities from these reforms. Governments that demanded the universal observance of the new slaughterhouse laws, however, forced religiously observant Jews to slaughter meat illegally, procure kosher meat from another source, or transgress Jewish law by stunning.

The political, social, and economic rearrangements of the late nineteenth century and early twentieth fundamentally changed the kosher butchering disputes. The growth of the middle class, the German unification of 1871, the political emancipation of German Jews, and the rise of a new kind of anti-Jewish animus contributed to significant shifts within German Jewish life. By the turn of the twentieth century, discussions of the *Schächtfrage* occurred with greater frequency and attracted attention from a wide range of individuals across the German middle class. Like the public controversies concerning circumcision, the debates concerning kosher butchering similarly underwent a radicalization. The availability of new methods for practicing Jewish rites and the increased attention to the alleged relationship between Judaism and blood brought the hostility with which discussants portrayed the Jewish rites to a new level. Increasingly, critics of both circumcision and kosher butchering relied on blood imagery and other anti-Semitic tropes to depict the allegedly brutal, premodern, and unassimilable character of the rites and, in turn, of Germany's Jews.

Even before the radicalization of the debates on *Ritualfragen,* discussants expressed fascination with the status, bearing, education, and self-control of the ritual practitioners. Throughout the *Ritualfragen,* regardless of the disputes' shifts in character and content, participants posed three questions concerning *mohelim* and *shochetim*: (1) What ought to be the characteristics that typify ritual practitioners? (2) If *mohelim* and *shochetim* failed to epitomize these attributes, would the ritual practitioner pose a threat to the Jewish community or the public at large? (3) And if the ritual practitioner demonstrated some kind of risk, what kind of supervisory body should intervene: the Jewish community (and if so, what kind of Jewish community) or the state (if so, what governing body)? Such conversations prescriptively offered formulations for what it ought to mean to be a Jewish man who operated under the watchful gaze of Jews and gentiles alike.

## MASCULINITY, MANHOOD, AND ANTI-SEMITISM

Since the 1990s, a history of masculinity has emerged that addresses the expectations and experiences of the men who composed the majority of society as well as those who were part of its minority. Concerned that these cultural histories of men privilege majority masculinities, some scholars have questioned the value of scholarship that omits the history of women from its center. Others, including Robert Nye, R. W. Connell, and Catherine Hall, insist that masculinity is useful as a historical category because of its ongoing interplay with the construction of a variety of different kinds of hierarchies, particularly those involving relationships of power, defined by gender, race, class, and kin. In their view, masculinity is a personal practice that is inexorably linked with its institutional and cultural contexts.[10]

The scholarship on Jewish masculinities has been fruitful in advancing our understandings of the power imbalances among men and of the varying ways in which individuals reinvent and reinforce gender difference and meanings.[11] It not only has established anti-Semitism's critique of the Jewish male body and manner, but also has analyzed the wide-ranging Jewish responses to these paradoxical presentations of Jewish masculinity. Moreover, a portion of this work has looked to the ways in which Jews have embraced and reformulated what they envisioned to be normative ideals of manhood, including the middle-class emphasis on codes of honor and bourgeois respectability. For European Jews of the middle class, the bourgeois preoccupation with moral discipline, economic success, and control of reproduction frequently served as strategies for integration. Just as bourgeois respectability linked men's power in the public sphere to men's position within the private reproductive economy, Jewish men of the middle class similarly asserted their ideal masculinity by establishing their authority vis-à-vis others in their community, most importantly women and Jewish immigrants from Eastern Europe, whom they somewhat pejoratively called *Ostjuden*.[12]

During the period evaluated here, German radical anti-Semites often pointed to the alleged brutality and deviancy of ritual practitioners.[13] Beginning in the 1880s, radical anti-Semites publicly imagined the Jewish butcher as a Jewish murderer, using Jewish ritual behavior to "prove" the truth of the blood libel charge. When blood libel charges were made during the Kaiserreich, officials and townspeople often blamed local ritual practitioners. In 1892, 1899, and 1900, police authorities arrested local Jewish butchers after children or young adults were found brutally murdered. The police suspected these *shochetim* because they believed them to be capable of decapitating and bleeding a human. A kosher butcher, they argued, would be called on to use brutal strength and constraining devices to hold down his victim; he would employ sharp knives to cut the victim; and he would know how to drain the victim's body of blood. A popular postcard from the Konitz affair of 1900 dramatized this link. The card depicted a man restrained in chains and surrounded by ten Jewish men (representing the quorum required by Jewish law for religious services). One man appeared to be decapitating the victim while another drained his blood into a bucket. The inscription read, "Remember 11 March 1900. On that day, the grammar school pupil Winter of Konitz was sacrificed by the *shochet*'s knife."[14] A decade later the journalist Hans Wehleid similarly demonstrated Jewish deviance by portraying the *shochet* as a savage creature overwhelmed by blood lust. His *shochet* "cut a single line across its [the animal's] throat. Out of this cut gushed a flow of blood."[15]

The circumciser also did not escape the attention of German anti-Semites. The anti-Semitic literature of the time maintained that *mohelim* were motivated by their brutality, blood lust, and economic greed. The radical anti-Semite Bernadin Freimut and other opponents penned polemical poems and essays that depicted *mohelim* as bloodthirsty creatures and infants as the prey of these

Die Beſchneidung

Bringt Vortheil — darum iſt ſie bei den Juden gebräuchlich.

200. Kikeriki. Wien 1912

"It makes a profit: that is why the Jews practice it." Reprinted from Eduard Fuchs, *Die Juden in der Karikatur: Ein Beitrag zur Kulturgeschichte* (Munich: Albert Langen, 1921), 194

malevolent actors.[16] Such attacks were particularly poignant after a series of syphilis epidemics followed the use of oral suction (*metzitzah*) by circumcisers. During these episodes, anti-Semites publicized the depravity of *mohelim*, particularly those who would apply oral suction to an infant's penis.[17]

In addition to painting the *mohel* and *shochet* in brutal, bloody strokes, anti-Semites also suggested that greed drove ritual practitioners to practice their craft. According to critics, avarice motivated *mohelim* to circumcise larger numbers of children, and *shochetim* to slaughter greater numbers of cattle. Substituting the word *penis* with *jewelry* and *jewels*, these texts suggested that greed drove the rite. One Austrian cartoon depicted an observant Jewish *mohel*, large scissors in hand, with piles of gold. Grotesque, with a large bulbous nose, bad teeth, tattered clothes, and sidelocks flying in the wind, the *mohel*'s caption read, "It makes a profit: that is why the Jews practice it."[18]

Carl Sedlaßek, the editor of the anti-Semitic *Generalanzeiger*, similarly accused Jews of profiting from kosher butchering. According to Sedlaßek, Jews intentionally sold infected or damaged meat, which Jewish law prohibited them from consuming themselves. Supposedly, when a *shochet* found a diseased animal, he would gleefully and greedily announce, "This is for the goyim!"[19]

## MORAL MEN OF THE JEWISH FAITH

The debates on *Ritualfragen* sparked another overlapping conversation concerning the character and behavior of *mohelim* and *shochetim*.[20] These discussions drew from middle-class signifiers of manhood. Looking to the ritual practitioners' education, patterns of consumption, work, and relations with women, Jewish participants offered a formulation of ritual practitioner behavior that mimicked the middle-class emphasis on bourgeois respectability. Such a preoccupation was not surprising. These Jewish men—physicians, rabbis, and Jewish national, regional, and urban communal leaders—often were themselves members of the Jewish *Bildungsbürgertum,* the educated middle class.[21] The discussions of *Ritualfragen* presented a zone in which these men could portray the ways in which they thought masculinity ought to be enacted in ritual and in gesture.

Discussants constructed an image of respectability for *mohelim* and *shochetim* that, like with *Bildung* itself, rested on education and cultivation. *Bildung* was a goal of the Enlightenment and of the German middle class. According to its precepts, education and character formation could bring about a man's self-improvement, and women could attain related modes of moral perfection by engaging in similar cultural practices. *Bildung* appealed to many Jews because it transcended religious and national distinctions. Men of any background could achieve civil and moral betterment if they were familiar with a certain corpus of knowledge and exemplified ethical behavior.

Participants in the debates on ritual questions drew from these concepts to imagine a ritual practitioner who was fully formed in intellect and character. Mirroring a general European belief that specialists ought to enjoy specialized knowledge and appropriate qualifications, they called for practitioners to be educated in two areas: in a religious corpus of some kind and in medical and/or veterinary training. Ritual practitioners, wrote one mid-century rabbi, "were to be learned masters of their craft, both medically trained and religiously knowledgeable."[22] "A *shochet*," a Jewish journalist commented, "is a communal servant whose character is verified by the community and who has the technical training needed for his work."[23] *Gebildete* ritual practitioners understood religious laws and were well versed in anatomy and science.

Guidebooks and prescriptive literature from the nineteenth and twentieth centuries emphasized the importance of instructing *mohelim* in anatomy and pediatric medicine and *shochetim* in veterinary and animal sciences and biology. A failure to attain such training on the part of the *shochet* allegedly could result in the production of nonkosher meat, the horrific disfigurement of animals, cruelty, and unbearable animal pain. A *mohel*'s poor medical training might lead to a child's impotence, the spread of disease, or even death.[24]

Over the course of the nineteenth century, Jewish communal councils and oversight boards increasingly established proof of professional training and knowledge as a requirement for a ritual practitioner's license (*kabbalah*). Influenced by the medical community's growing interest in the licensing and training of ritual practitioners and varying German authorities' increased supervision of circumcisers and butchers, the Jewish communal interventions called attention to the medical and veterinary corpus mastered by its ritual practitioners.[25] In this way, the reforms within the community differed from the state and city laws that demanded medical oversight and governmental intervention. The communal regulations included the mandate that *mohelim* be required to take preliminary surgical exams before the receipt of their license,[26] that *shochetim* periodically demonstrate their knowledge of basic animal science to their rabbis,[27] and that a *mohel* have sufficient medical training to observe a child for the days following his circumcision.[28] According to Rabbis Aub and Rothschild of Munich, "a license from the Jewish community validates that a *mohel* possesses a physician's knowledge."[29] Indeed, when rabbis and physicians extended licenses, they often remarked on the medical prowess of a candidate. "Hofmann did another circumcision today," wrote Rabbi Mayer (Baden-Baden) after he observed a ritual circumcision conducted by local Jewish teacher Simon Hofmann. "Kompter [a physician] and I were pleased. [Hofmann] was hygienic and surgically sound. He should be accepted as a *mohel*."[30] "I want to be a *mohel* in your community," wrote another candidate. "I have a letter from my rabbinical authorities and one from Dr. Lix of Mannheim who will verify my medical training."[31]

In addition to the acquisition of medical or veterinary training, the Jewish communal letters, guidebooks, and regulations concerning ritual practitioners emphasized the religious training of their communal servants. Religious education demonstrated not only piety but also moral worth. "A *shochet*, like a religious teacher," wrote one rabbi, "is a communal servant, trained in matters of Jewish law and learning." "They [*shochetim*] are young men who are appropriate to serve as community officers."[32] "Our *mohelim*," wrote another local rabbi, "are exemplary men. Moral men, trained in Judaism and its religious texts."[33] While the corpus of religious knowledge, like that of medical and veterinary knowledge, varied across German Jewish communities and often was dependent on a particular rabbi's strengths and interests, the portraits of the *shochet* and *mohel* consistently painted them as members of the *Bildungsbürgertum*, the German educated bourgeoisie.

For many of the discussants of *Ritualfragen*, ritual practitioners achieved this state of morality or exhibited exemplary behavior only partly because of their education and training. In addition to identifying knowledge as a key component of an ideal character, participants also touted discipline and self-control as crucial to respectability. These formulations mirrored nineteenth-century emphases on the restraining of physical urges and public displays of emotion. Norbert Elias and others have suggested that certain historical shifts during the modern era encouraged Europeans to adopt this value, part of what he has called the "civilizing process." In this schema, the upper class, and later the middle and working classes, articulated concerns that an inability to restrain one's physical urges and public displays of emotion could have harmful effects on society at large.[34] Respectability, then, became inexorably linked to self-control.

Guidebooks for *mohelim* and *shochetim* illustrated this emphasis. Clearly, while circumcision and kosher butchering rely on bodily control for their success, these conversations were particularly relevant during a moment when many members of the *Bildungsbürgertum* feared unruliness and portrayed the surgery and abattoir as places of blood and bodily fluids. The abattoir occupied a place of special concern. According to animal protectionists and sentimentalist activists, it attracted a wide range of unsavory characters who lacked self-discipline and control, and thus they promoted the passage of legislation excluding women and children from its domain.[35] Discussants of *Ritualfragen* echoed these calls and concerns. They offered portraits of ritual practitioners who exhibited calm and possessed control over their own bodies. They did not have "shaking hands," nor were they "prone to anger" or any other "kind of fits."[36] Mirroring the language of the temperance movement, mid- and late nineteenth-century Jews described the *mohel* and *shochet* as temperate individuals who avoided alcohol. "The *shochet*," German Jewish animal protectionist and journalist Albert Löw wrote, "must be a good moral man. He cannot be a drunk or an irascible man."[37]

Participants also emphasized neatness, suggesting that the public appearance of the *mohel* or *shochet* dictated his reputability. Dozens of nineteenth-century guidebooks and discussions championed the cleanliness and orderliness of ritual practitioners. Few places are as chaotic and bloody as the abattoir, and the *mohel* infrequently emerges from a circumcision untouched by bodily fluids. Still, discussants focused on the real or desired cleanliness and tidy demeanor of the practitioners. In his 1881 defense of kosher butchering to a local magistrate who had criticized the rite, Rabbi Cohn of Kattowitz described his *shochetim* as clean and orderly.[38] Two years earlier, Julius Dessauer had published a guidebook for *mohelim* in which he similarly emphasized that a circumciser (*Beschneider*) "should be ... clean. ... his hands should always be clean and his nails free of dirt.[39] Such an emphasis on the hands was not surprising. Since the beginning of the nineteenth century, participants in the *Ritualfragen* debates had called attention to the ritual practice of using a fingernail to uncover the corona (*periah*). Almost thirty years later, when Mayer observed Hofmann, he also commented on the circumciser's hygiene and that "he kept his tools in neat order."[40]

Moritz Daniel Oppenheim, *Der Gevatter Erwartet das Kind* (1867). Reprinted with the permission of the Leo Baeck Institute

Some of the visual images that accompanied texts on *Ritualfragen* reinforced these formulations. In advertisements for new fastening mechanisms and in sketches of proposed slaughterhouses, *shochetim* appeared perfectly clean and handsome despite the fact that they had just slaughtered cattle. In his sketches of a "painless shackling" device, S. Goldberg of Halberstadt, for example, portrayed a wide-eyed, smiling *shochet* standing next to a large contraption.[41] Few *mohel* guidebooks offered images of *mohelim*, but a number of popular paintings did. Moritz Oppenheim's (1800–1882) painting of a ritual circumciser, for example, portrayed the practitioner as youthful and effeminately beautiful, with full lips, a swarthy complexion, curly black cropped hair, and deep sparkling dark eyes.[42] Oppenheim's *mohel* and the *shochetim* of nineteenth- and early twentieth-century advertisements put forth an image of Jews that was in direct contradiction to one being promoted increasingly in popular culture and medical science. As Sander Gilman and others have shown, during the nineteenth century, observers of behavior and physique increasingly cast their gaze on Jewish bodies, insisting that Jews were ugly, physically unfit, and deformed. Oppenheim's *mohel* rendered distinctive Jewish characteristics in a positive rather than a negative light.

The legitimacy of the *mohel* or *shochet* also derived from his work practices, patterns of consumption, and relationships with women. For many participants, the reputability of a *mohel* or *shochet* hinged on certain choices that he made at work. In their view, legitimate ritual circumcisers employed new technologies rather than undertake the risky acts of *periah* with his fingernail or *metzitzah* with his mouth. Worried that circumcisers would spread contagion if they used their fingernails for *periah,* many Jewish physicians and writers strongly recommended that circumcisers use a clamp, endorsed by some rabbis and medical authorities, instead of their fingernails.[43] Critics also denounced the traditional practice of *metzitzah,* the oral sucking of the wound by the *mohel.*[44] Especially by the 1890s, when a glass tube had become available for oral suction and when a series of syphilis cases had been publicized, many professionals and Jewish leaders encouraged *mohelim* to cleanse the wound without getting any blood in their mouths or any saliva on the child's penis.[45] Accusing *mohelim* of spreading sexual infections through this practice, critics warned that *metzitzah* could lead to uncontrollable plagues of syphilis, tuberculosis, and gonorrhea. Sexual connotations also hovered over the deliberations, as evidenced by one writer's comment that it was "ethically problematic" that a grown man would suck an innocent newborn's penis.[46]

Similar discussions took place concerning *shochetim.* Participants in the *Ritualfragen* debates lauded those *shochetim* who utilized new, supposedly more humane, shackling devices. Rabbi Aron Kober of Breslau, for example, enthusiastically embraced a new shackling mechanism for his community and encouraged his *shochetim* to use it.[47] Rabbi Vogelstein of Stettin similarly pushed his colleagues to support other *Niederlegen* (putting-down) inventions, such as the one developed by Hugo Silberbach, "the perfect method of the present: painless . . . and swifter."[48] Both rabbis defended the reputability of those *shochetim* who utilized these devices and called into question those ritual practitioners who did not.

The discussions concerning these work choices were part of larger efforts during the nineteenth and early twentieth centuries to professionalize *mohelim* and *shochetim.* Influenced by general trends toward professionalization, Jewish communities encouraged their ritual practitioners to purchase professional kits and cases, which seemingly transformed the outward appearance of their communal servants to resemble physicians or veterinarians. *Mohelim* could purchase kits that included antiseptic solutions, sterile knives, and alcohol; the one sold by J. Bondi of Frankfurt also included a glass tube for *metzitzah* and a clamp for *periah.*[49] The circumcision cases resembled late nineteenth-century medical kits and were sold in medical specialty stores, a setting suggesting respectability and hygienic standards. Similar cases were available for *shochetim.* Michael Cahn of Fulda, for example, sold a kit for butchers and *shochetim* that included knives, stamps (to indicate that meat was kosher), and a carrying case.[50]

Finally, the respectability of the *mohel* or *shochet* could be seen by his status as a head of family. Local ritual practitioner associations, which mimicked other middle-class professional associations of the era, envisioned ritual practitioners as married men.[51] Anchoring notions of respectability in images of male ritual practitioners as husbands and fathers, these portraits drew on contemporary emphases. Women were envisioned as having the capability of providing havens for their husbands. They could ostensibly make sure that their husbands remained neat despite the filth and blood of their profession. Moreover, the presence of women might weaken the potential brutality encouraged by the cutting rituals. Participants in the ritual debates assumed that the abattoir was a violent space; just because the state banned women from entering the slaughterhouse did not end the perception that women could play a special mediating role in their husbands' lives.

By offering prescriptive formulations of the idealized ritual practitioner, discussants not only distanced *mohelim* and *shochetim* from the distasteful portraits of them presented by their anti-Semitic compatriots, but also valorized a much-critiqued Jewish religious practice and, in so doing, offered a strategy for integration. Much like the Jewish physicians studied by John Efron who reversed anti-Semitic criticism to affirm Jewish distinctiveness on their own terms, the Jewish participants in the debates on ritual questions subtly suggested ways in which Jews might integrate into the majority culture by adopting standards of bourgeois respectability both in ritual and in gesture.[52] Their formulations of the idealized adult male and his behavior aimed at furthering integration by promoting common ideas of male superiority.

The prescriptive portraits of the character and conduct of ritual practitioners also helped to reinforce certain hierarchies among Jewish men and between Jewish men and women. Despite the fact that most discussants could not have imagined a female ritual practitioner, several participants found it necessary to demonstrate the reputability and competence of their communal servants by contrasting them to women or children. Löw, for example, envisioned a *shochet* who was "neither a woman nor a child."[53] The Berlin association of *mohelim* similarly called for ritual practitioners to be "adult men."

Portraits of German Jewish male respectability were also sharply contrasted with the aggressive, untrained masculinity of their Eastern European co-religionists. Actively distancing German-speaking ritual practitioners from the "Ostjuden," many discussants criticized Eastern European–born *mohelim* and *shochetim* for the way they conducted their rites.[54] Eastern Jews supposedly were unlearned and smelled of garlic. They were of the wrong class. In his 1844 study, for example, M. G. Salomon juxtaposed the well-trained *mohelim* of Hamburg, who were "mostly . . . men of the middle class," with *mohelim* of Poland, who "made many mistakes."[55] In their censure of religiously observant circumcisers who lacked medical training, Jewish physicians M. Salomon and

Ellias Collin described these co-religionists as "horribly unenlightened, lacking all anatomical, surgical and therapeutic knowledge."[56] A few decades later, contributors voiced analogous anxieties. Participants in the fin-de-siècle debates on circumcision raised similar doubts, wondering whether syphilis outbreaks had been caused by *mohelim* from the community of "Ostjuden."

Similar complaints were lodged against *shochetim,* who could be suspect if they were born in Eastern Europe. Guidebooks criticized Eastern European practitioners who, in the eyes of the writers, were "patriarchal," a reference to both their traditionalist lifestyle and their gender relations. Participants in the disputes envisioned "Ostjuden" as transmitting a set of values that clashed with the modern German Jewish family ethic, which supposedly was more egalitarian.[57] By identifying the minorities within their communities as deviant, the contributors insisted upon their own reputability within the larger Jewish community. They constructed hierarchies according to gender, class, and nationality to paint themselves as ethical, moral, and deserving individuals.

The nineteenth-century discussions about ritual practitioners offered a portrait of domestic masculinity that was not too different from that formulated by non-Jewish German men. Over time, Jewish depictions of the ritual practitioner's discipline, morality, and conduct consistently referred to notions of a "reputable" manhood, describing practitioners as learned, disciplined, physically neat, and handsome. While conforming to German notions of male domesticity and civility, these normative claims about the Jewish man's character and public conduct also helped to create and maintain social and gender orders that benefited Jews. By insisting on the similarities of Jewish and gentile notions of manhood, Jewish contributors to the circumcision and kosher butchering debates allowed for Jewish integration into German society within a specifically religious framework. Yet, as scholars have shown in other contexts, nineteenth-century Jews simultaneously embraced this universality while insisting on their own differences.[58] They juxtaposed the disciplined ritual practitioner with the brutal, strong, and uncontrollable gentile butcher or unlicensed medical quack. These "unprejudiced, learned, moral, clean men of the Jewish faith" advanced Jewish integration and respectability.[59]

## NOTES

1. Letter, 30 September 1887, from Freie Vereinigung für die Interesse des orthodoxen Judenthums (hereafter Free Association), Neue Synagoge Berlin, Centrum Judaicum Archiv (hereafter CJA), 75BKa124, 152–153; Free Association, *Mittheilungen des geschäftsführenden Auschusses an die Vereinsmitglieder* (Frankfurt am Main: Louis Golde, 1887), vol. 2; Free Association, *Mittheilungen an die Vereinsmitglieder* (Frankfurt am Main: Louis Golde, 1897, 1898), vols. 8, 10.

2. Albert Löw, *Thierschutz im Judenthume nach Bibel und Talmud* (Budapest: F. Buschmann, 1890).

3. While the nineteenth- and early twentieth-century disputes concerning Jewish rites included Jewish and gentile participants, I am limiting my scope here to Jewish discussants.

4. Despite the Mishnah's stipulation that any Jew can be eligible to serve as a *shochet*, few women historically have done so. On the performance of gender, see Judith Butler, *Gender Trouble: Feminism and the Subversion of Identity* (New York: Routledge, 1993); and Butler, *Bodies That Matter: On the Discursive Limits of "Sex"* (New York: Routledge, 1993).

5. Barbara Evans Clements, "Introduction," in Clements, Rebecca Friedman, and Dan Healy, eds., *Russian Masculinities in History and Culture* (New York: Palgrave, 2002), 3.

6. This chapter draws from my *Contested Rituals: Circumcision, Kosher Butchering, and Jewish Political Life in Germany, 1843–1933* (Ithaca, NY: Cornell University Press, 2007). Also see Robin Judd, "The Politics of Beef: Animal Advocacy and the Kosher Butchering Debates in Germany," *Jewish Social Studies* 10, no. 1 (December 2003): 117–150; Judd, "Jewish Political Behaviour and the *Schächtfrage*, 1880–1914," in Rainer Liedtke and David Rechter, eds., *Towards Normality? Acculturation and Modern German Jewry* (Tübingen: Mohr Siebeck, 2003), 251–269; Judd, "Circumcision and the Modern German-Jewish Experience," in Elizabeth Mark, ed., *My Covenant in Your Flesh: Circumcision, Gender, and Culture across Jewish History* (Hanover, NH: University Press of New England, 2003), 142–155; and Judd, "German Jewish Rituals, Bodies, and Citizenship," Ph.D. diss., University of Michigan, 2000.

7. David E. Barclay, *Frederick William IV and the Prussian Monarchy, 1840–1861* (Oxford: Oxford University Press, 1995), xv.

8. While similar discussions took place sporadically elsewhere in Europe and in the United States, an analysis of these disputes in the German-speaking states suggests that the controversies over the rites were particularly important there.

9. The debates about the significance and danger of this rite continued into the Weimar period (1918–1933), involved Jews and non-Jews, and took place in a range of geographic and class settings.

10. See, for example, the positions adopted by Lisa Cody, "This Sex Which Seems to Have Won: The Emergence of Masculinity as a Category of Historical Analysis," *Radical History Review* 61 (1995): 175–183; R. W. Connell, "Review of *Meanings for Manhood: Constructions of Masculinity in Victorian America*," *Signs* 19 (1993): 280–284; Connell, "The Big Picture: Masculinities in Recent World History," *Theory and Society* 22 (1993): 597–623; Deborah Hertz, "Be Careful What You Wish For: Missing Women in the New Picture of Jewish Masculinity," in Dorothy Sue Cobble, Beth Hutchinson, and Amanda B. Chaloupka, eds., *Femininities, Masculinities, and the Politics of Sexual Difference(s)* (New Brunswick, NJ: Institute for Research on Women, 2004), 9–12; Catherine Hall, "The Rule of Difference: Gender, Class, and Empire in the Making of the 1832 Reform Act," in Ida Blom, Karen Hagemann, and Catherine Hall, eds., *Gendered Nations: Nationalisms and Gender Order in the Long Nineteenth Century* (Oxford: Berg, 2000), 107–136; George L. Mosse, *The Image of Man: The Creation of Modern Masculinity* (New York: Oxford University Press, 1996); Judith Newton, "Masculinity Studies: The Longed-For Profeminist Movement for Academic Men?," in Judith Kegan Gardiner, ed., *Masculinity Studies and Feminist Theory: New Directions* (New York: Columbia University Press, 2002), 176–192; Robert Nye, "Locating Masculinity: Some Recent Work on Men," *Signs* 30 (2005): 1937–1962.

11. Daniel Boyarin, *Unheroic Conduct: The Rise of Heterosexuality and the Invention of the Jewish Man* (Berkeley: University of California Press, 1997); Sander L. Gilman, *Jewish Self-Hatred: Anti-Semitism and the Hidden Language of the Jews* (Baltimore, MD: Johns Hopkins University Press, 1986); Gilman, *The Case of Sigmund Freud: Medicine and*

*Identity at the Fin de Siècle* (Baltimore, MD: Johns Hopkins University Press, 1993); Paula E. Hyman, *Gender and Assimilation in Modern Jewish History: The Roles and Representation of Women* (Seattle: University of Washington Press, 1995).

12. See, for example, Baader and Schüler-Springorum, this volume.

13. Sander Gilman's pathbreaking work has influenced my own scholarship on the history of Jewish ritual behavior as well as the work of countless others; see his *Franz Kafka: The Jewish Patient* (London: Routledge, 1996); *The Jew's Body* (New York: Routledge, 1991); "The Indelibility of Circumcision," *Koroth* 9, nos. 11–12 (1991): 806–817; and *Freud, Race, and Gender* (Princeton, NJ: Princeton University Press, 1993). Also see John M. Efron, *Medicine and the German Jews: A History* (New Haven, CT: Yale University Press, 2001); Eberhard Wolff, "Medizinische Kompetenz und talmudische Autorität: Jüdische Ärzte und Rabbiner als ungleiche Partner in der Debatte um die Beschneidungsreform zwischen 1830 und 1850," in Arno Herzig, Hans-Otto Horch, and Robert Jütte, eds., *Judentum und Aufklärung: Jüdisches Selbstverständnis in der bürgerlichen Öffentlichkeit* (Göttingen: Vandenhoeck & Ruprecht, 2002), 119–149; and Judd, "Politics of Beef," "Circumcision and the Modern German-Jewish Experience," and "German Jewish Rituals, Bodies, and Citizenship."

14. Another postcard, circulated after an 1899 ritual murder case (the Hilsner affair), similarly portrayed a bound maiden surrounded by three unkempt Jewish butchers. The reader would have known that they were butchers because the card labeled them as such. Interestingly, the man indicted was not a butcher but a cobbler.

15. Hans Wehleid, "Vom Schächten," *Hammer* (15 February 1911): 102.

16. Bernadin Freimut, *Die Jüdischen Blutmorde von ihrem ersten Erscheinen der Geschichte bis auf unsere Zeit* (Münster: A. Russell, 1895).

17. See chapters 3 and 4 in Judd, *Contested Rituals*. The laws of ritual circumcision mandate that the *mohel* draw out the wound's impurities and excess blood.

18. Eduard Fuchs, *Die Juden in der Karikatur: Ein Beitrag zur Kulturgeschichte* (Munich: Albert Langen, 1921), 194.

19. The Centralverein later successfully sued Sedlaßek for libel. "Fleischbesudelungs-Prozesse: Referat und Diskussion in der ordentlichen Versammlung des Central-Vereins deutscher Staatsbürger jüdischen Glaubens am 12. Oktober 1896," *Im Deutsche Reich* 10 (1896): 465–495.

20. Often, participants explicitly pointed to the presence of anti-Semitism in the disputes as one motivation for taking part in the discussions. See, for example, Hirsch Hildesheimer, *Herr Schlachthof-Direktor Heiz über das Schächten* (Berlin: Gutenberg, n.d.); letter, 15 December 1910, to Elb from Benjamin Hirsch, CJA, 75CVe1344, 425–426.

21. Frequently, these discussants took part in the disputes to position themselves in places of leadership, similar to the actions of German Jewish physicians who used languages of medicalization to assume positions of leadership and to publicly offer their images of the ideal Jewish community. See Efron, *Medicine and the German Jews*. Also see Wolff, "Medizinische Kompetenz und talmudische Autorität."

22. See the consistent articulation of this in Philipp Wolfers, *Brit Kodesh: Die Beschneidung der Juden eine Anweisung fuer Beschneider, Aerzte und Wundaerzte sich mit dem Ganzen der Weihe bekannt zu machen und die Handlung selbst nach Indicationen kunstgemäß und nach den esetzlichen Vorschriften vorzunehmen* (Hannover: Friedrich Ernst Huth, 1831); Levi, "Gießen, im November: Ueber die Verbindung des Schächterdienstes mit dem Lehreramte," *Allgemeine Zeitung des Judenthums* (hereafter *AZDJ*) (26 November 1855): 614–616; Wilhelm Landsberg, *Das Rituelle Schächten der Israeliten im Lichte der Wahrheit* (Kaiserslautern: Eugen Crufins, 1882); Naphtali Hirsch, *Die Freie Vereinigung für die Interessen des orthodoxen Judenthums: Eine Beleuchtung ihrer Aufgabe und seitherigen*

*Wirksamkeit* (Frankfurt: Louis Golde, 1900); Freie Vereinigung für die Interessen des orthodoxen Judenthums, *Mitteilungen an die Vereinsmitglieder* (Frankfurt am Main: Louis Golde, 1904), vol. 17.

23. J. Weigl, "Das Schächten vom Standpunkt der Physiologie, Hygiene, und Humanität," *Deutsche Israelitische Zeitung* (5 December 1912): 107, CJA, 75CVe1341.

24. See, for example, "Tagesgeschichte," *Allgemeine Medicinische Central-Zeitung* (1853): 311–312.

25. The medical knowledge required often drew from regulations or reforms offered by medical establishments or governmental bodies.

26. Order, 23 November 1814, and order, 10 November 1848 (no. 28) (Mannheim), Central Archives for the History of the Jewish People (hereafter CAHJP), GA II 49; order, 10 January 1883, concerning circumcision, CJA, 75BKa1 24, 62–63.

27. Order, 11 November 1883, issued by Rabbi Jacob Cohn, CJA, 75DCo1 27 11; and letter, 3 February 1890, from the rabbi of Erfurt to Katzenstein (*shochet*), CJA, 75AEr1 96 20.

28 "Aus Württemberg," *AZDJ* (30 March 1857).

29. Report, 14 January 1830, of the police authorities, no. 25,654, Staatsarchiv Munich, RA 33902.

30. R. Mayer, "Die Befähigung des Lehrer Simon Hofmann in Baden-Baden," CJA, 75Bka1 25 33.

31. Letter, 25 January 1911, from Salomon Oppenheimer to Groß. Oberrat Karlsruhe, CJA, 72 B Ka1 25 42.

32. Letter, 30 November 1906, to the Commission for the Defense of *Shechitah* from the Synagogue Community of Posen, CJA, 75CVe1 344 127.

33. Letter, May 1850, from Rabbi Schwartz, Hürben, CAHJP, inv. 6941.

34. Nobert Elias, *The Civilizing Process,* trans. Edmund Jephcott (New York: Urizen, 1978). According to Elias, this process originated with the decision by governments to take on increased responsibility for their inhabitants and for disciplining wrongdoing.

35. Dorothee Ingeborg Brantz, "Slaughter in the City: The Establishment of Public Abattoirs in Paris and Berlin, 1780–1914," Ph.D. diss., University of Chicago, 2003.

36. See, for example, Simon Bamberger, *Die Beschneidung: Eine populäre Darstellung ihrer Bedeutung und Vollziehung* (Wandsbek: Goldschmidt-Hamburg, 1913); Wolfers, *Brit Kodesh;* letter, 13 June 1912, from the Jewish community of Dresden to the Verband der deutschen Juden, CJA, 75CVe1 341 45; minutes, 9 May 1901, of the Commission to Defend *Shehitah,* CJA, 75CGe1 893, 90–94.

37. Löw, *Thierschutz im Judenthume,* 27.

38. Response, December 1881, from Jacob Cohn to the magistrate of Kattowitz, CJA, 75Dco127, 12.

39. Julius Dessauer, *Brit Olam Der ewige Bund: Die Beschneidung, vom ritualen, operativen und sanitären Standpunkte nach den besten Quellen* (Budapest: 1879), 19–20.

40. Report, April 1906, from R. Mayer concerning Simon Hofmann, CJA, 75Bka1 25, 33.

41. S. Goldberg, "Deutsches Reichspatent für stossfreies Neiderlegen von Grossvieh jeder Art zu Schlacht- und Operationszwecken," CJA, 75Cge1 893, 95–96; and letter, 21 April 1907, from the Verband to Robert Drucker, CJA, 75Cve1 350, 14. Also see Hugo Silberbach, "Neu! Niederlegenapparat, Neu!," CJA, 75Dco1 29, 112–113.

42. Oppenheim's painting received an overwhelmingly positive reception (he reproduced and expanded the series several times over the course of the 1870s). These images were in stark contrast to Yiddish literature's portrait of the strong, ultramasculine *shochet*.

43. Joseph Bergson, *Die Beschneidung vom historischen, kritischen und medicinischen Standpunkt mit Bezug auf die neuesten Debatten und Reformvorschläge* (Berlin: von Th. Scherk, 1844), 115–116; M. G. Salomon, *Die Beschneidung: Historisch und medizinisch*

*Beleuchtet* (Braunschweig: Friedrich Vieweg und Sohn, 1844), 45–48, 63; Klein, "Die rituelle Circumcision: Eine sanitätspolizeiliche Frage," *Allgemeine Medicinische Central Zeitung* 11 (June 1853): 365–366.

44. Interest in *metzitzah* was not new. Since Talmudic times, rabbinic authorities had debated whether the procedure was an essential part of the ritual of *brit milah*. Many commentators interpreted the mishnaic reference to *metzitzah* as a healing procedure rather than a necessary component of the *mitzvah* itself, in which case another healing procedure that applied suction could be substituted.

45. "Das Metsitsah-Glasröhrchen," CAHJP, inv. 855; Freie Vereinigung, *Mitheilungen an die Vereinsmitglieder* (Frankfurt am Main: Louis Golde, 1902), vol. 15; Chewrath Mohalim, *Statuten* (Frankfurt am Main: self-published, 1907). Cahn also invented devices for kosher butchering. See Michael Cahn, *Die Einrichtungen des Koscher Fleisch Verkaufs unter besonderer Berücksichtigung der Zeichnungs und Stempelungs-Methoden* (Frankfurt: Hofmann, 1901).

46. In addition to the criticism in the documents cited above, see Hamburg Jewish community council minutes, 11 May 1853, CAHJP, AHW 563, 30–32. Here, opinion shifted over time. While one group began questioning the character of men who utilized traditional techniques for *periah* and *metzitzah*, others in mid-century insisted that "good, moral men" were in the right to preserve the age-old methods. Such a view would become increasingly in the minority by the turn of the twentieth century, after mainstream Orthodox communities and organizations embraced the use of the glass tube and the clamp.

47. Letter, 22 June 1914, to Cohn from Aron Kober, CJA, 75DCol 29, 117.

48. Letter, 27 April 1907, from Julius Bier to Cohn, CJA, 75Dcol 28, 217; letter, 24 June 1907, to the Verband, CJA, 75Cvel 344, 159–160; letter, 1908, from L. Rosenak to the Bremen Jewish community, CJA, 75Cvel 344, 389; Rabbi Vogelstein quoted in Hugo Silberbach, "Neu! Niederlegenapparat, Neu!," CJA, 75Dcol 29, 112–113; Schwarzenberg & Co., "Beschreibung!," CJA, 75Dcol 29, 116; Albert Währer, "Schlachtmaschine" (1900), CJA, 75Aerl 96, 65; "Neue Schlachtmethode," *Der Israelit* 46 (1905): 620.

49. See Mohalim, *Statuten*.

50. Cahn, *Die Einrichtungen des Koscher Fleisch Verkaufs*.

51. Mohalim, *Statuten*.

52. Efron, *Medicine and the German Jews*.

53. Löw, *Thierschutz im Judenthume*, 27.

54. Bergson, *Beschneidung*, 115. Also see Ludwig Philippson, "Jährliche Rabbinerversamlungen, Die Beschneidungs- und Reformvereins-frage," *AZDJ* 10 (4 March 1844): 103; "Die Beschneidung," *AZDJ* 10 (1 March 1858): 129. Discussants also criticized them for burying people immediately after death, an issue that had been of concern since the late eighteenth century.

55. Salomon, *Beschneidung*, 92. Also see Gideon Brecher, *Die Beschneidung der Israeliten: Von der historischen, praktisch-operativen und rituellen Seite zunächst für den Selbstunterricht* (Wien: Franz Edl. v. Schmid and J. J. Busch, 1845), 40–45.

56. Salomon, *Beschneidung*, 66–70; Collin, "Ueber manch durch den Fortschrift der Medicin im Judenthum gedingte Reformen," in Z. Frankel, ed., *Zeitschrift für die religiösen Interessen des Judenthums, zweiter Jahrgang* (Berlin: M. Simion, 1845), 2:268. Also see similar comments in Bergson, *Beschneidung*, 112; and Brecher, *Beschneidung*. For an earlier description, see Wolfers, *Brit Kodesh*.

57. Brecher, *Beschneidung*.

58. On this scholarship, see Benjamin Maria Baader, *Gender, Judaism, and Bourgeois Culture in Germany, 1800–1870* (Bloomington: Indiana University Press, 2006); Jacob Borut, "'A New Spirit among Our Brethren in Ashkenaz': German Jews between Anti-Semitism and

Modernity in the Late Nineteenth Century" (Heb.), Ph.D. diss., Hebrew University, 1991; Borut, "The Rise of Jewish Defense Agitation in Germany, 1890–1895: A Pre-History of the C.V.?," *Leo Baeck Institute Yearbook* 36 (1991): 59–96; Evyatar Friesel, "The Political and Ideological Development of the Centralverein before 1914," *Leo Baeck Institute Yearbook* 31 (1986): 121–146; Till van Rahden, "Intermarriage, the New Woman, and the Situational Ethnicity of Breslau Jews, 1870s to 1920s," *Leo Baeck Institute Yearbook* 46 (2001): 125–150.

    59. Letter, 30 September 1887, from Free Association, CJA, 75BKa124, 152–153.

# 4

## A Soft Hero

*Male Jewish Identity in Imperial Germany through the*
*Autobiography of Aron Liebeck*

STEFANIE SCHÜLER-SPRINGORUM

Women write diaries, men write books. Women talk about their lives, men talk about the world. And when historians ask questions, they tend to ask female subjects about the private sphere and male subjects about the public sphere. At least since Karin Hausen's pathbreaking essay on the polarization of "gender characteristics," we know that this alleged division between the two spheres is part and parcel of a middle-class gender ideology. Indeed, Marion Kaplan has shown how useful an investigation of the "female sphere"—based primarily on private or personal sources—can be for our understanding of the "making of the Jewish middle class."[1] Yet, although this process was so very central to the entire nineteenth century, we still know very little about how it took place for the other half of humanity: for men. What effects did the development of a German Jewish bourgeoisie have on gender relations and gender models? Or, to put the issue differently: To what extent was the degree of involvement in this development, and the awareness of and assimilation into it, different for Jewish men and women? If we are looking for new gender-historical approaches to German Jewish embourgeoisement, it is high time to look at Jewish men as men—as gendered beings confronted with normative expectations. Scholars have typically viewed the public activities and positions of Jewish men—for example, programmatic or ideological writings published by the Centralverein or by Zionists—not only as the *official* Jewish history, but indeed as a straightforward reflection of Jewish men's attitudes. Their personal or "private" documents have thus far been studied essentially for references to "public" topics, and have not been seen as sources in their own right.

In this chapter, I present my reading of one such document, in order to explore the interpretive possibilities and to assess the limits of this kind of material as a source for Jewish gender history. I focus on the autobiography of the Königsberg businessman Aron Liebeck, written in 1928—when he was seventy-two years old—for the benefit of his family. This unpublished, 500-page document describes the life of the son of a poor provincial trader who rises to become a successful businessman and citizen of the East Prussian capital.[2]

Liebeck's life story is situated in the framework of a history of social ascent, the paradigmatic story for German Jewish history in the nineteenth century. The social-historical dimensions of this process, unique in European Jewish history, are by now familiar. While at the beginning of the nineteenth century, at least one-third of the Jews in Germany lived in grinding poverty, seventy or eighty years later a large majority of them enjoyed a secure middle-class existence. Simone Lässig has published an exhaustive study of this process, based on a vast body of source material, that investigates the cultural consequences of this rapid social transformation.[3] Like David Sorkin, Shulamit Volkov, and Marion Kaplan before her, Lässig combines demographic data, prescriptive texts, and autobiographies to describe the process through which Jews became part of the German middle class. In most cases these authors show awareness of the fact that their subjective sources, mainly the autobiographies that historians are so fond of, tend to tell us about the values of the educated middle classes, the *Bildungsbürgertum*, because members of those social groups left behind a disproportionate share of the extant memoirs.[4] Nevertheless, the conclusions derived from these sources—concerning values and norms as well as individual aspirations and experiences—are typically generalized to describe the German Jewish middle class as a whole.[5]

It is worth emphasizing that in the German Empire, this Jewish middle class was still clearly dominated by the world of merchants and traders: more than half of Germany's Jews made their living in trade, and the majority of these men were not highly educated, large business owners, but rather worked as small traders and shop owners, or as salaried employees and salesmen—as was the case with Aron Liebeck. Using the example of Liebeck's life history, I will call attention to how little we actually know about this core group of the German Jewish middle class, and how cautious we have to be when we draw conclusions, beyond the demographic data, about their historical experiences as businessmen, as Jews, and as men.

Christina von Hodenberg reminds us of the fact that this is not only a problem in German Jewish historiography, but it also applies to research into the German middle classes generally, where a similar tension divided the educated bourgeoisie from the ranks of the commercial classes. Indeed, while the bourgeois world was constituted on the basis of an economy characterized by capitalist and rational goals, the bourgeois "ideal of right living [*Ideal der Lebensführung*]" was from the beginning the "reading, studying citizen serving the state—in a word, a member of the educated middle class [*der lesende, studierende, staatsdienende Bürger—mit einem Wort, der Bildungsbürger*]."[6]

The major German research projects from the 1980s and 1990s on the history of the middle classes produced studies that focused almost exclusively—implicitly or explicitly—on the educated middle classes (*Bildungsbürgertum*).[7] Some have argued that the distinction between the "economic middle class [*Wirtschaftsbürgertum*]" and the "educated middle class [*Bildungsbürgertum*]" has been retrospectively constructed and therefore does not reflect historical realities, but the evidence for this assertion is not convincing,[8] and the opposite seems to be the case. The fact that the values particular to the educated middle classes arose as counter-tendencies to the "pernicious acquisitiveness of the mercantile world" points to inner tensions within the world of the middle classes. Of course, this does not mean that a member of the economic middle class was necessarily uneducated, but it remains to be established that there actually was a uniform "horizon of bourgeois values [*bürgerlicher Wertehimmel*]"[9] that, as many historians have assumed, extended over the homes of merchants and pastors, traders and teachers alike.

Taking an example from the history of masculinity, one may ask to what extent the duel, which entered the academic world from the military sphere, actually influenced conceptions of honor among young businessmen.[10] For German Jewish masculinity in particular, so far we can only draw conclusions from normative statements from the religious sphere or from the academic world.[11] We do not know to what extent these conclusions apply to the large majority of Jewish men, who were living in a business environment. Attempting to fill this lacuna with the example of a single life story is, of course, an audacious undertaking. Nevertheless I do believe that a close reading of Aron Liebeck's story not only offers a paradigm of Jewish advancement, but also yields significant insights into the self-construction and presentation of a particular Jewish male identity in Imperial Germany. I will concentrate on three aspects: social ascent, family and public life, and Liebeck's explicitly stated values and norms.

## SOCIAL ASCENT

On Aron Liebeck's sixty-third birthday, his children presented him with a handsomely bound notebook and asked him to record, "in chronological order, an approximate outline of his life" that could then serve as the starting point for a family history. Liebeck thought the idea too prosaic and feared that such a chronicle would provide only "a very blurred picture of my life and . . . work."[12] Instead, he set himself the more ambitious goals of placing his "achievements" into the proper context of his time and giving his entire autobiographical project a form that would let the reader know clearly where he himself wanted to be positioned within this context. The division of the chapters and their titles—"Meine früheste Jugend [My Earliest Youth]," "Meine Lehrjahre [My Apprenticeship]," "Meine Wanderjahre [My Traveling Years]"—are directly reminiscent of a bourgeois *Bildungsroman,* the classic German literary form that describes an individual's personal development and struggle to prove himself.[13] In Liebeck's case, this traditional literary structure does not provide a framework for the edifying and introspective reflections of a contented member of the bourgeoisie, but rather for the epic, even at times highly dramatized, story of a social climber.

Aron Liebeck, the youngest of seven children, was born in 1856 in the small East Prussian town of Lötzen. His father had started off as a door-to-door sales-man, but after years of hard work, he eventually managed to open a small shop. However, the business collapsed after the death of his wife, and Aron, who was a year old at the time, was sent to live with relatives, where he experienced the abject poverty of the Jewish lower classes.[14] At thirteen, he returned to Lötzen, where he was shocked to find his own family living in similar circumstances. Liebeck claims to have felt only "compassion intensified by emotional closeness [*seelisch vertieftes Mitleid*]" with his father, who lived "from hand to mouth" selling grain and lottery tickets: "When writing down these, my saddest memo-ries, my heart still shrinks with pain, thinking of my father who was haunted by food scarcity, bitter suffering and almost unbearable disease."[15] A few weeks later, Liebeck was sent to relatives in Berlin to be apprenticed as a shopkeeper—a mistake, as it turned out. The Berlin uncle, who ran a small textile business in Friedrichsfelde, was on the brink of bankruptcy and had taken his nephew as nothing more than cheap labor. Instead of the apprenticeship he had hoped for, Aron found himself hawking his uncle's wares door to door in the villages around Berlin. Feeling "misled and betrayed by fine words and hopeful promis-es," Aron eventually persuaded his uncle to help him find a real apprenticeship.[16]

At this point in the narrative, the author presents himself as the protagonist of his own story for the first time, as an individual agent responsible for his own fate, distinguishable from others by virtue of specific characteristics and, at the tender age of fifteen, already able to take charge of his life: "If I had been a brainless lad who was too lazy to think, I would have been able to continue with this life, but I did not want that, as I came to the conclusion that I could not educate myself here to the least degree about business, let alone academi-cally [*wissenschaftlich*]."[17] Liebeck leaves no doubt about his goal in life, namely "wealth and prestige,"[18] referring again and again to the poverty of his childhood and youth and to the misery of his family: "These are feelings that are etched in a child's mind for a lifetime."[19] In his accounts of important moments in his life, such as the circumcision of his first son, his first trip abroad, or the purchase of his first house, flashbacks to the poverty of his childhood effectively highlight the distance he has traveled since then.[20]

There are a number of indications that he indeed planned his career as care-fully as he describes it in retrospect. After his apprenticeship, for example, the self-confident "youth . . . who now wanted to take up the struggle for his exis-tence and win it" turned down a number of job offers in smaller towns, wait-ing for an opportunity to go to Königsberg. This was the provincial capital and the most attractive center for upwardly mobile youngsters, Jews and non-Jews alike, from the small surrounding towns and villages.[21] Liebeck assumed that opportunities there would give him a better chance to reach his long-term goal of financial independence.

After several ups and downs, he actually did achieve his goal twelve years later, at the age of thirty-four. By that time, he had begun to amass property and assets, and he managed to retain his holdings in spite of economic crisis and several failed construction projects and business partnerships. By the 1920s, he was able to enjoy the comfortable existence guaranteed by a secure, private income. He concludes the account of his social ascent as follows: "I do not hesitate to admit that every morning, upon freshly awakening, I thank fate again for having spared me from the need to work up to the last hour of my life or to be dependent on anybody."[22]

The exhaustive detail with which Liebeck recounts his thoughts, ideas, and financial deliberations—always in connection with some decision with far-reaching consequences—reveals the great importance he placed on the careful planning of his life: "Long hesitation was not my way . . . , but to change jobs carelessly and make unrealistic plans was against my nature, which always guided me to think and act logically."[23]

When we look at the way he recounts his career as a whole, we immediately notice the unusual structure of the story and the weight given to individual episodes: the emphasis on financial independence is betrayed by Liebeck's noting that, as he sees it, his *Wanderjahre* (years of travel, self-discovery) did not end until he was able to open his own business—in other words, at a time when he had already been married for ten years and had fathered three children. In such a way, he confirms the findings of Heinz-Gerhard Haupt and others who maintain that the emphasis placed on occupational or material independence remained the most important distinction between the *petite bourgeoisie* and the "great" bourgeoisie deep into the twentieth century. However, for many contemporaries who did not react as flexibly as Liebeck did, the pursuit of financial independence often proved to be a trap. This much-coveted goal was, in reality, often highly insecure, and one could easily slide back into a proletarian existence or even into poverty. Aron Liebeck could rightly count himself among the "happy few" who had managed to enter into the "arcane area of the bourgeoisie."[24]

It is all the more surprising, therefore, that the reader is not told much about the last twenty-five years of his career, a time when he had indeed reached a material plateau that secured his upper middle-class status, at least from an economic point of view. In contrast to this absence, the meticulous description of his social ascent covers nearly 300 pages. The focus of his self-representation, therefore, is the achievement of his ascent and a description of the character traits that made it possible.[25] These features are emphasized, and in fact made to appear extraordinary, through references to numerous counterexamples. That is, Liebeck's account is full of descriptions of various bankruptcies and tragic outcomes among relatives and acquaintances. He describes these misfortunes with a wealth of detail, seemingly relishing them, and he often singles out individual character traits as the cause of the tragedy. While some, for example his long-term boss Heinrichs, fail because of stubborn insistence on outdated principles, others come to ruin because of semi-legal practices or excessive spending.[26] Still others, such as his youngest brother-in-law, Hermann, are "unfortunately very untalented" and only by dying do they relieve their relatives—in this case, Liebeck himself—"of a heavy burden."[27] In Liebeck's view, most of these men simply lacked a strong will. He excuses his father's business failures by attributing them to a religiously determined "fatalism" which, he notes, "inhibits any serious striving toward a goal," while his friend Hurwitz was ultimately "not strong enough to shed his past as an employee." A boardinghouse colleague from the early Königsberg period is described in a less-than-flattering way: "One of the many people without any special qualities, who carry out their business duties in a habitual and mindless way, who are not self-indulgent, but also lack ambition and can only flourish under someone else's guidance."[28]

Noting all of these failures seems to have the primary function of showing Liebeck's own success in an even more dazzling light. And his secret—he leaves no doubt about it—is rooted in his character, his "firm determination to work hard and improve at all times."[29]

## FAMILY AND PUBLIC LIFE

Although bourgeois society allegedly valued achievement over origin, family background unquestionably played a double role in the fine game of distinction. Indeed, coming from a good middle-class family meant that one was socialized to feel confident and comfortable in important situations, and coming from a well-respected family armed one with a certain level of social cachet.[30] When it came to family background, Aron Liebeck's project faced a dilemma: his family was not presentable, and moreover he had not even grown up in it. He solved this problem of double rootlessness—real and psychological—by making a virtue of necessity and placing himself at the beginning of his own family history. His family of origin is dealt with fleetingly in several early pages, and he is then free to begin the "actual description of [his] life."[31] He portrays himself as a self-made man, even when it comes to family, and he consciously fashions himself into the patriarch, the progenitor of "the Liebecks," the founder of a new, bourgeois family tradition with which he attempts to compensate for his own rootlessness.[32]

Not surprisingly, then, Liebeck's description of his family life appears only in the description of his Königsberg years—in his exhaustive account of his bosses, Lachmanski and Löwenstein—and not in the early chapters about his childhood and apprenticeship in Lötzen and Friedrichsfelde. This focus on the bourgeois standards of the *Höherstehenden* (superiors) with whom he was in daily contact was, as Mario König stresses, not atypical for employees.[33] In this way, Liebeck had an opportunity, before his own marriage, to observe different models of domestic happiness. Lachmanski's wife, Laura, ran the Lachmanski home "in such an elegant way that it became a meeting point of distinguished personalities." In addition to regular social events on Friday evenings and on Sundays at lunchtime, guests were invited for lecture evenings and musical performances. Liebeck uses expressions like "crown of the house" to describe this woman who, "adorned with the radiant diadem of true femininity," succeeded in combining "domestic happiness" with an "agreeable lifestyle befitting their social rank"—in addition to educating the couple's six children.[34] Compared to this, the family lifestyle of the brothers Löwenstein seemed quite humble. These frugal and "quietly contented people" only socialized within a small circle of relatives and friends; they taught Liebeck through their example "that external glamour is not true happiness, and that happiness can be found in humble privacy."[35] The fact that the brothers also came from a poor background may have facilitated the identification. Furthermore, Liebeck was enough of a realist—at least in retrospect—to understand that it would have exceeded his later financial and cultural capacities (and those of his wife) to run a "great house" like that of the Lachmanskis, whom he admired but did not try to emulate.

For Aron Liebeck, family life was without a doubt a necessary component of the thoroughly bourgeois existence to which he aspired. He often notes that he would not have minded marrying a "totally poor girl," because he was concerned that a "well-to-do woman" might fail to appreciate his hard work, and that material dependence would disrupt the "natural order" of marriage. "I need and want a woman who will be loyal to me in all situations, one who will help me build and improve my existence, whom, as a consequence, I will have to love dearly who, though this remains unspoken, will owe me her happiness," he explains, adding later on: "I want to lay all that I am and all that I have at the feet of such a woman, even though she may not have more to contribute to our marriage than kind-heartedness, good sense and the earnest desire to make my happiness, to maintain it and continually increase it."[36]

The fact that Liebeck "authentically" describes his search for a wife in a passage of ten pages with direct speech and inner monologue shows the extreme importance that he placed on choosing the right partner and achieving "family happiness." Marriage and family were, as Karin Hausen has noted, "far from a sideshow in the history of the bourgeoisie and bourgeois society," and Liebeck shows unambiguously that the family setting was indeed an ideal place for constructing romanticized images of himself and others and, *en passant*, for determining both the emotional and the practical roles that the partners would have to play.[37]

In his account of his marriage proposal, Liebeck becomes an unexpected classical hero and his future wife the mirror of his achievements thus far. This role casting is clearly revealed by the following key scene in his autobiography. One day in the autumn of 1880, Aron Liebeck escorted home the cashier of the shop where he worked. In the ensuing conversation, the young woman showed interest in his life story, his disadvantaged childhood, and his assiduous ascent. When Liebeck realized "that her cheeks blushed and her gaze was glued to my lips, I was overwhelmed by overflowing emotions"—a crucial moment which, looking back, he can best express by borrowing from Shakespeare:

> In the midst of all this I suddenly remembered the deeply poetic confession of Othello to the Duke: "She loved me for the dangers I had pass'd, And I loved her that she did pity them." Had I not, like Othello, been a fighter from my earliest youth, even though my means may have been my wits rather than my arms? . . . What would have become of me if I had not used my formative years to improve my knowledge! One who follows the herd, nothing more! But here was a girl walking next to me who was moved to tears by the tri-fling story of my past; must she not have a wonderfully gentle, loving spirit? Besides, she was eminently hard working, honest and good. As I wanted to become a licensed bookkeeper . . . , Miss Zacharias would be the right, ideal career assistant for me.[38]

Thus inspired—emotionally moved and practically convinced—Liebeck made a spontaneous proposal to which "this dear sweet girl" from an Orthodox trading family assented with "a squeeze of her small trembling hand" after a brief moment of consideration.[39]

It would be far too speculative to try to measure the degree of affection between two people on the basis of an autobiographical text—particularly since what we have here is, of course, only one side of the story. But, as has been shown elsewhere, a "happy marriage" counted among the "essentials" of a successful bourgeois lifestyle, and the opposite is rarely found in (auto)biographical accounts.[40] Whatever the actual motives for this marriage were, it was important for Liebeck to describe it in a way that conformed to the bourgeois ideal of romantic marriage. This is shown by the very structure of his narrative. After fifteen years of marriage, Marie Liebeck dies of a stroke, and next to the courting scene, no other event is depicted as dramatically as her last hours and unexpected death. For her husband, this is a painful turning point. He suffers a nervous breakdown after Marie's death and feels that his life is "shattered" and stripped of its "value and direction." As a forty-year-old widower with three children, however, he has no choice but to marry again, quickly, and he finds an ideal second partner in a young cousin of his deceased wife. Franziska Rosenbaum distinguishes herself through "dutifulness" and "untrained, yet logically correct commercial knowledge" as well as the fact that she knows the children well and understands his own "idiosyncrasies" from earlier stays in the Liebeck home. She manages to transform "the dreary present into a better future full of promise for consolation and help." Toward the end of his memoirs, Liebeck is thus still able to present a happy family life in spite of the rupture caused by the death of his first wife.[41] The climax and, in a sense, the evidence of this are the extensive descriptions of the couple's silver wedding anniversary in 1922 and Aron's seventieth birthday four years later. On both occasions, he stresses the internal harmony of the family and the "successful events with all of our children," giving generous and detailed praise to the various artistic and poetic offerings, and including in his memoirs all of the poems dedicated to him as part of the festivities.[42]

The common characteristic of both marriages was a well thought-out life and work plan where gender roles were constantly being renegotiated and, quite clearly, adapted to the economic necessities of the day. This confirms Shulamit Volkov's impression that the Jewish family as an "institution" played a central and often underappreciated role in German Jews' social advancement and "assimilation."[43] The Liebecks seem to have carefully considered at all times how best to achieve particular short- or long-term goals. For example, marrying Marie Zacharias meant that the great project of financial independence had to be postponed for some time, since founding a family and establishing a home necessitated the security of a regular income. Nevertheless the bridegroom found it appropriate to announce, the day after the engagement, that his fiancée would leave her job, because she had to devote her time before the wedding to "receiving instruction in housekeeping and cooking." Thereafter, his wife worked at home for ten years, gave birth to three children, and provided her husband with a refuge where he could "rest at last after his strenuous travels." But when the time came to fulfill his long-cherished dream of financial independence, her professional skills were once again called upon.[44] The only way Liebeck's business could be at all profitable was with the help of each of his wives and, later, his oldest daughter.

Since the family's apartment was in the same building as the business, household and children could be cared for "on the side," or with the help of relatives who came to visit, sometimes for months—an arrangement that certainly did not follow the bourgeois model of keeping business and family life separate. This, incidentally, confirms Monika Richarz's findings on the division of labor in German Jewish families. Only a very elite social stratum of Jewish families lived up to the bourgeois ideal of separate spheres, and indeed only for a very short time; in the majority of Jewish middle-class households throughout the nineteenth century, wives and daughters actively contributed to the family income in various ways and for various reasons.[45] Liebeck's longing for financial independence seems to have been so intense that, for a while at least, he was willing to sacrifice the ideal of having a stay-at-home wife, which he thought so important for the bourgeois reputation of the family. The tensions between these aspirations must have been very strong, as becomes obvious when Liebeck's business does not live up to his expectations, and he has to close it down. Apparently somewhat relieved, he remarks that now everything is operating in a more respectable manner again. His wife and daughter are able to devote themselves once again to "the household and the education of the children," particularly in order to "further education, especially in music."[46]

Liebeck also experienced changes in his personal life, specifically in terms of his social circles and activities. Before marriage, Liebeck had socialized mainly with other unmarried young men. The narrative of his bachelor life shows that work-related socializing and his drive for social advancement were highly intertwined. With the exception of his relationship with an old school friend who, like him, came from a poor background, Liebeck always made certain that in his free time he had casual social contact with "socially higher" circles. However, his social ascent was only partially successful, betraying yet again the rigidity of bourgeois society's class structure. For example, when he was a young, salaried employee, he was only occasionally invited to his boss Lachmanski's home, but he quickly became a constant guest at the "coffee club" where Lachmanski's unmarried brother and business partner, Leopold, regularly invited other bachelors. As a bookkeeper in the Löwenstein firm, which was not quite as distinguished as Lachmanski's, he lived as a sub-tenant in the owner's sister-in-law's house, which facilitated "formal contact," and soon he received private invitations to Löwenstein's home. He appreciated this, he stresses, "very much."[47] Furthermore, Liebeck tried to "obtain some further education in social ways," and eagerly went to parties and dances. There, his dancing skills paved the "way to the best families," and he was even able to escort his boss's "adored" wife to the dance floor at a masked ball.

For a semblance of relaxation, he attended dances organized by clubs "whose members do not belong to the upper social class," where he could amuse himself in an uninhibited fashion. Similarly, he spent some evenings playing cards or billiards, leisure pursuits which were simply pleasurable and did not further his social ambitions.[48] His motivation to take part in the city's lively club life seems to have been varied: while the Kegelclub Samstagia (Samstagia Bowling Club), the Verein der Liederfreunde (Association of the Friends of Song), and the Dramatische Leseverein (Dramatic Reading Circle), of which he was a co-founder, were mainly patronized by young employees and tradesmen, membership in the Männerturnverein (Men's Gymnastics Club) was, as Liebeck still proudly stresses in retrospect, socially quite mixed. Hence, there were various reasons for him to join:

> But in the gymnastics club, I could not only strengthen my muscles, improve my health, make myself immune to the effects of bad weather, and avoid

youthful mistakes and indolence, but of equal utility, I found contact with like-minded men who lacked arrogance and prejudice, regardless of how rich they were or how high their position was in life. In the gymnastics club, everybody felt, moved and behaved as a member of the whole. When the game was over, many of us—I always—went to Krischnick's pub, where we held *Kommers* [drinking rituals]. It did not matter at all if I, the youngest, sat next to Mr. Rettig, the owner of a brewery, or to Louis Adamsohn, who was very rich.[49]

This relaxed bachelor's life ended abruptly after Liebeck's engagement. He immediately canceled his membership in all clubs, because he now spent every evening with his fiancée's family, something he saw as "self-evident." Had he remained an inactive member, he would have been spending money for the clubs "uselessly."[50] From this point on, he frequented the social circles of the family Zacharias and only kept contact with a few earlier acquaintances, most of whom also started families in these years. Henceforth, the Liebecks' social life—in addition to occasional outings to the theater or to a concert—consisted of periodic, mutual invitations within a group of young married couples who lived in the same neighborhood and with whom they also spent holidays at the coast. Within this social circle, which remained strikingly constant over the years, marriages and business partnerships were arranged and financial transactions negotiated. However, when they were playing cards, there was a relaxed social atmosphere "until morning."[51]

Another constant of Liebeck's life from bachelorhood through marriage stands out: the friends, colleagues, and acquaintances whom he describes in any detail are all Jews. The only possible exception could be his long-time boss Heinrichs, whose name does not appear in the membership lists of the Jewish community. But contact with Heinrichs seems to have been limited to the professional sphere: for example, Heinrichs declines when Liebeck invites him to his first son's circumcision. In his memoirs Liebeck feels the need to explain this refusal as consistent with his boss's practice of "never visiting social gatherings."[52] While the membership of the organizations in which he participated before marriage was apparently religiously mixed, with marriage his organized social life clearly shifted to the Jewish community. Having grown up in an Orthodox family, Liebeck belonged to various charitable associations and the B'nai B'rith lodge, something that we only learn about in passing in the memoir. There is also only scant information about his activities in the Verein für jüdische Geschichte und Literatur (Society for Jewish History and Literature), of which he was a co-founder:

> When the local club was founded, I immediately became a board member and a club poet. . . . The poems dedicated to the club . . . were written in a humorous style; in this sense they constituted, in a way, songs of praise to

the board members, once also to the ladies, and were the cause of enormous jubilation at the club celebrations [*Stiftungsfeste*]. With this kind of genial behavior, I attracted the members to me and my business; accordingly, I can say that next to my dear friend Birnbaum, I was one of the most popular club members.[53]

Membership in a community club was probably more appropriate to the status of a married bourgeois man than membership in a bowling club, but it becomes clear from his words that here—at least for Liebeck—the focus was less on the charitable work of the organization in question than on social life, indeed on professional and private contacts. To Liebeck, the bookkeeper, the associational life of the Jewish community provided highly desired access to the educated middle classes. He achieved his goal when he could count among his "dear friends" prominent community members like Rabbi Bamberger or Cantor Birnbaum—something he points out proudly and repeatedly in his memoirs.[54]

## VALUES AND NORMS

The skillful organization of middle-class family and social life was closely intertwined with the cultivation of respectability and education—elements often described as crucial in the development of a German Jewish bourgeoisie. George L. Mosse was the first to point out the ambiguity of these concepts for minority populations, that is, they could facilitate a higher degree of inclusion or indeed work to reinforce exclusion. Mosse stressed that *respectability* meant more than merely morality, integrity, and self-control, and individual characteristics such as bearing and physiognomy were also subjected to close scrutiny.[55] This analysis is easily confirmed by Aron Liebeck's life story. His lengthy memoirs include only two short descriptions of his own appearance—he was "of slight build, but strong," and as a young man he had "a full head of reddish hair . . . and an unassuming mustache"[56]—but the physical appearance of other characters is described with conspicuous frequency and detail, with good looks mostly, but not always, going hand in hand with a noble character. Furthermore, Liebeck seems to have given less weight to women's appearance than to the appearance of male friends and colleagues—a striking contrast to the role attribution generally held to be typical of the bourgeois world.[57] Women are described less often, in less detail, and in a strangely uniform manner. Only rarely does he comment that a woman is "interesting and pretty." Far more often, representatives of the opposite sex are characterized as being "stately" or "sweet" and frequently their features are described with diminutives, for example Liebeck's own "little woman [*kleines Weibchen*]" is portrayed as having a sweet and tiny hand (*Händchen*), a tiny mouth (*Mündchen*), and a tiny face (*Gesichtchen*).[58]

Such descriptions suggest, at least indirectly, that Liebeck might have felt physically superior to women, or at least that he felt a certain distance from them—a distance notably lacking in his portrayals of men, which are considerably more varied and often quite unusual in their choice of attributes. The men he felt close to were nearly always "beautiful people"; they were "well proportioned" and had "conspicuously attractive, manly traits" or "conspicuously lovely, pleasant features."[59] Note, for example, his description of an apprentice at Lachmanski's, who would eventually go on to have a career as an actor: "Max Behrend [was] a young man of about seventeen with a full head of jet-black hair combed back, fiery eyes contrasting strikingly with his pale complexion, a classical nose, a slim build."[60] Although such descriptions, of which there are many, seem to invite speculation about possible homoerotic bonding, I would like to stress a different aspect. By describing women and men differently, Liebeck confirms the hierarchical gender order in aesthetic terms. Men are more important, more meaningful, and even more beautiful than women; unlike women, they are physical and mental "personalities." Moreover, the "beautiful" men portrayed so lovingly by Liebeck are not described as having a military bearing. Indeed, he emphasizes quite the opposite characteristics. As Liebeck admits, the army as he had come to know it during his early days in Lötzen had always been a "place of horror" which filled him with "profound revulsion," particularly in view of the cases of ill treatment he had heard of in the Lötzen garrison.[61]

The widely accepted view among historians that a hegemonic form of military masculinity prevailed in Imperial Germany finds no support in Liebeck's memoir, suggesting that this model of masculinity had limits and had yet to permeate all parts of the East Prussian provinces. In other words, the close linking of citizenship, able-bodiedness, and masculinity that goes back to the early nineteenth century not only excluded Jewish men—to whom the rank of reserve officer, the emblematic bourgeois institution of masculinity and militarism, was still closed—but it also had a less explicit, but nevertheless significant bias toward the educated middle class and the aristocracy. Not only Jews, then, but all businessmen were seen as not "*satisfaktionsfähig* [worthy of dueling]."[62]

Clearly, not every bourgeois milieu in the empire was willing to subordinate itself to those military norms. This is shown by the growing criticism of dueling toward the end of the nineteenth century and also by a scandal that happened directly in front of Liebeck's door, so to speak, in Königsberg in 1894. There in the Börsengarten, a popular meeting place frequented by members of the bourgeoisie, an incident between a *Regierungsassessor* (young civil servant) and a Jewish businessman led to the demand for a duel. As a consequence, the establishment was boycotted by government institutions, the military, and the student fraternities.[63] The liberal commercial bourgeoisie of the city, however, supported the Jewish businessman, and Jewish as well as Christian merchants, it seems, found the militaristic attitude repellent. Consequently, Liebeck's attitude toward the military could have been rooted in both his religious background and his professional environment. What is clear is that he was no exception in his city.

Similar conclusions can be drawn from another noteworthy departure from the norms of "hard" masculinity: Liebeck's memoirs contain many instances of men "weeping bitterly" at a death, for example, and they feature men who are not ashamed to show their emotions in public. Liebeck notes his own "violent fits of tears" whenever he received the condolences of his customers after the death of his first wife.[64] Anne-Charlott Trepp and Rebekka Habermas have come across this type of "soft," emotional manliness when studying bourgeois German families of the late eighteenth century and early nineteenth, and since scholars have concluded that a *Gefühlskult* (cult of feelings) generally prevailed in bourgeois German culture in the earlier period, we might speculate that this kind of soft masculinity was still strong in some middle-class milieus in the late nineteenth century.[65]

It is certainly worth asking what, if anything, is specifically Jewish in the way Liebeck presents masculinity. The answer takes us back to the realm of aesthetics. Rather than masculine military swagger, his characters exhibit a specific form of "Jewish beauty" which, for him, combines good looks and a charisma that commands respect.[66] He describes a corn merchant, "knowledgeable only in theological matters," in the following words, which perfectly reflect Daniel Boyarin's term *Edelkayt*: Mr. Rabinowitz could have "served even Rembrandt as the model of a typically beautiful Jew: with his great stature, his noble features framed by a long, black beard, two intelligent, piercing and yet soft eyes shining behind his spectacles, everything about [him] combined to form a pleasant whole."[67]

I would argue that the most striking aspect of Liebeck's memoir is the form that he chooses for presenting his clearly distinct notion of masculinity. In spite of his rejection of the soldierly ideal as a male role model, Liebeck nevertheless sees himself as a "fighter," a role he often stresses in his autobiography and a quality he hopes to be remembered by in his (family) history. At the end of his memoirs, he writes, in the style of Goethe: "Without much ado, inscribe on my tomb: here was a man, and this means, here was a fighter."[68] The profession of bookkeeper, banal at first glance, is endowed with heroic dimensions by such statements, and Liebeck's intention, as he points out on many occasions, had always been to "succeed with honor in the momentous battle of commercial life."[69]

The concept of honor, a bourgeois male value which, as Ute Frevert has shown, was of central importance in the nineteenth century, is not clear-cut in the case of Aron Liebeck.[70] Indeed, the cultural norms of bourgeois identity have generally been defined in contradistinction to the "shallow materialism" of the financial world. To be sure, trade was the classic bourgeois occupation in the nineteenth century, and it goes without saying that property was the essential precondition for a bourgeois lifestyle, but members of the educated middle class held the "money bag" with his "petty-mindedness" in quiet contempt. "Unconstrained pursuit of gain" was seen as indecent, and ostentatious displays of one's riches were thought tasteless and disgusting. In general, this applied equally to the Christian as well as the Jewish economic bourgeoisie, but this highly charged dichotomy of bourgeois lifestyles opened up a space for anti-Semitic hostility, which Aron Liebeck certainly understood. This danger, to which every merchant was, in some measure, exposed by his occupation, could only be countered by the good bourgeois virtue of "modesty," by emphasis on a humble home and the "golden, middle path."[71] Furthermore, as a businessman, Liebeck could claim to possess the traditional concepts of professional honor—"fulfillment of duty, integrity of thought and action"[72]—and all of these words do appear often in his memoirs.

Nevertheless, his occupation as an independent bankruptcy trustee and financial consultant left him vulnerable to suspicions of dishonorable financial dealings. In one such case, the bankruptcy of one of his employers became the subject of a protracted trial and gave rise to years of coverage in the national press. Liebeck, who had been the senior bookkeeper of the business, was ultimately proven to have been "clean and honest." The immense significance that he attaches to salvaging his "good name" in this case is shown by the hundred or so pages in which he describes his work at the firm.[73] Perhaps because Liebeck's particular occupation was so precarious for the preservation of male honor, he fills his autobiography with exact details of private expenditures and income, increases in salary or rent, financial transactions and consultations, leaving out neither the price of lunch at a train station restaurant in 1882 nor the exceptionally inexpensive honeymoon in Switzerland that followed his second wedding.[74]

On the other hand, this remarkably public financial reckoning, which also includes all support given to relatives and acquaintances, stands in radical opposition not only to the bourgeois code of honor, but also to the way money was dealt with in the house of Lachmanski, an attitude that Liebeck mentions and admires. There, financial support was given in a "distinguished and discreet way"—a model which Liebeck seems to have followed to the letter, if not always in spirit. Liebeck demands that his "descendants" follow suit, and recalling his own fate, he urges above all that they support the education of "orphans and youngsters": "Also other charity work . . . should be an issue of honor for everybody who, now and in remotest times, carries my name. Only then will he continue to live in my spirit."[75] But his continuous and detailed emphasis on his "pecuniary circumstances"—despite the stigma—bears witness to the great tension that Liebeck carried within himself as a socially advancing businessman and bourgeois.

Liebeck's relationship to education, next to property the most important criterion of bourgeois distinction, reflects similar strains. Together with the description of social ascent, the implicit and explicit demonstration of education is the central thread of his literary project although, or perhaps because, as Liebeck admits, he did not possess the tangible educational credentials that were so important for the attainment of true bourgeois identity. "Since my earliest youth and until today, a secret trouble eats at me. In spite of all the efforts that I put into my continuous scholastic education, I was never able to transcend the status of an autodidact."[76] This dilemma is solved through the skillful styling of his male persona, at times reminiscent of the "helpless zeal" and the "unconditioned cultural persistence" of the *petit bourgeois*, so masterfully analyzed by Pierre Bourdieu.[77] In this way, the literary ambitions of the author who, according to his own statements, had a "purely natural, poetic vein" betray themselves over and over again in his autobiographical narrative. Especially in the first part, which is devoted to his "struggle" for social advancement, Liebeck succeeds in creating suspense in some passages by enriching them with direct speech. He also provides samples of his poetic ability by including, for example, some of the poems he dedicated to his first wife, which he saw as "partly serious, thought-provoking, partly lyrical, and glorifying her love," and which, he proudly remarks, cost him "not so much effort, but [provided] a lot of joy."[78] Furthermore, he repeatedly embellishes the descriptions of key moments in his trajectory by quoting the classics, thus making Schiller, Goethe, and Shakespeare constant witnesses to the drama of his life.[79]

Above all, Liebeck describes himself as a self-taught hero, a courageous and eager boy cut off from higher learning by external circumstances, that is, the social situation of his family. Although he had attracted early attention through his "quick perceptiveness" and "above-average achievement," he was prevented from attending *Gymnasium* (academic secondary school) first by a teacher and then by his own father. He was thus forced to vow "even then" that "throughout [his] life, he would seize every opportunity to educate himself further."[80] He reiterated this vow at various points in his life, so the chapter titled "My Self-Study" should be seen not only as the fulfillment of a childhood dream, but as the attainment of a goal that he consistently pursued. During his apprenticeship he met, for the first time, a sympathetic patron in the person of his junior boss, who recognized his "hot thirst for knowledge that could never be quenched" and provided him with books from his private library. This long-awaited access to education had enormous significance for Liebeck as can be seen from the dedication to this first benefactor, centered and underlined on the page: "Among all human beings whom I feel obliged to remember with never-ending gratitude, there will be in the first place, until my last breath, Mr. Louis Reinglass." Under his guidance, Liebeck read sometimes "feverish with excitement," sometimes "deeply touched," systematically making his way through works of high literature for the sake of—as he emphasizes over and over again—standing out "from the dull-witted crowd because of a great deal of knowledge."[81] As a young bookkeeper in Königsberg, he supplemented the knowledge acquired in this way with frequent visits to the theater, and he narrated these experiences as emphatically as the above-mentioned readings: "The moral strength in the theater flowed to the attentive spectator following the action with his heart and mind. I experienced it willingly and joyfully, as an overwhelming power. Grateful to a benevolent fate that made it possible for me to enjoy such high pleasures, I followed my inner instinct to educate myself by visiting the theater."[82]

While cultural and moral education, in Liebeck's view, were ideally combined in dramatic literature, fine art plays no role and music only a minor role in his autodidactic self-portrait. He emphasizes his "fine hearing and sense of tact," which he exercised in the Verein der Liederfreunde (Association of the Friends of Song), and his "extraordinarily deep and strong bass voice" when belting out *Kommerslieder* (drinking songs), which, according to his judgment, belonged to the "pearls of German poetic art." But generally, a concern with higher music was relegated to his daughters and sons.[83] When they surprised him at his silver wedding anniversary with an ambitious musical program, Liebeck saw "the dreams of his youth not only fulfilled, but far exceeded by reality." All of his children, with the exception of his eldest daughter, had studied at the university and were interested in "pure art"; all had become "useful members of humankind."[84] He had risen from being a poor autodidact to a provider of charity and thus was, at the end of his life, able to present himself as the patriarch of an educated and respectable middle-class family.

## A JEWISH MAN, A GERMAN *BÜRGER*

At times, Liebeck's memoirs seem almost to have been written deliberately to support the academic literature on the topic of *Bürgerlichkeit* in Germany—his story could scarcely be more germane had it been completely fabricated. With extraordinary consistency, on page after page, he cites the classic components of the "horizon of bourgeois values": using his own strength, with integrity and discipline; making the best of the assets that nature gave him; continuously working on his self-perfection; self-reliant outwardly and inwardly, yet at the same time moderate and caring toward his dependents and concerned with the general welfare. In this way, with great repetition, the Königsberg merchant presents himself in over 500 pages. In many passages, where his self-presentation appears to be strained and anxious, or where he violates unwritten codes and thus "betrays" himself to be the social climber that he is, he reminds us that he was not born with a silver spoon in his mouth and that he achieved everything through his own hard work.[85] His social ascent is the path of a small bookkeeper entering the middle class, and it also describes a common German Jewish trajectory. Generally, Jewish men experienced this ascent within the trade sector; then, their children and grandchildren received an academic education and could cross over into the typical professions of the educated middle class, and, since they were Jews, in most cases they entered the free professions.

The move from the countryside to the provincial capital was also typical for German Jews, as was a gradual abandonment of religious observance, which, in the case of Liebeck, can only be inferred or read between the lines—for example, in his move from a "ritualistically strict" to a "good Jewish" boardinghouse.[86] He never forgets to stress, however, that his "present worldview" is the result of "numerous inner struggles" and conflicts with his "Jewish-orthodox education" which, in his account, only appears marginally and mostly in negative terms. As was already noted, it was his Jewish teacher who prevented him from transferring to the *Gymnasium,* and only a short time later he regarded the "strict observance of orthodox-Jewish rituals" as responsible for his father's failure in his occupational life.[87] Instead, Liebeck's frame of reference is his town's well-to-do German Jewish middle class, the "highly esteemed" Jewish dignitaries and successful businessmen of Königsberg, who appeared to him as the "pride and adornment of the Jewish community."[88] Religiously, he seems to have been a follower of liberal Judaism, inspired by Immanuel Kant and Moses Mendelssohn, and of a humanistic culture in search of universal values.[89] His memoirs can be seen as the testimonial of a self-assured and successful Jewish man, completely lacking the inner conflict between German and Jewish identities that preoccupied such contemporaries of his as Walther Rathenau and Jakob Wassermann.

This points to two alternative ways of interpreting Liebeck's story. On one hand, it supports the distinction between the economic middle class and the educated middle class, not only, but also, as applied to German Jews. Thanks to the work of Monika Richarz, Marion Kaplan, and Shulamit Volkov, we now know a great deal about the acculturation processes of Jewish women, but similar research regarding Jewish men and masculinity is still lacking. Aron Liebeck's story, however, could provide evidence for the thesis that the great Jewish drama of modernity, the frequently observed conflict between "assimilation" and adherence to tradition, was different and less problematic for the broad mass of Jewish traders and merchants than for the academically educated men—writers or entrepreneurs, doctors or lawyers—on whose testimonies our research is so often based. Certainly the latter group, from their experiences at universities or in the army, had much greater exposure to the ideal of military masculinity— a form of masculinity that has been described as hegemonic in the German Empire—than their contemporaries in the economic bourgeoisie. We know next to nothing about the bourgeoisie's conceptions of masculinity and male identities; therefore, Liebeck's autobiography may inspire a reconsideration of the actual range and influence of this military masculinity. As has been shown, Liebeck does indeed describe his life with recourse to the contemporary ideals of manliness, heroism, and courage. Yet he skillfully adapts these traits to the requirements of his (in many ways) divergent life story. The result is a particular construction of manliness that involves, on one hand, an absolute rejection of military values and, on the other, the heroicizing of a man's role within his family and profession. Finally, what remains to be addressed is the question of whether this was a specifically Jewish constellation, or whether it reflects more general traits of the bourgeois culture of businessmen and merchants.

This interpretation refers to the great "unsimultaneity" of the Jewish bourgeoisie. On one level, Liebeck's story is a straightforward, classical account of social advancement. But when looked at in its historical context, this seems rather astonishing. Indeed, at the time of Liebeck's writing, the year 1928, the ideal bourgeois world, to which he so proudly belonged, had long been lost in a real and virtual crisis. Significantly, Liebeck's account is completely untouched by this. This absence could, of course, merely reflect the stubbornness that can come with old age, yet it also suggests that the great promise of bourgeois enlightenment, its evocation of an inclusive utopia which was so appealing to German Jews, remained symbolically powerful, even as it was being undermined in reality. That Liebeck's memoirs narrate a family story akin to the ones that have been described by Simone Lässig and Andrea Hopp for the period around the turn of the nineteenth century shows once again that the German Jewish middle class in the nineteenth century—indeed, the German middle class in general—was in no way a static social formation. The processes of social ascent were undertaken again and again, and accordingly produced new forms of masculine identity, which were much less homogeneous than the fixation on the traditions of the educated middle classes suggests. We should thus pay more attention to the dynamics, rifts, and changes that characterized the bourgeois gender order throughout the nineteenth century and attempt to put specific Jewish men's experiences into a broader perspective. Or, to put it the other way around: looking at diverse class- and culture-specific forms of masculinity forces us to question allegedly fixed assumptions in the history of German Jewry as well as the German *Bürgertum* in general, and thus highlights the necessity of further research into these areas from a gender-historical perspective.

NOTES

This chapter is based on a study published in German under the title "'Denken, Wirken, Schaffen': Das erfolgreiche Leben des Aron Liebeck," in Andreas Gotzmann, Rainer Liedtke, and Till van Rahden, eds., *Juden, Bürger, Deutsche: Zur Geschichte von Vielfalt und Differenz, 1800–1933* (Tübingen: Mohr, 2001), 369–394. I would like to thank Dr. Ingrid Laurien for translating parts of this paper and Lionel de Rothschild and Paul Lerner for their editorial help.

1. Karin Hausen, "Die Polarisierung, der Geschlechtscharaktere: Eine Spiegelung der Dissoziation von Erwerbs- und Familienleben," in Werner Conze, ed., *Sozialgeschichte*

*der Familie in der Neuzeit Europas* (Stuttgart: Klett, 1976), 363–393; Marion Kaplan, *The Making of the Jewish Middle Class: Women, Family, and Identity in Imperial Germany* (New York: Oxford University Press, 1991).

2. Aron Liebeck, "Mein Leben," unpublished typescript (Königsberg, 1928). The Leo Baeck Institute, New York, and the Germania Judaica Library, Cologne, hold copies of this work.

3. Simone Lässig, *Jüdische Wege ins Bürgertum: Kulturelles Kapital und sozialer Aufstieg im 19. Jahrhundert* (Göttingen: Vandenhoeck & Ruprecht, 2004).

4. Translating the German terms *Bürgertum, Bildungsbürgertum, Wirtschaftsbürgertum, Verbürgerlichung,* and so on presents tenacious problems which, alas, are crucial to my argumentation in this chapter. I have therefore chosen to use the German terms in some places, and in general to translate *Bürgertum* as "middle class" when I am referring to it as a social formation, and as "bourgeoisie" when I am dealing with its cultural dimensions. Of course, the two terms and their specific connotations cannot always be separated that cleanly. Equally clumsy, but nevertheless highly useful notions include "educated middle class" and "economic middle class" for *Bildungsbürgertum* and *Wirtschaftsbürgertum,* respectively.

5. David Sorkin, *The Transformation of German Jewry, 1780–1840* (New York: Oxford University Press, 1987); Shulamit Volkov, "Die Verbürgerlichung der Juden in Deutschland als Paradigma," in Volkov, ed., *Jüdisches Leben und Antisemitismus im 18. und 19. Jahrhundert* (Munich: Beck, 1990), 111–130.

6. Christina von Hodenberg, "Der Fluch des Geldsacks: Der Aufstieg des Industriellen als Herausforderung bürgerlicher Werte," in Manfred Hettling and Stefan Ludwig Hoffmann, eds., *Der bürgerliche Wertehimmel: Innenansichten des 19. Jahrhunderts* (Göttingen: 2 Vandenhoeck & Ruprecht , 2000), 79–104, quotation 79.

7. See the summary volume of the Bielefeld project: Peter Lundgreen, ed., *Sozial- und Kulturgeschichte des Bürgertums* (Göttingen: Vandenhoeck & Ruprecht, 2000). Notable exceptions are the articles of Youssef Cassis, Richard Tilly, and Patrick Fridenson in Jürgen Kocka, ed., *Bürgertum im 19. Jahrhundert,* vol. 2: *Wirtschaftsbürger und Bildungsbürger* (Göttingen: Vandenhoeck & Ruprecht, 1995), all of which deal with the economic elite; see also the works of Dieter Ziegler (editor of *Die wirtschaftsbürgerliche Elite in Deutschland im 20. Jahrhundert* [Göttingen: Vandenhoeck & Ruprecht, 2000]); and Heinz-Gerhard Haupt (*Die Kleinbürger: Eine europäische Sozialgeschichte des 19. Jahrhunderts,* ed. with Geoffrey Crossik [Munich: Beck, 1998]); and the dissertation that Andrea Hopp wrote in the context of the Frankfurt project, *Bürgertum: Jüdisches Bürgertum in Frankfurt am Main im 19. Jahrhundert* (Stuttgart: Steiner, 1997).

8. Uffa Jensen, *Gebildete Doppelgänger: Bürgerliche Juden und Protestanten im 19. Jahrhundert* (Göttingen: Vandenhoeck & Ruprecht, 2005), 20.

9. The catchy title of Manfred Hettling and Stefan Ludwig Hoffmann's article encouraged us to perceive *Bürgerlichkeit* as a cultural system: "Der bürgerliche Wertehimmel: Zum Problem individueller Lebensführung im 19. Jahrhundert," *Geschichte und Gesellschaft* 23 (1997): 333–359.

10. Ute Frevert, *Ehrenmänner: Das Duell in der bürgerlichen Gesellschaft* (Munich: Beck, 1991), 214–215.

11. See the chapter by Ben Baader in this volume, as well as Daniel Boyarin, *Unheroic Conduct: The Rise of Heterosexuality and the Invention of the Jewish Man* (Berkeley: University of California Press, 1997); Greg Caplan, *Wicked Sons, German Heroes: Jewish Soldiers, Veterans, and Memories of World War I in Germany* (Ann Arbor: University of Michigan Press, 2005); Miriam Rürup, "Jüdische Studentenverbindungen im Kaiserreich," *Jahrbuch für Antisemitismusforschung* 10 (2001): 113–137; and Christine G. Krüger, *"Sind wir denn nicht Brüder": Deutsche Juden im nationalen Krieg 1870/71* (Paderborn: 2006).

12. Liebeck, "Mein Leben," 1.

13. See Hettling and Hoffmann, "Der bürgerliche Wertehimmel"; Wilhelm Vosskamp, "Der Bildungsroman in Deutschland und die Frühgeschichte seiner Rezeption in England," in Kocka, ed., *Bürgertum*, 3:257–286.

14. The history of Jews in the East Prussian province in the nineteenth century is still relatively unknown; see, for example, Michael Brocke, Margret Heitmann, and Harald Lordick, eds., *Geschichte und Kultur der Juden in Ost- und Westpreußen* (Hildesheim: Olms, 2000); and the articles on cross-border migration in the area by Ruth Leiserowitz: "Die positive Grenzerfahrung: Jüdische Lebensläufe aus dem preußisch-litauischen Grenzgebiet," in Hans Hecker and Walter Engel, eds., *Symbiose und Traditionsbruch: Deutsch-jüdische Wechselbeziehungen in Ostmittel- und Südosteuropa* (Essen: Klartext, 2003), 111–121; and "The Traders of Wystiten: The Border as a Modernization Factor for Litvaks in Transnational Space in the 19th Century," in Jurgita Siauciunaite-Verbickiene and Larisa Lempertiene, eds., *Central and East European Jews at the Crossroads of Tradition and Modernity* (Vilnius: Center for Studies of the Culture and History of East European Jews, 2006), 319–331.

15. Liebeck, "Mein Leben," 27–28; for a general overview on working conditions and poverty in that period, see Marion Kaplan, ed., *Geschichte des jüdischen Alltags in Deutschland: Vom 17. Jahrhundert bis 1945* (Munich: Beck, 2003), 276–293.

16. Liebeck, "Mein Leben," 34–83, quotation 57.

17. Ibid., 73. For Liebeck, "scientifically" means "academically."

18. Ibid.

19. Ibid., 8.

20. See, for example, ibid., 280–281, 292, 371, 403–404.

21. Ibid., 99–100, 125, quotation 127; on Königsberg, see Stefanie Schüler-Springorum, *Die jüdische Minderheit in Königsberg/Pr. 1871–1945* (Göttingen: Vandenhoeck & Ruprecht, 1996), 43–58.

22. Liebeck, "Mein Leben," 379.

23. Ibid., 183.

24. See Heinz-Gerhard Haupt, "Kleine und große Bürger in Deutschland und Frankreich am Ende des 19. Jahrhunderts," in Kocka, ed., *Bürgertum*, 3:252–275, quotation 266.

25. The importance of personal achievement and independence are corrobated by Manfred Hettling, "Die persönliche Selbständigkeit: Der archimedische Punkt bürgerlicher Lebensführung," in Hettling and Hoffmann, eds., *Der bürgerliche Wertehimmel*, 57–78.

26. Liebeck, "Mein Leben," 128–129, 257, 340.

27. Ibid., 211, 260.

28. Ibid., 5, 136, 133.

29. Ibid., 127.

30. See Wolfgang Kaschuba, "Deutsche Bürgerlichkeit nach 1800: Kultur als symbolische Praxis," in Kocka, ed., *Bürgertum*, 3:9–44, 15–20, 29–30; and Michael Maurer, *Die Biographie des Bürgers: Lebensformen und Denkweisen in der formativen Phase des deutschen Bürgertums (1680–1815)* (Göttingen: Vandenhoeck & Ruprecht, 1996), 588–591.

31. Liebeck, "Mein Leben," 1–4, quotation 4.

32. Ibid., 219, 242.

33. Mario König, "Angestellte am Rande des Bürgertums: Kaufleute und Techniker in Deutschland und in der Schweiz 1860–1930," in Kocka, ed., *Bürgertum*, 2:220–251, 225.

34. Liebeck, "Mein Leben," 151–154.

35. Ibid., 194.

36. Ibid., 270–271, 204.

37. Karin Hausen, "'... eine Ulme für das schwankende Efeu': Ehepaare im deutschen Bildungsbürgertum: Ideale und Wirklichkeiten im späten 18. und 19. Jahrhundert," in Ute Frevert, ed., *Bürgerinnen und Bürger: Geschlechterverhältnisse im 19. Jahrhundert* (Göttingen: Vandenhoeck & Ruprecht, 1988), 85–117, quotation 88.

38. Liebeck, "Mein Leben," 200–202.

39. Ibid., 209.

40. See Hausen, "... eine Ulme für das schwankende Efeu," 88; Maurer, *Biographie des Bürgers,* 555–558.

41. Liebeck, "Mein Leben," 360–367, quotation 366–367.

42. See ibid., 383–391, 455–464, quotation 456.

43. Shulamit Volkov, "Erfolgreiche Assimilation oder Erfolg und Assimilation: Die deutsch-jüdische Familie im Kaiserreich," *Jahrbuch des Wissenschaftskolleg zu Berlin* (1982–1983): 373–387, quotation 376.

44. Liebeck, "Mein Leben," 210, 207.

45. Monika Richarz, "Geschlechterhierarchie und Frauenarbeit seit der Vormoderne," in Kirsten Heinsohn and Stefanie Schüler-Springorum, eds., *Deutsch-jüdische Geschichte als Geschlechtergeschichte: Studien zum 19. und 20. Jahrhundert* (Göttingen: Wallstein, 2006), 87–104.

46. Liebeck, "Mein Leben," 344–345, 374; see also Kaplan, *Making of the Jewish Middle Class,* 168–171.

47. Liebeck, "Mein Leben," 156, 150–151, 196; see also König, "Angestellte am Rande des Bürgertums," 230–236; Kaschuba, "Deutsche Bürgerlichkeit nach 1800," 22.

48. Liebeck, "Mein Leben," 171–172.

49. Ibid., 170–171, 179–180, 167–168.

50. Ibid., 221.

51. Ibid., 215–221, 241, 244, 259–262.

52. Ibid., 281.

53. Ibid., 353–354, see also 455.

54. Ibid., 144–146, 281, 354–356; on Bamberger's and Birnbaum's standing in the Königsberg community, see Schüler-Springorum, *Die jüdische Minderheit in Königsberg,* 108–110.

55. See George L. Mosse, "Jewish Emancipation: Between Bildung and Respectability," in Jehuda Reinharz and Walter Schatzberg, eds., *The Jewish Response to German Culture* (Hanover, NH: University Press of New England, 1985), 1–16; Volkov, "Verbürgerlichung," 111–130; Maurer, *Biographie des Bürgers,* 234–236.

56. Liebeck, "Mein Leben," 167, 231.

57. On bourgeois aesthetics in general, see Ulrike Döcker, *Die Ordnung der bürgerlichen Welt: Verhaltensideale und soziale Praktiken im 19. Jahrhundert* (Frankfurt am Main: Campus, 1994), 241; and Ute Frevert, *"Mann und Weib und Weib und Mann": Geschlechter-Differenzen in der Moderne* (Munich: Beck, 1995), 133.

58. Liebeck, "Mein Leben," 218, 26, 163, 208, 172, 188.

59. Ibid., 88, 144, 231; see also 197, 259.

60. Ibid., 177.

61. Ibid., 31–32. Liebeck's father took care of the Jewish soldiers stationed in the Lötzen garrison.

62. See Miriam Rürup, "Jüdische Studentenverbindungen im Kaiserreich," *Jahrbuch für Antisemitismusforschung* 10 (2001): 113–137; Frevert, *Ehrenmänner,* 214; and, more generally, Ute Frevert, *Die kasernierte Nation: Militärdienst und Zivilgesellschaft in Deutschland* (Munich: Beck, 2001); Christian Jansen, ed., *Der Bürger als Soldat, Die Militarisierung europäischer Gesellschaften im langen 19. Jahrhundert: Ein internationaler*

*Vergleich* (Essen: Klartext, 2004). For the debate on the concept of hegemonic masculinity, see Jürgen Martschukat and Olaf Stieglitz, *"Es ist ein Junge!": Einführung in die Geschichte der Männlichkeit in der Neuzeit* (Tübingen: Diskord, 2005), 81–93.

63. See Schüler-Springorum, *Die jüdische Minderheit in Königsberg,* 80; Frevert, *Ehrenmänner,* 288–296.

64. Liebeck, "Mein Leben," 365; see also 41–42, 118.

65. Anne-Charlott Trepp, *Sanfte Männlichkeit und selbständige Weiblichkeit: Frauen und Männer im Hamburger Bürgertum 1770–1840* (Göttingen: Vandenhoeck & Ruprecht, 1996); Rebekka Habermas, *Frauen und Männer des Bürgertums: Eine Familiengeschichte, 1750–1850* (Göttingen: Vandenhoeck & Ruprecht, 2000); Manfred Hettling, "Bürgerliche Kultur–Bürgerlichkeit als kulturelles System," in Lundgreen, ed., *Sozial- und Kulturgeschichte des Bürgertums,* 319–339, 332–333.

66. On the relationship between masculinity, male appearance, and respectability, see Mosse, "Jewish Emancipation," 6, 11. It is important to note, though, that Liebeck's form of "soft masculinity" is different in some crucial aspects—namely the focus on professional achievement—from that described by Anne-Charlott Trepp regarding the identity of early nineteenth-century middle-class men in Hamburg; see Trepp, *Sanfte Männlichkeit,* 401–402.

67. Liebeck, "Mein Leben," 215–216; also see 144.

68. Ibid., 485.

69. Ibid., 201.

70. See Frevert, *"Mann und Weib und Weib und Mann,"* 166–222.

71. See Manfred Hettling and Stefan Ludwig Hoffmann, "Zur Historisierung bürgerlicher Werte," introduction to Hettling and Hoffmann, eds., *Der bürgerliche Wertehimmel,* 7–21; Hettling, "Die persönliche Selbständigkeit"; and Hodenberg, "Der Fluch des Geldsacks."

72. Liebeck, "Mein Leben," 100.

73. Ibid., 231–339, quotation 337.

74. Ibid., 267a, 368.

75. Ibid., 153–154, 445.

76. Ibid., 391. On the importance of official education as a means of social distinction, see Peter Lundgreen, "Bildung und Bürgertum," in Lundgreen, ed., *Sozial- und Kulturgeschichte des Bürgertums,* 173–194; and Kaschuba, "Deutsche Bürgerlichkeit nach 1800," 29–34; for German Jews, see Mosse, "Jewish Emancipation"; Volkov, "Verbürgerlichung"; and Lässig, *Jüdische Wege ins Bürgertum.*

77. Pierre Bourdieu, *Die feinen Unterschiede: Kritik der gesellschaftlichen Urteilskraft* (Frankfurt am Main: Suhrkamp, 1996), 503–513, quotation 503.

78. Liebeck, "Mein Leben," 353.

79. Ibid., 16, 168–169, 240, 199, 300, 365, 381, 485.

80. Ibid., 59.

81. Ibid., 106, 120, 110, 112.

82. Ibid., 158–166, quotation 166.

83. Ibid., 170, 168.

84. Ibid., 456, 392, 444.

85. See Lässig, *Jüdische Wege ins Bürgertum,* 615–616, who argues that this type of social climber was relatively rare, even in the early nineteenth century. I would suggest, rather, that the first generation of achievers wrote less about it and we thus have fewer examples to scrutinize. When their sons and grandsons wrote family histories, they had already internalized the bourgeois standards of respectable self-representation— and this is also true for upwardly mobile families later in the century. Probably, if this

story had come down to us written by one of Liebeck's sons, it would sound completely different.

86. Liebeck, "Mein Leben," 60, 130–131, 196.
87. Ibid., 479–480, 5.
88. Ibid., 141–150, quotation 149.
89. Ibid., 130–131, 474–477.

# 5

## Performing Masculinity

### *Jewish Students and the Honor Code at German Universities*

LISA FETHERINGILL ZWICKER

In *The Loyal Subject* (Der Untertan), written between 1906 and 1914, Heinrich Mann produced a devastating satire of fraternity life. Mann's protagonist, Diederich, initially preferred to drink as a guest with a student fraternity called Neu-Teutons without formally joining them, but the members insisted that "the aim of the association of students, namely, training in manliness and idealism, could not be fully achieved by mere drinking, important as that was." It was participation in the student duels with swords that was central for this training in manliness. Thus, Diederich joined the Neu-Teutons, and since he slavishly followed the orders of others, he succeeded beautifully in the fraternity: "Everything was ordered in a loud voice, and if you followed orders you could live at peace with yourself and all the world." Diederich rejoiced in the scars on his face, which he received as a result of his duels: "His manly courage was threateningly inscribed on his countenance in the slashes which grooved his chin, streaked his cheeks, and cut their way into his closely-cropped skull. What a satisfaction it was to exhibit these constantly to everyone!" Diederich had "sunk his personality entirely in the students' *Corps* [fraternity] whose will and brain were his." As a result of his membership in the student fraternity, Diederich "was a real man, who could respect himself and who had honor because he belonged to it."[1] Yet in his obedience, he displayed the opposite of the values that fraternity men claimed to hold dear: firm independence, daring courage, and solid morality. The duel was to test a man's ability to stand up for himself and for what he believed. Instead, Mann showed how the ritual of the duel could reflect the opposite of those values: the fraternity man cravenly followed the orders of others and wilted under the pressure to take part in duels. Mann brutally exposed the hypocrisies of fraternity culture and undermined the claims of those men to embody true middle-class masculinity.

In Wilhelminian Germany, dueling fraternities dominated student life, but as the nineteenth century drew to a close, fraternity men met with a new hostility to the duel and to dueling culture.[2] In many ways, Heinrich Mann echoed the criticisms that had become common at the university. In 1902, the Catholic author Joseph von Riegger had already lampooned the fraternity ritual of the student duel in equally dramatic fashion. According to Riegger, if authorities wished to let students involved in duels go unpunished, then they should also refuse to punish young cobblers or tailors who attacked each other with their tools. Dueling culture produced men who were conceited, animalistic, brutal, mean, and immoral. Men subject to such a form of education could become only poor leaders of the German nation.[3]

During the Wilhelmine period, fraternity life and the duel were being increasingly criticized. Because of the well-organized anti-Semitic groups at universities and because Jewish students were excluded from many fraternities, historians have paid particular attention to the role of hostility against Jewish students.[4] Yet arguably the central dividing lines at universities in this period were between the dominant traditional dueling fraternities and a range of groups like the Free Students (Freistudentenschaft), Catholic students, and others who challenged the fraternities from the margins of student subculture. Jewish students could and did find their places within these battles. Certainly some Jewish students saw dueling in a similar light to Mann and Riegger. The memoir literature and the histories of Jewish dueling fraternities, however, also suggest that many Jewish students adopted the student honor code and the duel as their own, because they could use the student honor code to defend their place within student society.

This chapter examines two conflicts over honor and honorable behavior. I will consider the experiences of Jewish men in light of the competing ideas about masculinity in the context in which Jewish students lived. My aim is to create a nuanced understanding of the experience of Jewish students by highlighting the multiple areas of conflict between different groups at universities. While the universities were the sites of ugly anti-Semitism and many fraternities limited their membership to Christians, the honor code did provide opportunities for Jewish students to assert their own place within the student subculture, opportunities which were not open to devout Catholic students. Through participation in the duel, the male Jewish student could declare his honorable status, which contrasted with the position of those students who, for a variety of political, ideological, or religious reasons, did not take part in this "most German and most manly" of sports.[5] At the same time, the Jewish student who followed the honor code was also forced to face the increasingly vehement criticism of those who opposed the duel.

As a result of the work of George Mosse and Sander Gilman on the body and masculinity, historians have long noted the specific prejudices Jewish men faced in European society.[6] Discourses of race and gender shaped popular conceptions about the Jewish man, who was condemned for his alleged physical weakness and even considered unfit for the responsibilities of citizenship and military service. According to Mosse, Jews and other marginalized groups played an essential role as a "foil, projecting the exact opposite of true masculinity."[7] Defining oneself in opposition to an effeminate Other was thus at the center of the modern masculinity. Daniel Boyarin's controversial contribution to this literature described an alternate Jewish gender order, which is centered on *Edelkayt.* The ideal Jewish man, in Boyarin's reading, is the "gentle, timid, and studious male." He wants to rediscover and reclaim this "feminized Jew" and argues that "there is something correct—although seriously misvalued—in the persistent European representation of the Jewish man as a sort of woman."[8]

Evidence from the university context complicates the model of strong divisions between Jewish effeminacy and idealized Christian masculinity suggested in these works. Close attention to the academic context for Jewish-Catholic interaction indeed illustrates the fluidity of masculine norms. Although Jews did face anti-Semitism and charges of effeminacy, ideas about what constituted ideal masculinity were not clear or established. Some of the work on masculinity among educated elites has suggested that some groups embraced a form of androgynous masculinity. The research of Martina Kessel and Jens Ljunggren provides evidence that the ideal educated man was a "whole person" with the entire range of human (both male and female) characteristics.[9] He was androgynous in that he was "educated yet sensitive, energetic yet passionate, and capable of empathy." These men felt deeply, loved intensely, and understood beauty. The private sphere of family, friendship, and love was as important to them as the world of work. This form of androgynous masculinity contrasted with the masculinity of the military man, the modern entrepreneur, or the traditional artisan. By embracing a distinct set of ideas about what constituted ideal masculinity, this group of elite educated men distanced themselves from other parts of German society. Yet even among the educated elites, in the view of Kessel and Ljunggren, there was no consensus on what constituted ideal masculinity.[10]

This chapter will highlight the complex dynamics of German masculinity at universities through an examination of the German honor code as it was put into practice. Adolph Asch, the Jewish protagonist in the first incident I will describe, reacted to an insult, or performed his masculinity, in the same way that any other dueling fraternity student might have. Thus, he upheld traditional understandings of the links between the student honor code and idealized masculinity.[11] He took the side of those who dueled in the battle over masculinity and dueling culture at universities. I will also analyze a second incident in which Catholic students became involved in a dispute. Yet they did not duel and the conflict could not be resolved in accordance with the students' ideals, which emphasized manly independence and freedom. Like children appealing to parents or schoolchildren requesting help from the principal, Catholic students had to consult with the university administration in order to reestablish peace between the aggrieved groups. This resolution of the conflict was not consistent with a traditional understanding of the German honor code, to which we now turn.

## PERFORMING MASCULINITY, THE HONOR CODE, AND THE DUEL

It was the duel that enforced the student honor code and constituted the main activity of fraternities. Historically, German aristocrats and military officers had developed the duel to defend their honor against slights. By the end of the nineteenth century, students had created their own form of duel, which could take place without a specific cause or challenge, usually between members of two different fraternities. Students even had "dueling parties," in which two fraternities would meet and fight several duels. Fraternities created alliances for these dueling parties with those of a similar status and thus buttressed their reputation among students. Because the student duel had become such an important ritual within student life, universities offered practice areas and even advertised fencing teachers. Technically, these duels arranged between students were illegal, but within the academic community many believed that the duel was little different from other sports, and the regulations prohibiting duels were rarely enforced.[12]

Although university life was filled with ritual, the student duel provided a particularly rich opportunity for gendered performance. From the beginning of a challenge and the exchange of cards to the end and the duel doctor's work on the student after his duel, the entire process was scripted. In the event that a student was insulted, but it was not clear that the offense was intended, the student was to adhere to the following procedure. The injured student was to ask the student who insulted him if the offender's words were intended. If intended, the injured student was to ask for his opposite to apologize. Only when both students agreed on what had taken place, and only when the offender specifically and publicly refused to apologize could a duel be arranged. The particulars of the duel, including the type of weaponry, were then arranged through the intervention of an Honor Council, the constitution of which was determined by the universities. At the duel itself there were roles for fourteen men: the participants, one impartial arbitrator, two "seconds" who could break up the duel if necessary, two assistants to help in case swords needed to be straightened, two assistants to bring bandages or otherwise assist the duelers, two representatives of each fraternity involved in the duel, and one duel doctor. In front of all these witnesses, the duelers were to avoid showing any sign of fear. Each student was expected to wear a solemn mask of patient strength, and he who did not faced the risk of expulsion from his fraternity. Even after the duel had finished, as the duel doctor worked on the student, in some cases administering herbs so that the scar set deeply, the student was to betray no sign of pain. Throughout, the student was to show "manly" courage, and his calm silence would publicly demonstrate his fortitude. Martin Biastoch notes that for the *Corps* fraternity in Tübingen, after every dueling party, some of the pledges (candidates for full membership) had to be let go because of "unsatisfactory duels."[13]

Students not only fought practice or sport duels, but also duels of honor, which reestablished a student's reputation after an injury or slight. Students almost always fought these duels with swords rather than pistols, as opposed to the officer corps, which preferred the more deadly firearms. The members of the fraternity Franconia Corps SC in Tübingen, for example, fought 328 duels between 1871 and 1895, 40 of which were fought with heavy swords (*Säbel*) because of the serious nature of the offense, but no duels with pistols.[14] In addition to a decision about the kind of weapons involved in the duel, fraternities also had to determine if individual students could participate at all. Those deemed *satisfaktionsfähig* (literally, "able to give satisfaction") or competent to participate in this ritual were students or university graduates. Being considered *satisfaktionsfähig* was associated with honesty, courage, and honorable behavior. While membership in certain fraternities conferred this status, whole fraternities also could be declared unable to give satisfaction. As confirmation of their ability to give satisfaction, students were proud of the scars (*Schmisse*) on their faces, which they had earned through dueling and which they saw as proof of their honor, manliness, and courage. Students kept records of both the number of duels in which they participated and the number of scars that resulted from each dueling session. In the summer semester of 1902 the Germania fraternity in Jena fought eighty-four duels, members received twenty-one scars, and they made twenty-one scars on their opponents. German students' scars surprised Mark Twain, who reported, "They crisscross the face in angry red welts and are permanent and ineffaceable. Some of these scars are of a very strange and dreadful aspect."[15]

Not only the role of the scar, but also the technique of the student duel differs rather significantly from modern fencing. In the nineteenth-century student duels, the opponents remained mostly stationary and did not parry or retreat. Athletic lunges or finesse did not play a role, partly because each student was swathed in thick pads, making movement difficult. Standard duels, or sport duels, arranged without a cause or insult and called in German *Bestimmungsmensuren,* lasted fifteen minutes and were fought using weapons eighty-eight centimeters long (about thirty-five inches). The opponents stood about one meter apart with their swords in their hands and began the so-called weapon play, in which they took turns thrusting at the cheek or head of their opponent. Thrusts at other parts of the body were forbidden. Other than goggles, the students did not wear protective gear on their heads, in order to receive the scars that would reflect their manly character. Heavy silk bandages covered the arms and hands, where the combatants would absorb the thrusts of their opponents. Kevin McAleer compares the German duel unfavorably with the grace and athleticism of its French counterpart and describes the German sport as "a contest as sanguinary and brutal as it was dispassionate and robotic." In the view of the German participants in this ritual, however, the duel provided a way for the student to display the values most central in their worldview: a fearless courage in the face of an opponent and the strength to absorb blows. In the words of one fraternity man, "the outcome of a duel does not matter."[16]

It may well be that an increased emphasis on manliness and the focus on the role of the honor code compensated for the perceived loss of status for the academic class, which resulted from women's matriculation in the early twentieth century. Such arguments are consistent with the views of John C. Fout and his interpretations of the crisis of masculinity at the turn of the century.[17] Allowing women to study at universities and become doctors or teachers, in the view of some, undermined the status of the educated class. Students were the intellectual aristocracy of the German nation. The future of the German people was in their hands. They lived a life of full freedom that was allowed to no other group within German society so that they could focus all their efforts on the development of their personalities and on pursuing *Bildung* (cultivation). Because of contemporary gender norms, women could not live a life of full freedom, nor could women live outside the bounds of contemporary morality as was expected of male students.[18] It was in part the unique lifestyle of the student that helped to justify the unique honor code at universities. Women were not able to experience full freedom, and women had little to do with the honor code as it was understood at the time.[19]

The links between the honor code, the duel, and university study presented difficulties for many women students. For example, students in Göttingen elected two women as representatives of the medical faculty, and part of their duties as representatives was to wear the *Wichs* (full regalia with thigh-high boots, special jacket, and hat) of the medical faculty at university celebrations. Yet in the eyes of contemporaries, women would have looked ridiculous in *Wichs*. When this conflict became clear, the two women students were forced to resign their positions on the student council.[20] Apparently, no other suitable solution could be found. In the eyes of the university community members, the student representatives of the faculty must be able to wear the costume of the faculty. In a similar way, women could not participate in another ritual central to student life, the duel. The idea of women dueling in their long skirts or women with dueling scars was so inconceivable that it became the subject of student humor. The connections between the student, the honor code, and masculinity helped to make women second-class students at universities.[21]

## INTERPRETATIONS OF THE GERMAN
## HONOR CODE AND THE DUEL

In contemporary student imagination, honor was an essential element of university life. In his history of universities, Friedrich Paulsen wrote that the two most important aspects of honor were independence and courage: "the independence to follow one's own convictions of what is right and good and proper, not to bow to opinion because it is the dominating opinion." The honorable student also was bound by the truth: "veracity and frankness are among the things on which honor depends. . . . falsehood and breach of faith are, next to cowardice, the most disgraceful reproach."[22] While scholarship was the tangible product of university life, the honor code was supposed to discipline even those students who did not write dissertations to love truth and freedom. At universities, it was expected that students would live up to these ideals. Professors could expect complete honesty and the independence to tell the truth no matter the consequences. In university disciplinary records, rectors expressed their confidence in the absolute reliability of a student's word when he had sworn an oath.

Heinrich Mann's satire of student life would have been particularly distressing to fraternity men because Mann suggests that fraternity culture produced behavior in direct opposition to the ideals of the honor code. In *The Germans*, Norbert Elias uses the language of social science to make similar points. Elias differentiates between a "middle-class" moral system, which emphasizes "individualization" and "relative autonomy," and the "warrior strata's" honor code of the dueling fraternity with its "strict hierarchization of human relations, [and] a clear order of command and obedience."[23] Elias also stresses the ways that this "warrior code" produced an environment in which the strong were expected to dominate the weak. He argues that over the heads of all fraternity men hung the "ever present possibility of single combat," a "ubiquitous threat, which could at any time give the stronger man power over the weaker." Elias notes the attempts at reform, but nevertheless: "It was a pitiless human habitus. Basically people were brought up here to lash out hard whenever they realized they were confronted with a weaker person, making him immediately and unambiguously aware of their own superiority and his own inferiority. Not to do so was weakness and weakness was contemptible."[24]

Even the fraternity men of the nineteenth century might have admitted that there was a certain amount of painful truth in Elias's account. Some students, however, might have disagreed with Elias's analysis that the duel resulted in a display of superiority and inferiority. The deep importance of the decision to admit a student to participation in the duel would suggest that *all* who participated were seen as honorable. Fighting against a weak opponent would have done little to improve the status of the "winner." Students most admired the duelist who could show fearless courage in the face of the enemy's blows. Accordingly,

Paulsen's definition of honor, which was widely discussed in student literature, seems to be a direct refutation of Elias's characterization.

More convincing are the arguments of Peter Gay, who sees in the duel a particularly clear example of the role of violence in the nineteenth century as a whole; it was "an exercise in aggression checked by accepted rules."[25] The duel allowed the young hot-blooded student to unleash brutal violence against his fellows, but in a way that was accepted and even glorified by those around him. In this way, Gay argues, the duel was a "codification of adolescence":

> The *Mensur* [ritualized student duel] combined prohibitions and permissions, punishments and rewards, suffering and pleasure, with peculiar felicity. It provided ceremonials for establishing manliness, tests and substitutes for sexual prowess, and with its obsessively prescribed rules of procedure, a dependable framework within which youths could master the aggressive feelings that swamped them. Better still, the *Mensur* inflicted enough pain to gratify the most exacting superego.[26]

Similar to historians today, many students and academics of the nineteenth century debated the meaning of the dueling ritual. For the Jewish student, joining a dueling fraternity often proved particularly attractive. Already by becoming a university attendee, the young man had gained in status. Yet participation in a duel and the resulting dueling scar brought even greater recognition. Theodor Herzl imagined that a series of very public duels would raise the status of Jewry as a whole. In his diary Herzl detailed a fantasy in which he himself would take on the leaders of Austrian anti-Semitism and then either die heroically for his beliefs or be allowed a courtroom trial for murder, in which he could denounce anti-Semitism.[27] In a period in which ideas about what constituted ideal manliness were in flux, it may well have been particularly tempting for a Jewish young man to join with the duelers and prepare himself to participate in a ritual that *proved* his manly character and strength of purpose. In the first episode I will describe, although Adolph Asch did not actually duel, he followed the student honor code to the letter, and thereby (at least in his own view) gained status and the good opinion of those in his circle.

## ADOLPH ASCH AND THE DUEL AS DEFENSE AGAINST ANTI-SEMITISM

As a founding member of Jewish dueling fraternities and the author of a history of Jewish fraternities, Asch was particularly committed to the fraternity honor code.[28] Although Jewish fraternities remained small in size during the empire, they played an important role in the history of Jewish defense organizations. After the increase in anti-Semitism of the early 1880s, Jews began to form their own dueling fraternities, and by the 1890s Jewish dueling groups at five universities joined together to create a nationwide federation, the Kartell-Convent (KC), and to establish a network of alumni organizations similar to other fraternity federations.[29] By the early twentieth century, Jewish fraternities were well established at several German universities, including Berlin, Breslau, Würzburg, and Munich, and had even formed dueling contracts with other fraternities, a sign of their integration within student life.[30]

While groups of Jewish students had formed organizations in the past, this was the first time that they defined their organization specifically as Jewish and accepted only Jewish members. At the same time, they proclaimed their membership in the German nation. One alumnus declared in 1905, "[W]e will not allow one iota of our Germanness to be robbed from us!"[31] For the members of Jewish fraternities, it was culture that formed the nation. As one KC member explained, "[I]f blood made the German nation, then it would be split into 20 pieces." Instead, "land, language, art, education, literature, and common plans for the future—these make up the nation."[32] In the first issue of their newspaper, members of the Jewish fraternity in Breslau compared their own origins to that of the river Oder. Although the Oder has its source in Polish Russia, "who would have the courage to claim that Breslau and its Oder are un-German? [Are these origins] an obstacle to becoming the proudest German possession? No!"[33]

Jewish fraternities defended Jewish students against anti-Semitism at the universities and were especially visible in moments of heavy conflict. Their leaders, such as Benno Jacob, Leo Loewenstein, and Ludwig Hollaender, went on to play important roles in Jewish defense organizations during both the empire and the Weimar Republic. In addition to providing a forum in which students could practice dueling and defend their honor, the fraternities also offered instruction in the more subtle arts of carriage, speech, and behavior, aiming to create the ideal German Jewish man. One of the founders asked rhetorically: what is the ideal of the Jewish fraternity federation? "It is the education of the German-Jewish student to be a man and to assert and protect himself his whole life long as a man, as a Jew, and as a German."[34]

Fraternities also embedded the young, upwardly mobile student within Jewish society. These organizations offered numerous opportunities for professional development and helped to tie the Jewish student more closely to the Jewish community. One Jewish fraternity student, Julius Frank, reported that he was first drawn to the Salia at Würzburg when three elegantly dressed active members, with capes and sashes, appeared at his high school graduation ceremony and attentively recruited him.[35] Members also found wives through their fraternity contacts.[36] A wide range of Jewish leaders attended the 1914 celebrations for the twentieth anniversary of the federation of Jewish fraternities, including important Jews who were active in the political, religious, and economic life of the Jewish community and German society.[37] The attendance of such a diverse group within the Jewish community at a KC event testifies to the importance of the KC.

Jewish community leaders had long avoided forming specifically Jewish organizations because they believed these organizations might draw the attention of anti-Semites. However, Jewish fraternities broke this rule, and they set precedents for a generation of associations that publicly advertised the union of German national and Jewish identities.[38] In the two decades after the founding of the Jewish fraternities, other specifically Jewish organizations emerged. Most important for the history of the German Jewish community were the efforts of 200 Jewish leaders who, in 1893, came together to fight anti-Semitism and form a new organization, the Central Association of German Citizens of Jewish Faith (Centralverein deutscher Staatsbürger jüdischen Glaubens), in which Jewish fraternity alumni played an important role.[39] As I will show, Adolph Asch also saw himself engaged in the fight against anti-Semitism in his personal life.

Asch recorded in his memoirs that shortly after he had moved to Schneidemühl in Posen as an unpaid candidate for the civil service (*Referendar*), he began to spend time at the beer hall on the town square. Every day at lunch, Asch sat with other members of his social class at a regulars table (*Stammtisch*). From the start he suspected that some of the locals at his *Stammtisch* might have anti-Semitic views, concerns that he ended up discussing on an excursion of the Social Sciences Association of the Posen Academy. At the conclusion of the day, a Professor Dibelius, his neighbor on the train, invited Asch to spend time with him in Rauschen, a spa town near Königsberg. Asch agreed. When they were alone together in Rauschen, Dibelius said, "I am an alumnus and founder of the [anti-Semitic] Union of German Students." Asch responded, "[A]nd I am an alumnus of the K.C." Dibelius then explained, "I knew this and that is why I invited you. I observed you in the train and saw that you opened an invitation from the K.C."[40] Dibelius and Asch then spent the rest of the day together in deep and intense discussions of the "Jewish question." Dibelius professed an admiration for the aggressive defense against anti-Semitism practiced by the Jewish fraternities. In the matter of Asch's presence at the *Stammtisch* in Posen, Dibelius even assured Asch that his "mistrust [was] surely unwarranted. You can certainly continue to eat in the restaurant together with the other *Akademikern* [university graduates]." In this section of his memoir, Asch emphasizes his own openness and fairness; he was even willing to discuss the so-called Jewish question with someone who had founded an anti-Semitic organization. This introductory material then frames the following section in which Asch describes a conflict over honor.

Back in Schneidemühl, Asch continued to eat his lunch at the beer hall with other university graduates. One day as he was sitting with other men in his social circle he heard fellow *Referendar* Kuenzel lean over and ask a neighbor, "You aren't perhaps a Jew in disguise [*verkappter Jude*]?" Asch remembered that he waited until Kuenzel got up to go to the washroom; then, Asch approached him and asked, "When you used the words 'Jew in disguise' were you referring to me?" Kuenzel responded: "You may interpret my words however you would like." Asch replied, "Have at least the courage to take responsibility for what you have said." As Kuenzel was a former fraternity man, he naturally felt that his honor had been injured and stammered, "courage . . . ," and declared finally: "Yes, of course I meant you." With the words "I have heard enough," Asch left the restaurant immediately to telegraph his fraternity brother Max Cohn. It was necessary, wrote Asch, that Max come to Schneidemühl because of a matter of honor.[41]

At this point Asch was not sure if Kuenzel would demand a duel with light swords, heavy swords, or pistols. Although Asch had considerable experience with swords, he feared that his opponent would demand a battle with pistols. It was up to the newly constituted Honor Council to make the decision about the choice of weapon and to interview both parties, who swore on their honor to tell the entire truth regarding the incident. Included in the Honor Council was one of Asch's fraternity brothers, two members of the local *Stammtisch,* and one of Schneidemühl's *Gerichtsassessoren* (law students appointed as court officials after passing their second examination). After both Kuenzel and Asch separately described the details of what had taken place, the members of the Honor Council brought together the protagonists and explained that they had heard both testimonies and would consider what steps to take next. At the conclusion of the formalities there was some confusion as Kuenzel and Asch left the room, because both were politely trying to give the other the privilege of exiting first.[42]

Asch was then called back to the Honor Council and was told that in fact Kuenzel had not been referring to Asch when he made his comment. When Asch explained that Kuenzel had provided a different account earlier, the chairman of the Honor Council snapped, "The word of honor of your opponent is as valid as yours," to which Asch replied, "Of course, he has now spoken the truth." To conclude the incident, Asch asked for the following stipulations:

1. That *Referendar* Kuenzel revoke his statement
2. That Asch was correct in his assumption that he was welcome at the *Stammtisch*
3. That the members of the *Stammtisch* would be informed of the results of the Honor Council

Kuenzel accepted all of these conditions. Asch explained that he believed that he was acting in a correct manner and that "it became particularly clear that my behavior was perceived as appropriate when already on the day after the Honor Council had met, the city's prosecutor and the judge made clear attempts to greet me first and with special respect when I passed them in the street." Asch claimed that "the matter had been resolved in a way that was honorable for both sides," although in the history of the KC published in 1964 he also noted that he chose not to attend the *Stammtisch* again.[43] Asch had been vindicated in front of all the most important members of the community of Schneidemühl. He had shown courage and refused to accept an insult against the Jewish people as a whole. In this way he had defended not only himself, but also all his Jewish relations and friends. Asch's adherence to the academic honor code buttressed his belief in himself as a worthy member of the educated elite and an exemplary German man.

## CATHOLIC STUDENTS AND THE PROBLEM OF THE HONOR CODE

In contrast to Jewish students, most faithful Catholic students did not duel. As early as 1869 the leadership of the Catholic Church had declared absolute opposition to all forms of the duel, including the student duel with swords. By 1890 the church asserted that the Catholic who participated in a duel risked excommunication.[44] Catholic fraternities and associations emerged at universities to protect the Catholic faithful from the secular university environment and from the pressure to duel. Although dueling fraternities dominated student life, the Catholic associations grew considerably over the course of the empire, and by 1905 they were some of the largest student organizations. In Prussia about 30 percent of Catholic students joined Catholic student fraternities and associations.[45] Arguably, the rapid growth of the Catholic fraternities resulted in part from the intense focus on the duel in much of student life. Thus, by the eve of World War I, Catholic fraternities and associations increasingly elaborated a model of masculinity that defined itself in opposition to dueling culture. For the members of these organizations, independence and courage meant standing against the ritual of the duel. The men of Catholic fraternities held their values strongly and openly. Theirs were the sturdy shoulders that could bear the burden of the challenges faced by the church. Their masculinity was based on determination and loyalty.

Although not all Catholics opposed the duel to the same extent as the official organizations of the church, the conflict over the duel and the duel's association with masculinity deepened the divide between faithful Catholics and non-Catholics at universities.[46] Some dueling fraternity men saw direct links between the limitations that the Catholic Church imposed on students' academic freedom and Catholic students' refusal to duel.[47] Catholic men, it was argued, did not stand up for themselves in a manly defense of their intellectual independence, and they could not physically defend themselves in the duel. The differences between the constructions of masculinity presented by Catholic fraternity leaders and by dueling fraternities thus helped make confessional peace more difficult to attain. Despite the growing differences between Catholics and non-Catholics, it is nevertheless important to note, as Ute Frevert's work has demonstrated, that many Catholics did participate in duels. Moreover, some of the strongest opponents of the duel were non-Catholic leftist Liberals and Social Democrats.

In order to better understand the consequences of a principled refusal to take part in duels, I will discuss a conflict between the singing association Arion and the Catholic student fraternity Rappolstein. On 30 April 1895 in Strasbourg, Arion member Theodor Messerschmidt remembered that early in the morning of the same day, at about 1:30 AM, he had been the last to leave a local bar with a few of his fraternity brothers. As an officer in the organization he had paid the bill for the group. Until this point, he noted, all had been in a very good mood, but then, as a prank, some members of the Catholic fraternity Rappolstein, who had climbed onto the roof of the bar, decided to use the walkway as a latrine. Messerschmidt reported, "Urine was on us, running over our hats, jackets, etc. At first we began to yell. The gentlemen then disappeared very quickly; they did not approach us as one might expect in order to apologize." And it was an apology that Messerschmidt sought. Instead, several other members of the Catholic Rappolstein and a fellow Catholic fraternity, the Badenia, came to talk to the insulted Arion members, but still "not a single one of these gentlemen found it necessary to provide even the smallest word of apology."[48]

As was clear in his statement, Messerschmidt wanted some expression of regret, and the student honor code also held that the Rappolsteiners either should have apologized or should have arranged a duel. But as members of a Catholic fraternity, they could not duel, and the evidence suggests that they also wished to avoid apologizing. So the Rappolsteiners tried to steer clear of Arion members. The university records include some eight pages describing in detail Messerschmidt's attempts to gain an apology. Until early in the morning Messerschmidt searched for the Rappolsteiners who had been involved in this incident to give them the opportunity or to force them to apologize. Through Strasbourg's streets and parks the two groups circled each other. Messerschmidt became angrier and angrier. At the same time, he tried to keep the two groups of fraternity brothers separated in order to avoid a general brawl. There was more back and forth between the singing Arion members and the Catholic Rappolsteiners. They debated what had taken place. Messerschmidt suggested that a matter of honor was at stake because either one side or the other was misrepresenting the facts—and the different interpretations required a duel. One Catholic Rappolsteiner responded, "At 2 in the morning there is no such thing as word of honor [*Ehrenwort*]."[49] If this incident had involved non-Catholics, it seems probable that there would have been an exchange of cards in order to arrange a duel.

Instead, the evening ended with violence that was not regulated by the honor code. Messerschmidt pushed a Rappolsteiner named Criqui and knocked his cap off his head. If intentional, it was a sign that Messerschmidt aimed at humiliating Criqui. In the official proceedings that resulted from the incident, Messerschmidt denied boxing Criqui on the ears as "out of the question. If the gentleman's cap fell down while he was pushed, I could not say." Because of the violence, Messerschmidt presented himself to the rector to accept any punishment required. The rector then took the statements of the involved parties and tried to piece together the course of events. In his notes, the rector seemed to have been particularly concerned whether Messerschmidt boxed Criqui's ears and whether Messerschmidt intentionally pushed off Criqui's cap. The rector wrote:

> He [Messerschmidt] denied boxing Criqui on the ears. . . . the cap, though, could have fallen down. He seemed to remember that Criqui bent forward to the ground. In any case, however, he—Messerschmidt—never aimed at knocking off Criqui's cap. He was quite ready to state that he did not have the slightest intention to give Mr. Criqui a box on the ears.[50]

Rather than punishing either party, the rector negotiated a joint statement that both Messerschmidt and Criqui signed. The particulars were explained as follows:

> The [Catholic] Rappolsteiners acknowledge that one of their members provoked Messerschmidt and did not apologize quickly enough; therefore the Arion declare—in the presence of the university secretary—their regret without reservation.
> The Arion acknowledge and regret that on this evening things got out of hand and that they resorted to physical violence.[51]

The conflict thus ended with the apology that Messerschmidt had sought from the beginning, this time with the official stamp of university authorities. The tone of the rector's correspondence provides further evidence that Messerschmidt's pursuit of an apology was the accepted and appropriate way of dealing with this incident. A box on the ears or the knocking off of a cap was of great symbolic import. The time and energy the rector and the academic senate spent on this dispute, trying to understand the particulars, demonstrates the significance of conflicts over honor.

## JEWISH STUDENTS, CATHOLIC STUDENTS, AND THE HONOR CODE

One aspect of these affairs that strikes the modern observer is the formalistic way in which students resolved these disputes. In the first case, an Honor Council had to be formed, which had its own specific rules and procedures.

The council negotiated a statement that was presented to the *Stammtisch* members. In the second case, each participant had to sign an official document and affirm that he shared the rector's interpretation of the events. These episodes, furthermore, show clearly the ways that masculinity was "performed." In the first incident, events followed the script determined by the honor code; in the second, events deviated from that script and required the intervention of higher authorities.

The complexities involved in the resolution of these conflicts underscore the differences between the student and the nonstudent communities. The knowledge concerning the proper formation of an Honor Council or concerning the significance of the fraternity man's cap was the common property of Germany's "intellectual aristocracy," knowledge that Jewish students could fully share with their fellow students who were Christians. As befitting elites engaged in a common intellectual endeavor, students from different backgrounds interacted with other students as equals. Even the privileged *Burschenschaft* discussed the importance of equality and published articles that asked "are we not also guilty" of not treating all equally?[52] Arnold Ruge, the author of a turn-of-the-century book on student life, claimed:

> The student recognizes within his milieu no differences of rank [*Standesunterschiede*]. No one asks whether a student's father is an artisan or a government minister, one is simply a student. If he has a larger or a smaller monthly allowance, this does not alter his standing among his fellows. These are not the standards of value that one is accustomed to in practical life. If he is Christian, if Catholic or Protestant, or if he is a Jew, he is a student and that's that.[53]

While Professor Ruge's views may not have reflected the reality of student life, it is important to recognize that most students would have been aware of the ideal of the equality of all those who studied. In theory, the highly ritualized resolution of conflicts at universities could provide a means of integrating students from nontraditional backgrounds into university life. Common knowledge of the rules of university life could help make the Jewish or Catholic student feel connected to and part of the university community.

It was important, however, that all students took part in these rituals. The academic code of honor encompassed both the dignity of the individual and the reputation of the group. Each student bore the responsibility of defending his own independence, honesty, and courage, but at the same time, in acting in his own interest, he enhanced the reputation of the university community as a whole. Catholics' rejection of the duel complicated the already intricate rules of the student honor code. By not participating in the dueling ritual Catholic students were both failing in their duty as individuals to defend their own dignity and also injuring the honor of students as a whole, at least in the view of those who embraced dueling culture. In the second incident I have described, rather than offering a manly defense of their own interests or displaying courage in the duel, students were forced to appeal to a higher authority. Those involved might well have linked the Catholic students' refusal to duel with other areas where the Catholic student did not show manly courage. Students also used the term "manly courage [*Mannesmut*]" to describe the character traits required in the intellectual "battles" of university seminars. In following the teachings of the church, it was argued, the Catholic student did not show the intellectual independence necessary for the academic man.

Concern about Catholics and the duel only increased in the early twentieth century when waves of anti-Catholicism and hostility to the Catholic Center Party hit Germany.[54] Fraternities took the lead in anti-Catholic and anti–Center Party activism, and in 1904 the editors of one student newspaper argued that the "battle against the [Catholic] Center Party is the most difficult and the greatest political task of the present. . . . the fate of Germany depends on our ability to wrest ourselves from the grip of the ultramontane."[55] While Catholic students' refusal to duel exacerbated the prejudices they already faced, Jewish students, by contrast, took advantage of the rules of the academic honor code to defend their own place within student social hierarchies. The complex rules involved in redressing a slight, it could be argued, actually created more opportunities for members of minorities to assert their own dignity and honor. With the processes already in place and the rules known to all, the student needed no special contacts or high status to protect himself. Furthermore, through the duel itself the anti-Semite acknowledged the dignity and the worth of his Jewish opponent.

It is still necessary to ask, however: to what extent was the result of the procedure accepted by all? As we have seen, Adolph Asch claimed that the next day the judge and other notables greeted him with special respect, but at the same time, he did not return to the *Stammtisch*. Asch was a founding member of and chronicler of Jewish fraternities and was particularly committed to the academic honor code. Thus he might have been tempted to exaggerate the effectiveness of the duel as a means to defend Jewish honor. In his history of Jewish fraternities, Asch wrote that the founding of the KC had a particularly dramatic impact on reducing anti-Semitism, and he claimed that in the period from 1904 to 1914 in Breslau, "times had changed. Open vulgar anti-Semitism had ended thanks to the dashing and tireless battles of the [Jewish fraternity] Viadrina."[56] The information about the incident described above comes from Asch's memoirs, which, as Miriam Gebhardt has shown, often downplay anti-Semitism. Gebhardt has argued that historians should be aware that the writing of an autobiography involves processes of forgetting.[57] Yet even if we do not take Asch's account at face value, it still is important to consider the larger context of university life and the dynamic and fluid definitions of masculinity at universities and within German society in general. The views of convinced anti-Semites would change little as a result of a few duels. Dueling culture, however, did provide new opportunities for Jewish men to use gendered rituals to assert their own masculinity.

The proper settlement of disputes allowed for the participation only of men and only of those who had passed the demanding *Abitur* (exam for entrance to the university), about 1 percent of the German population during the empire. The number of men who were considered *satisfaktionsfähig* further narrowed the pool. They were members of an elite group who saw themselves as the future leaders of the German people and the embodiment of all that was best in German culture. At a time when women were entering universities and becoming doctors or teachers, the stress on the honor code as part of academic citizenship reinforced traditional gender hierarchies. Dueling culture as an avenue to status and prestige was fully closed to women.[58]

It was in part through the elaborate performances that have been discussed here, through tests of courage like the duel, that the boys who entered the university became German men. Anti-Semites certainly tried to restrict the participation of Jews in the dueling rituals, and anti-Semitic pressure meant that Jewish students could not become members of most fraternities.[59] Anti-Semites, however, were not successful in excluding Jews from dueling, and thus young Jewish men gained access to this ritual that symbolized ideal manliness in the eyes of many. It is certainly true that some anti-Semites called the masculinity of some (or, in certain cases, all) Jewish students into question, but it is also important to remember the larger context: devout Catholics were accused of lacking manly independence, some elite fraternity members of lacking manly self-control, the bookish students of lacking physical strength, and the sensitive "whole man" of lacking manly determination. As we have seen, contemporaries disagreed about the relationship of the duel and ideal masculinity. Mann and Riegger argued that the dueling student could be considered the opposite of the ideal man: arrogant, brutal, craven, and immoral. In contrast, in the view of Paulsen, the dueling student was firm, strong, courageous, and moral.

In his strict adherence to the German academic honor code, Adolph Asch could claim for himself a form of exemplary, courageous, and honorable masculinity that represented one of the different and competing models of masculinity in academic life. Through his membership in a German dueling fraternity, Asch had many opportunities to perform this type of masculinity he had opted for. On Sunday afternoons in Breslau, where the first Jewish fraternity was founded, male students in full dress paraded down Schweidnitzer Street and flirted with the ladies. Most fraternity men would have recognized the colored sash of each group; it was an open declaration: "We are Jewish. We are strong men. We are proud Germans." In his history of Jewish student organizations, Asch described the founding generation as "young men, but really men!" Peter Gay has persuasively argued, "A *Schmiss* [scar] on the face of a Jewish student had a particular poignancy: the scar was a symptom of defense, a proof of bravery, an assertion of equal status and manly self-respect."[60] Men such as the Jewish fraternity member Friedrich Solon wrote in their memoirs that membership in a Jewish fraternity had strengthened and solidified their Jewish identities.[61] The model of masculinity that Asch and other Jewish fraternity men embraced, however, was strongly informed by traditional student dueling culture and Protestant bourgeois norms. Men like Asch then made this model their own and also made it "Jewish" through the culture of their fraternity.

Michael Gross begins his book on anti-Catholicism with the provocative claim that "for obvious and irrefutable reasons, anti-Judaism in the nineteenth century and particularly anti-Semitism after the 1870s has received considerable attention from historians of modern Germany . . . yet the nineteenth century in Germany with its particular confessional divide, modern rationalizing culture, and secularizing social currents was arguably more a century of anti-Catholicism."[62] I would not go that far in describing the student subculture for the period of my study because in comparison to other parts of German life, anti-Semites had a particularly strong foothold at universities. It is important, however, to study the experiences of Jews and anti-Semitism in the larger context of social and political life. Standards of masculinity were used against Jewish men, but they were also used at various points against other groups within German society. Despite the ugly efforts of anti-Semitic agitators among students, men like Adolph Asch could employ the standards of masculinity and the honor code of student duel culture to defend themselves and other Jews against anti-Semitic insults.

NOTES

1. Heinrich Mann, *The Loyal Subject,* trans. Ernest Boyd, with a new portion trans. Daniel Theisen (London: Continuum, 1998), 18, 20, 24.

2. Ute Frevert, *Ehrenmänner: Das Duell in der bürgerlichen Gesellschaft* (Munich: Beck, 1991), 234–240; Peter Gay, *The Cultivation of Hatred* (New York: Norton, 1993), 17; Hans-Ulrich Wipf, *Studentische Politik und Kulturreform: Geschichte der Freistudenten-Bewegung 1896–1918* (Schwalbach: Wochenschau, 2004), 83–85; "Das Duell und der germanische Ehrbegriff," *Academia* 8, no. 12 (10 April 1896): 360–366; "Neues vom Duell," *Burschenschaftliche Blätter* 4, no. 11 (15 November 1896): 103; "Zur heutigen Mensurpraxis," *Burschenschaftliche Blätter* 5, no. 12 (1 December 1897): 131; "Burschenschaft und Mensur," *Burschenschaftliche Blätter* 11, no. 12 (1 March 1898): 289; "Die Leipziger Zweikampf gegen-Versammlung," *Burschenschaftliche Blätter* 3, no. 16 (1 November 1901): 56; "Zur Philosophie des Duells," *Academia* 6, no. 16 (15 October 1903): 169–171; E. H. Eberhard, "Die Anti-Duellbewegung und die deutsche Studentenschaft," *Academische Monatshefte* 10, no. 27 (1 February 1910): 334–336. On criticism of fraternity life by the Social Democrats, see "Numerus Clausus für ausländischen Studenten," *Burschenschaftliche Blätter* 2, no. 18 (15 October 1913): 335.

3. Joseph Riegger, *Das Duell* (Saugau: self-published, 1902). Excerpts of Riegger appeared in the newspaper of the *Corps,* "Von den deutschen Hochschulen," *Academische Monatshefte* 11, no. 14 (1 March 1903): 395.

4. Helmut Berding, *Moderner Antisemitismus in Deutschland* (Stuttgart: Suhrkamp, 1992), 26–37; Amos Elon, *The Pity of It All: A History of Jews in Germany* (Cambridge: Metropolitan, 2002), 216–220; Nortker Hammerstein, *Antisemitismus und die deutschen Universitäten 1871–1933* (Frankfurt: Campus, 1995); Konrad Jarausch, *Students, Society, and Imperial Politics: The Rise of Academic Illiberalism* (Princeton, NJ: Princeton University Press, 1982), 265, 271–274, 292–294, 355–356; Norbert Kampe, "Jews and Antisemites at Universities in Imperial Germany (I): Jewish Students: Social History and Social Conflict," *Leo Baeck Institute Yearbook* 30 (1985): 357–395; Kampe, "Jews and Antisemites at Universities in Imperial Germany (II): The Friedrich-Wilhelms-Universität of Berlin: A Case Study on the Students' Jewish Question," *Leo Baeck Institute Yearbook* 32 (1987): 43–102; Kampe, *Studenten und "Judenfrage" im deutschen Kaiserreich: Die Entstehung einer akademischen Trägerschicht* (Göttingen: Vandenhoeck & Ruprecht, 1988); Marion Kaplan, *The Making of the Jewish Middle Class: Women, Family, and Identity in Imperial Germany* (Oxford: Oxford University Press, 1991), 158; Jacob Katz, *From Prejudice to Destruction: Antisemitism, 1700–1939* (Cambridge, MA: Harvard University Press, 1980), 260–272; Karsten Krieger, ed., *Berliner Antisemitismusstreit 1879–1881: Eine Kontroverse um die Zugehörigkeit der deutschen Juden zur Nation* (Munich: Saur, 2003), 744–749, 764–769; Albert S. Lindemann, *Esau's Tears: Modern Anti-Semitism and the Rise of the Jews* (Cambridge: Cambridge University Press, 1997), 132–142; Michael A. Meyer, ed., *Integration in Dispute 1871–1918* (New York: Columbia University Press, 1996), 204–220; Oskar Scheuer, *Burschenschaft und Judenfrage: Der Rassenantisemitismus in der deutschen Studentenschaft* (Berlin, 1927), 38–43; Thomas Schindler, *Studentischer Antisemitismus und jüdischer Studentenverbindungen 1880–1933* (Erlangen: Selbstverlag der Studentengeschichtlichen Vereinigung, 1988); Shulamit Volkov, "Antisemitism as a Cultural Code," *Leo Baeck Institute Yearbook* 23 (1978): 41–43. For my views on anti-Semitism at universities, see Lisa Swartout, "Facing Antisemitism: Jewish Students at German Universities, 1890–1914," *Simon Dubnow Institute Yearbook* 3 (2005): 149–165. See also my book on students and politics: Lisa Fetheringill Zwicker, *Dueling Students: Conflict, Masculinity, and Politics, 1890–1914* (Ann Arbor: University of Michigan Press, 2011).

5. The duel as "most manly" of sports is from Curt Müller, *Couleurstudenten!?!* (Leipzig, 1893), 8.

6. George Mosse, *Nationalism and Sexuality: Middle Class Morality and Sexual Norms in Modern Europe* (Madison: University of Wisconsin Press, 1985); Sander Gilman, *The Jew's Body* (New York: Routledge, 1991); Klaus Hödl, *Die Pathologisierung des jüdischen Körpers: Antisemitismus, Geschlecht und Medizin im Fin-de-Siècle* (Vienna: Picus, 1997).

7. George L. Mosse, *The Image of Man: The Creation of Modern Masculinity* (Oxford: Oxford University Press, 1996), 6; Mosse, *The Crisis of German Ideology: Intellectual Origins of the Third Reich* (New York: Schocken, 1981), 196–199.

8. Daniel Boyarin, *Unheroic Conduct: The Rise of Hetereosexuality and the Invention of the Jewish Man* (Berkeley: University of California Press, 1997), 3.

9. Martina Kessel, "The 'Whole Man': The Longing for a Masculine World in Nineteenth-Century Germany," *Gender and History* 15 (2003): 1–31; Jens Ljunggren, *Känslornas krig: Första Världskriget och den tyska bildningselitens androgyna manlighet* (Stockholm: Scandia. Tidskrift för historisk forskning, 2004).

10. See Kessel, "The 'Whole Man,'" 2, 6, 8, 22.

11. Christian Helfer, "Formen und Funktion studentischen Brauchtums im 19. Jahrhundert," in Otto Neuloh and Walter Rüegg, eds., *Student und Hochschule im 19.*

*Jahrhundert* (Göttingen: Vandenhoeck & Ruprecht, 1975), 348. More recent conflicts over interpretations of the duel include Frevert, *Ehrenmänner;* and Kevin McAleer, *Dueling: The Cult of Honor in Fin-de-Siècle Germany* (Princeton, NJ: Princeton University Press, 1994), 119–158; for McAleer's criticism of Frevert, see 197–209. See also Frevert's review of McAleer in *Journal of Modern History* 69 (1997): 630. Hans-Ulrich Wipf stresses the pressure faced by those who chose not to duel. Wipf, *Studentische Politik und Kulturreform,* 85. Peter Gay introduces his book *Cultivation of Hatred* with an in-depth discussion of the duel, 9–33. See also Jarausch, *Students,* 244–246; Silke Möller, "Studienzeit als prägende Lebensphase: Organisierte und nichtorganisierte Studenten im Kaiserreich," in Harm-Hinrich Brandt, ed., *Der Burschen Herrlichkeit: Geschichte und Gegenwart des studentischen Korporationswesen* (Würzburg: Schöningh, 1998), 416–419; Karsten Bahnson, "Vorgeschichte und Gründung des Kösener Senioren-Convents-Verbandes," in Rolf-Joachim Baum, ed., *Wir wollen Männer, wir wollen Täten! Deutsche Corpsstudenten 1848 bis heute* (Berlin: Siedler, 1998) 45–83; Friedrich Kluge and Werner Rust, eds., *Deutsche Studentensprache* (Leipzig, 1895), 2:42–46.

12. Helfer, "Formen und Funktion studentischen Brauchtums," 350; Kurt Graeser, *Für den Zweikampf: Eine Studie* (Berlin, 1902); "Die Stellungsnahme des Strafgesetzentwurfs zum Zweikampf," *Burschenschaftliche Blätter* 4, no. 24 (15 November 1909): 78; Frevert, *Ehrenmänner,* 152, 256; Martin Biastoch, *Tübinger Studenten im Kaiserreich: Eine sozialgeschichtliche Untersuchung* (Sigmaringen: Thorbecke, 1996), 199; Biastoch, *Duell und Mensur im Kaiserreich am Beispiel der Tübinger Corps Franconia, Rhenania, Suevia und Borussia zwischen 1871 und 1895* (Vierow: SH, 1995), 9, 15–16; Jarausch, *Students,* 244; McAleer, *Dueling,* 120–127; Zwicker, *Dueling Students,* ch. 2.

13. Biastoch, *Duell und Mensur,* has the best description of the complexities of the student duel, 21–27. On the problem of "unsatisfactory duels," see "Über Mensurbeurteilung," *Burschenschaftliche Blätter* 1, no. 25 (1 April 1911): 9. High numbers of the *Burschenschaft* members of Franconia in Berlin were let go because of this problem. See Paul Weinrowsky, *Geschichte der Berliner Burschenschaften Franconia zum 50 Stiftungsfest, 1878–1928* (Berlin, 1928); Bernhard Schroeter, *Leben und Streben dem Vaterland: Die Geschichte der Burschenschaft Germania zu Jena Teil 1 Kaiserreich, Weimarer Republik und Drittes Reich* (Göttingen: KWD, 1996), 125–127, 142; Frevert, *Ehrenmänner,* 150; Gay, *Cultivation of Hatred,* 31; "Die heutige Mensur und ihren Folgen," *Burschenschaftliche Blätter* 9, no. 12 (1 February 1898): 228; Friedrich Schulze, *Die Fechtkunst mit dem Hau-Rapier* (Heidelberg, 1885); McAleer, *Dueling,* 142–144; Möller, "Studienzeit," 417; Walter Bloem, *Der krasse Fuchs* (Leipzig: Vita, 1906), 158–160; Fritz Jaeckel, *Geschichte der Burschenschaft Germania zu Greifswald 1861–1924* (Greifswald: Abel, 1924), 117.

14. Biastoch, *Tübinger Studenten,* 139.

15. Schroeter, *Leben und Streben dem Vaterland,* 133; Biastoch, *Duell und Mensur,* 28; Mark Twain, *A Tramp Abroad,* ed. Charles Neider (New York: Harper & Row, 1977), 36. Twain's book contains accurate descriptions of dueling culture; see chs. 4–7. See also Gay, *Cultivation of Hatred,* 11–12; Frevert, *Ehrenmänner,* 151; McAleer, *Dueling,* 145–149; Norbert Elias, *The Germans: Power Struggles and the Development of Habitus in the Nineteenth and Twentieth Centuries* (New York: Columbia University Press, 1996), 107.

16. "Ehre und Zweikampf," *Burschenschaftliche Blätter* 10, no. 26 (15 February 1912); Ludwig Caesar Roux, *Die Hiebfechtkunst: Eine Anleitung zum Lehren und Erlernen des Hiebfechtens* (Jena, 1885); Henner Huhle, "Nichts verändert das Fechten so—wie der Komment," *Einst und Jetzt* 34 (1989): 53–64; Biastoch, *Tübinger Studenten,* 162; Frevert, *Ehrenmänner,* 150–155; McAleer, *Dueling,* 120–127; Möller, "Studienzeit," 416–419.

17. John C. Fout, "Sexual Politics in Wilhelmine Germany: The Male Gender Crisis, Moral Purity, and Homophobia," *Journal of the History of Sexuality* 2 (1992): 388–421.

Between 1900 and 1909 the authorities finally admitted women students to German universities. Liberal Baden first opened the doors to women, and Prussia (1908) and Mecklenburg (1909) were the last states to make this step. In the United States and England, women gained admission to institutions of higher education earlier but to women-only courses of study. In Germany, in contrast, women could attend any institution. Some intermediate steps helped to pave the way for women's admission. A letter from 1871 provides evidence that women were attending courses at Heidelberg University, although in 1873 university officials decided that only the eight women who had begun their studies at Heidelberg could continue to attend classes. In 1889, Helene Lange opened the first college preparatory school for women, and by 1896 women could enter universities as auditors; by 1899 the first six women passed the *Abitur*. See "Zulassung und Immatrikulation von Frauen 1871–1900," *Strasbourger Post* (14 January 1900), for an overview of the ways that different universities dealt with auditors (Heidelberg Universitätsarchiv, RA 4623). See also Annette Kuhn et al., eds., *100 Jahre Frauenstudium: Frauen der Rheinischen Friedrich-Wilhelms-Universität Bonn* (Dortmund: Klio—Verein zur Förderung historischer Frauenforschung, 1996), 17; Patricia Mazon, *Gender and the Modern Research University: The Admission of Women to German Higher Education, 1865–1914* (Stanford, CA: Stanford University Press, 2003), 85–114.

18. Arnold Ruge argued that townsmen often looked on students warily because of their distance from middle-class customs. See Ruge, *Kritische Betrachtungen und Darstellung des deutschen Studentenleben in seinen Grundzügen* (Tübingen: C. J. B. Mohr, 1906), 119. On excuses for student excesses and laziness, see Gottlob Schrenk, *Des christlichen Studenten Beruf* (Halle, 1899), 6.

19. Frevert, *Ehrenmänner*, 214–232; Mazon, *Gender and the Modern Research University*, 19–22, 29–41; Möller, "Studienzeit," 410.

20. "Göttingen," *Burschenschaftliche Blätter* 6, no. 17 (15 June 1903): 138.

21. Mazon, *Gender and the Modern Research University*, 35, 45, 48; Frevert, *Ehrenmänner*, 214.

22. Friedrich Paulsen, *The German Universities and University Study* (New York: Scribner's, 1906), 271. Theobald Ziegler agrees and describes honor in the same words as Paulsen. Ziegler, *Der deutsche Student am Ende des 19. Jahrhunderts* (Leipzig, 1896), 61. See also Bloem, *Der krasse Fuchs*, 8.

23. Elias, *The Germans*, ch. 1, 97; Dietrich Heither and Michael Gehler make similar arguments in Heither and Gehler, eds., *Blut und Paukboden: Eine Geschichte der Burschenschaften* (Frankfurt: Fischer Taschenbuch, 1997), 61. See Frevert, *Ehrenmänner*, on the student code of honor, 134, and on the duel and the *Sonderweg*, 16; Gay, *Cultivation of Hatred*, 14–15.

24. Elias, *The Germans*, 107; Paul Grabein, *O alte Burschenherrlichkeit! Bilder aus dem deutschen Studentenleben* (Stuttgart: Union Deutsche Verlagsgesellschaft, 1900), 69.

25. Gay, *Cultivation of Hatred*, 9.

26. Ibid., 32.

27. Carl Schorske, *Fin-de-Siècle Vienna: Politics and Culture* (New York: Cambridge University Press, 1981), 160–161.

28. Adolph Asch, "Erinnerungen aus Posen und Berlin," Leo Baeck Institute, ME 18, 1–3; Adolph Asch and Johanna Philippson, "Self-Defence in the Second Half of the 19th Century: The Emergence of the K.C.," *Leo Baeck Institute Yearbook* 3 (1958): 122–139; Asch, *Geschichte des K.C. (Kartellverband Jüdischer Studenten), im Lichte der deutschen kuturellen und politischen Entwicklung* (London: self-published, 1964). For Jewish fraternities, see Keith H. Pickus, *Constructing Modern Identities: Jewish University Students in Germany, 1815–1914* (Detroit, MI: Wayne State University Press, 1999); Miriam Rürup, "Jüdische Studentenverbindungen im Kaiserreich: Organisationen zur Abwehr des Antisemitismus

auf 'studentischer Art,'" *Jahrbuch für Antisemitismusforschung* 10 (2000): 113–137; Alexander Seelos, "Jüdische Studentenverbindungen im deutschen Kaiserreich: Zwischen akademischen Abwehrverein, inner jüdischer Lagebildung, und Jugendbewegung," master's thesis, Munich University, 1992; Thomas Schindler, "'Was Schandfleck war, ward unser Ehrenzeichen . . .': Die jüdischen Studentenverbindungen und ihr Beitrag zur Entwicklung eines neuen Selbstbewusstseins deutscher Juden," in Harm-Hinrich Brandt, ed., *Der Burschen Herrlichkeit: Geschichte und Gegenwart des studentischen Korporationswesen* (Würzburg: Schöningh, 1998), 337–365. See also my articles: Lisa Swartout, "Segregation or Integration?: Honor and Masculinity in Jewish Dueling Fraternities," in Rainer Liedtke and David Rechter, eds., *Towards Normality? Acculturation and Modern German Jewry* (Tübingen: Mohr Siebeck, 2003); and Swartout, "Mut, Mensur und Männlichkeit," in Manfred Hettling, Andreas Reinke, and Till van Rahden, eds., *Ethnizität, Integration, Exklusion: Die Geschichte der Breslauer Juden im 19. und 20. Jahrhundert* (Hamburg: Schriftenreihe des Instituts für die Geschichte der deutschen Juden, 2003), 148–166.

29. The Jewish Union of Fraternities, the K.C., counted twenty-four Jewish fraternities in 1912: nine in the Bund jüdischer Corps (Berlin, Leipzig, Breslau, Munich, Charlottenburg, Strasbourg, Freiburg, Königsberg, Marburg); two Zionist fraternities in the Kartell zionistischer Verbindungen (Berlin, Munich); three in the Bund jüdischer Akademiker (Berlin, Munich, Strasbourg); seven in the K.C. (Breslau, Heidelberg, Berlin, Munich, Bonn, Freiburg, Darmstadt); and three affiliates ("K.C. Tendenz": Karlsruhe, Königsberg, Leipzig). See *K.C. Blätter* 10, no. 2 (July 1912): 204.

30. Asch, *Geschichte des K.C.,* 12, 79–80; Friedrich Solon, "Mein Leben in Deutschland vor und nach dem 30. Januar 1933," Leo Baeck Institute, ME 607, 8–9; "Semester-Bericht Winter 1905/06," in Ernst Fraenkel, *Viadrina suspensa! Vivat Thuringia! 40 Jahre im Kampf für Recht und Ehre* (Breslau: B. Elkeles, 1926), 42; *Kölnische Volkszeitung* (15 December 1905). Paul Posener reported that in 1896 the Breslau Viadrina counted thirty members for its Sunday stroll. Posener, "The Young Maccabees," Leo Baeck Institute, ME 83, 45.

31. Arthur Bein, "Akademische Freiheit und konfessionelle Korporationen," *Allgemeine Zeitung des Judentums* 119, no. 10 (10 March 1905): 114.

32. A. Lazarus, "K.C. Feier in Frankfurt a. M. am 1 Marz 1914," *Im Deutschen Reich* 2, no. 4 (April 1914): 170.

33. *K.C. Blätter* 1, no. 1 (1 October 1911): 1; Pickus, *Constructing Modern Identities,* 94–104; Asch, *Geschichte des K.C.,* 10–11, 137.

34. Benno Jakob, "Aus der Rede zur Fahnenweihe der Rheno-Bavaria," in *K.C. Blätter Festschrift* (New York: American Jewish K.C. Fraternity, 1946), 19.

35. "Salia Centennial 1884–1984," Institut für Hochschulkunde Archive, 1984, n.p.

36. Solon, "Mein Leben in Deutschland," 5.

37. Lazarus, "K.C. Feier in Frankfurt a. M."; *Literatur Wegweiser für den K.C.: Eine Übersicht über die für den K.C.er wichtigste Literatur* (Berlin: Schriftleitung der K.C. Blätter, 1926).

38. The works of Marion Kaplan, Till van Rahden, and Keith Pickus emphasize the flexible and changing nature of identity, and they tend to describe Jewish affiliation as a choice made in the personal realm. In contrast, Jewish fraternity students proclaimed their identity "in the full light of the public." Bruno Weil, "Der K.C. im öffentlichen Leben Deutschlands," in *K.C. Blätter Festschrift,* 12; Kaplan, *Making of the Jewish Middle Class,* 4, 11–12, 55, 84; Pickus, *Constructing Modern Identities,* esp. ch. 1; Till van Rahden, *Juden und andere Breslauer: Die Beziehungen zwischen Juden, Protestanten und Katholiken in einer deutschen Grossstadt von 1860 bis 1925* (Göttingen: Vandenhoeck & Ruprecht, 2000).

39. Avraham Barkai, *"Wehr Dich!" Der Centralverein deutscher Staatsbürger jüdischen Glaubens, 1893–1938* (Munich: Beck, 2002); Greg Caplan, "Wicked Sons, German

Heroes: Jewish Soldiers, Veterans, and Memories of World War I in Germany," Ph.D. diss., Georgetown University, 2001.

    40. For the Union of German Students (Verein deutscher Studenten), see Hedwig Roos-Schumacher, *Der Kyffhäuserverband der Vereine Deutscher Studenten 1880–1914/18* (Gifhorn: Akademischer Verein Kyffhäuser, 1986); Kampe, *Studenten und "Judenfrage,"* 23–51; Asch, "Erinnerungen aus Posen und Berlin," 1–2.

    41. Asch, "Erinnerungen aus Posen und Berlin," 2–3.

    42. Ibid., 3.

    43. Asch, *Geschichte des K.C.,* 64.

    44. Ignaz Klug, *Ideal und Leben: Eine Sammlung ethischer Kulturfragen* (Paderborn: F. Schöningh, 1913), 25.

    45. For detailed numbers of organized Catholics, see Christopher Dowe, *Auch Bildungsbürger: Katholische Studierende und Akademiker im Kaiserreich* (Göttingen: Vandenhoeck & Ruprecht, 2005), 304–318; for his discussion of masculinity, the duel, and Catholic students, see 99–104; for his conclusions on confessional relations and masculinity, see 132. Also see Frevert, *Ehrenmänner,* 157–158, 272.

    46. The literature on religious identity and conflict is large and growing. See, in particular, Helmut Walser Smith, *German Nationalism and Religious Conflict: Culture, Ideology, Politics, 1870–1914* (Princeton, NJ: Princeton University Press, 1995); and Margaret Lavinia Anderson's afterword in Smith, ed., *Protestants, Catholics, and Jews in Germany 1800–1914* (Oxford: Berg, 2001). See also Wolfgang Altgeld, *Katholizismus, Protestantismus, Judentum: Über religiös begründete Gegensätze und nationalreligiöse Ideen in der Geschichte des deutschen Nationalismus* (Mainz: Matthias-Grünewald, 1992); David Blackbourn, *Marpingen: Apparitions of the Virgin Mary in Nineteenth-Century Germany* (New York: Knopf, 1994); Olaf Blaschke, "Das 19. Jahrhundert: Ein Zweites Konfessionelles Zeitalter?," *Geschichte und Gesellschaft* 26 (2000): 38–75; Hartmut Lehmann, ed., *Säkularisierung, Dechristianisierung, Rechristianisierung im neuzeitlichen Europa: Bilanz und Perspektiven der Forschung* (Göttingen: Vandenhoeck & Ruprecht, 1997); Rainer Liedtke and Stephan Wendehorst, eds., *The Emancipation of Catholics, Jews, and Protestants: Minorities and the Nation-State in Nineteenth-Century Europe* (Manchester, England: Manchester University Press, 1999); Thomas Mergel, *Zwischen Klasse und Konfession: Katholisches Bürgertum im Rheinland, 1794–1914* (Göttingen: Vandenhoeck & Ruprecht, 1994); Thomas Nipperdey, *Religion im Umbruch: Deutschland 1870–1918* (Munich: Beck, 1988); Dietmar von Reeken, *Kirchen im Umbruch zur Moderne* (Gütersloh: Chr. Kaiser, 1999); Jonathan Sperber, *Popular Catholicism in Nineteenth-Century Germany* (Princeton, NJ: Princeton University Press, 1984).

    47. *Der Reichsbote* (27 February 1904), quoted in "Im freien Jena," *Academia* 11, no. 16 (15 March 1904): 348, 347; *Kolnische Volkszeitung* (19 April 1906) and (27 November 1905); *Badischer Landesbote* (19 February 1905); *Reichsbote* (10 August 1905), all in Geheimes Staatsarchiv Preussischer Kulturbesitz Berlin, 76 Va Sekt 1 Tit. XII, no. 25B; "Professor Bindung über Zweikampf," *Burschenschaftliche Blätter* 20, no. 6 (15 December 1905): 129.

    48. Undated letter to Disciplinaramt Strasbourg University from stud. med. Theodor Messerschmidt, Archives du Bas-Rhin, Strasbourg, 103AL197 [1895], n.p.

    49. Ibid.

    50. Ibid.

    51. Ibid.

    52. Dr. Heinz Potthoff, "Die Gleichheit der Studenten," *Burschenschaftliche Blätter* 10, no. 18 (15 February 1904): 234.

    53. Ruge, *Kritische Betrachtungen,* 173; Ziegler, *Der deutsche Student,* 246. The Jewish student Leopold Kessler, in "An Unfinished Autobiographical Memoir," Leo Baeck Institute

Archive, ME 1265, 15, wrote: "All students were equals whether rich or poor, and of whatever race or creed."

54. Matthias Erzberger, *Bilder aus dem Reichstagswahlkampf: Die Agitation der Zentrumsgegner, beleuchtet nach deren Wahlschriften* (Berlin: Germania, 1907); Smith, *German Nationalism and Religious Conflict*, 118–165; Margaret Lavinia Anderson, *Practicing Democracy: Elections and Political Culture in Imperial Germany* (Princeton, NJ: Princeton University Press, 2000), 133–147; Róisín Healy, *The Jesuit Specter in Imperial Germany* (Boston: Brill, 2003), 101–116; August-Hermann Leugers, "Latente Kulturkampfstimmung im Wilhelminischen Kaiserreich: Konfessionelle Polemik als konfessions- und innenpolitisches Kampfmittel," in J. Horstmann, ed., *Die Verschränkung von Innen-, Konfessions- und Kolonialpolitik im Deutschen Reich vor 1914* (Paderborn: Katholische Akademie Schwerte, 1987), 13–37.

55. "Demokratie und Kaisertum von Dr. Friedrich Naumann," *Burschenschaftliche Blätter* 5, no. 19 (1 December 1904): 118.

56. Asch, *Geschichte des K.C.*, 9–11.

57. Miriam Gebhardt, "Zur Psychologie des Vergessens: Antisemitismus in jüdischen Autobiographien vor und nach 1933," in Clemens Wischermann, ed., *Vom kollektiven Gedächtnis zur Individualisierung der Erinnerung* (Stuttgart: Steiner, 2002), 53–64.

58. Mazon, *Gender and the Modern Research University*, 35, 36, 44.

59. Schindler, *Studentischer Antisemitismus*; Kampe, *Studenten und "Judenfrage."*

60. Gay, *Cultivation of Hatred*, 26; Asch, *Geschichte des K.C.*, 37, 46.

61. Solon, "Mein Leben in Deutschland," 60.

62. Michael Gross, *The War against Catholicism: Liberalism and the Anti-Catholic Imagination in Nineteenth-Century Germany* (Ann Arbor: University of Michigan Press, 2004), 1.

# 6

## Whose Body Is It Anyway?

*Hermaphrodites, Gays, and Jews in*
*N. O. Body's Germany*

SANDER L. GILMAN

"N. O. Body" is a most appropriate pseudonym for Karl M. Baer (1885–1956) to have used when he sat down to pen his autobiography, which first appeared in 1907,[1] for being "nobody" was his way of seeing his body. It was doubly alienated (he writes "nobody" in English rather than German) because it was male as well as female, Jewish as well as German. This is how he imagined his earlier life raised to be a woman, Martha Baer, in a Jewish family in imperial Germany. But it is "nobody" that Odysseus tricks the Cyclops into answering when asked who has harmed him. "Who has hurt you?" "Nobody," the blinded giant responds. In his autobiography, written only a year after he was legally able to change his sex assignment from female to male, Baer is simultaneously the clever trickster and the damaged giant. His autobiography is a document of transformation, a physical one understood in the rhetoric of late nineteenth-century biological and racial science. For N. O. Body is also the signature under a sign asking for "an educated, desperate young man willing to make a last experiment with his life," which Theodor Herzl has his protagonist read in the paradigmatic Zionist novel of 1902, *Altneuland* (Old New Land). Our protagonist stops being Martha Baer and becomes Karl M. Baer, with Martha still lurking in the middle initial. He is, in an odd way, the "real" Gregor Samsa—a person who awakens one day in a body not his own.

On its surface Baer's autobiography is a remarkable fin-de-siècle document of "hermaphroditism," as the Berlin sexologist Magnus Hirschfeld (1868–1935) notes in his epilogue (109ff.). Its subject suffered from an incorrect gender assignment because of the apparent ambiguity of his genitalia as an infant. He was registered and treated as a female child rather than a male child, an error of assignment that became evident only at puberty. He was a "pseudohermaphrodite," to use the terminology of the day, as his body was hormonally and psychologically gendered male, even though his genitalia seemed at first glance ambiguous. Sex was defined by the appearance of the body and was dimorphic:

there were men and there were women. Anyone who was neither or both was seen as pathological.

The central argument of the autobiography is expressed on its opening page: "one may raise a healthy boy in as womanish a manner as one wishes, and a female creature in as mannish; never will this cause their senses to remain forever reversed" (7–8). No confusion about gender can exist except, as is the case here, through the fuzzy ineptitude of a physician, like the one at Baer's birth in 1885 (not 1884, as in the text) who stated that "on superficial inspection, the shape has a feminine appearance, ergo we have a girl before us" (9). But the autobiography shows that this was never the case. Baer was always a male, even when treated as a female. As Hirschfeld notes in his epilogue: "The sex of a person lies more in his mind than in his body" (110). For Baer, there was no ambiguity in his sense of discomfort as a woman caused by the outward appearance of his genitalia. His desires were male and heterosexual—from the games he wished to play to the women with whom he fell in love. But he had been assigned the gender role of a woman, which made his masculine desire seem perverse to him. The argument of the autobiography is that male children, however raised or treated, remain masculine in their intrinsic identity. This was very much against the tendency of the time and also against the practices of the later twentieth century.[2] Today, this sounds extraordinarily prescient.

After the 1960s, the gender reassignment surgery of children with "ambiguous genitalia" followed the view of scientists such as the Johns Hopkins psychologist John Money, who argued that it was culture not nature that defined gender.[3] It became usual to alter the external genitalia of babies with ambiguous sexuality to the female because of its greater surgical simplicity. These children were treated with hormones and raised as females. But since the 1990s a substantial literature has argued that Baer and Hirschfeld were right and Money was wrong. Gender is imprinted in as well as on the body; anatomy is *not* destiny. The primary case used by Money as his proof of the successful raising of a boy as a girl was that of David Reimer (known in popular culture as the case of John and Joan). He was one of identical twin boys, but a botched circumcision in 1966 led to the amputation of his penis at eight months and his being raised as a girl. Money announced this as proof that culture was the sole determinant of gender. But at twenty-five Reimer demanded to have his sexual identity as a man reconstituted. He had always felt himself to be male even in his culturally and hormonally reinforced role as a woman. By the early twenty-first century he had become a media darling and appeared on *Oprah*. In May 2004, he committed suicide at the age of thirty-eight.[4] His death was read as proof of how wrong Money was.

Reimer's life rebutted, as the first major reassessment of the case noted, the primary assumptions that everyone is psychosexually neutral at birth and that all healthy psychosexual development is dependent upon the appearance of the genitals.[5] This view, espoused by Money, argued from a set of assumptions based on the existence of hermaphrodites. He assumed that they were ungendered at birth. But who are these undifferentiated hermaphrodites? Do they not have a gendered identity from the very beginning of their lives? And is not their understanding of the meaning of gender also shaped by the historical world in which they are born? Certainly this was the case for the five-year-old Martha (Karl) Baer who, like Reimer, much preferred the games and toys of boys to those of girls even though the world treated him as it would a little girl.

The publication of Baer's autobiography in Germany is part of a fixation in the late nineteenth century and early twentieth with this surprisingly malleable category of the intersex individual, the "hermaphrodite." The "freakish" body, the body whose physiology did not reflect societal norms, has always fascinated European culture. From Petronius's representation in his *Satyricon* of hermaphrodites in first-century Rome to Velazquez's dwarf center stage in the Spanish court portrait of *Las Meninas* (1656) to the fantasies about sexual desire in Victor Hugo's *Hunchback of Notre Dame* (1831), Europeans have stressed physical difference as a way of defining the ever-changing boundaries of the "normal" and "healthy" body. Central to all of these representations was the need to "see" the physical difference of the body. Difference had to be physical even if the fascination was with the unseeable (and in these terms unknowable) aspects of what makes human beings different. Thus, ruminating about sexual desire and practices, such as homosexuality, which was in the process of becoming the subject of the medical gaze in the nineteenth century, did not have the same empirical claim as observing physical differences, such as those of the hermaphrodite.

In the late nineteenth century there was an explosion of autobiographical accounts of sexual difference that attempted to translate a fascination with behavioral or social aspects of sexual difference into physiological terms. One of the central metaphors for this difference was that of the "hermaphrodite." Virtually all of these attempts were cast as part of a new medical (or forensic) attempt to understand the psyche of "perversion." Homosexuals could only be judged by their acts; there seemed to be no way of seeing their difference in contrast to the healthy, normal body. How could one identify the homosexual? Could he (and at this point the "pervert" was always male) be as visible as the hermaphrodite? In a medical model the homosexual was inherently different from the healthy heterosexual, but was this difference an intrinsic one or could anyone be or become homosexual?

In the 1860s a German lawyer, Karl Ulrichs, provided an alternative model for a nonjudgmental account of "uranism," or homosexuality.[6] He hoped this would free the homosexual from the moral or medical taint that accompanied any representation of "perverse" sexual attraction or activity in the evolving medical model. He sought to defuse the legal status of the homosexual as a sexual criminal while avoiding the medicalization of homosexuality as a perversion. At the same time, liberals such as Richard Krafft-Ebing in his 1886 *Psychopathia Sexualis* also wished to free the homosexual from the charges of criminal sexual activity or moral depravity by medicalizing homosexuality and thus providing therapy rather than prison as the alternative. Ulrichs's argument was that the homosexual (and his references are exclusively to male same-sex desire and activity) is a "third sex," a natural alternative to the "two" sexes, male and female.

By the end of the nineteenth century physicians such as Magnus Hirschfeld applied the model of the third sex and sought a biological rather than a theoretical model. Of special interest to Hirschfeld were thus the "intermediate cases" of sexuality, the model for which was the hermaphrodite who, according to these accounts, was *both* female and male and thus *neither* male nor female.

Hirschfeld and the sexologists of the 1890s found it necessary to turn to the broader medical audience as well as the broader public with case material to prove their argument. While Michel Foucault had to excavate the complete version of the famous mid-nineteenth-century case of the French hermaphrodite Herculine Barbin from the Parisian archives of the Department of Public Health, it is much less difficult to find analogous cases of sexual difference in Germany after the 1890s.[7] This literature exploded in the medical writings of the day and quickly entered general public discourse.[8] Thus the autobiographical literature on homosexuality, cast in the model of the "third sex," uses the hermaphrodite as its concrete analogy for German consumption. The pioneering sexologist Havelock Ellis (1859–1939) wrote the first volume of his studies on sexuality collaboratively with the writer John Addington Symonds (1840–1893), which was published in Germany in 1896.[9] Symonds's autobiographical account of "this question of Greek love in modern life" was the core of this work, which was published the next year in Great Britain to the horror of his friends. Among other texts, Ellis included a detailed summary of "Ulrichs's views" on homosexuality as an appendix to the German original (and anonymously in subsequent English editions).

By 1900 there were hundreds of autobiographical accounts of sexual "anomalies," including hermaphroditism, available in the technical literature and some in the more popular literature. Magnus Hirschfeld's volume on "Berlin's third sex," with massive citations from autobiographies, appeared as volume 3 in the original urban sociological series *Metropolitan Documents,* widely sold in German bookstores prior to World War I.[10] "M. Baer" contributed a volume, *The International Trafficking in Girls,* an area of expertise that she had developed as a journalist, to the series in 1908. This series, edited by Hans Ostwald, formed the basis for many of the sociological studies of urban social groups in the 1910s and beyond. Most, like the Hirschfeld and the Ellis volumes, cut and pasted these into "scientific" discourses as firsthand "proofs" of the nature of sexual difference. Indeed, Hirschfeld even discussed the case of Baer, although anonymously, in an essay published in 1906.[11] Here, the hermaphrodite always served as the model for sexual difference, and the homosexual, the "third sex," was like the hermaphrodite in that he was to be found in nature.

This notion that the hermaphrodite can serve as the model for an understanding of male homosexuality is not merely an idiosyncrasy of the turn of the twentieth century. Michel Foucault writes in his *History of Sexuality*: "homosexuality appeared as one of the forms of sexuality when it was transposed from the practice of sodomy into a kind of interior androgyny, a hermaphroditism of the soul. The sodomite had been a temporary aberration; the homosexual was now a species."[12] This took place in the 1890s, the world in which Karl Baer lived.

As a literary trope, the modern notion of hermaphroditism as a metaphor for the impermanence of sexual dimorphism emerged at the same time. In 1891 we find a "magic seed" in Archibald Ganter and Fergus Redmond's novel (and then a remarkably successful play) *A Florida Enchantment* that transforms the protagonist and her servant into men. And Victorian and early twentieth-century erotica often turned on the confusion of sexual roles, in the form of androgynous characters or transvestism. Thus in *"Frank" and I* the reader discovers that the "female" lover of a young man turns out to be male, and in *Miss High-Heels* the hero, Dennis Evelyn Beryl, is transformed by his sister into a woman. Such purposeful sexual confusion is also at the core of Agatha Christie's early novel *The Man in the Brown Suit* (1924). And in 1928, with Virginia Woolf's *Orlando,* the full promise of the metaphor of hermaphroditism for the instability of sexuality identity is played out.[13] After that, it becomes a commonplace in the literature of the twentieth century.

In Germany, as in the rest of Europe, there was a steady stream of medical studies interested in hermaphroditism throughout the nineteenth century. But only with Magnus Hirschfeld's work in the 1890s was the *model* character of homosexuality stressed in such studies.[14] By then the hermaphrodite had become not only a model for, but also the etiology of, homosexuality. At the beginning of the twentieth century Hirschfeld published a long series of essays by Franz von Neugebauer (1856–1914) in his *Yearbook of Sexual Intermediate Stages*.[15] Neugebauer was the most important commentator on the biological nature of hermaphroditism within Hirschfeld's model during this period and was one of the researchers who referenced the case of Herculine Barbin in its pseudonymous extract in a scholarly study by Auguste Ambroise Tardieu in 1872. He argued that all children were born "bisexual" and that homosexuality was an inherent quality of brain development. But he was also convinced that women who desired to be male were less likely to have truly bisexual characteristics than a man who desired to appear as a woman. (The rationale is clear: why else would a high-status individual such as a male desire to be a low-status individual such as a woman? There is a social advantage to the male but never to the female.) A gynecologist in Warsaw and chief of staff at the Evangelical Hospital there, Neugebauer had systematically collected "930 observations of hermaphrodism in human beings; 38 of these were cases which had come under my own observation, and the rest I found dispersed in ancient and modern literature."[16] In his work he rethought the nosology of hermaphroditism. However, following Hirschfeld's model, he also understood the social consequences of such biological categorization. He clearly links hermaphroditism and homosexuality, as does Baer's image of the childhood sexual exploration and his young adult sense that he might be a lesbian: "It occurred to me alone, that I perhaps felt in that way" (64). As Neugebauer argued, this was not an unusual sexual confusion:

> The male or female character of the genetic sense of pseudohermaphrodites depends very often on the sort of environment in which they are brought up, that is to say, upon whether they are educated as boys or girls; it must be set down entirely to the influence of suggestion if a male hermaphrodite, owing to mistaken sex brought up as a girl, afterwards shows a feminine genetic sense, seeks to attract men and betrays perverse homosexual inclinations, and if when the mistake in sex is discovered he energetically opposes every attempt to make him abandon girls' petticoats, their way of life, and his feminine predilections and occupations, and if he declines to assume male attire and change his social position, and appear in future as a man. Such homosexual inclinations acquired by suggestion have in some cases been only temporary, and the male, though brought up by mistake as a female, has, sooner or later, recognized his virility, and has not hesitated to demand his social and sexual rights sometimes somewhat abruptly. There have been instances in which a male person, recognizing that his true sexual position had been misunderstood, has adopted male attire without consulting anyone, and without giving notice of the fact to the magistrate or any other authority; one such person found a mistress whom he put in the family way, and only demanded the adjustment of his social position on the evidence of that pregnancy—an incontestable proof of his manhood. In other cases the genetic sense with homosexual desire has persisted during the whole life of an hermaphrodite, whose true sex has been misunderstood; there have even been instances in which hermaphrodites of the male sex brought up as girls have, [when], too late, their true sex has been recognized, with all possible insistence demanded castration.

But this can lead to a sense of alienation if one does not resolve the question of sexual identity:

> The consciousness of being neither man nor woman, the constant and shameful fear that the malformation, though concealed with the utmost care, may some day betray itself and leave the sufferer to be the scorn and derision of those about him, are perpetually upsetting the mental balance and psychotic repose of the unfortunate pseudohermaphrodite, who racks his brain

demanding why he should be so afflicted, and seeking some way out of his miserable social position. Not daring to confide in anyone the poor hybrid passes his days and nights dwelling upon his lot; feeling excluded from the society of either men or women he cultivates solitude and avoids intimacy of any kind with anyone; he passes his nights in agony and tears; his health gives way, and he becomes suspicious, distrustful, shy, savage, irritable, irascible, vindictive, violent, and impulsive to an extent that may drive him to crime, or he becomes moody, apathetic, and melancholy, till at last he ends his days in self-destruction.

In imperial Berlin male cross-dressers could be arrested just because they appeared different. In Weimar Germany such cross-dressers (not necessarily homosexuals or hermaphrodites) were given identity cards to allow them to present themselves in public. Such a social danger of mis-seeing haunted the world in which Baer grew up. What would happen if one looked inappropriate for one's sex?

On December 2, 1891, a gendarme arrested a young girl of 19 on the platform of the railway station at Pilsen, on the suspicion of being a man disguised as a woman. It was in vain that the prisoner showed her personal papers, in which she was described as Marie Karfiol, born on such a day, at such place, and of such parents. In spite of her protestations, she was taken to the mayor's court, where medical evidence proved that there had been an error of sex, and that Marie K. was a male hypospadiac. She then admitted that at the time of her birth there had been some difficulty in determining her sex, but she had been brought up as a girl. At the time of her puberty suspicions as to the real state of the case had led to her being taken to see the mayor of her village and the priest; but no further action had been taken. Later on she abandoned herself to her fate, being ashamed to speak to anyone of her doubts. Her pretty hair was cut off and she was dressed in men's clothes; but in her novel attire she had a very timid yet wild appearance.

Thus, anxiety focused on the feminized appearance of the male. This runs like a red thread through Baer's autobiography. His female schoolmates will not play with him because their teachers call him a boy; equally telling is the fact that "street urchins also shouted 'Norbert' after me": he was seen as "something odd" in public.[17] When the adult Baer loses his passport on a trip to Hungary as a newspaper correspondent, the police see "her" as a disguised man, which is "very suspicious."[18] It is only the fact that a passerby recognizes her from her portrait in a women's magazine that rescues Baer. Being seen as different on the street was dangerous, especially if the assumption was that you were a feminized man.

Cesare Taruffi's classic monograph on hermaphroditism, originally published in Italian in 1902, appeared in 1903 in German. Here the notion that Hirschfeld had stressed—the hermaphrodite as model case—was spelled out in explicit detail. The model is always the feminization of the male as an answer to sexual dimorphism and sexual identity. Baer's life, as he recounts it after his transformation, is that of a feminized man, not that of a mannish woman. "Feminization" is here to be understood both in its general, cultural sense and in its specifically medical sense. Feminization or the existence of the feminized man is a form of "external pseudo-hermaphroditism."[19] It is not true hermaphroditism, but rather the sharing of external, secondary sexual characteristics, such as the shape of the body or the tone of the voice. The concept began in the middle of the nineteenth century with the introduction of the term *infemminsce* (to feminize) to describe the supposed results of the castration of the male.[20] By the 1870s, the term was used to describe the *feminisme* of the male through the effects of other diseases, such as tuberculosis.[21] Here is Baer's fantasy that the dropping of his voice was a sign of tuberculosis because "consumptives are often hoarse." One can see him reading in the medical (or popular medical) literature of the day, looking for a pathology that would explain his growing masculinization. He "coughed, suffered from backaches" and "in [his] lively imagination thought [he] felt all the symptoms mentioned in the book."[22] Indeed he later uses a feigned case of "consumption" to return home from his first job as an apprentice in a banking house "as my lungs had become weak."[23] But what he was doing was reversing the model: according to the literature of the time, diseases such as tuberculosis feminized men, precisely the problem from which he actually suffered. He had a need to see his state as an expression of a somatic pathology, but one that could be treated. "Feminization" was the direct result of actual castration or the physiological equivalent, such as an intensely debilitating illness. It reshaped the body.

Baer's autobiography is remarkable as much for its mode, masking its subject's identity, as for its candor. But Baer does something unique. He redefines his ancestry as "French" in order to explain his social difference:

> Our lineage is not German. Our forefathers came from France. My family is very old and proud of its family tree, whose beginnings reach back as far as the sixteenth century. For generations however, the descendants of this old family had moved up to the heights of existence, only to soon descend to the middling life of small shopkeepers. (13)

"French" was also understood in Baer's time as a racial category as well as a political one. Thus the arch-racist French count Joseph Arthur de Gobineau (1816–1882), widely read in Germany, argued the inherent superiority of the "Aryans" (Germans) over the "Celts" (French). Being "French" in Germany is a racial label that is mirrored on the body: "Our outward appearance alone is enough to easily distinguish us from the other inhabitants of Bergheim: black or brown eyes, brown wavy hair, and sharply defined southern European features are seldom found among the Saxons and Franconians of those mountain valleys."[24] These "French" bodies seem to be just as visible as the odd masculine body of the hermaphrodite.

Baer's French mask is transparent but it is also unnecessary as there is no reason in the argument of his autobiography for his identity to be anything but that of a hermaphrodite. It is the "somber gray [that] hung over our path through life."[25] Yet there was clearly a need to stress another category of difference that also affected his understanding of his own body. As Hermann Simon has brilliantly shown in his detective work that identified Baer as the author of N. O. Body's autobiography, Baer was not only a Jew but was also able to create a meaningful life for himself as an officer of the Berlin lodges of the Jewish fraternal organization B'nai B'rith (Brothers of the Circumcision).[26] That group seemed to have demanded neither educational certification nor birth records, as Baer fears at the end of his account. His lack of any formal education as male meant that his social role was truly damaged. He stresses this himself. But for B'nai B'rith, it was sufficient that he was a member of the Jewish community.

It is also the case that being Jewish and living uncomfortably as a woman were seen as parallels in Baer's self, at least in 1907. The volume is prefaced by an anonymous poem:

Over my childhood
Hung a threatening fist.
All my peaceful pleasures
Were shrouded in a mist.

The wounds this left were deep,
Like a dagger, stabbing me,
I could forget them, or dream them away. . . . . . . .
But healed—they never shall be.[27]

As the reader's introduction to the struggles of Martha to learn to be a young woman, this poem reflects the author's sense of a trauma beyond healing. Repression perhaps, but reconstitution never.

Baer borrowed (and slightly adapted) the text from his Zionist friend Theodor Zlocisti's *About the Path Home: Verses of a Jew* (*Vom Heimweg: Verse eines Juden;* 1903).[28] There, the lines clearly refer to Zlocisti's Jewish identity in the diaspora. The transformation of the politics of German Jewish identity into the politics of sexual identity leaves the "wound" unstated. Perhaps both are present. The notion that one is raised a "German" but is in fact a "Jew" seems to be a reality in the world in which N. O. Body lived. As a Zionist he acknowledges the impossibility (or at least the difficulty) of being a "German" while being a "Jew." Identity is fixed; no cultural forces can reshape it. The essential identity will eventually out. Jews remain Jews no matter what their upbringing, just as a man remains a man even though raised as a woman.

Baer becomes "French" rather than Jewish in his account in 1907 because the sexual implications of being Jewish were clear to him. Just as he transforms all of the Jewish holidays and practices into Catholic ones in his account of his early life, as Simon shows, so too does he desire to transform his Jewish body into a French one. (Being Catholic in late nineteenth-century Berlin, at the time of the *Kulturkampf* against the Vatican, was almost as exotic as being Jewish.) That the Jew was an anomalous sexual case was part of his world. For Baer and for the world in which he lived, the "damaged" genitalia of the male Jew, damaged through circumcision—though there is a debate as to whether circumcision can be inherited after generations—meant that the male Jew was already neither truly male nor truly female. He was, to use Ulrichs's coinage, a "third sex."

It is clear that the model that Ulrichs employed to characterize the homosexual as beyond the dimorphism of traditional sexual identity is analogous to the basic argument that Theodor Herzl used to establish Zionism. If the Jews were inherently "oriental," the basic argument in the Berlin anti-Semitic struggle of the 1880s, then the Jews should recognize their oriental nature, leave Europe, and return to Palestine. It is not a blemish but a recognition of their natural state. Being different in both cases is transformed from a pathological and stigmatizing identity to a positive one. Jews are Jews first and foremost; they may appear to be Germans but their essential oriental nature can only be repressed, never destroyed.

It is in the physiology of the male Jew that the myth of Jewish sexual difference is located. Circumcision, however, was not a powerful enough myth; the world of European anti-Semitism created the notion that male Jews menstruate. Menstruation is the sign of womanhood in Baer's autobiography. It is "a dark matter," because it had to do with "sexuality, and because one was then an adult." All of the girls in Baer's school "were 'it' already," so Baer too "arrived at school one morning, beaming. 'It' was there."[29] This "lie" continued for "ten years, in many countries and among strange customs, and it caused me many a worry."[30] Doubly so, for had Baer read further into nineteenth-century medical literature on the topic of male menstruation, by writers such as F. A. Forel and W. D. Halliburton, he would have found a fascination with male menstruation with regard to the problem of hermaphroditism as a sign of bisexuality.[31] Paul Albrecht in Hamburg argued for the existence of male menstruation which was periodic and which mimicked the menstrual cycle of the female through the release of white corpuscles into the urine.[32] The sexologist Paul Näcke provided a detailed discussion of the question of male menstruation and its relationship to the problem of male periodicity.[33] Näcke cited, among others, Havelock Ellis, who had been collecting material on this question for years. With the rise of modern sexology at the close of the nineteenth century, especially in the writings of Magnus Hirschfeld, male menstruation came to hold a special place in the "proofs" for the continuum between male and female sexuality.[34] The hermaphrodite, the male who was believed to menstruate, became a central focus of Hirschfeld's work. But all of this new "science" that used the existence of male menstruation still drew on the image of the marginality of those males who menstruated and thus pointed toward a much more ancient tradition.

The idea of male menstruation is part of a Christian tradition of seeing the Jew as inherently, biologically different. From the late fourth-century *Adversus Judaeos* (Against the Jews) of the early church father St. John Chrysostom through the work of Thomas Cantipratanus, the thirteenth-century anatomist, the abnormal and abhorrent body of the Jew marked the implacable difference of Jewish males. The argument was that male Jews menstruated as a mark of the "Father's curse," their pathological difference.[35] This view continued throughout the Middle Ages until the early modern period. The view that attributed to the Jews diseases for which the "sole cure was Christian blood" reappeared again as part of the blood libel accusations in the late nineteenth century.[36] It was raised again at the turn of the century in a powerfully written pamphlet by Daniel Chwolson, professor of Hebrew at the university in St. Petersburg, as one of the rationales used to justify the blood libel, that Jews killed Christian children (or virgins) to cure themselves. Chwolson notes that it was used to "cure the diseases believed to be specifically those of the Jews," such as male menstruation.[37] This version of the blood accusation ties the meaning of the form of the circumcised genitalia to the Jew's diseased nature.

These older charges about Jewish male menstruation and Jewish hermaphroditism reappeared with their reprinting in the nineteenth century.[38] By the end of the nineteenth century the arch-racist Theodor Fritsch—whose *Anti-Semite's Catechism*, first published in 1887, was the encyclopedia of German anti-Semitism—saw the sexuality of the Jew as inherently different from that of the German: "The Jew has a different sexuality than the Teuton; he will [not] and cannot understand it. And if he attempts to understand it, then the destruction of the German soul can result."[39] The hidden sign that the Jewish man is neither male nor female is his menstruation. The implicit charge of pathological bisexuality, of hermaphroditism, had traditionally been lodged against the Jewish male. (Male Jews are like women because, among other things, they both menstruate as a sign of their pathological difference.)

But Baer appeared to be a Jewish girl who did not menstruate, but he had to maintain the fantasy that he did. Was he, as he presumed in his first real job, merely an "anemic and poorly developed" girl, for whom "menstruation did not begin before the twenties"?[40] Or was he truly different? The question of ritual cleanliness during and after menstruation, the identification of his body as the antithesis of the menstruating Jewish male—here, the female who does not menstruate—is clarified only when he comes to understand his body as that of a healthy, Jewish male, who does not menstruate. Masculinity will out.

The resolution of Baer's conflict comes through a physician who recognizes him as a man and urges him to comprehend his desire for a woman as "a natural feeling."[41] All ambiguities are resolved—Baer claims—and the state resolves his question of identity by reassigning him as a man. He trains his new male body through exercise and sport. He becomes a "real" man except for "a slight furrow left behind from tight lacing." That mark remains written on the body. No circumcision marks Baer's new male body, but there is still a scar of his role as a woman. Yet the world into which he remakes himself is the world of a growing anti-Semitism in which the appearance of the Jew on the street was as "clearly" marked as that of the woman. Indeed, the closing of the public clinic for cosmetic surgery in Nazi Germany (1933) and the introduction of the yellow star in 1942 (1939 in Poland) both were aimed at making the invisible visible, because the fabled ability to recognize Jews at a glance turned out to be an anti-Semitic fantasy.

Baer fled to Palestine in 1938, when Germany was more obsessed by Jews than by the ambiguity of gender. He died in Israel in 1956.

NOTES

1. This chapter is a revised version of chapter 7 from my *Multiculturalism and the Jews* (New York: Routledge, 2006). I thank Routledge for permission to republish the material. All references are to the translation N. O. Body, *My Life as a Woman,* ed. Hermann Simon, trans. Deborah Simon (Philadelphia: University of Pennsylvania Press, 2005). Simon's 1993 German reprint presented the real identity of the anonymous author for the first time: *Aus eines Mannes Mädchenjahre* (Berlin: Hentrich, 1993). The original was published in Berlin by Riecke in 1907. On Baer specifically, see David Brenner, "Re(-)dressing the 'German-Jewish': A Jewish Hermaphrodite in Wilhelmine Germany," in Elazar Barkan and Marie-Denise Shelton, eds., *Borders, Exiles, and Diasporas* (Stanford, CA: Stanford University Press, 1998), 32–45. On hermaphroditism and transsexuality in culture, see Stefan Hirschauer, *Die soziale Konstruktion der Transsexualität: Über die Medizin und den Geschlechtswechsel* (Frankfurt am Main: Suhrkamp, 1993); Gesa Lindemann, *Das paradoxe Geschlecht: Transsexualität im Spannungsfeld von Körper, Leib und Gefühl* (Frankfurt am Main: Fischer Taschenbuch, 1993); Annette Runte, *Biographische Operationen: Diskurse der Transsexualität* (Munich: Fink, 1996); Jay Prosser, *Second Skins: The Body Narratives of Transsexuality* (New York: Columbia University Press, 1998); Kate More and Stephen Whittle, *Reclaiming Genders: Transsexual Grammars at the Fin de Siècle* (London: Cassell, 1999); Jason Cromwell, *Transmen and FTMs: Identities, Bodies, Genders, and Sexualities* (Urbana: University of Illinois Press, 1999). Of extreme importance is the work of Alice Domurat Dreger: "Doubtful Sex: The Fate of the Hermaphrodite in Victorian Fiction," *Victorian Studies* 38 (1995): 335–370; *Hermaphrodites and the Medical Invention of Sex* (Cambridge, MA: Harvard University Press, 1998); "A History of Intersexuality: From the Age of Gonads to the Age of Consent," *Journal of Clinical Ethics* 9 (1998): 345–355; "Jarring Bodies: Thoughts on the Display of Unusual Anatomies," *Perspectives in Biology and Medicine* 43 (2000): 161–172; and, as editor, *Intersex in the Age of Ethics* (Hagerstown,

MD: University Publishing Group, 1999). See also Helga Thorson, "Masking/Unmasking Identity in Early Twentieth-Century Germany: The Importance of N. O. Body," *Women in German Yearbook: Feminist Studies in German Literature & Culture* 25 (2009): 149-173.

2. The famed Philadelphia surgeon Samuel David Gross (1805–1884), the subject of Thomas Eakins's *The Gross Clinic* (1875), undertook a castration and reconstruction in the 1850s. See S. D. Gross, "Case of Hermaphrodism, involving the Operation of Castration and Illustrating a New Principle of Juridical Medicine," *American Journal of the Medical Sciences,* n.s., 24 (1852): 386–390.

3. This began as early as his Ph.D. dissertation: "Hermaphroditism: An Inquiry into the Nature of a Human Paradox," Harvard University, 1952.

4. Mireya Navarro, "When Gender Isn't a Given," *New York Times* (19 September 2004): 1, 6.

5. Milton Diamond and H. Keith Sigmundson, "Sex Reassignment at Birth: A Long Term Review and Clinical Implications," *Archives of Pediatric & Adolescent Medicine* 151 (1997): 298–304. One popular study is John Colapinto, *As Nature Made Him: The Boy Who Was Raised as a Girl* (New York: Perennial, 2002).

6. Hubert Kennedy, *Ulrichs: The Life and Works of Karl Heinrich Ulrichs* (Boston: Alyson, 1988).

7. Michel Foucault, ed., *Herculine Barbin: Being the Recently Discovered Memoirs of a Nineteenth-Century French Hermaphrodite,* trans. R. McDougall (New York: Pantheon, 1978). It is clear that the text was known to him from an extract in Auguste Ambroise Tardieu, *Question médico-légale de l'identité dans ses rapports avec les vices de conformation des organes sexuels, contenant les souvenirs et impressions d'un individu dont le sexe avait été méconnu* (Paris: J.-B. Ballière et Fils, 1872).

8. See Klaus Müller, *Aber in meinem Herzen sprach eine Stimme so laut: Homosexuelle Autobiographien und medizinischen Pathographien im neunzehnten Jahrhundert* (Berlin: Rosa Winkel, 1991).

9. Havelock Ellis and J. A. Symonds, *Das konträre Geschlechtsgefühl* (Leipzig: G. Wigand, 1896).

10. Magnus Hirschfeld, *Berlins drittes Geschlecht* (Berlin: Hermann Seemann, [1905]).

11. Magnus Hirschfeld, "Drei Fälle von irrtümlicher Geschlechtsbestimmung, Medizinische Reform," *Wochenschrift für soziale Medizin, Hygiene und Medizinalstatistik* 15 (1906): 614.

12. Michel Foucault, *The History of Sexuality,* vol. 1: *An Introduction,* trans. Robert Hurley (New York: Vintage, 1980), 43.

13. See Barbara Wedekind-Schwertner, *"Daß ich eins und doppelt bin": Studien zur Idee der Androgynie unter besonderer Berücksichtigung Thomas Manns* (New York: Lang, 1984); Andrea Raehs, *Zur Ikonographie des Hermaphroditen: Begriff und Problem von Hermaphroditismus und Androgynie in der Kunst* (New York: Lang, 1990).

14. The best summary of his views are in his textbook: Magnus Hirschfeld, *Sexualpathologie: Ein Lehrbuch für Ärzte und Studierende* (Bonn: Marcus and Weber, 1917).

15. His work is wide-ranging, from the early F. L. Neugebauer, *Zur Lehre von den angeborenen und erworbenen Verwachsungen und Verengerungen der Scheide: Sowie des angeborenen Scheidenmangels mit Ausschluss der Doppelbildungen* (Berlin: A. Th. Engelhardt, 1895), through to his classic essay Franz von Neugebauer, "58 Beobachtungen von periodischen genitalen Blutungen mestruellen Anschein, pseudomenstruellen Blutungen, Menstruatio vicaia, Molimina menstrualia usw. bei Scheinzwitter," *Jahrbuch für sexuallen Zwischenstufen* 6 (1904): 277–326. His views are summarized in Franz Ludwig von Neugebauer, *Hermaphroditismus beim Menschen* (Leipzig: Werner Klinkhardt, 1908).

16. I cite from his English-language summary essay: Franz von Neugebauer, "Hermaphrodism in the Daily Practice of Medicine: Being Information upon Hermaphrodism Indispensable to the Practitioner," *British Gynaecological Journal* 19 (1903): 226–263.

17. *My Life as a Woman*, 38.

18. Ibid., 86.

19. Cesare Taruffi, *Hermaphrodismus und Zeugungsunfähigkeit: Eine systematische Darstellung des Missbildungen der menschlichen Geschlechtsorgane*, trans. R. Teuscher (Berlin: H. Barsdorf, 1903), 96–103.

20. Ibid., 97.

21. Ferdinand-Valére Faneau de la Cour, *Du féminisme et de l'infantilisme chez les tuberculeux* (Paris: A. Parent, 1871).

22. *My Life as a Woman*, 41.

23. Ibid., 56.

24. Ibid., 14.

25. Ibid., 10.

26. Ibid., 113–136.

27. Ibid., 7; all punctuation per original.

28. Hermann Simon, "N. O. Body und kein Ende," in Marion Kaplan and Beate Meyer, eds., *Jüdische Welten: Juden in Deutschland vom 18. Jahrhundert bis in die Gegenwart* (Göttingen: Wallstein, 2005), 225–230.

29. *My Life as a Woman*, 50.

30. Ibid.

31. See, for example, F. A. Forel, "Cas de menstruation chez un homme," *Bulletin de la Société Médicale de la Suisse Romande* (Lausanne) (1869): 53–61; and W. D. Halliburton, "A Peculiar Case," *Weekly Medical Review and Journal of Obstetrics* (St. Louis) (1885): 392.

32. Paolo Albrecht, "Sulla Mestruazione ne maschio," *L'Anomalo* 2 (1880): 33.

33. Paul Näcke, "Kritisches zum Kapitel der normalen und pathologischen Sexualität," *Archiv für Psychiatrie und Nervenkrankheiten* 32 (1899): 356–386.

34. Hirschfeld, *Sexualpathologie*, 2:1–92.

35. Thomas de Cantimpré, *Miraculorum et exemplorum memorabilium sui temporis libro duo* (Duaci: Baltazris Belleri, 1605), 305–306.

36. Anatole Leroy-Beaulieu, *Israël chez les nations: Les juifs et l'antisémitisme* (Paris: Calmann Lévy, 1893), 166–167.

37. Daniel Chwolson, *Die Blutanklage und sonstige mittelalterliche Beschuldigungen der Juden: Eine historische Untersuchung nach den Quellen* (Frankfurt am Main: J. Kauffmann, 1901), 7, 207–210.

38. Chrysostomus Dudulaelus, *Gründliche und Warhafftige Relation von einem Juden aus Jerusalem mit Nahmen Ahassverus* (n.p.: n.p., [1602]), Diiir; reprinted as *Evangelischer Bericht vom den Leben Jesu Christi . . .* (Stuttgart: J. Scheible, 1856), 126.

39. Theodor Fritsch, *Handbuch der Judenfrage* (Leipzig: Hammer, 1935), 409.

40. *My Life as a Woman*, 64.

41. Ibid., 99.

# 7

## Toward a Theory of the Modern Hebrew Handshake

### The Conduct of Muscle Judaism

ETAN BLOOM

> More history is made by secret handshakes than by
> battles, bills, and proclamations.
>> —John Barth

My interest in handshakes began some years ago, when a friend of mine, Menashe, unexpectedly rejected my handshake.[1] He told me that I had pressed his hand too hard and demanded that I shake it more gently instead. His reaction, I believe, was connected to his decision to change the manner of his own handshake, returning to that of his late father, who had immigrated to Israel from Baghdad in the 1950s. My friend asked me, in particular, to stop giving him the strong slaps on the back and shoulders that Israelis call *chapcha*. Like many of my fellow countrymen, I had been fond of greeting my friends with a *chapcha* while handshaking.

This handshake with Menashe was perhaps my last authentic, modern Hebrew handshake. What had seemed spontaneous, friendly, and cool had been experienced as problematic by Menashe, leading to a kind of de-automatization of my handshaking. The interaction also inspired me to undertake some research on handshakes. For the present study, I interviewed and had conversations with more than 100 Israeli men and several women, as well as numerous Germans, Dutchmen, Bedouins, Egyptians, and Palestinians. The interviews were conducted in the early twenty-first century in conjunction with my larger investigation into the politics of the German Zionist Arthur Ruppin, who played a central role in the project of "culture planning" in Zionist Palestine. Under Ruppin's leadership as the first and most influential director of the Palestine Office (PO), contemporary ideas of *Arbeitswissenschaft* (science of work) and of the German eugenics movement informed the creation of a new Hebrew man and a modern Hebrew habitus in Palestine.[2] The modern Hebrew handshake was both a manifestation of and a motor for the formation of this distinct proto-Israeli cultural repertoire.

## METHODOLOGICAL FRAMEWORK: REPERTOIRE, HABITUS, AND CULTURE PLANNING

In a variety of disciplines, such as sociology, anthropology, semiotics, and cultural studies, the term *repertoire* is often used to denote the full number of options available to a group for managing its social life, while the context within which these repertoires function is labeled a *system* or *field*.[3] The concept of a repertoire emphasizes, as sociologist Ann Swidler puts it, the notion that "culture influences action not by providing the ultimate values toward which action is oriented, but by shaping a repertoire or 'tool kit' of habits, skills, and styles from which people construct 'strategies of action.'"[4] Itamar Even-Zohar has explained this concept in different terms, as "the aggregate of rules and materials which govern both the *making* and *handling*, or production and consumption, of any given product. . . . If we view culture as a framework, a sphere, which makes it possible to organize social life, then the repertoire *in* culture, or *of* culture, is where the necessary items for that framework are stored."[5]

Underlying the concept of the repertoire is the understanding that the so-called toolkit, or "aggregate of rules," which regulates culture does not evolve on its own, through "natural causes." Rather, social "nature" or "reality" is itself a product of the repertoire's history. In one form or another, a culture's repertoire thus must be taken into consideration in any historical analysis. In fact, our very perceptions and sense of history can themselves be seen as products of our repertoire; in this way, the currently hegemonic repertoire determines our past and shapes our future. By inquiring into the characteristics and mechanics of the repertoire we thus gain insight into the connections between past, present, and future in all their interrelatedness. In this vein, social reality is understood as coming into existence when human agents or other forces act on cognitive structures. This mode of conceiving of reality as evolving within certain cognitive frameworks can be applied to virtually anything either *of* or *in* the world, but particularly to social structures, and it lends itself well to historical analysis.[6] As Bourdieu puts it, "these structuring structures are historically constituted forms and therefore arbitrary in the Saussurian sense, conventional, 'ex instituto' [by an arbitrary institution] as Leibniz said, which means that we can trace their social genesis."[7]

This conceptual framework forms the basis for Even-Zohar's concept of culture planning, which denotes the initiation and operation of a culture plan as well as its reevaluation and revision when the needs of a social field change.[8] Culture planning takes place successfully when a dominant group succeeds in imposing a repertoire on a social field. By doing so, the leaders generate a social cohesiveness which allows them to institute a certain regime of personal and institutional interactions within that field. The ability of a group to impose its repertoire is dependent on its success in gaining control over what Bourdieu calls "statist capital [*capital étatique*]."[9] In other words, such a group has to create a centralized administration in order to control the different bodies and institutions that are responsible for the distribution of both symbolic capital (such as the education system, the press, and the arts) and material capital (such as national banks, public foundations, and property that is in private hands). A group that is able to impose a repertoire on a social field can be referred to as a dominant group and its repertoire as the dominant repertoire. Moreover, according to Even-Zohar, the identity of a group is connected to a specific repertoire: "one indivisible repertoire for one group." The dominant repertoire is also always closely related to a particular group's habitus, which evolves whenever a certain repertoire succeeds in taking hold within the group.[10]

This is the conceptual framework that I bring to bear on the following inquiry into the early history of the modern Hebrew repertoire, as well as into the habitus that this repertoire generated for both individual and collective practices. In other words, this chapter explores the process by which the modern Hebrew repertoire took shape within what was to become the dominant group and the development in the course of which this repertoire created certain patterns of behavior, or the particular habitus, of the modern Hebrews and, later, Israelis. I am using Bourdieu's concept of the habitus, which he defines as "a set of dispositions which incline agents to act and react in certain ways. The dispositions generate practices, perceptions and attitudes which are 'regular' without being consciously co-ordinated or governed by any 'rule.'"[11] Accordingly, the history of the habitus is the history of social memory. Yet in distinction to the repertoire, the memory that finds expression in the habitus is understood in this chapter not only as an ideological or symbolic abstraction, but also as a force that shapes and regulates the body. Thus I follow Talal Asad, who has suggested that "the concept of habitus invites us to analyze the body as an assemblage of embodied aptitudes, not as a medium of symbolic meanings."[12]

Studying the Palestinian Zionist handshake sheds light on the making of the modern Hebrew man's repertoire as well as on the process by which the habitus has come to manifest itself in his body. In addition, it can deepen our understanding of the modes of embodiment that emerged among young Jewish immigrants in Zionist Palestine at a time when the ambitious German Jewish cultural planner Arthur Ruppin sought to engineer a new Hebrew society. Researching handshakes might seem an unlikely endeavor for a historian, but as I will show in this chapter, the history of gestures provides a window into the development of the habitus. By interpreting and accounting for a gesture like the handshake, which forms an integral part of the habitus, we can gain new insight into how German Jewish cultural and political leadership shaped Zionist Palestine, and thus broaden our understanding of the origins of modern Israeli society. The human body is as much a historical document as any charter, diary, or parish register (though unfortunately it is much harder to preserve), and it deserves to be studied accordingly.

At the end of the twentieth and the beginning of the twenty-first century, a number of studies on handshakes appeared in print, most of them written by anthropologists, linguists, or psychologists. The majority of these studies examine gestures broadly as forms of nonverbal communication within a scholarly field known as "kinesics."[13] But gestures, and in particular handshakes, have received little attention from historians, since it is difficult to study something as fleeting as bodily comportment and motion in the past; it is much easier to observe these human interactions in their present-day manifestations. Thus, my inquiry into the emergence of the modern Hebrew handshake, which evolved within a relatively brief period of time, is a foray into a largely undeveloped field: the history of human gestures.

## MODERN HEBREWS

My use of the term *modern Hebrews* is historically specific. It reflects the way in which the members of the Jewish intelligentsia and Zionist groups in Europe and Palestine in the late nineteenth century thought of and represented themselves. Particularly in Palestine, Zionists portrayed themselves as the successors of the ancient Hebrews and thereby distanced themselves from the traditions of the Jewish *galut* (exile) and the alleged degeneration caused by it. In distinction to diaspora Jews and reformers of Judaism, these modern Hebrews aimed at reviving ancient Hebrew culture. Seeking to emulate the heroes of Hebrew antiquity, they named their Zionist sports clubs and paramilitary organizations after such figures as Samson, Bar Kokhba, Yehuda Hamaccabi (Judas Maccabeus), Simon bar Giora, and others. However, as historian George L. Mosse has noted in regard to Zionist revivalism, the physical appearance so essential to the makeup of the new Jew or the modern Hebrew was a product not of biblical times, but of the late nineteenth-century classical revival in Germany. Moreover, Mosse observed that "the conditions of the *galut* Jews, out of their original soil, were to be blamed for their stunted bodies, for in Biblical times they had produced strong men who could compete on equal terms with Greek athletes or Nordic barbarians."[14]

This distinction between Jews and Hebrews can be found in the writings of the earliest Zionist thinkers. The writer Micha Berdyczewski (1865–1921), for instance, argued that "Jews have the choice of being either the last Jews or the first Hebrews."[15] One of these "first Hebrews," Avshalom Feinberg,[16] wrote to his friend Segula Bekman: "We are the children of our land, we are not from the *galut* and the ghetto, and we are not ill with a black-mood. . . . Oh you Hebrew! Don't be a Jew [*yehudia*]."[17] Feinberg's injunction to Bekman that she think and act as a Hebrew, rather than as a Jew, indicates that both men and women were expected to embody the new ideal of Hebrewness. His negative attitude toward "Jewish" and "Jew" was also quite typical of many other new Hebrews. According to Rachel Elboim-Dror, Zionist youths of pre-state Palestine often used the word "Jew" itself as a curse, and in their diaries and letters the epithet *yehudonim* bore a meaning similar to "kikes."[18]

The new social field in Zionist Palestine was thus built not by Jews, but by Hebrews. Workers organized under the General Federation of Hebrew Workers; the first teachers under the Hebrew Teachers Association; and soldiers joined the British army in the First World War under the Hebrew Regiment. Banners in Zionist demonstrations called for "Hebrew work" and a "Hebrew state." The slogan for Hebrew-language revivalism was *Ivri daber Ivrit* (Hebrews, speak Hebrew). The university in Jerusalem was referred to as the first "Hebrew university," Tel Aviv as "the first Hebrew city," and so on. In short, the distinction between Jews and Hebrews was crucial to the formation of Zionist culture and identity in pre-state Palestine.[19] Zionist identity, in fact, formed in large measure as a direct reaction against anti-Semitic representations of *galut* Jews in Europe, and the Zionist movement owed much of its success to the tension between the traditional notion of a religiously defined Jewish community and the Zionists' more secular conception of a Hebrew nation or race.

After the Holocaust and the establishment of the State of Israel, these distinctions and tensions became gradually subdued. In part, this was a result of the Israeli leadership's active efforts to position the new state as the undisputed representative of *all* Jews in the world. Moreover, the distinction between Jews and Hebrews was rendered obsolete when large waves of Jewish immigrants from Europe and elsewhere entered the country and thus effectively "re-Judaized" it.[20] Still, the division between Jews and Hebrews continues to exist in contemporary Israel—albeit in a repressed and muted form—and the resulting tensions are far from being resolved. Yet common usage and popular history books have blurred the distinction, so that the terms *Jew* and *Hebrew*—once so important to the formation of Zionism—have become more or less synonymous in today's discourse.[21]

Both the cultural and political context and the reference system in relation to which the German and Eastern European Zionists developed their notion of "Hebrewness" was European society. The new society in the Zionist settlements of the land of Israel/Palestine was engaged in an intricate dialogue with Europe and gradually established its own repertoire in reaction to negative European perceptions and descriptions of Jews. From the very beginning of the Zionist movement, its founders and leaders actively sought to prove their competence to non-Jewish Europeans. This desire for European recognition found expression, for instance, in the words of the legendary warrior Yosef Trumpeldor,[22] who migrated to Palestine in 1912: "If only the Gogols, and the Dostoyevskis," he wrote, ". . . could see the brave and bold chaps [the pioneers], they would have depicted their Jewish characters differently."[23] In a similar vein, the influential German Zionist, sociologist, and political economist Franz Oppenheimer (1864–1943)[24] believed that Zionist activity should be aimed at improving the image of Jews worldwide and at making the Jews who intended to remain in Europe "proud" of their "working brothers" in Palestine.[25]

Indeed, the new Zionist culture of Palestine idealized the active and courageous fighter and the productive agricultural worker. An examination of the relationship between the repertoires of Europe and of Zionist Palestine shows that the qualities promoted by the Zionists were the exact opposite of the negative stereotypes ascribed to Jews by European culture.[26] Europeans traditionally conceived of Jews as greedy, materialistic, effeminate, and lacking in creativity, productivity, and courage, while Zionists saw the new Hebrews as masculine, brave, hardworking, active, creative, innovative, original, and following socialist ideals and other worthy goals. Where Jews were thought to be overly intellectual, Hebrews despised excessive intellectual reflection. Europeans regarded Jews as unhygienic, prone to sickness, and primitive, whereas Zionists were invested in improving the hygiene and health of individuals and the nation and in praising the advantages of technology and modernity. Jews were also said to be antisocial and overly compassionate. Thus, the modern Hebrews celebrated themselves as loyal to state and community, and believed their uncompromising dedication to the cause of their people to be culminating in the ideal of "cruel Zionism."[27]

It is important to note that Zionists understood these negative stereotypes of Jews not simply as symbolic constructions, but as very real and concrete physical flaws, which they set out to correct. This is illustrated, for instance, in a report that the Ministry of Education and Culture published in 1953. Zvi Nishri, its author and one of the first modern Hebrew gymnastics teachers in Palestine,[28] claimed:

> [T]he shortcomings ascribed to us by the nations of the world—cowardice, evasion of military service, hatred of physical work, degenerate bodies (crooked backs), etc. etc.—have disappeared over time thanks to the physical education that we have begun to foster, and thanks to the national spirit that has come to pulsate among the people of our nation.[29]

## DESCRIPTION OF THE MODERN HEBREW HANDSHAKE

The modern Hebrew handshake is emblematic of male Hebrew body language generally.[30] I am not suggesting that all Hebrew men give this handshake in the exact same manner, nor even that they shake hands at all. Rather, I argue that an examination of the modern Hebrew handshake can give us insight into the ways in which modern Hebrew and Israeli men are expected to behave, and I claim that this handshake has played a role in shaping and regulating male body culture in Zionist Palestine.

The modern Hebrew handshake came into existence in the early decades of the Hebrew cultural ascendancy in Palestine, where it was developed almost exclusively by men, particularly by those working in the agricultural sector and those with military training. Until quite recently, this would have included the majority of Israeli men. It is a strong, firm handshake, similar to that of the Germans and unlike, for instance, the relatively mild handshake of the Dutch. As noted earlier, it is sometimes accompanied by a strong slap on the shoulder or back, known among Israelis as *chapcha*. The word *chapcha* comes from the Arabic-Iraqi dialect and literally denotes a tap or hit on the head. Yet whatever the origins of the modern Hebrew handshake or some of its components, they were not the reason for its acceptance and growing popularity in Zionist Palestine. Rather, this handshake became part of the modern Hebrew repertoire because it was a means by which Zionist men could express and demonstrate that they were no longer "old Jews" but had become "new Hebrews."

The modern Hebrew handshake and its accompanying *chapcha* are considered informal greetings in contemporary Israel. However, within certain contexts they have become formalized. This is most notably the case in the well-respected infantry units of the military; the closing ceremonies of basic military training (*tironut*) in these units are the most formal context in which the handshake is used. There, the *chapcha* marks the male recruit's transformation into a fully qualified soldier. At the ceremony, the commander forcefully strikes the recruit on the shoulder, neck, or chest, and the recruit, for his part, has prepared his body to receive the hit "like a male [*kmo gever*]."[31] Each commander has his own style, and either the *chapcha* can follow a firm handshake or both can be delivered at the same time. My interviews and observations indicate that the memory of this moment tends to be cherished by the soldier for many years, and when he and his commander meet again, no matter how much time has elapsed, the commander will usually greet him with a short *chapcha* to acknowledge their particular bond. With this *chapcha*, the two men renew their special, hierarchical relationship, which is not unlike that of a father to a son. The soldier—even if he has long since been promoted to the rank of officer himself—never gives the *chapcha* to his former superior.[32]

A 2005 article in the front section of *Yediot Acharonot,* Israel's largest daily newspaper, on a farewell party for the Israeli chief of staff, General Moshe (Bugi) Ya'alon, observed that the general opened the event by giving "*chapchot* [plural of *chapcha*] to his commanders" and "kisses to their wives."[33] Ya'alon's manner of treating the commanders and their wives differently thus points to the gendered dimension of *chapchot;* the Zionist and Israeli repertoire of body language is highly gender-specific. As is the case in most other societies, particular gestures, such as *chapchot* in Zionist Palestine and Israel, serve to demarcate the cultural and social spaces of men and women.[34] Women have been excluded from and are still marginal in the three fields in which the handshake and the *chapcha* have featured most prominently: the army, diplomacy, and business. In the Jewish context, the traditional prohibition for a man to touch a woman other than his wife is likely to have reinforced women's exclusion from these realms.[35]

An examination of handshakes among women has been, unfortunately, beyond the scope of my research, and the history of women's participation in the Zionist movement is a scholarly field in its own right.[36] The few women whom I did interview, however, told me that the *chapcha* usually irritates them, and that they prefer to kiss and hug when greeting one another.[37] Some of the women remarked rather pointedly that any man who gave them a *chapcha* was—as one of them put it—an "insecure jerk." Furthermore, whereas the men shared many stories about handshakes with me and related them to important events in their lives, my female interviewees did not report similar experiences. Although some of them expressed an interest in my research, their reasons were different from those of the male interviewees: men discussed handshakes to explore the history of their own relationships and identities, while women were intrigued to learn about a male realm from which they were kept at a distance. Nonetheless, more women have been receiving the *chapcha* since the 1980s due to a relatively modest increase in female soldiers in the Israeli army. Women who fulfill such traditionally male roles as tank drivers, shooting instructors, and border police officers are sometimes given the *chapcha* during the ceremonies that mark the completion of their training.[38] These *chapchot,* however, do not have the same meaning as those given to male recruits—even if there is no discernible difference in the way they are delivered. My admittedly limited evidence suggests that when the *chapcha* is administered to female recruits, it is often intended to make them feel what it is like to be a man and a soldier rather than to induct them into the military brotherhood as equals. It might be an example of what Bourdieu called "symbolic violence." If so, it would establish the women's inferiority and invite female self-deprecation.[39]

Handshakes appear to play an important role in the fashioning of Israeli male identity, while women have a much more ambivalent relationship to them. The specific handshake under discussion here is a constitutive part of the Israeli male repertoire. It is the ideal handshake for men who want to be seen as masculine by their peers.

One of the distinguishing features of the modern Hebrew handshake is that it exposes those who fail to shake in the expected manner to public rebuke. In modern Hebrew and Israeli culture,[40] a man acts appropriately when he expresses his goodwill toward another man who shakes too softly by admonishing him and saying, "Press hard! Like a male! [*Tilchatz chazak! Kmo gever!*]."[41] One thirty-year-old man told me that he had always been aware of this expression, but the only time he ever took it seriously was when he heard it from a classmate whom he regarded as an alpha male (partly because his friend was success-ful with women). My informant further believed that improving his handshake might make him, too, more popular with female students.

The importance of, and the tension around, vigorous, masculine handshak-ing is illustrated in the story of a left-handed Ashkenazi man in his early for-ties whom I interviewed. Born in Jerusalem and raised for several years on a kibbutz, he later, as a young man in the military, wanted to be accepted by his infantry unit comrades as a worthy fighter. Thus, he invested much time, energy, and focus into strengthening his right hand so that he could shake with it in the required manner. Unfortunately, he had great difficulty learning to do it in a way that seemed natural and spontaneous, and his awkward, deliberate man-ner always gave him the feeling that he failed to have the true experience of an appropriate handshake.

The first Jewish immigrants to the modern Hebrew cultural space in Palestine must have likewise felt self-conscious and awkward in their efforts to be manly Hebrews. Initially, they must have felt like *schlemiels* (Yiddish for "habitual bungler" or "dolt") in relation to the European men with whom they compared themselves. Men from religious backgrounds and some of the *miz-rachim,* or so-called orientals, whom I interviewed expressed similar feelings, since members of these two groups have generally not fully adopted modern Hebrew identities and continue to practice the Jewish tradition of gently touch-ing, rather than shaking, hands.

Scholarship on the history of Jewish handshakes and of Jewish kinesics is scarce. Yet personal observations, interviews that I have conducted, and texts that mention these issues in passing indicate that hand touching belonged to the cultural repertoire of Sephardic, *mizrachi,* and Ashkenazi societies. In particular, Jewish men used the hand touch in two contexts. When they con-ducted business, the practice was known as *tki'at kaf* (literally, "to thrust the palm of the hand"),[42] and it marked the parties' agreement to a deal that had been negotiated. Perhaps since biblical times,[43] Jewish men used this touching of hands to signal that they assumed full responsibility for fulfilling the terms of the contract they thereby entered into.[44] Second, Jewish men touched each other's hands during times of celebration, such as weddings and holidays. Hand touching appears to have been accompanied at such events by kissing either the hand or cheek or by hugging, and it was thus not the dominant component of the interaction. Certainly it was not as central as it has been in Christian Europe and in modern Hebrew society.

It is likely that handshaking developed in the context of European court politics and was initially practiced by warriors, knights, diplomats, and court-iers.[45] The Jewish practice of hand touching, by contrast, forms part of a culture that was shaped by rabbis and sages. This difference in origin may account for the different meanings of handshaking and hand touching. Unlike the European elites, Jews developed a strong aversion to bloodshed. Under the influence of rabbinic and prophetic teachings and due to their experience as an often-victimized minority, unable to protect itself militarily, Jews came to consider war the trade of Esau, meaning the gentile world. In particular for European and Middle Eastern Jews, engagement in warfare figured only in their mythical past or their messianic future, but it did not belong in their present lives.[46] This is why Jews have at least since the end of the Talmudic age written relatively little about the politics and moral dilemmas of warfare, with Maimonides being a notable exception.[47]

My inquiry into the rabbis' relationship to handshaking has led me primarily to twentieth-century texts from Palestine, in which the authors dismiss handshaking altogether and claim that by doing so they represent traditional Jewish views. According to the renowned rabbi Shlomo Zalman Auerbach (1910–1995) of Jerusalem, for instance, "it was not customary in our dwelling places [bimkomoteinu] to bless by stretching out the hand, except when someone came in off the road or in times of simcha [celebration, such as weddings, bar mitzvahs, holidays]."[48] Rabbi Abraham Isaiah Karelitz (1878–1953), better known by his pseudonym Chazon Ish ("vision man" or "vision of man"), declared that "a man's hand is not ownerless [hefker], so that anyone can grab it whenever he likes."[49] The Sephardic sage of Jerusalem, Chacham Shlomo Eliezer Alfandari (d. 1930), known as the Holy Grandfather (Sabba Kadisha), noted that he avoided the practice of shaking hands entirely because it "cannot be found in the Torah or the Talmud, and because it follows the laws of the Gentiles [chukei hagoyim]."[50]

These three rabbis might have followed the opinion of Maimonides and other sages when they advised Jews to avoid physical touching, and thus worldly temptation, as much as possible. According to rabbinic teachings, the sense of touch is the lowest of the senses both because it allows one to perceive an object only through direct physical contact (an epistemological source that is the opposite of abstraction or reflection) and also because it is the dominant sense used in adultery. Quoting Aristotle, Maimonides emphasized the animal-like and dangerous nature of the sense of touch several times in his *Guide for the Perplexed*:

> There must be an absence of the lower desires and appetites, of the seeking after pleasure in eating, drinking, and cohabitation: and, in short, every pleasure connected with the sense of touch. Aristotle correctly says that this sense is a disgrace to us, since we possess it only in virtue of our being animals; and it does not include any specifically human element.[51]

However, it is notable that these strictures did not seem to apply to the traditional Jewish practice of hand touching. The dangerous or sensual aspects associated with the practice appear to have become sublimated into its spiritual meaning, and the hand touches of rabbis came to be seen quite literally as a means by which spiritual energy was transmitted from the rabbi to another man.[52] Halakhic or religious justifications do not account fully for the handshake's rejection by these three early twentieth-century Jerusalem rabbis. Rather, it is likely that Auerbach, Karelitz, and Alfandari were expressing in their critique of the handshake their opposition to the modern Hebrew repertoire that was emerging in Palestine at the time.

Evidently, the modern Hebrew handshake arose in a radically different context than the traditional Jewish hand touch, and it carried a very different cultural meaning. The hand touch and the Zionist handshake are distinguished from each other in intent, form, and origin. The modern Hebrew handshake is closely related to its European antecedents, particularly to those of Germany.[53] Nevertheless, it is also distinct from its European progenitors. In order to understand these differences, we must take into account the relationship between the modern Hebrew and the European (especially the German) repertoires and their attendant habitus.

## HYPERCORRECTION

The cultural symmetry that I described earlier—wherein modern Hebrew culture fashioned itself in direct opposition to European anti-Semitic stereotypes—suggests a clear case of what Bourdieu called "hypercorrection." He explained that hypercorrection in the sociological sense results from "the disparity between knowledge and recognition, between aspirations and the means of satisfying them—a disparity that generates tension and pretension. . . . This pretension, a recognition of distinction which is revealed in the very effort to deny it by appropriating it, introduces a permanent pressure into the field."[54]

"Tension and pretension" emerge when a subordinate group or individual starts to question cultural preconceptions about their own inferiority. These groups or individuals then set out to prove—to themselves and to others—that they are indeed fit to possess whatever they are deemed to lack, or to perform whatever they are deemed unable to do, by the dominant group. Thus, they seek to (re)create a repertoire utterly unlike the one traditionally conceived for them by those who have the power to set the cultural standards in the society. In their efforts to produce this repertoire, they tend to be greatly concerned not to display any of the shortcomings that their imagined betters have ascribed to them in order to denigrate or stigmatize them. Typically, this anxiety leads to the imposition of strict and even excessive measures of self-control on the behavior of the previously subordinate group, which go far beyond the ways in which the group being emulated regulates its own comportment.

The modern Hebrew handshake, like numerous other modes of behavior in Zionist Palestine, bears this mark of hypercorrection. It is essentially a radicalized form of the European (particularly the German) handshake, and thus the pressure that is applied during this handshake appears to be greater than that of most of its European counterparts.[55] Likewise, both the *chapcha* that accompanies the modern Hebrew handshake and the explicit demand to shake hands like a "male" stem from the need to overcompensate (or hypercorrect) for the effeminacy, passivity, feebleness, and bodily unfitness so often ascribed to Jews by other Europeans (especially by Germans) in the nineteenth century. The new Zionist cultural space in Palestine thus produced a new, more virile Jewish male body in direct response to the allegedly deficient masculinity of Jewish men in Europe; in other words, the more macho Hebrew handshake arose as an externalized corrective to internalized stereotypes of Jewish inferiority.

## SPEED

With the beginning of the Second Aliya (the second wave of Jewish immigration) in 1903, the social field of Zionist Palestine entered its self-proclaimed "practical phase." Particularly after the establishment of the Palestine Office (PO) in 1908, a new sense of urgency came to characterize the politics of the Zionist leadership.[56] As I have described elsewhere in more detail,[57] the PO's culture planning introduced an emphasis on establishing the material and cultural units of modern Hebrew society most speedily and thereby profoundly altered the Palestinian social field. In fact, the Palestine Office succeeded in dramatically transforming the conditions and the structure of society in Palestine within a very short period of time. At great speed, land purchases increased, settlements expanded, and economic activities diversified and intensified. This acceleration of Zionist settlement politics was driven by a conscious desire to "create facts," even at the expense of quality. Speed thus took precedence. For instance, the construction of the first Hebrew city, Tel Aviv, was executed as quickly as possible without careful and well-ordered urban planning. The city founders were aware that they lacked the necessary manpower, materials, and experience to construct a city; nonetheless, they deemed the rapid construction of a city that would create "demographic facts" as being more important than the quality of their product. For this reason, the builders tended to take an ad hoc approach to fashioning Tel Aviv; the result was predictably cheap and low-standard housing and urban development.[58]

Thus, the enormous rate at which the Zionist settlement in Palestine grew in the first decade of the twentieth century was not merely a function of a great many immigrants haphazardly entering the country, nor of investors coincidentally taking increased interest at that time. Rather, the expansion resulted from a deliberate policy formulated and pursued by the Zionist leadership in order to accumulate political, symbolic, and material capital for the Zionist project by speedy development. Indeed, almost from its inception in 1908, the PO was

proclaiming its policies in Palestine to be economically and socially successful—far earlier than any factual basis for such claims existed.[59] This propaganda
of practical Zionism was aimed at inducing the Hebrews in Palestine to work
even faster and thereby to sustain the new image of a hardworking, masculine,
and productive people and nation. In the same vein, Zionist leaders propagated notions of a model Hebrew body and created an entire pantheon of ideal
types and heroes to celebrate.[60] "[H]astily we are to make history," Yosef Haim
Brenner from the Zionist youth organization Ha-poel Hatzair observed pre-
sciently in 1912. "How we rush to sanctify things which can be sanctified only
over the breathing space of generations."[61]

According to Norbert Elias, it takes "centuries" for the "fortunes of a nation" to "become sedimented into the habitus of its individual members."[62] In
the case of the modern Hebrews, this process of sedimentation, by which a
repertoire becomes a habitus, took less than three decades. In fact, haste became an inherent feature of Zionist Palestine's social field. In his memorable
lecture to the Eleventh Zionist Congress, the German Jewish director of the
Palestine Office, Arthur Ruppin, stressed the importance of haste in his organization's culture planning: "Our work is urgent . . . we must inherit the land as
soon as possible. . . . It must also be the concern of each individual. We are at a
great beginning and we must pave the way for those who will come after us."[63]
This notion that modern Hebrews must act quickly before it is too late helped
to accelerate the process of sedimentation. Similar to the ways in which Tel
Aviv was erected in haste, a new modern Hebrew repertoire was forged and
disseminated among the young immigrants of the Second Aliya, who were
mostly between seventeen and twenty-one years of age when they arrived in
Palestine.

Their cultural identities were shaped in great haste, and this dimension of
speed is embodied in the modern Hebrew handshake. As a fairly simple gesture,
the handshake could easily serve as a vehicle for expressing the intent to act.[64]
The handshake is a transmitter, or an "action sign."[65] It operates as what sociologist Ann Swidler has called a "strategy of action," by which both concrete bodily
acts and the abstract mental ideas of a repertoire can be mobilized.[66]

## SELECTIVITY

Even though the element of haste played an important role in respect to the
hypercorrection that took place in Zionist Palestine, the speedy establishment
of modern Hebrew society was not achieved in an utterly chaotic manner. The
factor of speediness consistently came into conflict with another pressing need
of the Zionist field, namely selectivity, or the differentiation between potential
immigrants. In this regard, the PO followed the lead of German eugenicists, and
like their German counterparts, Palestine Office administrators were particularly

interested in the process of social selection (*soziale Auslese*).[67] Thus, since its inception, the PO had been searching for high-quality *Menschenmaterial* (human material) to serve as the base for creating a healthy *Volkskörper* (national body).[68] At the same time, the PO did everything it could to prevent supposedly negative, dysgenic elements from entering Hebrew Palestine. In his lecture to the Fifteenth Zionist Congress in 1927, Ruppin explained his policy in sober terms: "Some believe that in Palestine a higher type of human [*höherer Menschentyp*] will develop by itself. I do not share this belief. What we sow today, we shall reap tomorrow."[69]

The PO's directors thought of themselves as being engaged in shaping a society still in its early stages of development, and they considered this phase of the nascent Hebrew society as critical. They believed that bold experimentation was required to create an exemplary social unit that would form the nucleus of future Hebrew life worlds. In this formative phase, the men and women who participated in the project were expected to show discipline of both body and mind and a strong commitment to working toward the racial health of the collective. Consequently, Ruppin agitated in a number of different forums for "quality immigration." He consistently emphasized that "the future composition of the Jewish population in the Land of Israel" depended on an appropriate "selection of human material."[70] In his *Sociology of the Jews* from 1930, Ruppin argued that, unlike Europeans, "the Jews have never engaged in a 'self-cleansing' of their race, but have rather allowed every child, be it the most sickly, to grow up and marry and have children like themselves." He went on to suggest that "in order to retain the purity of our race, such Jews must abstain from childbearing."[71]

Historical research has shown that the Palestine Office indeed applied eugenic principles in both Palestine and Europe when it assessed candidates for immigration.[72] According to one estimate, Ruppin's strict policy of selection led to the rejection of about 80 percent of those who tried to migrate to Palestine between 1912 and 1918.[73] These policies formed part of the PO's plan to create a network of training farms and model agricultural settlements through which Ruppin and the Zionist leadership pursued two primary goals. First, the directors of the PO wanted to establish tighter control of lands owned by the Zionist movement; second, through selection and a healthy lifestyle, they aimed at fabricating a stock of "good" *Menschenmaterial.* They hoped that the racial characteristics of this improved *Menschenmaterial* would eventually become dominant in what was to emerge as the old-new Jewish species that Ruppin liked to call "the Maccabean type."[74] It is telling that the term used to designate the new social unit in Palestine, Yishuv, refers to the collective Zionist settlement in the land of Israel/Palestine as well as to the inhabitants of the settlements. The word thereby reflects the profound link between land and people in modern Hebrew culture.

As I have described elsewhere at length,[75] Ruppin's *Weltanschauung* was based on a *völkisch* nostalgia for what he thought was the lost racial purity of the Jewish people. However, he also believed that scientific intervention could restore the collective of racially pure Jews and rescue it from extinction. Although he conceded that such racial purity could not be fully reestablished in his own time, since the true traits of the Jewish *Volk* had been badly compromised and diffused, he was convinced that with the right methods, the Jewish race could regain its purity and strength in the future.[76] Ruppin was an ambitious social scientist who perceived himself to be, in the words of the German eugenicist Fritz Lenz, the *geistige[r] Führer des Zionismus* (intellectual leader of Zionism).[77] Ruppin had faith in the potential of the Jewish race, and he regarded the training farms and the settlements that he had helped establish as "laboratory experiment[s] directed at the future."[78] In his view, these institutions were exceptionally well suited for identifying and expunging "the unfit [*die Ungeeigneten*]."[79]

The first training camp was established in Kinneret on the banks of the Sea of Galilee, and was followed by the creation of a network of small communal settlements that later became known as the *kvutzot* (collective groups). The establishment of these training farms and *kvutzot* was not a local development in which the Zionist leadership responded spontaneously to conditions and problems in Palestine, as the traditional historiography would have it.[80] Rather, the PO's group system was inspired by innovations in the German labor market, where at the turn of the twentieth century eugenics had gained influence and a new science and politics of labor relations had taken shape. At the crossroads of science, medicine, and government-directed social policy, a novel *Arbeitswissenschaft* (science of work) emerged which generated new models of management in the factories and new patterns of relationship between factory owners and laborers.[81] In particular, the new approach encouraged managers to bind the workers in their factories more closely to the workplace through a system of codes and measures, which sought to mirror family relations and were designed to give meaning to the workers' lives. They helped foster an emotional connection between the workers and their factories.

This new brand of labor relations in Germany, which came to be emulated by Palestinian Zionists, was often referred to as the "Stumm system," named for its most dedicated and powerful advocate, the steel industrialist and conservative politician Karl Ferdinand von Stumm (1843–1925). Though Stumm had worked primarily in the Saar, his management models were soon accepted by a large number of important factories in Germany.[82] In order to curb the influence of independent labor organizations, Stumm's managerial system combined far-reaching new rules that increased discipline at the workplace with an extensive array of social provisions, designed to attract a core of highly loyal workers (*Arbeiterstamm*). In this system, the employer figured as the "provider"

(*Brotgeber*) and was a father figure to the workers, who thus were to think of themselves as his dependents (or children) in the larger factory "family." Stumm, in his capacity as the director of a steel factory in the town of Neunkirchen, often referred to himself as being the head of a "family of workers" (*Arbeiterfamilie*).[83]

In a manner quite similar to the German Stumm system, Ruppin referred to the workers at the *kvutzot* as his "sons," which soon earned him the nickname "The Father." His style of managing the network of training farms and settlement groups with the aid of meticulously kept statistics, careful planning, and close monitoring of the workers, as well as his focus on the workers' physical health and capacity for productivity, likewise resembled the Stumm system.[84] As the German employers did in their factories, Ruppin imbued the work performed in the Zionist settlements with a significance far beyond its economic benefits.

Ruppin consistently reminded the young immigrants of the Second Aliya that he considered them partners in the creation of a new society.[85] In the same vein, German workers were told that they labored toward the betterment of their "family," not merely to earn a wage. The Stumm system endowed factory work with a moral quality and a dimension of sacredness, so that factory workers began to cherish the supposedly moral aspects of their own hard labor. They came to consider work as a means of self-improvement and identified it with values such as orderliness and moderation, which they thought deterred individuals from idleness or morally corrosive activities. The company's social welfare services thus did not simply address the workers' material needs; rather, they were inspired by the company's much wider ambition to refine and elevate the morals and intellects of their workers. Through income savings, loan programs, and housing cooperatives that offered workers financial means to purchase their own homes, the company tried to inculcate in workers the values of thrift, conservation, sobriety, moderation, obedience, and loyalty to the factory family.[86] Company officials often monitored the activities of their workforce for immoral conduct, keeping a particularly keen eye on the sexual and marital lives of their employees. Younger workers could be dismissed from their factory job for illicit (nonmarital) cohabitation. At some firms, workers who wished to marry were even expected to seek the approval of their employer before taking their vows.[87]

According to the principles of the Stumm system, the loyal core of workers, or *Arbeiterstamm* (literally, "trunk of workers" or "work tribe"), was to look upon the factory owner as a father figure, and the young immigrants at the *kvutzot* considered Ruppin their fatherly leader. Ruppin regarded these young men not only as sons but also as the nucleus of a future pure Jewish race, and in the years to come the Palestine Office would rely heavily on the members of the *kvutzot* for disseminating to the growing immigrant population the repertoire that the Zionist leadership sought to foster in its program of culture planning. The PO used the young workers from the *kvutzot* as a pool of high-quality *Menschenmaterial* from which it staffed the numerous positions in the Yishuv's expanding bureaucracy; these young men were often appointed as messengers, instructors, clerks, and managers.[88] Moreover, the leadership of the influential labor movement in Jewish Palestine and, later, Israel would emerge from the ranks of the *kvutzot* members. Thus, this group of people indeed continued to produce and reproduce the modern Hebrew repertoire, long after the Palestine Office itself had become defunct.[89]

In order to resolve the conflict that the PO experienced between the need to act fast and the need to be highly deliberate in its efforts to build a modern Hebrew society in Palestine, the Zionist leadership drew inspiration not only from the Stumm factory system but also from the German military. In the decade it operated in Palestine, the PO was committed to a focus on rigor and a tight organization. Zionist leaders were not particularly interested in adopting Prussian modes of actual warfare,[90] but they closely studied Prussian methods of applying military modes of operation to civil society. "Our condition here," Ruppin wrote in 1919, "is similar to that of an army. . . . When there is a well-trained standing army, it is easy to augment it with large numbers of new men every year, training them alongside already competent soldiers."[91] Ruppin's introduction of military categories into the managing of civil society constitutes one of his most lasting and significant contributions to modern Hebrew culture.[92]

In 1919, the same year that Ruppin compared the situation in Zionist Palestine to that of an army, the Jewish population in Palestine comprised an estimated 56,000 inhabitants. By May 1948, when the State of Israel was founded, that number had swelled to 650,000. In only thirty years, more than a half million Jews had migrated to Zionist Palestine.[93] The influx of such a large number of immigrants to the region within such a short time helped to make the PO's vision for the speedy development of modern Hebrew society a reality. In addition to achieving its goal of external expansion, the Palestine Office was successful in laying the foundations for the modern Hebrew habitus and the repertoire that came to characterize Palestinian Zionist and Israeli society. For this purpose, the Palestine Office drew on models from German labor relations and the Prussian military, and Zionist leaders implemented a program of both internal selection and conditioning of their population. In fact, the Zionist leadership not only created a system of norms but also instituted modes of sanction against those who deviated from the modern Hebrew code of conduct in any way.

## THE CONFLICT BETWEEN SPEEDINESS AND SELECTIVENESS AND ITS IMPACT ON THE HANDSHAKE

The PO's conflicting aims to simultaneously act fast and work toward producing a high quality of new modern Hebrew people may have helped give birth to the *chapcha*. At odds with accepted codes of European behavior, the forceful gesture of the modern Hebrew handshake and its accompanying *chapcha* are unlikely to be of purely European origins. Although German and Israeli attitudes toward the handshake bear similarities, there are also some significant differences. As noted earlier, both cultures stand out by favoring very firm handshakes, and they place a great deal of importance on handshaking as a social practice.[94] They differ vastly, however, in their conceptions of personal space, both in actual physical and in social terms. If a German person is dissatisfied with another person's handshake, he or she will almost never raise the issue directly but may discuss it with others;[95] an Israeli, on the other hand, is likely to correct a "soft shaker" straightforwardly. He (or sometimes she) does so out of a sense of cultural goodwill, even if it entails publicly humiliating the soft shaker.[96] Thus, German and Israeli conceptions of what one can and cannot appropriately say to another—and hence their ideas of what conduct is required to respect an individual's personal space—are quite distinct. The *chapcha* not only possesses the directness of the Israeli tendency to reprimand, but it also violates European standards in regard to its proxemics (the distance between people while they are interacting) and its haptics (the way people touch each other).[97] It is my contention that this component of the modern Hebrew handshake is informed by the European repertoire only insofar as it is the result of hypercorrection and as it is influenced by German ideas of eugenics and social selectivity.

In the eugenics program that Ruppin and other Zionist leaders in Palestine and Europe implemented, the new immigrants themselves were to play a decisive role. It had to be the young men of the *kvutzot* who eliminated whatever unfit and undesirable elements had entered Palestine (a role that accorded nicely with the Stumm system's basic principles). Ruppin made the point quite explicitly: "We are delegating the task of putting away people of antisocial inclination largely to the *kvutzot* themselves."[98]

The Palestine Office had carefully designed the social space of the *kvutzot* to fulfill the eugenics and selective purposes. "[The *kvutza*] enables members to develop close relationships and to truly know each other in the course of several years," Ruppin explained. On the basis of this intimate knowledge of each other, the collective then could "reject those members who are not qualified for work or for social life."[99]

The PO aimed at putting the members of the *kvutzot* under great social and psychological pressure. It created an ethos according to which everything within the *kvutzot* was the property of the collective, including the very thoughts of the individuals. One of the *kvutzot*'s characteristic regulations stated, for instance, that "all privacy disturbs the common work."[100] Private discussion was virtually impossible, and conversations among *kvutza* members tended to be inquisitive and intrusive. The young people were encouraged to make intimate "confessions" to the entire *kvutza*, in the course of which *kvutza* members investigated and "corrected" each other's thoughts and emotions. This system, which was designed to test the young and to weed out the unfit, undermined rather than fostered an atmosphere of solidarity and often made *kvutza* members feel isolated and lonely.[101] Golda Meir, who was accepted by *kvutzat* Merchavia only on her third attempt to join it,[102] recounted that the intrusion into the members' personal space led to the departures of "thousands."[103]

I suggest that it is within this context that the modern Hebrew handshake and especially the *chapcha* developed. By means of this forceful gesture, a group member could invade his comrade's personal space, which not only was permitted but was a highly desirable mode of conduct in the social world of the *kvutzot*. When they performed the modern Hebrew handshake, the young men of the *kvutzot* became agents of social selection and thus assumed a highly respected role. Later, the *kvutza* members disseminated the practice of the handshake and the *chapcha* among the masses of Jewish immigrants who arrived in Palestine, and the modern Hebrew handshake itself evolved into an instrument of selectivity. With the help of this gesture, its practitioners participated in what Ruppin had conceived as the natural eugenics process, or the self-cleansing of the modern Hebrew *Volk* in its ancestral homeland.

## CONTROLLING THE TOOL: FROM THE HOE TO THE RIFLE

> In the new environment that is to be created, not the
> book shall be in the lead, but the shovel and the hoe.[104]

The young, mostly male immigrants who arrived in Zionist Palestine during the formative years of 1903–1921, as part of the waves of immigration that historians call the Second Aliya (1903–1914) and the Third Aliya (1919–1923), had to prove that they were capable workers. Initially, the young immigrants had to convince land owners to employ them for agricultural work,[105] and later they needed to pass the rigorous selection process of the PO's agricultural training farms and settlements. In order to obtain work and to survive in the early years of the new Hebrew social field, young men were forced to demonstrate their aptitude as agricultural laborers, and evidence from a great many stories, songs, and personal recollections of this time suggests that the most important test was working with the *turiya* (hoe). The ability to control the hoe was highly regarded among those who would become the dominant group in the social field of Zionist Palestine.[106] To acquire the skill of working the hoe—or the "tool" as they called it[107]—was to win the respect of one's fellow workers and of the native Arabs, who often seemed to doubt the masculinity of Jewish men.[108] It also offered an opportunity to obtain work in the agricultural settlements called *moshavot*, where skilled workers could even be promoted to be supervisors.

The Palestine Office, which was established five years after the first immigrants of the Second Aliya began arriving, considered work with the hoe to be a "fire test,"

Workers at Kibbutz Ma'ale Hahamisha, 1938. With permission from the Central Zionist Archives

as Ruppin put it.[109] For Ruppin, the ability to work with the tool determined the quality of an individual in the PO's quest for good *Menschenmaterial.* The Palestine Office was engaged in testing and scrutinizing the new immigrants in order to ensure that they were indeed fit to be members of the dominant group—the trained core of the army to which newcomers could be added, as Ruppin put it in his comparison of 1919. In the terms of contemporary cultural studies, these immigrants were to become the reproducers of the new modern Hebrew cultural identity.[110]

Yet mastery of the hoe was not simply understood as evidence of the immigrants' masculinity and productivity, but it was also seen by the Palestine Office as an indication of the young men's biological link with the ancient Hebrews. Apparently, Ruppin and the PO subscribed to a distinctly German, *völkisch* conception of a people's (*Volk's*) bond to its ancestral soil, and they regarded a man's ability to work the land with his hoe and to fertilize it as proof of his connection to the soil. According to the Zionist leaders, this skill confirmed that an immigrant possessed the racial makeup of the ancient Hebrews.[111] And, by having a strong handshake, the male pioneer not only conveyed that he was capable of working the hoe—which in itself carried significant cultural and material capital at the time—but his new Hebrew, masculine body was also an expression of his connection to the soil of his ancestors.

## ACTIVISM

An important shift in the development of the handshake occurred with the second generation of modern Hebrews (*tzabarim*). Having been born to immigrant parents, they were the first modern Hebrews to be native to Palestine, and they came of age in the 1930s and 1940s. They witnessed the second Arab-Palestinian revolt (1936–1939) and the rise of "activism," the new military strategy designed to quell the revolt; they also experienced the emergence of paramilitary units, including the elite fighting forces of the Haganah, known as the Palmach (literally, "strike force") in the early 1940s.[112] Within these units, the ideal of the agricultural worker was partly replaced by that of the warrior for pre-Israeli youth. Indeed, the demand to be "active"—physically active as well as proactive—had always been present in the modern Hebrew repertoire, but it was only at this juncture that it became a dominant feature. Now, the youth were encouraged to divert their enthusiasm to the military sphere and to perform great acts of courage; controlling the "tool" in this period no longer meant toiling with the hoe, but firing with the rifle. The political and strategic ideology that came to the fore in this era, called activism, had as its motto a Zionist interpretation of the Talmudic phrase "*ha-ba le-horgecha hashkem le-horgo* [arise and kill first he who comes to kill you]."[113] It stressed the need for preemptive warfare in self-defense and promoted the notion that the struggle over the land in Palestine would be determined by force.[114]

The first generation of pioneers had understood their *Lebenskraft* (vital force, life energy, enthusiasm)[115] to be evidence of their connection to the ancient Hebrews of biblical Israel. The younger modern Hebrews who had been born in Palestine did not feel the same need as their parents to prove a connection to the land, and they expressed their *Lebenskraft* now in the form of military activism. A song from the period illustrates their worldview and politics:

> There is still in this world
> Such a kind of people,
> For whom justice is an eternal candle at their feet.
> They loathe activity [*aktiv*]
> And they have much to say,[116]
> While explosions make the windows shudder . . .
> But—
> We shall stay forever—activists! [*aktivistim*]
> With every ship that's breached—activists!
> While around us the storm is blowing—activists!
> We always break through wall and gate—activists!

...
Fed up with talk and chatter—activists!
To the shore with Stens[117] we came—activists!
...
Until thousands more come here—activists![118]

The *chapcha* may have arisen in the period of activism because of its distinctive physiological effects: it activates the sympathetic nerve system[119] and instills the body with a sense of preparedness and a desire to be active. However, the *chapcha* is not simply a slap or tap meant to stimulate or encourage its recipient (as one frequently finds in sports), but as I have discussed above, it can be a marker of a hierarchical relationship. Moreover, insofar as it constitutes an invasion into another person's physical space, the *chapcha* also possesses an element of "justified cruelty" or "healthy cruelty."[120] The idea of healthy cruelty was common in the eugenics movement, which held that even though processes of social selection might appear cruel to people who did not think modernly, they were not only natural but also necessary for the continued existence and progress of human races. Ruppin and the Palestine Office adopted this concept, like they did so many others, for the new Zionist repertoire they had set out to fashion. In their *Weltanschauung,* the mercifulness of *galut* Jews was a sign of diaspora Jewry's degeneracy and weakness. Thus, the concept of healthy cruelty was designed to overcome the frightened and excessive compassion of the *galut* Jew and to erase the memory of such behavior from the collective consciousness and the bodies of modern Hebrews. Zionist leaders created a comprehensive ideology to effect such a transformation of the Jewish people's mode of conduct and to obliterate the existing cultural memory from among them. I believe that a well-performed *chapcha* was much more effective than words when it came to erasing the traces of feebleness and degeneracy from the Jewish body.

## CONCLUSION

It was likely in the 1940s, when the *tzabarim* of the Second Aliya were coming of age, that the modern Hebrew handshake attained its distinctive status as a common informal gesture in Zionist Palestine. The young members of the Palmach especially developed a liking for the handshake and in particular for the *chapcha,* which they regarded as less formal than the shaking of hands. As part of the handshake or on its own, the *chapcha* became an expression of affection or, as one of my interviewees described it, it constituted "extreme intimacy." Another interviewee, in his attempt to reflect on it from the distance of time, described the *chapcha* of his youth as a type of "violent intimacy."

It seems that the particular kind of *chapcha* that took shape among the young men of the Palmach emerged out of a need for friendship and intimacy which conflicted sharply with the hypermasculinity the fighters were meant to exhibit. Expected to avoid all displays of gentleness, tenderness, and any other comportment that might be judged feminine, the troops appear to have developed the *chapcha* as a kind of emotional safety valve. It allowed them to express intimacy while retaining elements of masculine aggression and even cruelty. Thus, through hypercorrection, the *chapcha* helped repress elements of the supposedly effeminate behavior that was thought to characterize social and cultural Others, such as Jewish men of the old *galut* (*hayehudonim*), *mizrachim* or oriental Jews, and Muslim or Christian Arabs.

When Ruppin wrote about the modern Hebrews who had been born in the land of Israel/Palestine, he referred to them as "the Maccabean type," a new sub-race that he believed his culture planning had brought forth. In his last book, *The War of the Jews for Their Existence* (1940), he described the process through which the Jewish bodies of young immigrants had become Hebrew bodies. *Galut* Jews, he wrote, knew how to be brave, yet only in a

> passive way: they knew how to endure suffering . . . but they have not had to develop courage in the active sense. War, which is the most common cause for the display of courage, has not touched [the sons of] Israel directly, but only indirectly. They have been subjected to the depravations of war, but not to the bravery and grandeur that comes with warfare. Thus when the new era dawned, they remained at the margins, full of fears and without desire to fight, while Christians possess personal courage and a spirit of war.[121]

However, the "new Jew" of the 1940s, the modern Hebrew whom Ruppin observed more than thirty years after the establishment of the Palestine Office, had converted his inherent courage from the ability to passively endure hardship into active bravery. Ruppin continued:

> The new conditions under which the Hebrew youth grew in the land have endowed him with new qualities. He has freed himself from his fear and his sense of inferiority and become brave and high-minded. . . . Nowhere else is there such a high percentage of young men who are willing to face danger and perilous enterprises and to sacrifice their lives as in the land of Israel. The younger generation of this land is a new type of Jew, perhaps most akin to the Maccabean type from our distant past.[122]

The "new conditions" to which Ruppin alluded were—to a significantly greater extent than is typically acknowledged—products of the *Weltanschauung* of *Muskeljudentum* and of Zionist leaders' intervention. With their program of culture planning, Ruppin and his collaborators had succeeded in generating a new modern Hebrew habitus, and the modern Hebrew handshake is one of that habitus's manifestations. My analysis of this handshake has shown that it has been shaped by and embodies a number of aspects and dimensions that all characterize the modern Hebrew habitus itself: the drive for speedy development; selectivity and productivity; the function of hypercorrection; militarism; and the ideology and strategy of activism. Moreover, an investigation into this gesture makes us aware that in Israeli society, the dominant Zionist ideology is not only "out there" as an abstract concept or materialized in the policies of bureaucrats or in ceremonies of the state and other institutions. Rather, Ruppin's victorious Zionism is also "in here," indelibly engraved on our bodies and lodged in the most intimate layers of our being, since it structures the ways in which we, as members of this society, feel, think, judge, and act.

As for my own handshake, after experimenting for a time with hand touches, I returned to the modern Hebrew handshake and soften it only when meeting my friend Menashe or when attending synagogue. With most of my fellow Israelis, I press as firmly or as hard as ever, and I enjoy including a warm *chapcha* here and there. I have tried to convince Menashe of the truth in the saying "when in Rome, do as the Romans do"—but he is stubborn, he has patience to wait for the world to come around, and he is willing to pay the price of marginalization for his principled stance.

NOTES

1. I would like to thank Ben Baader for inspiring and supporting this project, and I thank Evan Bernier for his editorial assistance with this chapter.

2. Etan Bloom, *Arthur Ruppin and the Production of Pre-Israeli Culture* (Boston: Brill, 2011).

3. Itamar Even-Zohar, ed., *Polysystem Studies*, a special issue of *Poetics Today* 11, no. 1 (1990); Ann Swidler, "Culture in Action: Symbols and Strategies," *American Sociological Review* 51, no. 2 (1986): 273–286.

4. Swidler, "Culture in Action," 273.

5. Itamar Even-Zohar, "Factors and Dependencies in Culture: A Revised Draft for Polysystem Culture Research," *Canadian Review of Comparative Literature* 24, no. 1 (March 1997): 15–34, http://www.even-zohar.com, quotation 20; see also Even-Zohar, "The Making of Repertoire: Survival and Success under Heterogeneity," in Guido Zurstiege, ed., *Festschrift für die Wirklichkeit* (Darmstadt: Westdeutscher, 2000), 41–51.

6. Ernst Cassirer called the structures within which reality takes shape "symbolic forms," and Emile Durkheim called them "forms of classification." These are different ways of expressing the same idea in different theoretical traditions. See Pierre Bourdieu, "Rethinking the State: Genesis and Structure of the Bureaucratic Field," in George Steinmetz, ed., *State/Culture: State-Formation after the Cultural Turn* (Ithaca, NY: Cornell University Press, 1999), 53–72, 67.

7. Ibid. Bourdieu made a similar statement when he discussed what he called "ritual practice": "To bring order is to bring division. . . . the limit produces difference and the different things 'by an arbitrary institution,' as Leibniz put it, translating the 'ex instituto' of the Scholastics. This magical act presupposes and produces collective belief, that is, ignorance of its own arbitrariness." Bourdieu, *The Logic of Practice* (Cambridge: Polity, 1990), 210.

8. See Itamar Even-Zohar, "Culture Planning, Cohesion, and the Making and Maintenance of Entities," in A. Pym, M. Shlesinger, and Daniel Simeoni, eds., *Beyond Descriptive Translation Studies: Investigations in Homage to Gideon Toury* (Philadelphia: John Benjamins, 2008), 277–292. Culture planning must be understood as a flexible and dynamic implementation of a repertoire, in which the plan operates more like a jazz standard than a score for a symphony.

9. Bourdieu, "Rethinking the State," 57.

10. Even-Zohar, "Making of Repertoire," 42.

11. Pierre Bourdieu, *Language and Symbolic Power* (Cambridge, MA: Harvard University Press, 1993), 12.

12. Talal Asad, *Genealogies of Religion: Discipline and Reasons of Power in Christianity and Islam* (Baltimore, MD: Johns Hopkins University Press, 1993), 75.

13. Kinesics includes the study of proxemics (the distance between people while they are interacting) and of haptics (the way people touch each other).

14. George L. Mosse, *Fallen Soldiers: Reshaping the Memory of the World Wars* (New York: Oxford University Press, 1991), 166.

15. Micha Josef Berdyczewski, *Changing Values* (Heb.), quoted in Shmuel Almog, *The Jewish Point: Jews in Their Own Eyes and in the Eyes of Others* (Tel Aviv: Sifriat Poalim, 2002), 93 (Heb.).

16. Avshalom Feinberg (1889–1917) was born in Gederah, Palestine, and studied in France. He returned to Palestine to work at the research station in Atlit. During World War I, he became a founder of the NILI underground organization, which assisted British forces in occupying Palestine and thereby ending Turkish rule in the region.

17. Quoted in Rachel Elboim-Dror, "'He is Coming, from Within Us Comes the New Hebrew': On the Youth Culture of the First Immigrations," *Alpaim* 12 (1996): 104–135, 123 (Heb.).

18. Ibid. This term was still in use in the twenty-first century. In 2002, a member of the Israeli parliament, Zvi Hendel, called the American ambassador, Dan Kerzer, a *yehudon,* and when he apologized for it, Hendel explained: "I meant a small person and mistakenly I said small *yehudon.*" Smadar Shmueli, "Storm in the Knesset," *Ynet,* internet version of *Yediot Acharonot,* the biggest daily in Israel, www.ynetnews.com, 9 January 2002. During a public debate over former MP Avraham Burg's controversial assertions about the character of the Jewish state, Burg applied the term to himself: "in the prevailing terminology here [in Israel]: [I was] a *yehudon.*" Ari Shavit, *Divorce Certificate* (Heb.), *Musaf Haaretz,* 7 June 2007. Perhaps not surprisingly, many of the angry responses to Burg described him not only as "stinking," "poor," and a "traitor," but also as a *yehudon.* On the use of *zhid* (or *yehudon*) as designating "sickness" in Israeli culture, see, for instance, Amos Oz, *In the Land of Israel* (Tel Aviv: Am-Oved, 1983), 73.

19. For a discussion and bibliography of the large and varied scholarly literature on these issues, see Rakefet Sela-Sheffy, "'What Makes One an Israeli?' Negotiating Identities in Everyday Representations of 'Israeliness,'" *Nations and Nationalism* 10, no. 4 (2004): 479–497, 480–481.

20. For a description of the tensions in the 1950s, see Etan Bloom, "The Reproduction of the Model of 'the Oriental' in the Israeli Social Field: The 1950s and Mass Immigration," M.A. thesis, Unit of Culture Research, Tel Aviv University, 2003.

21. For information on the "Canaanite movement," which in the 1940s and 1950s unsuccessfully tried to stem the blurring of Jewish and Hebrew identities, see Bloom, *Arthur Ruppin,* 13.

22. Trumpeldor was a military hero, already hailed in the 1905 Russo-Japanese War. He was killed in 1920 in one of the formative battles of Palestinian Zionist military history,

at Tel Hai, and his supposed last words—"It is good to die for our country"—became an inspiration to generations of patriots in Israel.

23. Quoted in Amos Elon, *The Israelis: Founders and Sons* (Jerusalem: Schocken, 1971), 137 (Heb.).

24. As an expert on colonization projects all over the world, Oppenheimer became Theodor Herzl's advisor and formulated the first program of Zionist colonization, which he presented in 1903 to the Sixth Zionist Congress. Merchavia, established in 1910 as the first cooperative settlement, was based on Oppenheimer's ideas.

25. Franz Oppenheimer, *Der Zionismus, Wege zur Genossenschaft: Reden und Aufsätze* (Munich: Max Hueber, 1924), 214–229, quotation 220.

26. On the symmetrical relationship between Zionism and modern anti-Semitism, see Even-Zohar, "The Emergence of a Native Hebrew Culture in Palestine 1882–1948," in Even-Zohar, ed., *Polysystem Studies*, 175–191; John Milfull, "Imagining Jew(ess)es: Gregor von Rezzori's Memoirs of an Anti-Semite: An Aetiology of 'German' Anti-Semitism," in Milfull, *Why Germany?* (Providence: Berg, 1993), 105–117.

27. On this concept, common in Palestinian Zionist discourse, see Avraham Sharon, *The Theory of Cruel Zionism* (Tel Aviv: Am-Oved, 1944) (Heb.).

28. Zvi Nishri was a gymnastics teacher in Palestine beginning in 1907. Nishri, *A Summary of the Physical Education History* (Tel Aviv: Ministry of Education and Culture, Department for Physical Training, 1953).

29. Ibid., 56.

30. In Brechtian terms, we might consider the handshake a kind of *Gestus;* the combination of gesture, facial expression, and body language is deliberately used to create meaning and communicate a message.

31. In the Zionist settlements in Palestine and in Israel, there have been many slang terms and expressions to denote this ideal masculine male: in the pre-state period *zachar alfa* (alpha male), later *akbar gever* (very male), *achla gever* (good male), *gever amiti* (real male), *gever lainyan* (capable male), *gever retzini* (serious male), and in the latest Israeli version *gever-gever* (male-male).

32. Hierarchy is extremely important, because Jews were often accused of being insubordinate. "Our greatest fault," wrote the Zionist leader Max Nordau, "is stubbornness and the refusal to acknowledge the value of our fellow man, he who is from our own race. It is an egregious shortcoming of ours that we fail to subordinate ourselves to his command." Nordau, "What Is the Meaning of Gymnastics for Us, the Jews?," in his *Zionist Writings* (1902; rpt., Jerusalem: Zionist Library, 1960), 2:82 (Heb.).

33. Zvika Brot, "Bugi Soger Cheshbon," *Yediot Acharonot* (2 May 2005): 15.

34. There is a large literature on the relationship between nonverbal forms of communication, physical comportment, and gender. Empirical studies indicate that in their nonverbal modes of expression, women generally convey more emotion than do men. However, when women interact with men rather than other women, they tend to avoid direct eye contact and physical touch and thus assume a more passive stance. Likewise, they allow men to establish dominance by letting them dictate interpersonal proxemics. Jennifer Huwer, "Understanding Handshaking: The Result of Contextual, Interpersonal and Social Demands," senior thesis project, Haverford College, 2003, 27–32; J. W. Lee and L. K. Guerrero, "Types of Touch in Cross-Sex Relationship between Coworkers: Perceptions of Relational and Emotional Messages, Inappropriateness, and Sexual Harassment," *Journal of Applied Communication Research* 29, no. 3 (2001): 197–220.

35. When Rabbi Ovadia Yosef won the Israel Prize in 1970, he refused to shake the hand of Prime Minister Golda Meir because she was a woman. This kind of behavior is still accepted by most Orthodox rabbis.

36. Women have related in a variety of ways to Zionism's masculine rhetoric and program. As Jewish men were expected to become physically fit to match the new nationalist ideal, so too were Jewish women. Thus, some women embraced Zionism's masculine emphasis and sought equality by attaining strength, prowess, and endurance. Yet from a very early stage of Palestinian Zionism, other women rejected a gender equality that denied the physical distinctiveness of men and women. They answered Ahad Ha-Am's call to embrace their "natural" roles as "enlightened Jewish mothers" who would raise children for the benefit of the nation. However, both the Palestine Office and, from the 1920s on, the labor movement believed that only physical labor on "the land" could free women, just as it could free the entire Jewish people. As historian Gerald Berg has argued, it was hard physical labor and productivity—not their female gender—that stood at the core of women's identities in the formative period of Palestinian Zionism; likewise, it was the culture of the *galut*—and not men—that Jewish women saw as the source of their oppression and the oppression of the Jewish people more generally. Gerald M. Berg, "Zionism's Gender: Hannah Meisel and the Founding of the Agricultural Schools for Young Women," *Israel Studies* 6, no. 3 (2001): 144, 146, 156.

37. Hugging and kissing are typical female behaviors according to Huwer, "Understanding Handshaking"; and Lee and Guerrero, "Types of Touch in Cross-Sex Relationship."

38. In the late 1940s, on the eve of the founding of the State of Israel, an estimated 20–30 percent of all members in the Zionist military forces and paramilitary units in Palestine were women. It is possible that some of these female combatants in fact adopted this kind of handshake. Yet in Israeli society today, a woman is not expected to perform it.

39. Bourdieu uses the concept of symbolic violence to denote a particular form of social compulsion. The exercise of symbolic violence entails no physical violence nor even the threat of it, and it does not involve any orders by an authority. Rather, it operates by creating the perception that an individual or group is superior, exclusive, and distinguished. It leads to self-deprecation among its victims, who consequently refrain from competing against those exercising symbolic violence. Pierre Bourdieu and J. C. Passeron, *Reproduction in Education, Society and Culture* (London: Sage, 1977), 4.

40. Since the end of the 1980s and the appearance of the metrosexual repertoire, small segments of the male Israeli population have adopted new modes of handshaking interactions, which I am not considering here. These still-marginal developments seem to be connected to the fact that during the 1990s, the percentage of men not serving in the Israel Defense Forces and the social acceptance of this choice both increased dramatically.

41. Sometimes, the expression takes the form of a command, such as "Be a male! [*Tihye gever!*]." Other times, it is expressed less directly, as when, for example, one hears "What is the matter with you? You didn't eat breakfast today?" Moreover, "be a male" is an expression commonly used by men to convince other men to do something fair, decent, or brave or simply to do somebody a favor. When a man fulfills such an expectation or wish, he can be described as someone who *yatza gever* ("came out as a male"). Note that I am translating the Hebrew word *gever* as "male" and not as "man," for which the Hebrew is *ish*. *Ish*, which is still used in spoken Israeli today, denotes a moral man in traditional Jewish texts, such as in Pirkei Avot (Ethics of the Fathers) 2:5: "*Bemakom shein anashim hishtadel lihiyot ish* [In a place where there are no men, strive to be a man]." The shift from *ish* to *gever* reflects Zionism's influence on the Jewish repertoire, as it stresses the importance of masculinity and makes virtue a function of gender rather than of ethics.

42. The verb *litkoaa* is also used for describing the act of thrusting a tent stake into the ground. It seems that for the ancient Hebrews shaking hands bore some similarity to thrusting a stake, an action that was common at that time.

43. See, for instance, Proverbs 17:18 and Job 17:3.

44. The touching of hands was used particularly when it came to obligations to pay back a loan or when two parties agreed on a prospective marriage (*shidduch*). However, biblical texts also warned against engaging in the practice of "thrusting hands." See, for instance, Proverbs 11:15 and 22:26.

45. This is only one of several possible explanations for the origin of the European handshake, since conclusive evidence is lacking. Deborah Schiffrin, for instance, has contended that handshaking was already practiced in ancient Greece as a sign of friendliness, hospitality, and trust. Peter Hall and Dee Ann Hall believe that it was developed much later in medieval Europe, when kings and knights grasped each other's hands as a show of their good faith. The handshake demonstrated that neither party bore concealed weapons nor intended any harm. Other scholars have traced the handshake's roots to Renaissance court life. Philip Busterson, for instance, has argued that it was introduced at the Tudor court by Sir Walter Raleigh in the late sixteenth century. See http://www.squashmagazine.com/vcm/ squashmagazine/COLUMNS/shake_it_up.html. Herman Roodenburg has situated the handshake's emergence in the context of a much larger shift in Europe toward more egalitarian social values, noting that it gradually replaced such common signs of deference as bowing, kneeling, and curtsying. See Roodenburg, "The 'Hand of Friendship': Shaking Hands and Other Gestures in the Dutch Republic," in Jan Bremmer and Herman Roodenburg, eds., *A Cultural History of Gesture* (Ithaca, NY: Cornell University Press, 1992), 152–189; Peter Hall and Dee Ann Hall, "The Handshake as Interaction," *Semiotica* 45 (1983): 249–264; Deborah Schiffrin, "Handwork as Ceremony: The Case of the Handshake," *Semiotica* 12, no. 3 (1974): 189–202, reprinted in A. Kendon, ed., *Nonverbal Communication, Interaction, and Gesture* (New York: Mouton, 1981), 237–250; Keith Thomas, "Introduction," in Bremmer and Roodenburg, eds., *A Cultural History of Gesture*, 1–14.

46. The high regard for military power and the establishment of a Jewish army have perhaps been the greatest innovation of the modern Hebrews. These innovations bespeak both a radical change in the political status of Jews and a profound revolution in the Jewish repertoire and habitus. Nevertheless and regardless of the low esteem for warfare in rabbinic culture, Halakhah had never developed a principled pacifist position. According to rabbinic texts, it is legitimate to conduct not only a necessary war (*milchemet chova*), or a war of self-defense against an aggressive other, but also an unnecessary war (*milchemet reshut*). Only in the messianic age will human nature radically change and the worldly peace that the prophets foretold be established. On the rabbis' position toward war, see the bibliography in Nahum Rackower, *Treasure of Law* (Jerusalem: Harry Fischel Institute, 1975), 201–205 (Heb.). See also Ehud Luz, "The Moral Price of Sovereignty: The Dispute about the Use of Military Power within Zionism," *Modern Judaism* 7, no. 1 (1987): 51–98.

47. Luz, "The Moral Price of Sovereignty," 53.

48. Shlomo Zalman Auerbach, *Shlomo Customs*, 3 vols. (Jerusalem: published independently by the rabbi's grandchildren, 2004) (Heb.), quoted in Eldad Nakar, *My Bones Will Say: Body Language as Halacha* (Jerusalem: Casuto, 2006), 99 (Heb.).

49. Nakar, *My Bones Will Say*, 99.

50. Ibid.

51. Quoted ibid., 350–351.

52. There are many stories about the supposed "spiritual energy and heat" which some rabbis are said to possess in their touch. Such popular beliefs are not unlike those once held by medieval Christians regarding the healing power of a saint's touch. In some Jewish communities, hand touching in the synagogue takes place when the worshiper who made *aliya latorah* (who was reading from the Torah) returns to his seat. The idea seems to

be that the man who touched the Torah carries in his hand some of its holiness, which he is then able to pass on to his fellows.

53. An American journalist in the early 1950s aptly described the German handshake as a "ritual which begins with energy, like an instantaneous shot," and a distinct German way of shaking hands appears to have existed at least since the end of the nineteenth century. Beginning in the late twentieth century, however, younger generations of Germans abandoned this powerful handshake. It was often seen as old-fashioned and overly formal. This change in greeting habits coincided with the shift from the pronoun *Sie* to the less formal *Du*, when young people address each other. Yet in the twenty-first century, the handshake has been revived, at least in certain parts of Germany, and has reentered the youth repertoire. On the history of the German handshake and its culture, see Carola Otterstedt, *Abschied im Alltag, Grußformen und Abschiedsgestaltung im interkulturellen Vergleich* (Munich: Iudicium, 1993).

54. Bourdieu, *Language and Symbolic Power*, 62.

55. In most manuals of Western manners, it is considered poor taste to demonstrate one's dominance by shaking too aggressively. Interestingly, researchers of body language have claimed to find a correlation between the strength of an individual's handshake and his or her personality. Some have posited that a strong grip usually denotes an aggressive, overbearing, self-important, and socially incompetent individual. These results were found to be independent of the participants' gender. In gender-specific analyses, stronger handshakes appeared to indicate deficient social skills in men and a tendency to domineering behavior in women. See Jan Astrom, "Introductory Greeting Behavior: A Laboratory Investigation of Approaching and Closing Salutation Phases," *Perceptual and Motor Skills* 79 (1994): 863–897.

56. The ideology of "practical Zionism" gained influence in Palestine at the turn of the twentieth century. It promoted the use of what it called practical methods to achieve Zionist goals, such as promoting Jewish immigration and founding rural settlements and educational institutions in Palestine despite the lack of progress in the political and diplomatic arenas. This doctrine was propagated most notably by members of the Second Aliya, who began settling in Palestine in 1903. Importantly, the Palestine Office, which was established in Jaffa in 1908 by Arthur Ruppin and represented the World Zionist Organization within Palestine, also embraced this practical approach. For a decade, the PO acted as the central agency overseeing Zionist settlement in Palestine, and it formed the core of the administrative institutions that directed and coordinated all Zionist activities in the land. In 1918, the PO was replaced by a number of other institutions, including the Jewish Agency.

57. Etan Bloom, "The 'Administrative Knight'—Arthur Ruppin and the Rise of Zionist Statistics," *Tel Aviv University Year Book for German History* 35 (2007): 183–203 (Heb.); Bloom, "Arthur Ruppin and the Suppressed German Nationalist Sources of the Zionist Labor Movement," *Mitaam: A Review of Literature and Radical Thought* 11 (2007): 71–94; Bloom, "What 'the Father' Had in Mind: Arthur Ruppin (1876–1943), Cultural Identity, *Weltanschauung* and Action," *History of European Ideas* 33, no. 3 (2007): 330–349.

58. Yaakov Shavit and Gideon Biger, *The History of Tel Aviv: The Birth of a Town (1909–1936)* (Tel Aviv: Ramot, 2001), 20–21 (Heb.). See also Barbara E. Mann, *A Place in History: Modernism, Tel Aviv, and the Creation of Jewish Urban Space* (Stanford, CA: Stanford University Press, 2006); and Joachim Schlör, *Tel Aviv: From Dream to City* (London: Reaktion, 1999). The rapid expansion of Tel Aviv is a prime example of Palestine's enormous growth in the early twentieth century. The city's population grew from only 200 in 1908 to 2,000 in 1914, and was 30,000 by 1924—an increase of more than fifteen times within the span of only ten years. Shavit and Biger, *History of Tel Aviv*, 100.

59. Michael Berkowitz, *Zionist Culture and West European Jewry before the First World War* (Chapel Hill: University of North Carolina Press, 1993), 146.

60. For a list of these heroic models, see Yehonatan Frenkel, "The 'Yizkor' Book of 1911," in Yehuda Reinharz and Anita Shapira, eds., *Essential Papers on Zionism* (New York: New York University, 1996), 422–453.

61. Quoted ibid., 445.

62. Norbert Elias, *The Germans: Power Struggles and the Development of Habitus in the Nineteenth and Twentieth Centuries* (New York: Columbia University Press, 1996), 19.

63. Alex Bein, ed., *Arthur Ruppin: Chapters of My Life, Diaries, Letters and Memoirs* (Tel Aviv: Am-Oved, 1968), 2:219 (Heb.).

64. Like most other gestures, the handshake and the *chapcha* do not fill a gap left by language, but rather have a function that is independent of spoken utterances.

65. For further explanation of this concept, see B. Farnell, "Moving Bodies, Acting Selves," *Annual Review of Anthropology* 28 (1999): 352–354.

66. Swidler, "Culture in Action," 273.

67. On the interest of German eugenicists in social selection, see Christopher M. Hutton, *Race and the Third Reich: Linguistics, Racial Anthropology and Genetics in the Dialectic of Volk* (Cambridge: Polity, 2005), 99.

68. Ruppin described the role of eugenics in his culture plan in the article "Die Auslese des Menschenmaterials für Palästina," *Der Jude* 3 (1919): 373–383.

69. Arthur Ruppin, *Briefe, Tagebücher, Erinnerungen,* ed. Schlomo Krolik (Königstein: Jüdischer Verlag Athenau, 1985), 181.

70. Arthur Ruppin, "The Selection of Human Material" (1919), in Bein Alex, ed., *Thirty Years of Building in the Land of Israel: Lectures and Articles* (Jerusalem: Shoken, 1936), 63 (Heb.). Ruppin's immigration policies marked a radical change from the approach that the World Zionist Organization had taken since the 1880s, according to which Palestine was to be a refuge for Eastern European Jews, regardless of their racial makeup. In contrast, Ruppin aimed his eugenics program only at a segment of the collective that was generally called "the Jews." He believed that this exclusivist strategy was necessary in order to sustain the existence of what he considered to be the Jewish race and nation. Unlike Herzl, who wished to solve the burning problems of the masses in the Eastern European Pale of Settlement, Ruppin suggested that those who did not qualify for migration to Palestine should go to the United States. Arthur Ruppin, *The Jews of Today: A Social Scientific Study,* trans. Y. H. Brener (Moriah: Odessa, 1914), 206 (Heb.).

71. Arthur Ruppin, *Soziologie der Juden,* 2 vols. (Berlin: Jüdischer Verlag, 1930), quoted in Meira Weiss, *The Chosen Body: The Politics of the Body in Israeli Society* (Stanford, CA: Stanford University Press, 2002), 2. Ruppin promoted the "selection of human material" throughout the 1920s and 1930s. Daniel Karpi, ed., *Jabotinsky: Letters 1930–1931* (Jerusalem: Jabotinsky Institute, 2004), 14 (Heb.).

72. Meir Margalit, "The Question of the Classification of Immigrants in the First Period of the Mandate—Ideology, Policy and Practice," in Yechiam Weitz, ed., *Contemporary Judaism, Zionism, the State of Israel and the Diaspora* (Jerusalem: Hebrew University Press, 1999), 243–280 (Heb.).

73. Gur Alroey, *Immigrants: Jewish Immigration to Palestine in the Early Twentieth Century* (Jerusalem: Yad Izhak Ben Zvi, 2004), 173 (Heb.).

74. Arthur Ruppin, *The Jews Fighting for Their Existence* (Tel Aviv: Mosad Bialik and Devir, 1940), 287 (Heb.).

75. Bloom, "What 'the Father' Had in Mind."

76. Although *Volk* was used in German-language Zionist publications, some of the specific meaning and significance of the term was lost when it was translated into Hebrew

and English. George L. Mosse has noted that in the context of German culture the concept of the *Volk* has significantly different connotations than its approximate English equivalents, "nation" or "people." More than a group of people whose members share some form of connection with each other, *Volk* has a strong transcendent dimension, refers to a unity that goes beyond itself, and implies a bond to a particular land. George L. Mosse, *The Crisis of German Ideology: Intellectual Origins of the Third Reich* (New York: Grosset and Dunlap, 1964), 4ff. Hans Kohn has stressed that Zionism was shaped by the German model of nationalism, which rejected the "Western civic ideals" and the democratic and universalistic models of the American and French Revolutions. See Kohn, "Zion and the Jewish National Idea," in Michael Selzer, ed., *Zionism Reconsidered: The Rejection of Jewish Normalcy* (London: Macmillan, 1970), 187.

77. Fritz Lenz, untitled review of Ruppin's *Soziologie der Juden*, in *Archiv fur Rassenund Gesellschafts-Biologie, einschliesslich Rassen- und Gesellschaftshygiene* 26 (1932): 436–438.

78. Quoted in Shilo Margalit, *The Attempts of Colonization: The Palestine Office 1908–1914* (Jerusalem: Yad Izhak Ben Zvi, 1988), 203 (Heb.).

79. "Die Kwuzah," *Jüdische Rundschau* 29: 7 (November 1924): 521–522; Schlomo Krolik, ed., *Arthur Ruppin: Briefe, Tagebücher, Erinnerungen* (Königstein: Jüdischer Verlag Athenau, 1985), 135.

80. For example, Anita Shapira contends that "the actual state of affairs in Palestine" led to the creation of the first group. See Shapira, "The Origins of 'Jewish Labor' Ideology," *Journal of Israeli History* 5 (Spring 1982): 110.

81. Anson Rabinbach, *The Human Motor: Energy, Fatigue, and the Origins of Modernity* (Berkeley: University of California Press, 1992), 23.

82. Ibid., 189–202, 218–219; Dennis Sweeny, "Work, Race and the Transformation of Industrial Culture in Wilhelmine Germany," *Social History* 23 (January 1998): 36–50.

83. Sweeny, "Work, Race and the Transformation," 36–37.

84. In the German Saar region, employers had likewise begun in 1906 to organize groups of particularly "healthy and work-capable [*arbeitsfähig*] employees" from among their workers. See *Studien und soziale Aufgaben sowie deren Lösung* (Völklingen, 1906), quoted in Sweeny, "Work, Race and the Transformation," 49. On the plans of the Monist League to establish breeding colonies, see Daniel Gasman, *The Scientific Origins of National Socialism: Social Darwinism in Ernst Haeckel and the German Monist League* (London: Macdonald, 1971), 152.

85. Ruppin's attitude was also shaped by his highly critical assessment of the First Aliya. As Ruppin's critique of the practices common in the Baron administration shows, his thinking was clearly influenced by the principles of the German *Arbeitswissenschaft*: "The third mistake was that the system of administration blocked the development of a spirit of independence among the colonists. . . . It is for this reason that the Jewish colonist does not feel the same responsibility as the farmer who accepts the risk of his own decisions." Arthur Ruppin, "The Picture in 1907," address to the Jewish Colonization Society of Vienna, 1908. Available in English translation at http://www.geocities.com/Vienna/6640/zion/essential. html, 3.

86. Ibid., 40.

87. Furthermore, workers were fined or even fired for drinking, and they were expected to report on the drinking habits of their colleagues. As a rule, those under forty who were suspected of excessive drinking and thereby seemed to represent both a moral threat and a potential economic burden on the company's sickness fund were dismissed immediately. Ibid.

88. Lissak found that almost 50 percent of the political functionaries (*askanim*) in the 1930s and 1940s came from the *kvutzot* (collective groups) and the kibbutzim, which derived from the collective groups. The same research also indicates that the political leaders in the young Israeli state achieved their high positions at a very young age, 50 percent of them within their first ten years in Palestine and 40 percent on a fast track of between one and six years. Lissak called these extraordinarily rapid careers the "leaping-over mobility of the 'founding fathers.'" Moshe Lissak, *The Elites of the Jewish Community in Palestine* (Tel Aviv: Am-Oved, 1981), 37, 42 (Heb.).

89. Almost all the friends and collaborators whom Ruppin mentioned in his diary later became members of the Knesset (the Israeli parliament); several even became Israeli ministers, prime ministers, and presidents. Most of them had begun their careers as agricultural workers in the training farms and settlements that Ruppin had supervised. Examples include President Yitzhak Ben Zvi; Minister of Transportation David Remez; key Labor Zionist Berl Katznelson; Yosef Sprinzak, MP; Zvi Yehuda, MP; Yosef Baratz, MP; Shmuel Dayan, MP; Avraham Herzfeld, MP; Shlomo Lavi, MP; and Aharon Zeitling, MP. See Bein, ed., *Arthur Ruppin*, 2:58–59.

90. However, Ruppin and the PO discreetly supported all Zionist military organizations in the Yishuv. Ruppin, for instance, offered financial and moral support to the paramilitary unit known as the Jaffa Group and to its leader, Eliahu Golomb, who later became a founding member of the Hagana (the leading underground organization of the Yishuv and the cradle of the Israeli army, the IDF). See Ahuvia Malkin, *The Biography of Eliahu Golomb, the Activist, 1893–1929* (Tel Aviv: Am-Oved, 2007), 94–95 (Heb.).

91. Ruppin, "Selection of Human Material," 375.

92. The most important unit of Zionist workers during the years of the Third Aliya (1919–1923) was called the "work regiment" (*gdud haavoda*). Its organization was based on a combination of the Stumm system and military modes of operation.

93. Yinon Cohen, "From Haven to Heaven: Changing Patterns of Immigration to Israel," in Daniel Levy and Yfaat Weiss, eds., *Challenging Ethnic Citizenship: German and Israeli Perspectives on Immigration* (Oxford: Berghahn, 2002), 36.

94. On the importance of the handshake in German society, Carola Otterstedt elaborates: "Mit dem Reichen der Hand offenbart der Grußpartner seine Gefühle, seinen Charakter und seine momentane seelische Verfassung: 'Er hat einen laschen Handdruck.' 'Sie kann ja ganz schön zupacken.'" Otterstedt, *Abschied im Alltag*, 92.

95. This tends to happen when the handshake was considerably weaker than expected, that is, when there was a significant disparity between the shaker's masculine image and the strength of his handshake.

96. This directness is known in Hebrew as *dugri*, which comes from Arabic. It developed in opposition to the allegedly excessive intellectualism of the *galut* Jew and was part of a broader trend toward more straightforward, plainer modes of conduct and styles of expression in Zionist Palestine. Elboim-Dror, "He Is Coming," 127. *Dugriness* (from *dugriyut*), which can also be translated as "truthfulness," probably also developed in contradistinction to European stereotypes of the unreliable and cunning Jew.

97. According to many of the European and American handshaking instruction guides found on the internet, a gesture like the *chapcha* is unacceptable. To quote from just one: "do not put your free hand on the other people's shoulders . . . while shaking hands. By so doing you exceed what is socially acceptable and invade other people's personal space." Dona Cardillo, "The Uncommon Handshake," http://www.dcardillo.com/articles/handshake.html. On the appropriate handshake, see also John Samuel, "Handshake," http://www.askmen.com/money/successful/success5.html.

    98. Ruppin, "Selection of Human Material," 65.

    99. Ibid.

    100. Ofaz Aviva, ed., *The Book of the Group* (1925; rpt., Jerusalem: Yad Izhak Ben-Zvi, 1996), 8 (Heb.). See also Zigfrid Landshot, *The Group* (Jerusalem: Yad Tabenkin, 1944; rpt., Tel Aviv: Keter, 2000), 56–58 (Heb.).

    101. Bloom, "Arthur Ruppin," 261–262.

    102. It was not unusual for applicants to try many times before being admitted to the collective groups, since admittance was severely restricted.

    103. Golda Meir, *My Life* (Tel Aviv: Maariv Library, 1972), 75 (Heb.).

    104. Yosef Klausner, "A World Being Formed/Created," *HaShiloch* 29 (1913–1914): 204 (Heb.).

    105. Shmuel Dayan (the father of Moshe Dayan) described how he and his friends stood in the marketplace of a town called Kfar Saba, waiting to be examined by the pedantic *mashgiah* (supervisor) of a farm. Shmuel Dayan, *Jubilee of Degania* (Tel Aviv: Shtibel, 1935), 9–10 (Heb.).

    106. Many Second Aliya immigrants wrote in their memoirs about how they had to "conquer the hoe," as they frequently put it.

    107. In early Israeli slang, the word "tool" (*kli*) referred to, among other things, the hoe. After the 1930s, this use fell out of fashion, but *kli* continues to mean "rifle" or "gun" as well as "alpha male" and "penis."

    108. In the pioneers' diaries, one often finds stories about "productivity contests" between Jewish pioneers and Arab workers. For instance, Naftali Avrahmiyahu, recalling his work in Gedera in 1909, mentions how he "competed with two Arabs" in cutting grapes: "it was like a struggle until eventually the Arab worker asked me to stop the competition." Quoted in Tamir Nachman, ed., *People of the Second Aliya: Memories, Chapters* (Tel Aviv: Center for Education and Culture, 1972), 12 (Heb.). These descriptions are likely to be accurate and reflect the pioneers' desire to prove that they were not inferior to—and were even better than—the Arabs in terms of productivity and their natural connection to the soil. In addition, Arab men claimed to be authentically masculine, and the tension between Arabs and Jewish pioneers thus included a gendered dimension too.

    109. The full quotation is: "If today the agricultural workers' diligence is greater than it was ten or fifteen years ago, then the credit must first be given to the workers for their selection work among the *kvutzot*. From the thousands that have passed through the *kvutzot*, a great many have been discarded, perhaps even most of them. Those who stayed were those who passed the fire test." Ruppin, *The Agricultural Settlement of the Zionist Organization in the Land of Israel (1908–1924)* (Jerusalem: Dvir, 1928), 42 (Heb.).

    110. Bloom, "What 'the Father' Had in Mind," 330–344; Bloom, "Arthur Ruppin," 173–350. For more on the monitored selection system, see Margalit, "Question of the Classification." The rigorous selection process implemented during the PO's heyday began to slacken toward the end of the 1920s following the Fourth Aliya (1924–1928), when about 67,000 new immigrants (half of them from Poland) arrived. Although the directors of the PO and, later, of the Jewish Agency in both Palestine and Eastern Europe had suggested maintaining a strict selective policy when distributing immigration certificates, this proved in many cases impossible. Many of the new immigrants did not match the Jewish Agency's criteria. The European branches of the agency were often staffed by inadequately trained, unprofessional workers and were weakened by favoritism, partisan politics, and even bribery, which hastened the process's decline. For a fuller discussion of the subject see Aviva Halamish, "'Selective Aliya' in the Zionist Idea: Practice and Historiography," in Anita Shapira, Jehuda Reinharz, and Jay Harris, eds., *The Age of Zionism* (Jerusalem:

Zalman Shazar Center, 2000), 185–202 (Heb.); Halamish, *A Dual Race against Time: Zionist Immigration Policy in the 1930s* (Jerusalem: Yad Izhak Ben-Zvi, 2006), 440–448 (Heb.).

111. As I have argued elsewhere, these ideas were inspired by the *völkisch* brand of German nationalism, which sought to regenerate German men, to increase their courage and strength, and to make them feel "at home" in the natural landscape of their fatherland. Bloom, "Arthur Ruppin," 225–227. See also Gasman, *The Scientific Origins of National Socialism*, 7.

112. The Palmach was a precursor of the IDF, whose most important founders and leading commanders had been members of this paramilitary organization.

113. Talmud Bavli, Sanhedrin 72a. See also the biblical text on Moses's war against the Midianites: "Vex the Midianites and smite them, for they vex you" (Numbers 25:17–18).

114. Since then, activism has been the worldview of many leaders, including Yitzhak Sadeh (the founder and leader of the Smash Troops), David Ben-Gurion, Moshe Dayan, Ariel Sharon, and many others. It is still the dominant military strategy of Israel today.

115. Pioneer "enthusiasm" was an important concept in the labor movement of Zionist Palestine and Israel, where it was regarded as a defining virtue of the modern Hebrew. However, the PO's culture planners believed that enthusiasm was a scientific category that possessed objective validity. According to the new *Arbeitswissenschaft*, anxiety, fear, and panic (often seen as typical attributes of Jews) could eventually lead to a "paralysis of the will" that resulted from a "lack of nervous energy." Quoted from Rabinbach, *The Human Motor*, 168. Ruppin held that the First Aliya's evidently weak link to the land had caused the decline of the immigrants' "enthusiasm," which he had already defined in his *Darwinismus und Sozialwissenschaft* (1902) as the vital force, or *Lebenskraft*, of individuals or a people. The concept of *Lebenskraft* had first been elaborated by the German scientist Alfred Ploetz (1860–1940), and contemporary scholars understood it to be connected to the concept of *Vitalrasse* (vital race), which referred to a population with good genetic lines of transmission (*Erblinien*). This doctrine of "vitalism" saw life as progressing toward a harmonious final stage, since it held that all cells and organisms have an innate drive toward a more whole or harmonious form. See Hutton, *Race and the Third Reich*, 17, 27. On Ruppin and vitalism, see Derek Penslar, *Zionism and Technocracy: The Engineering of Jewish Settlement in Palestine, 1870–1918* (Bloomington: Indiana University Press, 1991), 86; Alex Bein, ed., *Arthur Ruppin: Chapters of My Life, Diaries, Letters and Memoirs* (Tel Aviv: Am-Oved, 1968), 1:22 (Heb.).

116. The first part of the song reflects the dissatisfaction of native modern Hebrews with the first generation's, in their view, overly tolerant attitude to the Arabs, as well as that generation's tendency to talk instead of act.

117. A Sten is a British submachine gun with a rate of fire of around 500 bullets per minute.

118. Haim Hefer and Haim Guri, *From the Palmach Family: A Collection of Tales and Songs* (Jerusalem: Palmach Members Organization, 1978), 155, my translation.

119. The sympathetic system is the part of the nervous system which takes over in dangerous situations, when immediate and effective responses are required in order to fight or to escape.

120. For a fuller discussion of the concept of healthy cruelty, see Bloom, *Arthur Ruppin*, 241–249.

121. Ruppin, *The War of the Jews for Their Existence* (Tel Aviv: Bialik Institute & Devir, 1940), 287 (Heb.).

122. Ibid.

# 8

## Friedrich Gundolf and Jewish Conservative Bohemianism in the Weimar Republic

ANN GOLDBERG

Friedrich Gundolf (1880–1931), the influential Weimar literary scholar and Heidelberg professor, was in many ways a classic Jewish Wagnerian.[1] The notion of "Jewish Wagnerianism," which derives from the Jewish studies scholar Daniel Boyarin, refers to those Jewish men in the late nineteenth and early twentieth centuries who fled the effeminate, queer, hysterical Jew of fin-de-siècle anti-Semitic discourse by embracing an aggressive masculinism of Western culture.[2] Coming of age at the turn of the twentieth century, Gundolf fled his Jewishness in the most literal sense, choosing as his mentor the neo-Romantic poet-prophet Stefan George (1868–1933). The gentile George gave Gundolf a figurative home, not only as his chosen disciple, but as a member of an inner circle of poets and scholars gathered around the "master" in an exclusive, cult-like, and misogynist *Männerbund*. As author of pathbreaking literary histories on Caesar, Goethe, George, and others, Gundolf became the chief academic spokesman of the George circle, embracing a worldview that, hostile to much of modernity, celebrated the genius superman and a transcendent spirit. Analogous to Freud's heterosexualizing of the psyche and Herzl's masculinist Zionism—each, in Boyarin's analysis, tied to internal conflicts over Jewishness and gender—Gundolf's romantic conservatism can be linked to his intense ambivalence about race, a fact connected in turn, I will argue, to ongoing conflicts in his life over gender and sexuality.

Yet, Gundolf's life in many ways also challenged the notion of Jewish Wagnerianism. It did so literally: Gundolf's god (George) was a homosexual, and Gundolf's long-time lover and, later, wife, Elisabeth Salomon (1893–1958), was an emancipated "new woman," the sort whose very existence threatened Western traditions of male dominance. It also did so in the categories of thought through which Gundolf interpreted his experiences as a Jew and a man. This chapter explores these issues by examing Gundolf in terms of his relationship with Salomon and in terms of the broader milieu of Weimar culture. The milieu of Weimar bohemianism, to which Gundolf and Salomon belonged, opened up alternative lifestyles and new possibilities for imagining the self, indeed, for the transcendence of old gender, ethnic, and political divisions. It made possible Gundolf's unconventional relationship with Salomon, but it also brought him agonizing personal conflicts in the form of his master's jealous hatred of Salomon and the choice Gundolf therefore faced, but sought to evade, over many vacillating years between Salomon and George, lover and prophet, physical love and metaphysical ideal, new woman and *Männerbund*. At once conservative insider and racial outsider, tormented by his conflicting personal attachments, Gundolf experienced in acute form some of the key racial and gender divisions of his time.

This discussion of Gundolf and Salomon is based on their unpublished correspondence, an extraordinarily extensive set of about 1,400 letters spanning the length of their relationship, from 1914 until Gundolf's death, which reveals the lived experience of two people at the center of German and European culture in the early twentieth century.[3] Gundolf and Salomon were self-conscious letter writers.[4] This fact, together with the inevitable performing of the self that is in the nature of letter writing, is something I have kept in mind as I have explored the self-conscious, staged personas of the letters. I am also interested in the deeper levels of experience the letters reveal, that is, the psychodynamics of the relationship and the individual psyches of the couple. Thus I have paid close attention to the dreams, jokes, and mundane associations the two wrote about, material which, to be sure, was shaped and censored by the writing self, but which also provides partial access to less-conscious realms. Their dreams, in particular—about sex, longing, jealousy, rage, rejection, abandonment, impotence, imprisonment, and powerlessness—communicated the difficulties of negotiating the polarities and ambiguities of identity within this relationship and in its times.

Gundolf's life was made up of conflicts that, in interesting ways, mirrored the broader divisions of Weimar Germany. On the one hand, his membership in the conservative George circle involved a radical rejection of modern feminism and the new woman. Speaking the language of romantic conservatism—the celebration of genius, spirit, and charismatic leadership against the tide of soulless materialism and the egalitarianism of modern society—the George circle excoriated women's emancipation and, despite a mixed Jewish-gentile membership, contained elements of anti-Semitism. Cultish and homosocial, the group saw its mission in religious terms as a search for purity and spirit, for "priestly" discipline, asceticism, and transcendence. These values were defined in "radical distinction from everything soft . . . feminine . . . [and] sensual."[5] Women were physically banned from the group's sacred space—the "globe room" in Karl Wolfskehl's Munich home where George and his disciples, dressed in Roman togas and laurel wreaths, recited poetry and feasted on dates and wine. Alhough distancing himself from the far right's extreme racism and from politics altogether, George was a leading voice in the rightist critique of contemporary society. Within Weimar's culture wars, this put the George circle in opposition to urbanism, democracy, economic rationalization, and notions of modernity connected with feminism, sex reform, and other progressive movements that envisioned the reshaping of gender and sexuality along more egalitarian lines. Two great contemporary symbols of that modernity were the new woman and the Jew.

Gundolf shared his group's anti-feminism and its condemnation of the "godless . . . emancipated woman."[6] But paradoxically Gundolf was also deeply in love with just such a woman. Salomon, raised in a progressive, middle-class Silesian family (her father, a physician, was a supporter of women's rights),[7] attended the radically innovative, coeducational Freie Schulgemeinde, run by the youth movement cult figure and Nietzschean Gustav Wynecken, and later attended university, earning a doctorate in economics with Alfred Weber. She subsequently supported herself for years as a single woman, working as a *Pressereferent* (press officer) in Vienna and as a journalist, translator, and private tutor in Rome. She loved sports and modern dance (doing some performing herself), cavorted in the mountains skiing and hiking with friends, kept a (sub-letted) apartment in Berlin, and, during the years she waited for Gundolf, had other love affairs (Gundolf and Salomon did not marry until 1926). At the same time, she struggled with depression and anxiety, job and housing discrimination, terrible financial difficulties, the "disgrace" of being an unmarried woman, and fears of aging, alone and poor. She was, in her own words, a "contemporary woman," experimenting with newly won sexual and social freedoms while painfully aware of "emancipation's" high price.

Gundolf's striking openness to Salomon, despite his anti-feminism, was in part a function of his psychological need for a woman capable of tolerating his slave-like attachment to George. Salomon's emancipation (or, at least, her ability to tolerate the single state) was necessary if Gundolf were to maintain the delicate and ultimately impossible balance between his attachments to George and to Salomon. And it was her emancipation, in turn, that enabled her to accommodate for years the needs of these two men, providing her with the economic and geographic mobility and psychological resources to abandon the scene in Germany, where she was the object of hostility (George) and ambivalence (Gundolf).

More broadly, Gundolf's relationship with Salomon was possible in the context of Weimar's intellectual milieu, where left and right, feminists and antifeminists, shared a critical discourse of modernity and bourgeois society. The terms of this discourse were a utopian search for authenticity, feeling, and soul—in community, art, the unconscious, nature, the vital body—as antidotes to the deadening conformity and alienation of mass industrial society. This postliberal rhetoric could be found across the political spectrum: from socialists to *völkisch* nationalists; from the George group and other rightist circles to the German youth movement (itself split into progressive and *völkish*, anti-Semitic groups), in which Salomon had been immersed since her youth; and from anti-feminists to feminists. Within the fluid and hybrid intellectual milieus of the Wilhelmine and Weimar eras, impulses long associated with the right—neo-Romanticism, anti-materialism, Social Darwinism, eugenics—merged and intersected with socialism, feminism, sex reform, and other progressive movements. Furthermore, despite their many differences, German feminists (moderates and radicals alike) shared with anti-feminists a maternalist rhetoric that emphasized the inherent differences of the sexes and cast women's nature (and hence, women's primary social roles) as nurturing and caregiving.

It was this fluid intellectual and political environment that brought the pair together in their unconventional relationship, and that opened up new possibilities for imagining the self and for living out the experiment of gender emancipation as conservative bohemians. It also contributed to the conflicts and split allegiances of Gundolf's life, as well as confusion and anxieties about issues raised by the new terrain of women's emancipation and bohemianism: the boundaries of sexual experimentation, female independence, and gender difference; how or whether one should try to reconcile happiness, bourgeois security, and freedom; and the ambiguities of being at once intellectual insider and racial outsider.

On the one hand, Gundolf was immensely attracted by and fascinated with Salomon's emancipation—what he called her "courage," "internal restlessness," "enthusiasm," and "fire." He encouraged her professional achievements and emancipated lifestyle, and he had no trouble envisioning an ideal of transcendence for his female lover. A quintessential unworldly professor ensconced in his secure university position, Gundolf seems to have derived vicarious pleasure from Salomon's talent for living life fully in the present, even from her transgressions. In fact, he demanded her emancipation as a condition of their relationship. When, in the 1920s and struggling financially, Salomon began to long for marriage and security, he pushed her to uncompromisingly stay the course of a higher, emancipated, anti-bourgeois ideal: "You want to combine enjoyment, freedom, peace, and bourgeois comfort, but this goes against the laws of life. Whoever wants to lead a stimulating, dubious [*bedenklich*] life must also accept the dangers it brings."[8] In response to her distress about whether she should enter into a marriage of convenience to a Canadian, he sounded like an individualist feminist: they were no longer living in "patriarchal primitive society . . . where women were little better than animals or slaves or mothers. . . . A woman [now] lays claim to being a 'personality,' an independent person, [and] can exist for herself."[9]

At the same time, he agonized over Salomon and her unconventionality. The reasons had partly to do with the continued power of patriarchal ideals in their relationship and in the society. Salomon's wild partying at the end of the war and her announcement, in the early 1920s, about her plans (transient, as it turned out) to become a film actress, gave him qualms (he warned she would develop a "film soul"). When Salomon bobbed her hair—a symbolically charged gesture of female emancipation in the 1920s—Gundolf reported having a dream that turned this emancipatory act into a scene of subordination: "Last night, I dreamt that Aga[10] held you prisoner and mistreated you: you were forced to cut your hair and serve her dressed as a page, and I could not help you."[11]

Gundolf's relationship with Salomon—a vital, independent, sexually emancipated woman—overwhelmingly attractive on one level, also evoked deepseated fears about emasculation, dependency, and loss of control. "The power of the love that binds me to you terrifies me," Gundolf wrote Salomon in partial wonderment. "I still don't understand it—the causes of such strong feelings."[12] Over and over he called her "dangerous" and talked of love as enslavement and bewitchment. Salomon was his "*Herrin* [master]," the "*Schicksalgöttin* [master of his fate]," and a "*schwarze Hexe* [black witch]," and he her slave, not unlike the cowering black dancer of his dream (described below).[13] She took possession and feminized him, making him, he joked, "impregnated with Mega Musel."[14] These fears pervaded his dreams, some of which featured disturbing and seductive images of lesbian sex and powerful women, including one in which Salomon drank him down "slowly, gulp by gulp."[15] In these dreams, sex was often coupled with death wishes (e.g., Gundolf decapitated, followed by a feeling of being "calmed").[16] Elsewhere in the correspondence, writing of Salomon's demonic, sensual powers, he chanted, "Oh love, I'd like to be burned with you on the same funeral pyre."[17]

Gundolf's ambivalence toward gender and sexuality was compounded by and linked to his Jewish identity. On the one hand, despite the outer trappings of his public persona, Gundolf felt a certain affectionate identification as a Jew, and this helped bond him with Salomon, an entirely secular and assimilated Jew who shared his ambivalent ethnic identity. On the other hand, Gundolf had internalized the language of anti-Semitism, steeped as he was in a rightist discourse that had racialized the critique of modernity, equating as "degenerates" Jews, feminists, and the left. One way he found to relieve the psychological tension produced by this contradiction was his famous wit and humor. When, at the beginning of their relationship in the first days of World War I, Salomon reported on being singled out on a train for interrogation by the military police (implicitly, she suspected anti-Semitism), Gundolf wrote back jokingly: "I [anticipated] that with your *black hairness*, which doesn't let the *blondness of your heart* make itself felt, you wouldn't get through [the train ride] without being pestered."[18]

These sorts of jokes were ways of articulating and neutralizing troubling truths about anti-Semitism. The reality in August 1914 was that at an unprecedented moment of national unity—the *Burgfrieden* at the beginning of the war that welcomed into the political fold even the vilified socialists in a domestic civic peace—Salomon as Jew, despite her strong German patriotism (her blonde heart), was more outcast than ever. Playing with the *völkisch* categories of black-Jewish versus blonde-Aryan,[19] the joke turned the anti-Semites' exclusive and literal Aryan blondness against itself—into a metaphor applied affectionately to a Jew's inner self. Gundolf was soon making a practice of expressing his affection for Salomon with sobriquets that similarly played with the stigma of Jewishness: she was his "black, Silesian witch [or devil]," for instance, which managed in one phrase to incorporate three anti-Semitic slurs.

Elsewhere, Gundolf spoke directly of the contradictions of his two racial lives. During the war years, anti-Semitism still seemed fairly distant and manageable, and Gundolf, in his pedagogical mode, dispensed hopeful advice about how to live with the doubleness of the German Jew. One way, he wrote to Salomon, was to treat identity as a form of role playing, shifting identities at will—what today is called "situational ethnicity." The "deep, internal feud" in German Jews between their Jewish and German identities, he counseled her, was based on a false dichotomy. One simply lives as both, alternating and adjusting to the context: with certain people one is Jewish, with others German.

While ethnicity helped bond Gundolf and Salomon, it also functioned as a metaphor for gender and sexual anxiety. This is evident in a dream Gundolf reported. "Last night," he wrote to Salomon in Vienna, "I dreamed you were breaking in a Creole woman," adding, "as is well known, there was no opposition." "I saw you in front of me with the expression of an animal tamer and a black, pale, frightened female dancer."[20] With its images of racial hybridity, colonial subjugation, and female power, the dream used the language of race to articulate both the attractions toward and fears about sex and the new woman. Salomon, of course, was not "well known" as an animal tamer, but she was known to exercise a powerfully attractive force on Gundolf which, like the Creole dancer in the dream, he felt incapable of resisting. She was, as he affectionately put it, his "black *Seelenherrin* [master of his soul]."[21] Foregrounding the themes of disempowerment and divided identity (symbolized by the radical Otherness of the mixed-race, colonized woman), the dream suggests something of Gundolf's ongoing internal struggles about allegiance and loyalty (his lover versus his master), as well as about deeper fears in his relationship with Salomon.

Gundolf's answer to the dilemma of the feminized, racialized Jewish Other came in a 1914 poem to Salomon. Written several weeks before the outbreak of World War I and the aforementioned train incident, after another encounter Salomon had had with anti-Semitism, the poem was meant as consolation and encouragement. Addressing Salomon as a daughter of Zion, the poem set out the thousand-year-old suffering of the Jews, proposing as a solution the notion of the sower:

Dich, tochter Zions, die in unsern sonnen
Zu unserem wort und unserer not gereift
Hat manchmal noch der trübe wind gestreift
Als wärst du der gefängnis nicht entronnen.

Das tränenvolle wehen das die weiden
Erzittern liess an wassern Babylons.
Ist noch dein blut gedenk des klagetons
Um deiner väter dir vershollne leiden?

Macht dich ihr tausendjährig schicksal wach
Für schmerzen die nicht deine sind, befehle
Die du nicht zu vollziehn brauchst? Deine seele
Trotzt noch und tränt vom fernen ungemach.

Wirf ab die bürde murrender Hebräer
Und heb in heutig licht dein schwarzes haar!
Sei schön für das was wird: verlass die schar
Der stoppel-leser, komm zur schar der säer![22]

Though rejecting certain aspects of Jewishness, the poem was less about flight from or the denial of race than it was about redemption and the recreation of the self, *while* being a Jew. It rejected one kind of Jew—the "grumbling Hebrews" burdened by the past, still sorting the stubble, and hence, by inference, stigmatized, shameful outsiders. And it offered as an alternative the sower—an image of fecundity, depth, and creativity. The sower allowed one to be Jewish with dignity, even with pride (to raise one's black hair), because he represented an empowered inner self divorced from the racialized and stigmatized Jewish body.

The sower's qualities were, on the one hand, those Gundolf associated with (male) genius—with Caesar, about whom he wrote in similar agricultural imagery, and with the master himself, George. On the other hand, strikingly, Gundolf saw no contradiction in applying the emancipatory sower ideal to his female lover. And, indeed, Salomon took up the challenge, pursuing the ideal in her life as a modern woman and, in doing so, radically refashioning the notion of women's identity by appropriating a hitherto male, bourgeois ideal of "wholeness" (*Gesamtmensch*).[23]

In this way, Gundolf's thinking about race and gender identity diverged significantly from that of the Jewish Wagnerian. The binary implicit in the Jewish Wagnerian, according to Boyarin's formulation, was between the passive, meek, effeminate rabbinic scholar and the aggressive, homophobic, masculinist muscle Jew.[24] The binary implicit in Gundolf's thought, by contrast, was aggressive careerism and materialism (associated with modern industrialism, Jews, and new women) versus a transcendent pure realm of art, spirit, and intellect, a realm that was determined not by race or even gender, but by an aristocracy of talent and sensibility. Here, the flight from Jewishness involved carving out an intellectual realm for Jews and women free from social constraints and discrimination.

A dream Gundolf had on the night before Weimar's first national election (January 1919) starkly expressed the binary at work in his mind. Rather than the hopeful imagery of the sower (transcendence of the Jewish body), it presented an uneasy and starkly dichotomous image of race and self, one indirectly reflecting, it seems, the political realities of growing anti-Semitism. The dream came during a period when Gundolf's writing on the Romantic poets was not going well. Communicated in a letter discussing, with resignation and relief (it could have been worse) and sarcasm (silly women voters), the elections, the dream suggests in its ambivalence a parallel between internal and political divisions:[25]

> Caesar issued me a passport [*Reiseausweis*] with the help of a local Jewish *Streber* [social climber], obligingly [*verbindlich*] and ironic. . . . apparently he knew about my spleen (which isn't doing well). I am reading Dilthey's Schleiermacher and everywhere come upon chasms and gaps in my knowledge [*Bildung*] and mental powers [*Kraft*] so that sometimes I despair. At those times I'd like to put my head in your lap until I have no more thoughts and feel only what you let me feel.[26]

The dream was literally about identity (documented by the passport), an identity that, at the moment, was struggling with professional self-doubts and feelings of inferiority as Gundolf compared himself to his former professor, the philosopher Wilhelm Dilthey. The "irony" was that securing the passport required the joint efforts of two wholly opposite figures: Caesar and the Jewish *Streber*. These were figures of enormous symbolic resonance, tropes of opposites, in Gundolf's worldview and in the culture battles of Weimar. While Caesar represented a lost world of nobility and charismatic authority, the Jewish *Streber* symbolized the detested modern age—its materialism, its empty, loud ambitions, and its social leveling. The social climber was an emblem of a society that, at the moment of the dream, was forcing itself in the most dramatic way on Gundolf's consciousness in the form of the election and the political chaos in the streets of Berlin. Merging professional, racial, and political anxieties, the dream image can be seen to stand, among other things, for the internal divisions of a German Jew who was at once celebrated scholar and "inferior" Jew, insider and outsider, and who, having internalized anti-Semitism, cast his lot with a gentile elite—the Caesars and the Georges—while finding solace in his Jewish lover.[27]

Gundolf's binary worldview makes sense in terms of Weimar's intellectual and political milieu. It can be located as well in a style of thought identified by Gerald Izenberg and Jacques Le Rider in Austro-German intellectuals and artists at the turn of the twentieth century.[28] This thought, which was far from confined to ambivalent conservative German Jews like Gundolf, embraced (albeit with great ambivalence) "the feminine" in the self as a source of creativity and transcendence. The "idealized feminine" was, in turn, associated with "Nietzsche's *Übermensch*," someone who "lived in her body" and "legislated her own values."[29]

An ambivalent idealization of the feminine is precisely what one sees in Gundolf, whose muses and love objects were a new woman and a homosexual poet, but whose work made him a Jewish Wagnerian. There were interesting connections, in this sense, between the private and public aspects of Gundolf's life—the literary critic espousing a version of the Nietzschean superman and the man who dreamed of himself as a disempowered, feminized racial hybrid. The Creole dream posed agonizing dilemmas (of race and sex, power and identity) whereas Gundolf's work offered solutions: wholistic visions of an empowered and unified self—the *Gesamtmensch* whose highest embodiment was found in genius leaders like George. Gundolf's creation in his writing of a mythology of the great man and his search for a world-historical savior, it seems, were linked (though not reducible) to a more personal search for redemption. This involved a journey from the (sexed and racialized) body to a transcendent soul, spirit, and culture; from the Jewish *Streber* to Caesar and George. The tragic irony of Gundolf's case is that, while fleeing the Jewish *Streber*, he contributed in his work to a climate of illiberalism on which his enemies, the anti-Semites, fed and would soon triumph.

NOTES

1. This chapter is a revised and shortened version of my "The Black Jew with the Blond Heart: Friedrich Gundolf, Elisabeth Salomon, and Conservative Bohemianism in Weimar Germany," *Journal of Modern History* 79, no. 2 (2007): 306–334. I thank the *Journal of Modern History* for permission to republish it.

2. Daniel Boyarin, *Unheroic Conduct: The Rise of Heterosexuality and the Invention of the Jewish Man* (Berkeley: University of California Press, 1997).

3. Until recently, the correspondence was in the private possession of my mother, Ruth Goldberg, who inherited it as Salomon's niece. It has since been transferred to the Deutsches Literaturarchiv in Marbach, Germany, where it is available to scholars. Most, but not all, of the letters have survived. Missing documents include many of Salomon's early letters to Gundolf and a few later miscellaneous letters (or parts of them) by Salomon and Gundolf. These missing letters, I believe, contained material that Gundolf or Salomon did not want publicly known and were intentionally destroyed. My citations indicate which of them wrote the letter and give the date on which it was written or, when this information is lacking, the postmark date (if available).

4. The couple were acutely aware of their letters' posthumous value. Salomon expected them to be used by Gundolf's biographer (who has not yet materialized) and, having preserved them with the utmost care, managed to get them out of Nazi Germany when she fled to London in 1934.

5. Nicolaus Sombart, "Männerbund und politische Kultur in Deutschland," in Thomas Kühne, ed., *Männergeschichte-Geschlechtergeschichte: Männlichkeit im Wandel der Moderne* (Frankfurt am Main: Campus, 1996), 141.

6. "Einleitung der Herausgeber," *Jahrbuch für die Geistige Bewegung* 3 (1912): v–vi. Gundolf and Friedrich Wolters were the editors of the journal and, hence, presumably, the authors of the piece.

7. Max Salomon, her father, corresponded with Helene Lange, Ellen Key, and Marie Stritt, and was a co-founder of the Freie Schulgemeinde. The letters are in Elisabeth Salomon's *Nachlaß* (this author's possession).

8. Gundolf, 6 October 1920.

9. Gundolf, 23 June 1921.

10. Agathe Mallachow (Aga) and Gundolf had an affair in Berlin during World War I that resulted in the birth of a daugther (Cordelia Ottilie Mallachow, born 30 November 1917). Gundolf's refusal to marry Aga caused conflicts and legal battles for the rest of his life.

11. Gundolf, 14 October 1920.

12. Gundolf, 31 May 1920; 1921 letter (more precise date impossible to decipher) with drawing of two naked women; n.d., ca. March 1921.

13. Gundolf, 31 May 1920; 12 January 1919.

14. Gundolf, 4 February 1921. "Musel" was Salomon's nickname.

15. "[A]nd yet I remained full and shook with fear about whether I could satisfy you, and I couldn't, so amazing was your thirst." Gundolf, 1(?) April 1921; 14 October 1920.

16. Gundolf, 21 September 1920.

17. Gundolf, 16 May 1921.

18. Gundolf, 10 August 1914.

19. Sander Gilman, *Jewish Self-Hatred* (Baltimore, MD: Johns Hopkins University Press, 1986), 7; Gilman, *Freud, Race, and Gender* (Princeton, NJ: Princeton University Press, 1993), 19ff. Houston Stewart Chamberlain, for example, called Jews a "mongrel race"; Hermann Wagener called them "White Negroes." On Weimar Jews and the exotic, see Michael Brenner, *The Renaissance of Jewish Culture in Weimar Germany* (New Haven, CT: Yale University Press, 1996), 130.

20. Gundolf, 17 May 1921.

21. Gundolf, 31 May 1920.

22. Gundolf, Heidelberg, July 1914. The uncapitalized nouns are in the original. My rough translation of the poem: "You, daughter of Zion, who in our suns / matured to our word and hardship / sometimes grief-stricken / as though you had not escaped from prison. / The tearful fluttering that made the / pastures tremble at the shores of Babylon / your blood still remembers the suffering / of your fathers. / Does their [fathers'] 1,000-year fate make you / aware of the pain which is not yours / and give you commands which you do not need to follow? / Your soul is still defiant and sheds / tears from far off. / Throw off the burden of grumbling Hebrews / and raise your black hair in today's light / Be beautiful for that which will be: leave the throng of those who sort the stubble / and join the throng of the sowers."

23. See, e.g., Salomon, 3 November 1920. Martina Kessel, "The 'Whole Man': The Longing for a Masculine World in Nineteenth-Century Germany," *Gender and History* 15, no. 1 (2003): 1–31, shows for the nineteenth century how women used the discourse of the "whole man" to "voice their desires or criticise male claims to dominance and control." Salomon, extraordinarily, went far beyond this to claim for herself the ideal itself.

24. Boyarin, *Unheroic Conduct*.

25. Gundolf, 20 January 1919. A government of the moderate left, Gundolf opined, was the best outcome for the present because it was necessary to placate the workers in order to avoid the nightmare scenario of their further radicalization and a communist revolution.

26. Ibid.

27. Gundolf's disassociation of himself from the Jewish *Streber* was a never-ending life task that, one senses, ate at him. Two years later, his internal divisions were on full display as, reacting to the new virulence of anti-Semitism, he wrote in a moment of terrible prescience: "Wenn ich jetzt an die Zukunft der Deutschen und der Juden denke, so dank ich Gott, daß wir Freude und Fülle miteinander gehabt haben, die niemand mehr uns rauben kann und die aufgehoben ist in Gottes Busen—denn die Zukunft sieht bös aus. Was die Deutschen in der Welt sind, das sind die Juden in Deutschland und wenn die Anständigen nicht verhungern so schlägt man sie vielleicht doch in absehbarer Zeit einmal tot. *Du weisst, ich bin eigentlich kein Judenfreund, wenn auch nicht ungern und nicht ohne Stolz Jude,* aber der heutige Antisemitismus ist der läppischste, subalternste und unbilligste der je war, und ehrt die Opfer die er trifft. Bisher haben wir noch nicht grad märtyrerhaft gelebt, aber manchmal mein ich, es könnte uns noch so etwas wie ein Martyrium blühen." 13 April 1921, my emphasis.

28. Gerald N. Izenberg, *Modernism and Masculinity* (Chicago: University of Chicago Press, 2000); Jacques Le Rider, *Modernity and Crises of Identity* (New York: Continuum, 1993).

29. Izenberg, *Modernism and Masculinity,* 17.

# 9

## A Kinder Gentler Strongman?

### Siegmund Breitbart in Eastern Europe

SHARON GILLERMAN

Through his spectacular displays of strength, bending iron and biting through chains, Siegmund Breitbart had become one of Europe's most popular entertainment sensations in the 1920s. Breitbart performed his feats of strength in a variety of typical masculine personas, but the most well known and frequently reproduced image of him was as a Roman centurion. Breitbart frequently made his grand entrance onto the stage riding in a chariot pulled by four white horses while accompanied by two men on horseback blowing trumpets to announce his arrival. The centurion was an intriguing figure to have become the strongman's signature persona, since, alongside his being an icon of popular culture, Breitbart was arguably the most visible performer of Jewish masculinity at the time. Known as Siegmund the *Eisenkönig* (Iron King) to the non-Jewish Central European and Polish-speaking public, and as *der moderner Shimshon hagibor* (modern Samson the hero), *unzer yiddisher gibor* (our Jewish hero), or his first name, Zishe (sweet), in Yiddish, Breitbart performed his masculine feats of strength for a wide range of audiences who likely had very different associations with the centurion's ancient symbol of martial masculinity. What values and sensibilities did Breitbart's diverse audiences bring to their reading of his centurion? Was Breitbart's centurion a figure who embodied imperial dominance, or was he a symbol of cultural resistance? Did Breitbart's centurion in particular and his masculine performances of strength more generally suggest that he had internalized gentile notions of masculinity and abandoned, or buried, traditional ideals of Jewish masculinity?

To explore Breitbart's projections of masculinity as a means for reflecting on the complexities of Jewish identity and the processes of cultural production, I turn to Homi Bhabha's notion of mimicry for the way it highlights the mutual interpenetration and construction of identities among dominant and subordinate groups. In his essay "Of Mimicry and Man," Bhabha places great emphasis on the mutuality of this interrelationship, even within an existing power differential as is inherent in the colonial paradigm.[1] Bhabha shows how

Breitbart as a Roman centurion.
With permission from © Gary
Bart, 2001, world rights reserved

colonial strategies for exercising power were meant to keep colonized people in a subordinate position by offering them the possibility of being just like the colonizers. At the same time, however, he argues that when those who were colonized mimicked the colonizer, their acts, rather than making them exactly like the colonizers, ultimately produced something distinctive. "In order to be effective," writes Bhabha, "mimicry must continually produce its slippage, its excess, its difference."[2]

Mimicry, Bhabha suggests, can never perfectly reproduce the Other. Moreover, and central for the argument I will develop in this chapter, it creates the possibility of cultural innovation and difference, even helping at times to subvert the very values it seeks to imitate. It is my aim to use Bhabha's "Of Mimicry and Man" to explore constructions of Jewish masculinity in Central and Eastern Europe through analyzing the performances of the Yiddish-speaking Polish strongman Siegmund né Zishe Breitbart. As I follow Breitbart into the Eastern European cultural realm from his home in Berlin, I seek to find some of the ways in which his performances of masculinity drew from and integrated certain typical German ideals and images of masculinity while engaging with and integrating key values from traditional Jewish culture.

In his book *Unheroic Conduct,* Daniel Boyarin utilized Bhabha's theory of mimicry to explain the decline of a unique form of Jewish masculinity with modern Jews' embrace of normative gentile ideals of masculinity. He argues there was a distinctly Jewish construction of masculinity, one that valorized the gentle and studious male against the martial ideals of manhood found in the surrounding gentile culture. This ideal of *Edelkayt* (nobility and gentleness), rooted in the Babylonian Talmud and remaining deeply embedded in Eastern European Jewish culture, formed a countertype to European notions of manliness, and as such, represented for Boyarin an act of cultural resistance, "a valuable and assertive historical project of Jewish eastern European culture."[3] For Boyarin, it is modernity in general, and the nineteenth century in particular, that foretells the radical denouement of this ideal within Jewish culture. Focusing most pointedly on Zionism as the site for the undoing of traditional notions of a gentle masculinity, Boyarin presents Herzl's appropriation of European values and behaviors as an example of what Bhabha has called "colonial mimicry." He employs Bhabha's notion of mimicry to underscore one of the central arguments about Jewish masculinity: with the invention of Zionism, the "colonized becomes just like the colonizer, sometimes even more than [the colonizer] is himself."[4] Displaying little originality or agency, Boyarin's Herzl offers a wholesale capitulation to the ideal of an exclusionary nationalism and an embrace of the dominant (non-Jewish) form of masculinity.

While Boyarin's reading of Bhabha stresses the complicity of the colonized in reproducing their own subordinate position, I instead seek to highlight the ways in which such "mimicry" in Breitbart's performances also came to represent a new cultural product, one that in certain instances may have also operated to undermine or redefine the "original." I will identify some aspects of Jewish agency and parody in Breitbart's performances of masculinity, even as he embodied some of the most visible attributes of what we may call for the purposes of our discussion the "ideal of German masculinity." Breitbart's body-centered performances appeared to intentionally yet ironically exemplify the ideals of modern masculinity, which, as George Mosse has argued, were intimately linked with the ideals and functioning of normative society.[5] These ideals and the moral qualities associated with them were promoted through a set of powerful images which derived from Greek ideals of male beauty, particularly as represented in classical sculpture. This masculine stereotype functioned to mark outsiders such as Jews as insufficiently masculine.

Yet even while Breitbart was exemplifying German masculine ideals, this analysis will also suggest that a dichotomized view of a gentle ("traditional") Jewish masculinity, on the one hand, and a ("modern") capitulation to gentile culture, on the other, does not do justice to the range of conceptions of Jewish

Breitbart as Hercules. With
permission from © Gary Bart,
2001, world rights reserved

Slegmund Breitbart, Eisenkönig

masculinity available to Jews at the time. Based on the Breitbart example, I will
propose that in place of conceiving only two forms of masculinity that were
mutually opposed to one another, we instead consider the Jewish masculinities
that Breitbart performed, and that were perceived by different audiences, as a
loose and flexible assemblage of images, a mosaic, or even a cacophony of divergent discourses.[6] This is not to suggest that there were no culturally dominant
forms of masculinity, but it does point to the existence of multiple images and
discourses that may help to broaden our understanding of how Jewish masculinities were conceptualized and performed at various times and places.

Breitbart's performances can serve as a useful means through which to explore conceptions of Jewish masculinity not because he was typical but because
his performances can be read as symbolic cultural texts. Viewed in this way,
any performance can be analyzed as a site of cultural negotiation, an occasion
upon which a culture or society can reflect upon and define itself. While gender

studies and performance studies scholars use the language of performance to shed light on the constructed nature of gender representation in everyday life, a study of Breitbart offers up literal performances of gender that can be analyzed for what they might say about cultural worlds beyond the theater.

Breitbart's performances also constitute a particularly rich arena for exploration because of the passionate engagement of his audiences and the vivid record of public responses to the Jewish strongman that can be found in the press. Breitbart's performances also extended beyond the stage. Indeed, much of his public followed his offstage ventures and activities with intense interest. His involvement in scandals and lawsuits, his defense against his anti-Semitic critics, and his physical assaults on them were documented in their every detail by the Jewish and general press. Thus, while his performances of masculinity were indeed unique, they reflected his acute awareness of his audiences, their sensibilities, and their desires. Most important for the purposes of this chapter, the reception of Breitbart's performances on- and offstage suggests possibilities for conceptualizing Jewish masculinity in ways that existing models have not yet fully addressed.

The core of Breitbart's act was to display the strength of his beautifully sculpted male body in a succession of hypermasculine poses—in the costume of a bullfighter, as a Roman centurion, or skimpily clad as Hercules. With his broad shoulders, steely muscles, high cheekbones, and beautifully proportioned facial structure, Breitbart sometimes positioned himself against a backdrop of images from ancient Greece. Onstage, he moved fluidly between a range of archetypal masculine postures, adopting the armor of the Roman gladiator in one act and just as readily becoming the western cowboy in the next, thereby undermining any fixed notion of self and Other, Aryan or Jew.[7]

As a performer on the vaudeville stage, Breitbart drew from an arsenal of images and stage personas to craft an entertaining show that would satisfy the tastes of his audiences. Breitbart's Roman centurion visually represented the relationship of empire, militarism, and manliness. In the body of the centurion, physical strength, masculinity, and imperial power all came together to form a potent symbol of personal and national regeneration. Particularly after the First World War, the warrior image of masculinity assumed added significance in the German cultural realm with its emphasis on the combined qualities of courage, sacrifice, and a will of steel.[8] The deepening association of militarism and manliness, in turn, also forged a renewed link between masculinity and nationalism. Interestingly, this image of the masculine warrior appears to have been meaningful for non-Jewish and Jewish audiences alike. In the Warsaw Yiddish daily *Moment,* Breitbart's obituary was accompanied by a photo of him as the fabled Roman warrior.[9]

It is possible to read these performances of Roman military might as reinforcing contemporary ideals while simultaneously challenging them. Breitbart clearly admired Rome as the embodiment of military and imperial ideals. According to one report, Breitbart had a personal library containing more than 2,000 books on the history of the Roman empire.[10] Yet he also appropriated Rome as a symbol of resurgent Jewish military power. In a particularly audacious move, he placed in a leading German trade journal a full-page advertisement that boasted an oversized Star of David.[11] Accompanying the star was German text: "Take note of two words. Siegmund Breitbart." The following appeared in both German and Latin: "In hoch signio veritas vincet [In this sign the truth will prevail]," the words pronounced by the angel to Emperor Constantine as he went to battle under the sign of the cross in 312 CE.[12] By transposing Constantine's battle cry, acclaiming a new Christian empire, into a rallying cry for Jewish military conquest, Breitbart was able to simultaneously admire and challenge the ideal of imperial (Roman) power. At the same time, he seems to have contested the narrative of exclusive nationalism, incorporating himself as a representative of the very enterprise that would otherwise exclude him and, by extension, his people. In so doing, he overturned—perhaps for a few moments onstage and likely only for certain members of his audiences—the ideal of an exclusionary nationalism as he himself embodied it onstage.

Yet alongside Breitbart's sometimes ironic appropriation of images that, under other circumstances, might have excluded him as a Jew for many in his Eastern European audiences, he also appeared to project images that reinforced explicitly Zionist ideals. Those who viewed him from a Zionist perspective could read his beautiful male Jewish body as a symbol of national strength and the personification of the new Jewish man. Clearly, Breitbart assumed a posture on- and offstage that promoted such associations. He was known, for example, to appear flanked by the Zionist flag, and he also performed his feats of strength posing as Bar Kokhba, the second-century failed military figure who was resurrected by Zionists as a model of militant Jewish nationalism. In Warsaw, Breitbart refused to return to a popular restaurant after the band had declined to play *Hatikvah,* the Zionist hymn and future Israeli national anthem, to greet the strongman. A supporter of the Jewish settlement in Palestine, Breitbart published a congratulatory notice in the Hebrew press on the occasion of the opening of the Hebrew University on Mount Scopus in Jerusalem in 1925.[13] Even among non-Jews, he selectively, but unabashedly, associated himself with Zionism. Beyond Breitbart's own use of specific images that called upon Zionist symbols, Eastern European Jews were particularly inclined to see the strongman as a figure who offered a forceful answer to Jewish powerlessness.

Beyond his performance of personas that embodied images of an imperial Roman masculinity or even Zionist ideals of manliness, Breitbart's appearances in Eastern Europe also employed images that reflected the values of the softer and gentler Jewish man—much along the lines of what Boyarin characterized as the ideals of rabbinic and premodern Eastern European Jewish masculinity. In Poland, for example, Zishe Breitbart displayed deep admiration for the traditionally high-status roles of Jewish religious and secular men: rabbis, writers, and intellectuals. In fact, he seemed to crave their approval. The Warsaw Yiddish daily *Haynt* reported that on a visit to that city in 1925 Breitbart built a new fence around the grave of the great Yiddish writer Y. L. Peretz, since the existing one had fallen into disrepair. On another occasion, Breitbart performed for the Jewish Literature Association in Warsaw. Asked by members of the association to write a letter of endorsement that the group could use in its advertisements, Breitbart, according to the event organizer, "held the pen and wrote in Hebrew with the same intensity and concentration with which he bent iron."[14] Not entirely successful on either the first, second, or third tries, his labored writing exercise was attributed to the fact that he was "trying to throw in a lot of Hebrew words to impress the writers."[15] Breitbart cultivated friendships with Yiddish and Hebrew writers and was particularly pleased to be seen in their company. He was also proud to write his autobiography and have it published, though his book was ghostwritten by the Yiddish writer Ber Kutscher.

What becomes clear in the Eastern European Jewish context (and also applies to immigrant populations in Germany) is that many Yiddish-speaking consumers of culture perceived Zishe in ways that were not always consistent with the hypermasculine ideal that formed the content of his onstage performances. One reporter and admirer even described Zishe in terms that epitomized Boyarin's characterization of "traditional Jewish masculinity." When he went to meet "Zishe the athlete," the reporter expected to find a man with enormous muscles and a big stomach, a tough guy. Instead, he characterized Breitbart as "the embodiment of *Edelkayt*."[16] Thus, while confirming a conceptual divide between the ideal of *Edelkayt*, on the one hand, and the ideals of a muscular masculinity, on the other, this writer nevertheless seemed to suggest the possibility of transcending that divide by showing how Zishe was deeply rooted in, and belonged to, Eastern European Jewish culture.

In a similar way, the chief rabbi of the Orthodox Jewish Community (Adass Yisroel) in Berlin, Dr. Esra Monk, portrayed Zishe as a figure who challenged the simple dichotomy of the physical against the spiritual. Monk knew Zishe Breitbart personally, yet he saw no contradiction that a man who was called "modern Samson the hero" could also possess such a tender and childlike demeanor. "It is greatly symbolic," noted Monk in his eulogy in October 1925, "that for a man who broke chains, it was enough for one person's good word to melt Zishe's heart [render his heart soft as butter]."[17] It was as though Monk were mounting a defense of Breitbart not only against a traditional Jewish critique but also against Boyarin's use of the term *goyim naches,* a pejorative Yiddish term for European Christian culture and its masculine values such as war making, dueling, and, one would presume, bodybuilding.[18]

While some Jewish observers found in Zishe aspects of the traditional *Edelkayt* ideal, many others seem to have understood him through a model of manliness that was associated with the *shtarker* figure (Yiddish; literally, "strong one"). In Eastern Europe, representations of strong Jewish men were thus not produced exclusively by Zionists. Indeed, at about the same time as the Zionist new Jewish man began to be included in the iconography of the Zionist movement, the figures of the *ba'al guf* (Hebrew; "tough guy") or *shtarker* also began to appear in Yiddish literature.[19] These images, which circulated widely in the early twentieth century, were produced in no small part by the same historical circumstances that led to the creation of Zionism. In the Eastern European Jewish context, the experience of political disenfranchisement and physical vulnerability, combined with rising violence and a desire among Jews to exercise some form of self-defense, led to the rise of the *shtarker* and the *ba'al guf* in Yiddish literature.

One of the most famous depictions of the *ba'al guf* in this literature appears in Sholem Asch's "On Kola Street" (1905–1906), which vividly portrays a clear split in Jewish society between the majority, who embraced the scholarly ideal, and the uneducated, unruly rabble who lived on Kola Street. In Asch's story, the rabbinic elite had no use for these unsavory figures, that is, until anti-Jewish violence befell their community. Then, and only then, the scholars put their lives in the hands of these fishmongers, porters, and physical laborers. During normal times, "the street of the scholars . . . felt very much ashamed of Kola Street."[20] Although the tough guys of Kola Street were not Zionists per se, neither was Kola Street in the diaspora. On Kola Street, noted Asch, no Jew was ever beaten.

As the Sholem Asch story illustrates, the ideal of self-defense, and the physical strength required to carry it out, were key characteristics of the *shtarker* figure. This helps explain how Breitbart was integrated so readily: the interpretive framework of Eastern European Jews already existed. Coming from a family of blacksmiths, Breitbart worked in a trade that depended largely on physical labor and strength, and much of his public persona among Eastern European Jews was connected with his resolve to further self-defense among the Jews. He once confessed his desire to be the general of an army that would seize Eretz Yisrael for the Jewish people.[21] And there were numerous stories circulated and published of Breitbart defending himself or the public from anti-Semitic attacks. But perhaps the richest evidence of the public's view of Breitbart as a defender of the Jewish people can be found in the popular expression "Were a thousand Breitbarts to arise, Jewish persecution would cease."[22]

Also characteristic of the *shtarker* figure was the place he assumed on the lowest rung of the Eastern European Jewish class hierarchy. What characterized members of this Jewish underclass, as the literary historian Warren Rosenberg has argued, is that, in addition to their socioeconomic status, occupational profile, and level of education, members of this group tended to use violence in ways that violated the ideals of the rabbinic elite.[23] Here again, Zishe Breitbart could have easily been cast in the mold of the *baʾal guf.* Breitbart's background—growing up in a poor working-class Jewish neighborhood in Lodz—was, according to his own report, filled with violence. His career and his autobiography were littered with examples of his own violent acts, which began in the schoolyard when he was a young boy. During the height of his fame in Vienna, he was convicted of assault against a competitor. And in Lublin, his performance was banned by authorities because Breitbart "got even with several Christians" who were mocking and taunting Jews.[24]

If his framing in the east was to some degree rooted in the image of the *shtarker,* Zishe nevertheless moved himself beyond the socially marginal status traditionally relegated to that figure by appearing to transcend the division between the values of the Jewish religious establishment and Polish Jewry's violent but sometimes necessary underclass. Zishe's attempt to heal this divide is evident in his efforts to win the sympathy and support of figures of rabbinic authority. In one such encounter with a leading Hasidic rabbi, the Radziner rebbe in Warsaw, he succeeded in breaking down the perceived divide between rabbinic values and muscles. While the rebbe had initially forbidden his disciples from attending Breitbart's performances (which was to little effect since Hasidim were known to flock to them anyway), the rebbe eventually summoned Breitbart to his home for a private performance, anxious to see for himself what was behind the Breitbart phenomenon. According to numerous reports, after spending two hours with Breitbart, the rebbe was so impressed with Breitbart's feats that he gave Breitbart his approval, his *hechsher* (rabbinical certification of purity), as it were; in turn, Breitbart donated thirty pounds of Passover flour to the rebbe's community, displaying his familiarity with the community's values, and departed with the rebbe's blessing.

Despite the efforts of his rabbinic supporters to break down the perceived division between the gentle man and the man of strength, Breitbart could also serve as a symbol of the social outsider who helps hasten the demise of the social order. In a cartoon entitled "The New Divorce Epidemic," which appeared during the height of the Breitbart mania in Warsaw, Zishe is represented both as an object of erotic attraction and as a figure who, like the *shtarker,* stands outside the bounds of normative Jewish society.[25] The setting is a *beit din*—a religious court consisting of three rabbis or learned Jewish men that is convened to arbitrate and make decisions about matters of religious law. On the bench sit the rabbis, receiving a long line of women who are dragging their husbands behind them to initiate divorce proceedings. "What do you want?" the rabbi asks the first woman in line. The woman replies, "I want a divorce." "Why?" the rabbi follows up. "Because ever since I laid my eyes on Breitbart, I can't look at my *shlemazal* husband any more." Beyond this lighthearted commentary on Zishe's appeal to women, the cartoon offers a pointed commentary on what the author

"The New Divorce Epidemic," *Moment* (13 March 1925).

portrays as a skewed Jewish gender order consisting of overly strong women dominating their effeminate men.

In this critique, Zishe represents the anomalous or modern Jewish male who embodied contemporary ideals of strength and beauty (*Kraft und Schönheit*) and modern masculinity, in contrast to the identifiably Jewish weak and scholarly men who appear in the cartoon as husbands or rabbis. At another level, by positing an irresolvable split between elite religious values, as represented by the rabbis, and the physical drives of women, the cartoon also offers a distinctly Jewish version of the traditional opposition of high and low culture. Viewed from this perspective, Zishe's presence, although he is visually absent, serves to destabilize the status quo, letting loose the normal social restraints that reined in female passions, and sets in motion phenomena that led women in particular to violate the sanctity of the family, challenge religious authority, and upset the social order of Eastern European Jewish society.

What makes the report of a Jewish divorce epidemic in Warsaw all the more intriguing is the existence of a parallel and nearly identical text in a satirical, anti-Semitic paper in Vienna. Appearing during a four-month period when the city's inhabitants were consumed with "Breitbart fever," the newspaper *Kikeriki*, which had regularly mocked the Eastern European Jewish obsession with

Breitbart, published a tongue-in-cheek column written from the point of view of a neglected husband. The writer complains that his Breitbart-crazed wife, who bought tickets to see the strongman four nights in a row, talks dreamily about Breitbart the hero while complaining about her own husband's manly inadequacy.[26] This column reflected what was widely noted in the Viennese press at the time: women were the ones caught up in the frenzy and the daily traffic jams outside the theater. Many observers, psychoanalysts among them, weighed in on why Viennese women fell for Breitbart, despite sexual repression and racial hatred. To be sure, the image of love-struck women mobbing popular male performers, especially bodybuilders, was nothing new; similar reports appeared about the strongman Eugen Sandow in his time.[27] In both the column and the cartoon, however, we find a common critique of women's consumption, which formed part of a larger theme in the rise of mass culture and its emphasis on the seemingly uncontrollable passions propelling female consumption and desire.[28]

Whereas Boyarin used the concept of mimicry to represent more or less capitulation to the dominant non-Jewish ideal, a conception of mimicry that focuses more on the agency and resistance of the colonized offers a more subtle model for tracing the emergence of Jewish masculine ideals and their relationship to gentile ones. Reading Bhabha in this way allows us to see how Breitbart's performances of gender recombined various elements of the German masculine stereotype that functioned as a comment on and even parody of some of the more militant and racialized forms of German masculinity. In the process, we see the agency of the performer to juxtapose symbols and shift their meanings while interacting with multiple publics in a variety of cultural settings. Breitbart's performance of a muscular Judaism incorporated and played with German masculine ideals in ways that both approximated and exaggerated the images of the warrior and the associated attributes of dominance, strength, and will, and it is precisely these sites that reveal examples of excess and slippage. Through Breitbart's physical embodiment of the German masculine stereotype and his adaptation of some of its symbols, we can identify in his performances not a simple surrender of Jewish uniqueness, as Boyarin argues about modern Zionists in general, but a cultural innovator who projected images that spoke to, and resonated with, audiences in widely different cultural contexts.

Like other performances of resistance, Breitbart reaffirmed important ideals of German masculinity and of a new version of Jewish masculinity, and undermined them both at the very same time. It is in this way that we may identify both agency and originality—not merely imitation and capitulation—in Breitbart's performances, which drew from the German masculine stereotype, Zionist ideals of the new Jewish man, the image of the *shtarker,* and the ideal of the gentle and learned Jewish man. "Cultures are never unitary in themselves," wrote Bhabha, "nor simply dualistic in the relation of self to other."[29] As a lens into Eastern European Jewish culture and the process of cultural adaptation,

Breitbart's performances and the reception of him in Eastern Europe attest to a complex confrontation with and interpenetration of a diverse array of cultural sensibilities and values.

From this brief analysis, we can see that, far from representing any unified notion of masculinity, Breitbart combined and projected multiple conceptions and images of masculinity. He was able to move about easily, crossing boundaries within and outside Jewish society, and he put together images that otherwise might not have been seen as compatible. That parts of the Jewish public could see Breitbart as the embodiment of *Edelkayt,* while also viewing him as a tough guy who would fight and defend his people, clearly suggests the coexistence of multiple ideals of masculinity that were not mutually exclusive but could be altered, remixed, and manipulated. Rather than seeking to trace one coherent or uniform discourse that remained static over time, I have sought to illustrate how sometimes opposing attributes of masculinity coalesce in unpredictable ways: in both Breitbart's performances and his audience's readings of them.

Onstage, as Breitbart imitated the forms of the colonizers and infused old archetypes with new meanings, his audiences engaged in a similar process. Thus, when a journalist for *Haynt* at Breitbart's funeral in Berlin reported that his admirers had lost their Jewish Siegfried, he was doing more than simply equating Breitbart with the mythical, dragon-slaying Germanic hero. Indeed, in the simple appropriation of the Germanic national hero and the transformation of Siegfried into a Jewish idiom, Breitbart's fans challenged, as Bhabha anticipates, the very construct of the colonizer. Wagner's Siegfried symbolized an essential Germanness that embodied heroism, strength, and dominance, but the mythical Breitbart was no simple copy of the original. This we can see in the eulogy for the new Jewish national hero, when Rabbi Monk of Adass Yisroel gave voice to a unique and specifically early twentieth-century Jewish meaning of strength, manliness, and heroism among the thousands of Eastern European Jews who came to the cemetery to honor and mourn Zishe Haim ben Yitzhak Halevi.[30] While his physical powers were the embodiment of might, noted the rabbi, "his soul [was] the embodiment of poetry."[31]

NOTES

1. Homi Bhabha, "Of Mimicry and Man: The Ambiguity of Colonial Discourse," in his *The Location of Culture* (New York: Routledge, 1994), 85–93.

2. Ibid., 86.

3. Daniel Boyarin, *Unheroic Conduct: The Rise of Heterosexuality and the Invention of the Jewish Man* (Berkeley: University of California Press, 1997), 4.

4. Ibid., 17.

5. George L. Mosse, *The Image of Man: The Creation of Modern Masculinity* (New York: Oxford University Press, 1996).

6. I borrow this phrase from Caroline Bynum, "Why All the Fuss about the Body? A Medievalist's Perspective," *Critical Inquiry* 22, no. 1 (1995): 7.

7. For further elaboration on this theme, see Sharon Gillerman, "Samson in Vienna: The Theatrics of Jewish Masculinity," *Jewish Social Studies* 9, no. 2 (2003): 65–98; and Gillerman, "Strongman Siegmund Breitbart and Interpretations of the Jewish Body," in Gideon Reuveni and Michael Brenner, eds., *Emancipation through Muscles: Jews and Sports in Europe* (Lincoln: University of Nebraska Press, 2006), 62–77.

8. Mosse, *Image of Man,* 110–113.

9. *Moment* 235 (13 October 1925): 4.

10. "Breitbart, Modern Samson: First American Appearance of Jewish Superman," *American Hebrew* (28 September 1923): 497.

11. *Das Programm* (3 February 1925): n.p.

12. Don Gifford, *Ulysses Annotated: Notes for James Joyce's Ulysses* (Berkeley: University of California Press, 1988), 94.

13. Dan Almagor, "Dress Rehearsal for Independence: The Foundation of the Hebrew University of Jerusalem 75 Years Ago," *Ariel* 111 (1999): 29.

14. *Haynt* 59 (10 March 1925): 7.

15. Ibid.

16. Ibid.

17. *Haynt* (13 October 1925): 4.

18. Boyarin, *Unheroic Conduct,* 38.

19. David G. Roskies, *The Jewish Search for a Usable Past* (Bloomington: Indiana University Press, 1999), 29–30; Roskies, *Against the Apocalypse: Responses to Catastrophe in Modern Jewish Culture* (Cambridge, MA: Harvard University Press, 1984), 141–143. According to Roskies, the "ba'al guf entered fiction in response to the ideological demand that Jews stop abdicating the physical realm for the spiritual." Roskies calls this figure a "proto-Zionist hero of action."

20. Sholem Asch, "On Kola Street," in Irving Howe and Eliezer Greenberg, eds., *A Treasury of Yiddish Stories* (New York: Schocken, 1973), 260–275.

21. "Zishe Breitbart," *Yiddisher Morgen Zhurnal* (14 October 1925).

22. Personal communication with Gary Bart, a descendant of Zishe Breitbart, 14 November 2004.

23. Warren Rosenberg, *Legacy of Rage: Jewish Masculinity, Violence, and Culture* (Amherst: University of Massachusetts Press, 2001), 68.

24. *Moment* 122 (28 May 1925): 10.

25. *Moment* 62 (13 March 1925): 7.

26. "Aus dem Tagebuch des Herrn von Sumper," *Kikeriki* (11 February 1923): 2.

27. David Chapman, *Sandow the Magnificent: Eugen Sandow and the Beginnings of Bodybuilding* (Champaign: University of Illinois Press, 1994), 52, 75.

28. On this theme, see Rita Felski, *The Gender of Modernity* (Cambridge, MA: Harvard University Press), 1995, 73; for a discussion of gender, consumption, and Jewishness, see Paul Lerner, "Consuming Pathologies: Kleptomania, Magazinitis, and the Problem of Female Consumption in Wilhelmine and Weimar Germany," *WerkstattGeschichte* 42 (Summer 2006): 46–56.

29. Bhabha, *Location of Culture,* 36.

30. *Haynt* (13 October 1925): 4.

31. Ibid.

# 10

---

## Family Matters

---

*German Jewish Masculinities among Nazi Era Refugees*

JUDITH GERSON

Recalling his close relationship with his father, Henry Salfeld wrote in his memoir that his father was anxious to bring up his son as "a proud Jew and also a German patriot." Elected to head the local chapter of the Reichsbund jüdischer Frontsoldaten (RjF; Association of Jewish Combat Veterans), Richard Offenbacher remembered that every year on Memorial Day he led a parade of its members and delivered a speech in front of the war memorial at the Jewish cemetery. Taken from the memoirs of German Jewish refugees during the Nazi era, these are only two instances among many that reference the writers' lives as Germans and as Jews. In the first example, the terms are literal—a proud Jew and a patriotic German—while in the second case, being German and being a Jew are evoked through organizations and behaviors.[1]

The writers as well as the readers of these memoirs rely on interpretations that express the complicated, varied, and vexed relationships between being German and being Jewish. Indeed it makes sense to read the memoirs in this way, because these are the terms the writers often use. Moreover, the Jewish question and, arguably, the German question represented persistent concerns in public discourse in Germany long before and in the decades following emancipation. Yet if we were to read the tensions in these memoirs over the meanings of being Jewish and German as solely reflecting those identities, our knowledge would be incomplete. The experiences of being Jewish and German are also gendered experiences and thus the meanings of masculinity both shape and are shaped by the meanings of being Jewish and German. Integrating an analysis of masculinity with an analysis of Jewish and German identities enables a more comprehensive and appropriately more complex understanding of German Jewish masculinity.

This chapter considers the range of practices and expressions of masculinities among German Jewish refugees: people who fled Nazi-controlled Europe between 1933 and 1941, and resettled in New York City before the war's end. I will begin with an overview of the project and information about the people who are at the center of my inquiry. Then I will describe the primary evidence for my research and summarize my conceptual understanding of gender relations before embarking on an analysis of German Jewish masculinities among these refugees.

## PROJECT OVERVIEW

Evidence for this chapter comes from a larger study of German Jews who fled Germany between 30 January 1933, when Hitler assumed power, and 23 October 1941, the date after which Germany prohibited emigration. Many refugees who resettled in the United States were forced to take circuitous routes and make lengthy intermittent stops. The refugees included in this study arrived and resettled in New York City as early as 1933 and as late as May 1945, when the Allies declared victory in Europe.[2] My decision to concentrate on this immigrant group and its relationship to the Holocaust stems from the relative scarcity of knowledge about people who escaped from Nazi-controlled Europe before the "final solution" was implemented.[3] Juxtaposing the scholarship on the Holocaust and on migration, I elaborate our knowledge of German Jewish immigrants through an analysis of identity practices in daily life. *Identity practices* refer to people's thoughts, actions, and feelings that mark their memberships in groups or, conversely, their marginality or exclusion from them.[4]

For this analysis, I concentrate on forty-one largely unpublished memoirs, usually written in English, by people who generally claim to speak for themselves or their families alone. Most of these documents are housed in the archives at the Leo Baeck Institute or in the archives of the U.S. Holocaust Memorial Museum. In addition I read essays by former German Jews submitted to two essay contests: a 1939 Harvard-sponsored contest, "My Life in Germany before and after January 30, 1933," and a 1942 YIVO-sponsored contest, "Why I Left Europe and What I Have Accomplished in America."[5]

Most commonly, the memoirs were written in the 1970s, 1980s, and 1990s when the writers were in their sixties, seventies, and eighties, reaching the end of their lives. At times writers wove letters and passages from diaries into their narratives, but more often they wrote from memory, which they asserted had not eroded over the years. Traumatic memories may surface years after the events, and thus it is not surprising to encounter this gap in time between the events and their recording in memoirs. Holocaust collective memory and commemoration are central and valued elements of Jewish American, Western European, and Israeli cultures, and these memoirists were among many witnesses who wanted to testify before the end of their lives, cognizant that theirs was the last generation of survivors.

## GENDER RELATIONS

It has long been established that gender is socially constructed. Gender operates at all levels of social life, ranging from intrapersonal processes and interpersonal interactions to cultural practices and larger institutional formations, such as the military, the family, and the state. Like all contributions to this volume, my analysis of patterns of masculinity among German Jewish refugees starts from the premise that masculinity does not possess a single or unified form but rather presents itself in a variety of configurations. The content and form of masculinity are neither random nor predetermined but instead constitute and are constituted through the configurations of being German and Jewish, which vary over time and place. The various forms of masculinity are neither co-equal nor merely different from one another but instead connote power relations. A hegemonic definition of masculinity exists in relation to subordinate, complicit, and marginalized forms of masculinity. With this framework in mind, I turn to the evidence in the memoirs to explore the meanings of masculinity among Jewish refugees from Germany.[6]

## FAMILY FRAMES

Men wrote more than half of the memoirs I read, in contrast to the more common pattern of memoir writing being the province of women. This apparent anomaly is particularly interesting because these memoirs are not the typical masculine narratives of selfhood filled with tales of individual accomplishments and personal demonstrations of intelligence, cleverness, and strength, resulting in notable achievements and success.

These family memoirs stand in marked contrast to that of Aron Liebeck, who stresses his hard work, careful planning, and ultimate triumphs despite an early life marked by personal hardships and in contrast to others' ongoing misfortunes. Whereas Liebeck "presents himself as the protagonist of his own story, as an individual agent responsible for his own fate," the engine and the center of his family's life, the refugee memoirs are narratives not of independent men who triumph but rather of family men who recognize their kin as their major source of satisfaction and pride.[7]

Their families were patriarchal with a male head of the household who was thought to be the most powerful and also the most knowledgeable. Given most German Jewish men's decline in economic and social status before emigration and the hardships upon resettlement, writing family memoirs was a legitimate way to recuperate some respect and authority. Similar to the efforts of Aron Liebeck, these memoirs were a vehicle to account for and reconstruct male honor in a manner compatible with the "soft manliness" of the urban German bourgeoisie, which placed priority on the father's role in family life.[8]

Yet there is also an underlying similarity between the women's and men's memoirs that transcends any bifurcated definitions of gender. Most of the men as well as the women cite their families as the reason for deciding to write their memoirs. In the introductions, prefaces, and occasional letters which accompany the unpublished manuscripts submitted to archives, men are as likely as women to dedicate their memoirs to their children or grandchildren. Sometimes they acknowledge the children or grandchildren by name as the impetus for their writing, thanking the younger generation for encouraging them to record their past. They write because they want their families to know what happened, and in this sense the memoirs represent lasting contributions to the legacies of their families and an important resource for their continuation. Memoir writing not only contributes to one's family legacy but also constitutes part of a larger complex of caretaking of one's family. The men's focus on their families suggests that not just women believe family continuity is important.

Many memoirists invoke the biblical injunction to remember the past, *zakhor*, and to teach it. In Jewish culture and religion, remembering the dead is one way of perpetuating and honoring their memory. In these memoirs, the family is the primary locus of memory. It unites generations to one another by teaching the younger ones about their ancestors whom they did not know. Collective memory, or how a group remembers the past, is often a source of clues for how a group thinks about its collective identity. Analysis of these memoirs provides unquestionable evidence that German Jewish practices of memory and identity are family-centered. Writing about a family life that was destroyed, moreover, is a redemptive act. It recovers the past for an audience of kin who are living proof that evil did not triumph. Ernest Hausmann expresses this connection toward the end of his memoir: "My primary aim in putting together this history of the Hausmann and Weingartner families during a most troubled time is to give my grandchildren some sense of their heritage. Hopefully it might also help to guide them to be more caring persons."[9] This familial orientation both provides a sense of purpose for the writers and diminishes much of the self-absorption that might normally accompany memoirs. Like other parents and grandparents, Hausmann sees his grandchildren as representing the possibility for a more just world.

While most memoirists tend to be parents or grandparents, other people write memoirs as well. Childless narrators occasionally mention a cousin, niece, or nephew as the rationale for writing, or are driven by a more general desire to pass on their heritage and knowledge to others. The expressed and immediate audience for the memoirs frequently is other family members. The younger generations not only are the intended audience but suggest a sense of purpose. Children and grandchildren are proof that the "final solution" was incomplete. Writing for younger generations may also have guided the authors in their decisions about what to include and exclude, though they are never explicit about this. Concerns about protecting younger readers from full descriptions of some of the terrors they experienced might explain and help writers rationalize their avoidance of full or extensive accounts of brutality. Though this omission is far from universal, references to atrocities are relatively sparse.

Thus these memoirs, even the published ones, are largely family matters. Not only is the family the catalyst for their writing and their expressed audience, the family is the modal frame and the most frequently mentioned category of analysis. The substantive emphasis on family is evident in the ways narrators describe their daily lives in Germany and upon resettlement in the United States. It is also apparent in their retelling of their family and communal history. But this emphasis on the family should not be understood as suggesting that little else occurs in these texts. There are wonderful passages about the importance of the natural landscape in their lives—their hikes and bike trips. There are detailed descriptions of their school years, association and club memberships, and employment. And there are also horrifying passages about the increasing harassment and brutality, and the deaths of kin and friends. But even many of these references are explicitly tied to family life.

Memoirs have a narrative structure and sequence, which in the case of these texts often begins with the telling of the family's life in Germany. Frequently this is a genealogical project as writers trace their family's history back for centuries, knowledge which is both a source of pride and a basis for an oblique expression of their right to a residence-based citizenship. Ernest Hausmann is quite specific in his assertions, chronicling his family's existence in Baden back to the Thirty Years' War (1618–1648) and noting that the chaos of those years probably meant early records were destroyed. This longevity brought considerable grief to one of his cousins, who proved in a school assignment that their family had been resident in Germany longer than that of any of her Aryan classmates.[10]

Others relate a more general history of Jews living in a particular locale. Joseph Adler opens with a short history of the Jews in Frankfurt in the Middle Ages. Henry Buxbaum narrates a short history of the Jews in the Frankfurt ghetto, where he claims all Jewish families in Germany had their roots. His father's family was lost to them, having migrated to America in the nineteenth century, and perhaps as a consequence, he is one of a handful of men who focus on their matrilineal heritage. He explains:

> [M]y grandfather Loeb Mayer's people belonged to the original core of the ten or so Jewish families who had settled in Reichelsheim in the early or mid-1700s. One hundred years later, they had multiplied into one of the largest rural congregations in South-Hessia, certainly in the Odenwald region. They were typical of the many communities in the Hessian countryside. With their intense Jewishness, their clannishness which as a rule did not extend beyond the family—only that such a family, as we remember, included everybody up to the nth cousin with its in-laws. . . . This was the setting where 110 or so years ago, in 1864, my mother had been born.[11]

Unlike some former Jews who used genealogical documents as proof of conversion to Christianity a generation or two earlier, or as evidence of their mixed ancestry to secure protection against the Nazi regime, these German Jews sought to legitimate their rights to German citizenship by proving their residence in Germany over the centuries. A few memoirs make this connection explicitly and succinctly. Alfred Gruenspecht writes, "When our small community in the German countryside was first threatened by the Nazis, Papa began to record a list of the names of the members of our two families on his side—the Gruenspechts and the Heinemanns (the family of my father's mother). . . . He must have had a premonition of the tragedy that was to come."[12]

Though there are numerous similar tales of families who can document their existence in Germany since the seventeenth or eighteenth century, others without an extensive genealogical record instead occasionally provide detailed accounts of their parents or grandparents. Fred Sternberg writes with admiration for his grandfather, a founder of the Turnverein and an important person in the Jewish community. He describes his grandparents' home with its four bedrooms on the second floor, two more on the third, a large kitchen, a living room, and a basement where coal and potatoes were stored. Ernest Hausmann also depicts his grandparents' home, vividly recalling the unheated room where he slept and the toilet facilities, which he judged to be "clean but primitive." Others lovingly remembered grandparents, aunts, and uncles in vivid detail, portraying frequent large family gatherings.[13]

If family life is the most visible and recurrent theme of these memoirs, military service is certainly the second most frequent emphasis. Though initially it might appear that these are distinct foci, a closer look reveals that military service mattered because it was the instrument on which men and their families depended to secure their rights to citizenship and to bestow honor on them and their families. For these German citizens of Jewish faith, men's military service in World War I represented the pinnacle of acceptance as German men and German citizens—a definition of masculinity, which simultaneously linked national identity to gender identity. The paramount symbol of this allegiance was the Iron Cross, a medal awarded for valor. Men who received the Iron Cross mention it in their writings, and so do their wives, sisters, mothers, and children. More than half of the memoirs contain one or more references to military service as a mechanism through which they claimed their national identity—either referring to their own or a relative's service. There was a shared sense of betrayal when German Jews recognized that honorable military service did not guarantee them the rights and privileges of full membership in the German state.

At times military service provided the foundation for assessing the current situation. Talking about his father, whose family had lived in a small town for more than two centuries, Alfred Mayer writes, "Some of my father's friends realized that all the Iron Crosses and medals bestowed by the late Wilhelm II for valor in World War I had lost their value." Reiterating a frequently voiced theme of Jewish men serving the German state, a daughter is explicit about her resentment: "My father, like many Jews, was a good German and insisted on enlisting voluntarily in the Army in World War I. . . . How grateful the Germans were to us later on!" Upon returning home after six months in Dachau, Fritz Ottenheimer's father threw his war medals into the trash. Gerhard Bry pens, "Father volunteered for World War I service so that nobody could say that Jews let German Goyim do the fighting and dying needed to protect our families." Sarcasm but more often anger and despair erupted when German Jews realized that their military service ultimately meant nothing and would offer them no durable protection.[14]

The contested issue of military service was a vexed subject for Jews years earlier as well. Alfred Wolf writes poignantly of his father, who was a soldier from 1888 to 1889: "He often told me proudly what a good soldier he was and how he excelled in soldiering, shooting, gymnastics, marching." His father was admitted to the reserve officer training corps and passed the course, only to be told by an apologetic captain:

> [I]t was by mistake that he was admitted to the course . . . and of course being a Jew he could not be promoted to lieutenant of the reserve. And that was that. My father told me this story often, especially when the First World War was started and I wanted to volunteer. . . . The refusal made a profound and lifelong-lasting impression on Papa, and was a hurt and insult which he never forgot and forgave.[15]

The volume and intensity of these references seem commensurate with the troubled, complicated, and contested history of the relationship among the state, military service, and citizenship for Jews living in Germany, which varied among the states before the unification of Germany and alternated between more progressive and restrictive periods before and after 1871. Regardless of the locale or time period, legal statutes often guaranteed equality of opportunity, but in actual practice, discrimination against Jews persisted.[16] A few guideposts will provide additional context for understanding the frequency and force of references in the memoirs to military service.

At the end of the eighteenth century, when non-Jewish German men rejoiced in their exemptions from military service while concurrently insisting on the privileges it conveyed, Jewish men tethered their goal of full civic inclusion and privileges to their right to be able to serve in the military. Jewish men considered military service their entrance card into Prussian civil society and the basis of their social and political freedom.[17] The Edict of 11 March 1812 granted formal citizenship and equal rights to Jews in Prussia. Jews were now subject to military conscription but prevented from becoming officers, thus leaving the issue of full equality unresolved in practice. Nonetheless more than 700 Jews, more than half of them volunteers, fought for Prussia during its 1813–1815 Wars of Liberation. Those numbers increased to 7,000 Jewish soldiers during the Franco-Prussian War of 1870–1871.[18]

In the period after 1871, Jewish efforts to gain acceptance in German society concentrated on the reserve officer corps, despite ongoing discrimination in other institutions of Jewish and secular life. Serving in the reserve officer corps brought two prized advantages. Reserve officer appointments meant honor and prestige, and opened the doors to various civil service and professional occupations. For Jewish men long marginalized, both of these rewards were significant. In the immediate aftermath of German unification and recent military victories, Jews appeared less of a threat to the homogeneity of the officer corps, and some did succeed in becoming reserve officers.

Throughout Western and Central Europe, World War I was collectively remembered as the Great War and for Jews and non-Jews alike, the war and military service were pivotal experiences organizing collective memory.[19] Fighting for Germany gave Jews the opportunity to serve alongside their Christian countrymen, ostensibly strengthening the ties between them. Furthermore, military service enabled Jewish soldiers to demonstrate their loyalty to the state, exhibit their courage and bravery, and thus prove baseless the persistent stereotypes of their physical weakness and cowardice.[20] The war was the defining crucible for forging a heroic, nationally and ethnically proud, military masculinity.

It would be a mistake, however, to assume there was consensus within the Jewish community concerning military service. For many, the rabbinic ideal of Torah study and Talmudic culture meant that the peaceful resolution of disputes and avoidance of armed conflict remained exalted values. Violent physical activities were *goyim naches*—the pleasures of Christian life. Though disdained in Jewish culture, these pursuits were at the same time an important arena for judging and determining Jewish inferiority.[21] Moreover, military service temporarily protected certain groups of German Jews from some forms of discrimination and exclusion during the early years of the Third Reich. Initially, the RjF won the right for combat veterans to avoid dismissal from their civil service and from some professional jobs, their children remained in school, and wounded veterans continued to receive disability payments from the state.

Several writers expressed their distress over the injustice of military service and their family's losses, and some enumerated the temporary advantages they had. Joseph Adler, who received the Iron Cross on 27 January 1917, Kaiser Wilhelm's birthday, wrote, "The children were in school, I could work, and I thought we could squeeze through. I had the Iron Cross and the Front Fighter *Orden* (a war medal) from Hitler's government. In this respect we were a little better off than the other Jews. After all, we stayed because Germany was our *Vaterland* and German our mother language." "In Germany, as a front soldier,

I still had certain privileges [in 1938] under Hitler, which made the negotiations with the Gestapo and the *Deviesenstelle* [*sic*] (foreign exchange) somewhat easier." Whether they wrote ultimately with irony, anguish, anger, or disbelief, German Jews assumed their military service offered them the protections of and guaranteed their rights as citizens of the German state. During the early years of the Nazi regime, the occupational and educational privileges extended to some Jews who fought for Germany in World War I perpetuated a false sense of comparative safety.[22]

How did the memoir writers represent the accelerating forms of exclusion, harassment, and brutality? One common way was to write as succinctly as possible about the trauma. Readers cannot know for certain whether the scarcity of material was an accurate portrayal of their experiences, or if the writers were trying to protect themselves or their offspring from their anguished memories. One of the more puzzling omissions of this sort is Klaus Loewald's memoir, entitled "My Kristallnacht," which assumes but does not discuss the pogrom. Others, like Fred Sternberg, listed the names of or their relationships to those killed: "It was painful to look back. Dad's two sisters and two brothers and their whole families disappeared in the Holocaust. So did three of my cousins and their families and five of Mother's cousins. But life here had to go on."[23]

Occasionally the memoirs contain fuller narratives of atrocities. Martin Gumpert knew about many forms of terror but only wanted to describe those he witnessed, which he reported in significant detail.[24] In an award-winning essay for the YIVO contest, Paul Nickelsburg described his and other Jewish men's internment in Buchenwald during the November 1938 pogrom, and his report is among the most wrenching accounts to read. After some men were deprived of food and drink for three days, they were driven to shacks, where there was no room to lie or sit properly.

> In addition to the general excitement and anxiety, it produced fits of anguish and hysteria. They [the prisoners] yelled and screamed and cursed each other and tried to get out. Suddenly some came down with diarrhoea. . . . The Capos . . . would not let them out. . . . The Capos drove them back with cudgels. Now, Hell broke loose, yells, howling, blows, curses. . . . Many soiled their garments, the stench inside became nauseatic. . . . Within the barracks, frantic hysteria rose to a climax. Some went insane.[25]

> I am writing about these things with great reluctance, and I am saying only as much as absolutely necessary considering the purpose of this report. Much more might be said, more details might be given of instances of cruelty that happened any day, evidence that the stories of almost unbelievable crimes of the Nazis which reached this country cannot be dismissed. But it is not my purpose to arouse the reader[']s feelings with descriptions of atrocities.[26]

The most salient exception to the relative sparseness of accounts of hardship derives from the effects of the Nazi regime on working men's livelihoods, a prominent part of the manuscripts written by adult men. Even though the narrators tell of the forced change of residences which their families endured, and are concerned about their children having to leave or change schools, none of these passages approach the intensity and extent of the words devoted to men's labor. There are innumerable references to men who lost their jobs or whose work was constrained by restrictive legislation. Many shopkeepers and businessmen write about the 1 April boycott, and others mention that both before and after this date they lost customers, though some fared better than others. Ultimately the consequences were devastating, but in the first years of the Third Reich, the effects were more variable. Fritz Ottenheimer describes the first of April 1933 in Constance, with a sound truck moving through the streets, commanding people not to buy from Jewish stores. In response, his father returned home to retrieve his bag of World War I medals, and substituted those medals for the shirts usually displayed in his store window. "A number of people who knew my father's military record stepped up to a storm trooper and explained [that] Ludwig Ottenheimer was a good German, a disabled war veteran, who had done more than just his duty for his country. 'Surely you would not deny him the right to make an honest living!'"[27]

Other memoirists despaired, and several felt isolated and helpless. Henry Buxbaum, a physician, writes:

> In the spring of 1937, depressed from the increasing attacks of an implacable enemy, a feeling of helplessness took hold of me. They had made me a stranger and an outcast in my own country. I was step by step cut off from its life: A wall of bricks was going up around me, isolating me in their midst, condemning me to die a slow death. My practice was coming to its inevitable end.[28]

Helmuth Perlmann explains that on the first of January 1934, Hitler required all Jewish brokers to have permission cards to continue to work, which meant Perlmann was among the first to lose his job: "First I felt desperate and figured life had finished for me. They had me cut off from . . . what was my very existence. Finally, [I] said to myself: You have to start something else. There must be other ways to make a living."[29] Consoling himself that it might be better for his health anyway, he began selling wrapping paper and bags. Succeeding in his new business, he nonetheless admonished himself: "I should have realized that Hitler was out to destroy all the Jews of Germany as he had written in his book 'Mein Kampf.' . . . My exclusion from the Stock-Exchange at the end of 1933 should have taught me a good lesson. If I was smart I should have foreseen what every Jew had to expect from the Hitler-Regime."[30]

Whether to emigrate was a tormented decision for many men in the early 1930s. For some, like Martin Gumpert, a widower, it appeared to be an individual decision: "I knew I had to amputate my heart. I had loved Berlin, I had loved Germany, I had loved Europe. It is difficult to determine the point where one's usefulness for one's country ceases to exist, where one acknowledges defeat or clings to the right to continue life without threat, without unbearable restrictions of freedom and dignity." But many others linked their decision to the importance of their employment to their family's well-being; when income and job security were taken away from them, they recognized the necessity of leaving. Richard Offenbacher describes his decision to leave Germany in these words: "Anyway, conditions in Germany did not improve; the Nazis became more and more brutal, aggressive and violent, and it was evident that the free world (at least at that time!) was standing idly by, and doing nothing to stop Hitler. My dear father had died in 1937. So, the time had come not only to think of, but to prepare for our emigration."[31]

Indeed as Richard Offenbacher implies, the decision to emigrate was more difficult if family members stayed behind. In this vein Leo Grebler worries about severing family ties: "In 1935, the notion of going to the United States was a little frightening to us. All of our families were still in Europe although a few had left Germany. Stationing ourselves somewhere in Europe would make family meetings and contacts with friends easier." Joseph Adler pointedly expresses his anguish at having to leave his mother and sister, Bertha: "Can you do it, have you not the obligation to protect her, to hold her hand in the last moment of her life? She was always understanding, always forgiving, and now I had to go, to save my wife and children. The thought I could not and have not saved my mother and Bertha will torment me the rest of my life."[32]

While family ties were a responsibility and an obligation, they also were an asset and a resource. American kin were sources of information and advice about the procedures for immigration and, most important, were potential providers of affidavits of support, needed to secure visas to the United States. Helmuth Perlmann proudly recounted the story of his wife's clever idea of going to the Hamburg public library to find all the Perlmanns in the New York City telephone book so they could write to them for affidavits, which they did.[33]

Age made a significant difference in how men approached the prospect of leaving Germany. Children's transports enabled young people like Ernest Stock to leave Frankfurt with his younger sister on a Catholic-sponsored train to France. Some adolescents and young men thought their hometowns provincial and thus looked forward to leaving. Moreover, the younger generation had not built up their hopes, developed honorable reputations, and accumulated resources, all of which their fathers, uncles, and grandfathers had secured through years of hard work and military service, offering ostensible protections to their elders and making it harder to leave. Nor did the young men have the experiential knowledge which yielded the false belief that anti-Semitism might again loosen its grip, as it had in the past. In these ways, boys and young men seemed freer to leave than adult men, girls, and women. Girls had the added burden of their parents' assumption that they needed protection and should not be allowed to emigrate on their own. Thus some young men, like Alfred Mayer, who had recently finished *Gymnasium,* assessed their situation differently than their elders. But this does not mean that leaving their families was easy. Mayer writes:

> My own life took a serious turn when in the fall of 1934 an affidavit arrived from America for both myself and my brother, who was one year younger than I. Where joy and jubilation would have prevailed in many Jewish homes, welcoming the opportunity to leave the country in an orderly fashion, such was not the case in my home. Remember, it was 1934 and business was still only slightly damaged, and leaving home was a far cry from reality. It remained for me to confess that I had asked for these affidavits behind my parents' back. . . . As April 1935 approached my heart grew heavy at the thought of parting with all the loved ones whom I had to leave behind and whom, in all certainty, because of their age, I would never see again. But the thought of adventure in the "New World" ignited a spark in me which, while it made me self-supporting for the first time in my life, would give me the great opportunity to engage in rescue work to bring people out of Germany. The second task turned out to be far greater than the first.[34]

There is relatively little attention in the memoirs to the actual work of preparing for departure despite the strict requirements that émigrés obtain exacting affidavits of support before applying for a visa at one of four U.S. consulate offices and then be approved to leave Germany only after payment of increasingly larger taxes and levies. Even though there are scant details of such preparations (obtaining the documents that required governmental stamps of approval, occupational training, language study, property sales, and so forth), writers do note the hurdles. Henry Buxbaum describes his desperation and helplessness in 1937 and 1938 as he searched for a country that would take him. Fritz Ottenheimer writes, "A letter from the U.S. Consulate—at last! Our application was approved—we could go! There was no time to lose." Upon his release, Ottenheimer's father, who had been in Dachau, made all the required arrangements, including securing train and ship tickets, obtaining approval for shipping their possessions, filing the required forms, and telegramming relatives. Ernst Marcus recalls that his "preparations for emigration consisted of a few English lessons. My wife was better prepared. . . . She learnt dressmaking and tailoring at a time when she had not had a thought [of] using these talents professionally upon emigration." Among the notable exceptions to these succinct accounts are a few stories of adventure and risk, such as Kurt Lenkway's trip by train from Cologne to the last railway station on the Rhine and then by kayak on the river before crossing the Dutch border.

These departures are a stark contrast to the circumstances of the many men who were arrested and interned on Kristallnacht, who were unable to assist their families. As a consequence, the actions and resourcefulness of many of their wives proved crucial. Thus both the brevity of the references to preparations for emigration as well as their absence confirm Marion Kaplan's conclusion that much of the logistical work of emigration was women's work.[35]

The invisibility of preparation is also suggestive of the ways in which men might have dealt with questions of their own efficacy in the decision-making processes. Some struggled with their delays and tried after the fact to make sense of the timing of their decisions. Men wrote touchingly about the difficulties of "giving up" on their life's work or losing their fight against anti-Semitism. Others expressed remorse about not knowing or understanding the meanings of the events unfolding before their eyes. These failures represented their failures as men and went to the essence of their manliness. They no longer could provide for their families, who depended on their income, and even worse, they no longer could guarantee their safety.

Frequently these accounts include instances of self-blame and self-recrimination, which no doubt were buttressed by messages the authors had received in various public settings—they "should have known better," should have "left earlier," and so forth. An important element of modern Western masculinity revolves around men's competence and efficacy and their abilities to shape their own destinies. These men's heightened sense of responsibility underscored a sense of their own agency, and exaggerated their abilities or the possibilities they could have acted otherwise. Had they done something differently, they might have been able to save their parents and siblings, aunts and uncles. According to this hegemonic definition of masculinity, therefore, they were not true men because if they were, they could have somehow safeguarded their kin.

At the same time, there is a competing explanation evident in the memoirs, which effectively robbed men of their own sense of free will. There are multiple references to being on the "last train" to leave Germany before they closed the border or the "last ship with a kosher kitchen" that sailed before the war started. This means that an emigrant left toward the end of the period after which many if not most escape routes were closed.[36] Yet sometimes this memory of being last, such that trains no longer took Jewish passengers or ships no longer sailed, does not always match the historical record now available to us. What the memory of being "last" connotes is the very real anxiety that must have circulated widely in communities of German Jews and that must have been experienced deeply in the guts of many preparing to leave. Being last, moreover, suggests luck, good fortune, and the importance of chance. In framing their successful escape in terms of luck, the authors minimize their own sense of agency and erase their own actions and preparations for immigration. Labeling themselves as lucky meant they were effectively no different than those who did not escape. Minimizing their own agency in this regard may also have lessened some of the guilt that burdened them.[37]

The accounts of arrival in New York City are a motley mix of first impressions. Invariably there are descriptions of the Statue of Liberty, or Manhattan, or Hoboken, or occasionally Ellis Island, where they docked. They worried about having the necessary documents and finding those who awaited their arrival. Some liked the tall buildings and crowds, marveled at the subway, and took pride in being able to recognize landmarks, while others thought of everything as a jumble. Many hated the weather especially if it was summer. These first impressions are important, but it was a gendered family that defined their resettlement, in several ways.

First, family yielded the rationale for work. Men accepted whatever work they could find to provide for their families or at least contribute to the household income. They used their knowledge of trade and commerce to find the best jobs they could, often working more than one job, and quitting initial jobs for better-paying ones. Fred Sternberg's father peddled candy bars in downtown New York and according to his son's account seemed satisfied with the work. Familial necessity also offered the rationale for men's acceptance that they were no longer the sole wage earners and now their wives and older children routinely labored as well. Immigrants often turned to their sponsors or extended family to get leads for possible jobs. One of Alfred Mayer's relatives offered him a job as a meat cutter. Henry Landman's father arrived in New York before him and found Henry a job in the fur business. Still others relied on their identification as Jews to activate sympathetic connections with other Jews to find jobs. As one man describes it, "I decided to go into my own 'business'—peddling. I went to Allen Street on the lower East Side in Manhattan where I was fortunate enough to find a nice Jewish man who gave me 20 dozen neckties free . . . to get a start." Others accepted jobs for which they had no qualifications and soon got fired. A few families, such as the Gruenspechts, kosher butchers, were able to reestablish the family business. Occasionally immigrant men could draw on business or social ties they had made in Europe, which yielded job opportunities or leads to possible employment. Conversely several men expressed distress over not being able to find sufficient employment, as Meinhardt Lemke's resume reveals. With a doctoral degree from Breslau, Lemke continued to write poetry, while working as a machine operator and then a bookkeeper in New York.[38]

Securing a job upon resettlement was essential to men's self-concept as men. Employment demonstrated that they could provide for themselves and for those who depended on them—a core element of a family-based masculinity and thus a significant accomplishment. If immigrants arrived alone, they were as concerned as men with families about saving money for their relatives, whom they hoped would soon follow. Though many physicians studied for the medical licensing exams and restarted their medical practices in the United States, attorneys were not as likely to practice law in their new homeland since their legal training and experience were of little use in the United States. Younger men essentially started their work lives in their new homeland, and many of these men would eventually enlist or be drafted. Regardless of their age upon arrival or their previous occupations or professions in Germany, men mostly took whatever jobs they could find. Most of the men writing memoirs had worked in small businesses—either as employees or owners. There were also men who failed to restart their work lives, but they did not leave many records, as the act of memoir writing screens out the less successful. The men who wrote stressed the importance of family and took pride in being resourceful and making a living however they could.

Second, men also worked tirelessly to secure affidavits and bring remaining family members out of Europe. Several described the ways they would split their days or weeks between their places of employment, on the one hand, and refugee and governmental agencies, and shipping companies, on the other, to try to secure their relatives' immigration. A sample of letters in the files of the National Council of Jewish Women indicates men signed if not wrote a majority of the letters seeking help securing affidavits and passage for kin.[39] Indeed, a number of men considered the work they did to get their families to the States as supremely important. Alfred Mayer worked feverishly with his brother to guarantee the safety of family members who remained in Germany. They searched for distant relatives in New York and contacted several unfamiliar wealthy kin, imploring them for affidavits. By 1936 they began to see the results of their efforts, and the brothers provided room and board for numerous family members upon their arrival. Fred Sternberg's family collected sufficient funds to help him migrate to New York from Buenos Aires, where he had settled five years earlier. Describing their reunion, he wrote, "Finally in April 1941 I arrived in New York. After my ship docked, I spotted Father, Mother, Bernhard and Betti, Uncle Max and Aunt Selma, and I was so overwhelmed by my emotions and could not hold back my tears." Henry Landman also acknowledged crying when he "ran into my family's arms." Arriving in New York a year after his parents and sisters, Landman, then nineteen, described how his father "picked up my valises, looked at me with pride, and simply said, 'Let's go home.'" They made their way home, Landman continued, and "I was pleased to see that my father was known in the neighborhood. Strollers would nod their heads in recognition and I felt that my father had taken his appropriate place in this community, as he had in Augsburg."[40]

The vitality of kin ties was also visible through the support men gave to family members upon their arrival and during the early months and years of resettlement. Though it would be a mistake to think this pattern was universal, and some men justifiably complained about financially secure relatives who refused to help their immigrant kin, men often wrote with gratitude for the help in finding jobs and the regular stipends they received. In numerous letters, Jacob Mann thanked his cousin for the monthly $50 checks: "Not only that we thank you for bringing us to this country, but you have besides this dealt with us in such a generous and wonderful manner, that we are always afraid that we will prove to be too much of a burden to you."[41]

Third, the context of family life was the source of many of the deepest pleasures and some of the most profound distress. Some of the most moving passages in the memoirs refer to extended family life. Alfred Gruenspecht writes how his family of six Gruenspecht and six Braunschweiger relatives plus cousin Bertel's parents lived together in a six-room apartment for two weeks. "But we truly enjoyed each other's company," he says. Gruenspecht's memoir is filled with rich descriptions of an active extended family life in New York, which included weekly and occasionally more frequent visits between households and numerous business ties. He refers to his, his siblings', and his cousins' participation in the U.S. military during the war and provides details about family weddings, births, bar mitzvahs, and deaths. These are not merely factual reports but stories often told with some emotional force. Paul Nickelsburg's memoir provides an exemplar of the meaning of family life. Writing of the value of a family table with abundant food, his passage could have easily been penned by a woman:

> We ate breakfast. The food which is eaten in its homes is an important feature of a country, as important as its climate and its language. Notice how it tastes and how it nourishes you, and you will learn an important part of geography. American food is rich and reflects the abundance of this country. My first drink of milk here was a sensation to me, creamy and sweet, and every time I have milk with my meals it gives me the same enjoyment. Grandma was beaming. She liked to have a big crowd around the table and plenty of food on it; she always has been used to it with her eight children.[42]

The family was also the locus of considerable pain, particularly as people learned the fate of relatives who had remained in Europe. Sons and brothers were also killed serving in the U.S. military. Alfred Gruenspecht memorializes one of his brothers-in-law, who had volunteered to go on a mission: "Justin, his pilot and his gunner were killed. The War Department telegram announcing Justin's death arrived at the Seitenbach home on April 17, 1943, the Sabbath directly preceding Passover. The whole family was plunged into deep mourning."[43]

## CONCLUSIONS

Ample evidence in these memoirs demonstrates there are multiple forms of masculinity in practice. Hegemonic masculinity in German society was defined primarily through the bonds between military service and citizenship.

The emphasis on military service in the memoirs reflects the cultural salience in German Jewish life of the military as the mechanism to secure full citizenship and solidify the integration of Jews into German society. German Jews, a subordinated group, believed that military service, especially service with honor, would guarantee their rights and privileges as citizens of the German state. When the German state denied German Jews their citizenship, it did so by dismantling the rights of men, which German Jewish families had assumed were theirs because their husbands, brothers, and uncles had served fully and honorably in the military.

Frequent references in the memoirs to genealogy and the longevity of family residence on German soil also speak to the relationship between hegemonic and subordinated forms of masculinity, albeit in a less direct way. Claiming to have lived in Germany for centuries is a defensive posture. A subordinated group might cite its continued residency to legitimate itself, but a dominant group would have no need for such a defense since its existence is assumed to be valid and is taken for granted.

The emphasis on employment in the memoirs also points to an important understanding of dominant and subordinate masculinities. While in Germany, men's ability to provide for their families was a sign of their successful participation in hegemonic patriarchal life. The significance attached to the loss of jobs and earnings in the decision to emigrate signals another form of exclusion of German Jewish men from participation in hegemonic masculinity. Finding a job and earning a living in the United States was not a way to regain a semblance of hegemonic masculinity but instead represented a tacit acceptance of a subordinated masculine life, one that valued the family in more intense and expressive ways than back in Germany.

German Jewish men's orientation to their families was primary. The genealogical emphasis along with the extensive discussions of military service and citizenship provide evidence that this was not solely or primarily a domestic notion of family life but a public or civic-oriented family life.[44]

The resettlement process introduced a different type of family life. Men spearheaded efforts to secure the safety of loved ones still in Europe. The narratives also emphasize a more privatized notion of family, even though the boundaries between households and extended kin were open and malleable. When read in the American context of a postwar United States, it is understandable that the refugees, like native-born Americans, retreated to their families and sought to remake a sense of a normal life. Though there are comparable emotionally evocative descriptions of family life before emigration, the passages about family life in the United States appear more prominent than earlier discussions, in part because the memoirists seem to value their families more than ever. It is tempting to suggest that in order to emigrate refugees had to detach themselves from their families, try to bracket their significance, and could only embrace them again upon successful resettlement. But it is equally as likely that the emotional force these memoirists, both men and women, give to their kin and to family life reflects their advanced years.

Had these men and their families not lost their rights as citizens of Germany, perhaps a civic sense of masculinity would have remained more prominent even in their new homeland. It is interesting to note that only a few memoirs mention the naturalization process and here what the writers talk about is getting their "first papers"—the initial step to becoming citizens. Yet it would be premature to conclude that accordingly the forms of familial masculinity practiced in the United States were exclusively privatized. Certainly, male immigrants were glad to be Americans and said as much clearly. Many worked in a number of ways, often as volunteers, to make their new homeland a better, more just world. But there is no doubt that, above all, their families mattered most to them. The family and not the state defined their masculinity.

Finally, the emphasis on family life in these memoirs suggests that German Jewish men and women were more alike than different. Though men stressed their jobs more than their sisters and wives did in their writings, these jobs were important because they enabled the men to contribute to and help sustain family life, while they concurrently affirmed their manhood, albeit in different ways after migration. In their emphasis on family life, we witness men adopting many of the forms of caring and expressions of emotionality more commonly associated with women's lives. Thus the legacy of these memoirs written by German Jewish immigrants remains a family-centered understanding of their lives in Germany, the destruction of the Holocaust, and the processes of immigration and resettlement. They demonstrate that in traumatic times, German Jewish women and men were more alike than we might have believed.

NOTES

I would like to thank the volume editors for their wise guidance and insightful comments.

1. Henry Salfeld, "Little Stories from the Past: In the USA: The Past," Memoir 1010, MM II 25, Leo Baeck Institute, New York, 4; Richard Offenbacher, "65 Years Devoted to the Study and Practice of Medicine, 1889–1975," Memoir 480, MM 60, Leo Baeck Institute, New York, 40.

2. In 1933, a half million Jews lived in Germany—less than 1 percent of the population. Until October 1941, the Third Reich encouraged Jews to leave, but the prospects for emigration and resettlement were increasingly restricted by the mid-1930s. The actual number of Jews from Germany who settled in the United States, and specifically in New York City, remains difficult to determine. Germany and its territories expanded and thus how German émigrés were counted changed. The U.S. Immigration and Naturalization Service classified entrants "by races or peoples" and not religion. Until 8 November 1943, when it was dropped, the term "Hebrew" was used as a proxy to count Jewish immigrants.

Between 1933 and 30 June 1944, 132,012 refugees from Germany and Austria arrived in the United States, and 120,661 immigrants arrived as part of the German and Austrian quota during that time period. Maurice Davie et al., *Refugees in America: Committee for the Study of Recent Immigration from Europe* (New York: Harper, 1947), 33–37; Herbert Strauss, "Jewish Emigration from Germany: Nazi Politics and Jewish Responses (II)," *Leo Baeck Institute Yearbook* 26 (1981): 359, table IV. The number of arriving immigrants was small at first, and the largest proportion of immigrants arrived from July 1938 through June 1940, with Jewish immigrants from Germany almost half of the 157,000 refugees. Steven M. Lowenstein, *Frankfurt on the Hudson: The German Jewish Community of Washington Heights, 1933–1983: Its Structure and Culture* (Detroit, MI: Wayne State University Press, 1989), 47, 276n15. After the war, approximately 30,000 German Jewish refugees resided in the northernmost section of Manhattan, Washington Heights, making it by far the largest enclave of German Jews in the United States. Sarah A. Ogilvie and Scott Miller, *Refuge Denied: The St. Louis Passengers and the Holocaust* (Madison: University of Wisconsin Press, 2006), 77.

3. Despite this relative scarcity, several outstanding sources exist and have influenced my work. See Marion Berghahn, *German-Jewish Refugees in England: The Ambiguities of Assimilation* (New York: St. Martin's, 1984); Atina Grossmann, *Reforming Sex: The German Movement of Birth Control and Abortion Reform, 1920–1950* (New York: Oxford University Press, 1995); Marion A. Kaplan, *Between Dignity and Despair: Jewish Life in Nazi Germany* (New York: Oxford University Press, 1998); and Lowenstein, *Frankfurt on the Hudson*. While each of these books is pathbreaking, Lowenstein's volume, which focuses on German Jewish immigrants in Washington Heights, provides an important foundation for my own work. Though it is impossible to adequately summarize his research here, several findings are particularly pertinent to understanding gender. German Jewish refugee families tended to adhere to a traditional gender division of labor within the home, with women doing virtually all the domestic work. Extended family ties were common in the neighborhood with multigenerational households a common phenomenon and family gatherings among households a frequent occurrence. Upon arrival, women often had an easier time finding jobs than their husbands did, as they were usually younger, more adaptable, and also better suited to the widely available jobs as maids. Lowenstein's interviews indicate that women's relative occupational success was upsetting to some of their husbands, who traditionally had been the economic mainstays of their families. But German Jewish women continued to be employed in significant numbers even after economic hardships had eased. Although the largely Orthodox and Conservative congregations made little room for women's leadership and influence, the exclusion was far from complete, and women also held a number of influential positions in German Jewish secular organizations in the community. Lowenstein, *Frankfurt on the Hudson*, 58, 92–96, 279n8.

4. Since I am interested in routine patterns of daily life, I excluded memoirs and essays written by well-known people, as they were more likely to have led exceptional lives in some respects. For an analysis of Jewish everyday life in Germany see Kaplan, *Between Dignity and Despair;* and Trude Maurer, "From Everyday Life to a State of Emergency: Jews in Weimar and Nazi Germany," in Marion A. Kaplan, ed., *Jewish Daily Life in Germany, 1618–1945* (New York: Oxford University Press, 2005). For an analysis of identity practices, see Judith M. Gerson, "In Between States: National Identity Practices among German Jewish Immigrants," *Political Psychology* 22 (2001): 179–198.

5. For an insightful introduction to the Harvard essay contest, see Harry Liebersohn and Dorothee Schneider, "Editors' Introduction," in *My Life in Germany before and after January 30, 1933: A Guide to a Manuscript Collection at Houghton Library, Harvard*

*University* (Philadelphia: American Philosophical Society, 2001), vol. 91, pt. 3, 1–30. The authors note the disparate experiences of persecution, which were shaped in complex ways by each writer's occupation and residence. A quarter of the memoirs were written by women who took responsibility for the emotional well-being of their families. My analysis challenges this gender division of family caretaking. For an outstanding introduction to the essays submitted to the YIVO contest, see Jocelyn Cohen and Daniel Soyer, "Introduction," in Cohen and Soyer, eds. and trans., *My Future Is in America: Autobiographies of Eastern European Jewish Immigrants* (New York: New York University Press, with the YIVO Institute for Jewish Research, 2006), 1–17.

6. The idea that inequalities and differences are co-constitutive and co-vary emanates from feminist theories of intersectionality. *Intersectionality* refers to the differences and inequalities in identities, social practices, cultural ideologies, and institutional arrangements as well as the interactions among them, which both reflect and produce power. For a fuller explication of intersectionality, see Hae Yeon Choo and Myra Marx Ferree, "Practicing Intersectionality in Sociological Research," *Sociological Theory* 28 (2010): 129–149; Kimberlé Crenshaw, "Mapping the Margins: Intersectionality, Identity Politics and Violence against Women of Color," *Stanford Law Review* 43 (1991): 1241–1299; Kathy Davis, "Intersectionality as Buzzword: A Sociology of Science Perspective on What Makes a Feminist Theory Successful," *Feminist Theory* 9 (2009): 67–85; and Leslie McCall, "The Complexity of Intersectionality," *Signs* 30 (2005): 1771–1800. For analyses of the variability of masculinity, see Daniel Boyarin, *Unheroic Conduct: The Rise of Heterosexuality and the Invention of the Jewish Man* (Berkeley: University of California Press, 1997); George Chauncey Jr., "Christian Brotherhood or Sexual Perversion? Homosexual Identities and the Construction of Sexual Boundaries in the World War One Era," *Journal of Social History* 19 (1985): 198–211; R. W. Connell, *Gender and Power: Society, the Person, and Sexual Politics* (Stanford, CA: Stanford University Press, 1987); and Connell, *Masculinities* (Berkeley: University of California Press, 1995).

7. Schüler-Springorum, this volume, 93.

8. Gregory A. Caplan, "Germanising the Jewish Male: Military Masculinity as the Last Stage of Acculturation," in Rainer Liedtke and David Rechter, eds., *Towards Normality? Acculturation and Modern German Jewry* (Tübingen: Mohr Siebeck, 2003), 159–184.

9. Ernest Hausmann, "A Family during Troubled Times: The Hausmanns & the Weingartners; 1934–1944," Memoir 886, MM II 12, Leo Baeck Institute, New York.

10. Ibid., 1–2.

11. Joseph Adler, "The Family of Joseph and Marie Adler: Jews in Germany, German Jews in America," Memoir 971, MM II 21, Leo Baeck Institute, New York, 2–13; Henry Buxbaum, "The Emigration of Two Generations 1900–1938," Memoir 76, MM 14 260, Leo Baeck Institute, New York, 78.

12. Alfred Gruenspecht, "Alfred Gruenspecht Memoir," RG 10.123, box 18, acc. 1994. A0254, U.S. Holocaust Memorial Museum, Washington, DC, 1.

13. Fred Sternberg, "Memoirs," Memoir 1295, MM III 6, Leo Baeck Institute, New York; Hausmann, "Family during Troubled Times," 3.

14. Alfred Mayer, "Road to Exile, 1932–1953," RG 02.190, acc. 1994.A314, U.S. Holocaust Memorial Museum, Washington, DC; Gretel Baum-Meróm and Rudy Baum, *Kinder aus gutem Hause: Children of a Respectable Family,* ed. E. R. Wiehn (Konstanz: Hartung-Gorre, 1996), 93; Fritz Ottenheimer, "*Hineini*—Here I Am!" Memoir 1007, MM II 24, Leo Baeck Institute, New York; Gerhard Bry, "Resistance," Memoir 73, MM 13 273, Leo Baeck Institute, New York, 11.

15. Alfred Wolf, "Memoirs," Memoir 263, MM 82, Leo Baeck Institute, New York, 14–15.

16. Werner T. Angress, "Prussia's Army and the Jewish Reserve Officer Controversy before World War I," *Leo Baeck Institute Yearbook* 17 (1972): 19–42.

17. Ute Frevert, *A Nation in Barracks: Modern Germany, Military Conscription and Civil Society,* trans. Andrew Boreham with Daniel Brückenhaus (Oxford: Berg, 2004), 65.

18. Todd Presner, "Muscle Jews and Airplanes: Modernist Mythologies, the Great War, and the Politics of Regeneration," *Modernism/Modernity* 13 (2006): 702.

19. Jay Winter, *Sites of Memory, Sites of Mourning: The Great War in European Cultural History* (Cambridge: Cambridge University Press, 1995).

20. Presner, "Muscle Jews and Airplanes," 705–706.

21. Boyarin, *Unheroic Conduct,* 42.

22. Ibid., 56; Adler, "The Family of Joseph and Marie Adler."

23. Klaus G. Loewald, "My Kristallnacht," Memoir 1203, MM II 39, Leo Baeck Institute, New York; Sternberg, "Memoirs," 13.

24. Martin Gumpert, "Autobiography, 1897–1950," Memoir 223, MM 31, Leo Baeck Institute, New York, 209–215.

25. Paul Nickelsburg, "Why I Left Europe and What I Have Accomplished in America," RG 102, box 14, file 168, YIVO, New York, 21–22.

26. Ibid., 24.

27. Ottenheimer, *"Hineini,"* 8.

28. Buxbaum, "The Emigration of Two Generations," 25.

29. Helmuth Perlmann, "Why I Left Europe and What I Have Accomplished in America," RG 102, box 13, file 146, YIVO, New York, 2.

30. Ibid., 2–3.

31. Gumpert, "Autobiography," 215; Offenbacher, "65 Years Devoted to the Study and Practice of Medicine," 42.

32. Leo Grebler, "German-Jewish Immigrants to the United States during the Hitler Period: Personal Reminiscences and General Observations," Memoir 416, MM 29, Leo Baeck Institute, New York, 27; Adler, "The Family of Joseph and Marie Adler," 89.

33. Perlmann, "Why I Left Europe," 8.

34. Mayer, "Road to Exile."

35. Buxbaum, "The Emigration of Two Generations," 7; Ottenheimer, *"Hineini,"* 37; Ernst Marcus, "My Life in Germany before and after 30 January 1933," MS Ger91*57M-203, Houghton Library, Harvard University, 45; Kurt Lenkway, "This Small Piece of History: The Escape from Germany and Three Years Later the Successful Immigration to the United States of America of the Family Lenkway," RG 02.065*01, acc. 1992.A0117, U.S. Holocaust Memorial Museum, Washington, DC, 9–10; Kaplan, *Between Dignity and Despair,* 127–135.

36. The editors of this volume wisely suggested that being the "last" also is a clever narrative device, which heightens the drama of the story.

37. By contrast, Ruth Wajnryb finds that camp survivors who wrote recollections of the Holocaust tended to emphasize events in which they exercised their own or a collective sense of agency. Wajnryb, *The Silence: How Tragedy Shapes Talk* (New South Wales, Australia: Allen & Unwin, 2001), 211.

38. Sternberg, "Memoirs"; Mayer, "Road to Exile"; Henry Landman, "A Return Home: Henry Landman as Told to Ralph Lopez," RG 02.194, acc. 1994.A339, U.S. Holocaust Memorial Museum, Washington, DC; Rosalyn Manowitz, *Reflections on the Holocaust* (New York: Hebrew Tabernacle Congregation of Washington Heights, 1978), 154; Gruenspecht, "Alfred Gruenspecht Memoir"; Meinhardt Lemke, "Meinhardt Lemke Collection 1905–1962," AR 4235, MF 1027, loc. B26/2, Leo Baeck Institute, New York.

39. In the files, these letters are organized alphabetically. I read and counted the letters of people whose last names began with the letters G, M, R, and S.

40. Mayer, "Road to Exile"; Sternberg, "Memoirs," 12; Landman, "A Return Home," 151.

41. Jacob Mann, letter to a cousin, 17 February 1941, Mann and Mandelbaum Family Correspondence, RG 19.016*01, acc. 1991.A.01, U.S. Holocaust Memorial Museum, Washington, DC.

42. Gruenspecht, "Alfred Gruenspecht Memoir," esp. 48; Nickelsburg, "Why I Left Europe," n.p.

43. Gruenspecht, "Alfred Gruenspecht Memoir," 85.

44. Lenore Davidoff, personal communication, 2003.

# CONTRIBUTORS

## EDITORS

**Benjamin Maria Baader** is Associate Professor of European History and co-coordinator of the Judaic Studies Program at the University of Manitoba. He is author of *Gender, Judaism, and Bourgeois Culture in Germany, 1800–1870* (Indiana University Press, 2006) and articles on German Jewish women's and gender history and historiography.

**Sharon Gillerman** is Associate Professor of Jewish History and Director of the Edgar F. Magnin School of Graduate Studies at Hebrew Union College, Los Angeles. She is author of *Germans into Jews: Remaking the Jewish Social Body in the Weimar Republic* and numerous articles on German history, Jewish history, and the history of gender and masculinity.

**Paul Lerner** is Associate Professor of History and Director of the Max Kade Institute for Austrian-German-Swiss Studies at the University of Southern California. His book *Hysterical Men: War, Psychiatry, and the Politics of Trauma in Germany, 1890–1930* won the Cheiron Prize for best book in the history of the human sciences. He has co-edited *Traumatic Pasts: History, Psychiatry, and Trauma in the Modern Age* and has published articles on the history of psychiatry, Jewish history, and the study of consumer culture in Germany.

## AUTHORS

**Etan Bloom** received his Ph.D. in Cultural Studies from Tel Aviv University in 2009. He is author of *Arthur Ruppin and the Production of Pre-Israeli Culture* and articles on Zionist history. He is director of *Hypercities Tel Aviv–Jaffa,* a digital research and education project sponsored by UCLA, Tel Aviv University, and Bezalel Academy of Arts and Design.

**Judith Gerson** is Associate Professor of Sociology and Women's and Gender Studies at Rutgers University. She is editor (with Diane Wolf) of *Sociology Confronts the Holocaust: Memories and Identities in Jewish Diasporas.*

**Sander L. Gilman** is Distinguished Professor of the Liberal Arts and Sciences and Professor of Psychiatry at Emory University. A cultural and literary historian, he is author or editor of over eighty books, most recently *Obesity: The Biography* and the edited volume (with Jeongwon Joe) *Wagner and Cinema* (Indiana University Press, 2010).

**Ann Goldberg** is Professor of European and German History at the University of California, Riverside. She is author of *Sex, Religion, and the Making of Modern Madness* and *Honor, Politics, and the Law in Imperial Germany*.

**Andreas Gotzmann** is Professor and Chair of Jewish Studies at the University of Erfurt. He is author of *Jüdisches Recht im kulturellen Prozeß, Eigenheit und Einheit, Jüdische Autonomie in der Frühen Neuzeit*, and numerous articles on Jewish history and culture.

**Robin Judd** is Associate Professor of History at the Ohio State University. She is author of *Contested Rituals: Circumcision, Kosher Butchering, and Jewish Political Life in Germany, 1843–1933* and articles on Jewish history, gender history, and ritual behavior.

**Stefanie Schüler-Springorum** is Director of the Center for Research on Anti-Semitism, Berlin. She is author of *Die jüdische Minderheit in Königsberg/Pr. 1871–1945* and *Krieg und Fliegen: Die Legion Condor im Spanischen Bürgerkrieg* and editor (with K. Heinsohn) of *Deutsch-jüdische Geschichte als Geschlechtergeschichte: Studien zum 19. und 20. Jahrhundert*.

**Lisa Fetheringill Zwicker** is Associate Professor of History at Indiana University, South Bend. She is author of *Dueling Students: Conflict, Masculinity, and Politics, 1890–1914*.

# INDEX

agricultural work: Jewish worker relations with Arab workers, 170, 184n108; kvutzot, 166, 167, 168, 169–70, 183nn88–89, 184n109; Lebenskraft, 172–73, 184n115; mastery of the hoe, 170–71; military activism, 172–73; selected immigration for, 165–66

Albrecht, Paul, 147

Alfandari, Shlomo Eliezer, 161, 162

animal protection campaigns, 74, 80

anti-Catholicism in Germany, 129, 131

Anti-Semite's Catechism (Fritsch), 148

anti-Semitism: blood libels, 76, 148; effeminate Jewish man, 1, 2, 64; of George circle, 187; in Gundolf-Salomon correspondence, 190–91; Jewish fraternities, 121, 122, 129, 130; Jewish question, 15, 123; male menstruation, 1, 147; Nazism, 7, 13–14, 63, 213–14, 217–18, 219, 222; responses to, 123–25; riots, 32, 33, 46n19; Zionist identity as response to, 156

Arbeitswissenschaft (science of work), 152, 166, 182n85, 184n115

Arndt, Ernst Moritz, 63

Asad, Talal, 154

Asch, Adolph, 116, 121, 123–25, 129–30, 131

Asch, Sholem, 204

Auerbach, Shlomo Zalman, 161, 162

ba'al guf figure, 204, 205, 209n19

baal habayit (head of the household), 26, 27–28, 35, 41–42

bachelorhood, 26, 99–100

Baer, Karl M.: feminine identity as Martha, 146; fraternal organization membership, 146; French identity assumed by, 145–46, 147; gender identity of, 139, 145; Jewish identity of, 146; on menstruation, 147, 148; sexual identity, 143, 144, 148–49; social difference, 145. See also "N. O. Body" (pseud. for Karl M. Baer)

Barbin, Herculine, 141

Bekman, Segula, 155

Berdyczewski, Micha, 155

Berg, Gerald, 178n36

Berkowitz, Michael, 14

Beyfuss, Ruben Benedict, 43

Bhabha, Homi, 197–98, 199, 207

Biale, David, 6–7

Bildung, 10, 13, 78, 119

Bildungsbürgertum (educated middle class), 78, 80, 91, 92, 103–104, 109n4

Bildungsroman, 92–93

blood imagery, 1, 75, 76–77, 147–48

B'nai Brith, 100, 146

body: assignment of sexual identity, 138–40, 143–44, 149; hygiene, 77, 80, 82, 88n44, 88n46; hypermasculinity, 2, 13, 17n2, 162–63, 173–74, 197–98, 200–203; the muscular Jew, 2, 13, 155–57, 170–71, 192; physiogamy, 81, 101–103. See also handshakes

Bourdieu, Pierre, 12, 105, 149, 153–54, 159, 162, 175n7, 178n39

Boyarin, Daniel: Bhabha's theory of mimicry, 199, 207; decline of Jewish masculinity and embrace of gentile ideals of masculinity, 199; Edelkayt, 103, 116, 199, 202–203; goyim naches, 203, 217; on Jewish modes of masculinity, 3, 58, 60, 63; Jewish Wagnerianism, 186, 192

Breitbart, Siegmund, 2, 13, 197, 198; as defender of the Jewish people, 204–205; Edelkayt of, 199, 202–203; as embodiment of strength and beauty (Kraft und Schönheit), 206; gentile culture, 199–200; German masculine stereotype, 207; hypermasculinity of, 2, 13, 200, 202, 203; Jewish identity of, 202, 203–205; Jewish masculinity performed by, 199–203; "The New Divorce Epidemic" cartoon, 206; Roman imperial power, 197, 198, 200, 201–202; women's attraction to, 205–206, 207; Zionist associations of, 202, 207; as Zishe, 197, 198, 203, 204, 205, 206, 208

Burgfrieden, 190–91

Cassirer, Ernst, 175n6

Catholicism, 11, 55, 115–17, 125–26, 128–29, 130–31

Central Association of German Citizens of the Jewish Faith (Centralverein deutscher Staatsbürger jüdischen Glaubens), 123

chapcha, 152, 158–59, 163, 169, 173–74, 177n32, 183n97

Chazon Ish (Abraham Isaiah Karelitz), 161, 162

children: education of, 54, 56, 61, 188; excluded from abattoir, 80; fathers and, 26–27, 53, 62; financial support for children born out of wedlock, 31, 40; illegitimacy, 25; as memoir audience, 213–14; mothers' impact on, 54;

Printed and bound by CPI Group (UK) Ltd, Croydon, CR0 4YY

13/04/2025

14656543-0001